# THE ART OF THE PRINTMAKER
# 1500-1860

# THE ART OF THE PRINTMAKER 1500-1860

Roger Baynton-Williams

A&C Black • London

First published in 2009 by
A & C Black Publishers Limited
36 Soho Square
London W1D 3QY
www.acblack.com

ISBN: 978-1-4081-1266-3



CIP Catalogue records for this book are available from the British Library and the U.S. Library of Congress.



Commissioning Editor: Linda Lambert
Managing Editor: Sophie Page
Insides designed by Penny Mills
Cover designed by James Watson
Proof-read by Julian Beecroft

This book is produced using paper that is made from wood grown in managed, sustainable forests. It is natural, renewable and recyclable. The logging and manufacturing processes conform to the environmental regulations of the country of origin.

Printed in Singapore by Star Standard Industries Pte Ltd.

# CONTENTS

# PREFACE

I joined my father's print-selling business when I left school, having taken an interest in it since he returned from the war in 1945. It was not long before I realised that there was a mystique about the art of printmaking, even some confusion in the minds of enthusiastic collectors. It seemed to me that an important part of enjoying prints is an understanding of the way they were made, the artistry and craftsmanship that was required. Much more galling is the number of people who denigrate prints as some cheap reproductive system without being aware of how they were made.

This book has come into existence in an odd way round. Some 30 years ago, I began to collect prints that were good, distinctive examples of each printing method, not necessarily aesthetically good or valuable or rare examples. Gradually, I managed to buy various printing materials, plates and blocks, and these are unique. The collection soon became of value from the point of view of being able to show the different printing methods simply and clearly, and the difference between good, bad and indifferent examples of the same print. I was then asked to put the collection on exhibition, which I happily agreed to do, and I was enormously encouraged by the enthusiastic reception the exhibition received. Since then, the exhibition has been shown at over 40 venues in the British Isles. Whenever the opportunity arose, I continued to add to the collection, improving it all the time. I think I have now reached the point where it would be difficult to find better examples, considering that the collection was made for the purpose of illustrating the differences in the various printing methods.

All this time, I had in the back of my mind that the collection was the basis for a book on the subject. The exhibition has the advantage of showing the original prints, while the book relies on faithful reproduction of the prints, but the quality of modern printing has achieved the required result. Hopefully, the text will make the subject easier to understand.

If it was not for the fact that the early printmakers are so underrated as artistic craftsman, the book would probably not have been written. Very few of their names are mentioned within the pages, but the names of individuals who made prints are not crucial to the book, which deals more with their methods and craftsmanship. However, my thanks are due to all of them for giving me so much enjoyment.

My thanks are extended to my wife, Sarah, and my sons. Many of my colleagues in the trade have generously given me first refusal when they have found suitable items for the collection. Some of the plates and blocks, where I have not been able to trace original prints taken from them, have been printed by either John Land at the Printing Workshop at Amberley Museum, West Sussex, or by Susanne Smith of Arundel, West Sussex, and I am very grateful to them for their assistance and encouragement. The Printing Workshop at Amberley Museum has a wide range of printing equipment, and there is usually a printing press in operation. It is well worth a visit.

By no means least, I thank Roger Biggs for giving so much of his time to reading the transcript. He used not to know about prints, which is why I volunteered him as a suitable reader; I wanted to make sure that a 'non-print person' could understand my descriptions. We are still good friends.

# A GENERAL INTRODUCTION

Most of us gain a little experience of printing a picture during our school days, perhaps using some crude and simple method, but printing for all that. My first, and last, attempts happened when I was eight years old. My art master was dismissive of the results. The class had been making prints using potatoes, cut in half so a design could be made on the flat surface. Most of them had produced a butterfly or a flower or something simple. When finished, the potato is dipped in poster paint and stamped onto paper. I was more ambitious. I tried to produce an image of an antiquated van that used to deliver paraffin around the village, and my picture bore little relation to reality. Though the general shape was nearly right, I failed dismally in the attempt at making the wheels look anything like the right shape. I could not get anywhere close to making the front wings of the van look as though they were highly polished; the introduction of white to create reflections only made the van look completely dilapidated.

My second attempt was, I soon discovered, even more ambitious. Again using a potato, I tried to make a monogram of my initials, hoping to be able to use the result as an ordinary rubber stamp. It had to be done in reverse in order to obtain a negative, but it never occurred to me to do it by reversing a piece of tracing paper. In the same way as the van wheels, the letters gradually became smaller and smaller in my effort to perfect the shape. It was never finished. At an early age I conceded that I would never make an engraver. In my early teens I came to the conclusion that I would never make an artist, either. As I grew older and began to take more interest in early prints, I realised I had reached these conclusions in the right order. The skill required by an engraver to create a realistic picture in black and white, or, more often, to produce a faithful copy of another person's picture, without the assistance of colour, is a mixture of mastering the art of engraving, being a competent draughtsman and a highly competent artist, and mastering the techniques of perspective and anatomy, with some knowledge of chemistry and science, all in one.

Prints can be made by using any material that can transfer an image onto paper, capable of repeating the same image several times. At the time, my potato was, to me, a serious attempt at printing, but while the system might have suited a class of school children, and taught me a little bit about printing, it was not a practical material. Over the years, printmakers have experimented with all kinds of materials in an effort to produce prints easily and cheaply. While some of these attempts were undoubtedly more suited to the task than a potato, they are not the concern of this book. From the beginning of printmaking until the middle of the 19th century, there were three recognised materials which were used to make the prints that are likely to be found on the market. These were wood, metal and stone, and these are the ones on which I will concentrate.

Later on in the book I have explained the principles of the recognised methods used in making old prints, keeping my descriptions as simple as possible. I have no doubt that experienced engravers and printers, as well as a few collectors, will think that I have over-simplified the subject, ignoring the frustrations and failures that easily occur. David Strang's *The Printing of Etchings and Engravings,* published in 1930, contains one chapter, 50 pages long, dealing with the method of wiping the surface of the plate clean immediately prior to printing, while I have described the matter, in a very simplified form, using not much more than 50 words. In the introduction to the same book, Martin Hardie, a printmaker and print historian, describes the plight of the printer:

> Wait until you stand, black aproned to the armpits, black to the elbows with oily ink, black across your cheek and nose where you have smeared the perspiration off, looking spitefully at a small plate on the jigger – a very devil's playing card grinning at you with a black and oily face. Sometimes you win, and sometimes you lose; and you usually end by being grateful to the professional printer who can carry off the satisfactory proof that, by good luck more than guidance, you have achieved, and can repeat it faithfully and easily for fifty times or more.

The engraver's craft, while not so messy, was equally frustrating. It required infinite patience to engrave a metal plate or a block of wood or stone, using skill to produce light and shade in the scene, reflections in water, textures which might vary from rough cloth to fine silks and satins, and from a laurel bush to a fir tree, all in the same picture. This, and a lot more besides, is seen in the illustration of Whitton, plate 10 (page 24). Such matters teased the ability of even the finest engravers to the limit. The mid-18th century engraver of the print, William Woollett, who lived and worked near Leicester Square in the centre of London, is reputed to have fired a small cannon from the roof of his house every time he completed the engraving of a plate as a celebration, sometimes in the middle of the night. The area then was more densely residential than it is now. I have not found any record of the reaction of his neighbours; his activities would have done little to endear himself to anyone, with the possible exception of other engravers, who might have understood Woollett's elation. It is no coincidence that Woollett's name occurs several times within this book.

There are some interesting tales that provide useful insight into the trials of an engraver. One of Woollett's first engraved works was *Niobe* after a painting by Richard Wilson, published by Boydell, who agreed to pay Woollett a fee of 100 guineas (£105). At the time Boydell considered the amount to be outrageous, but before long it was clear that Woollett was struggling to finish the engraving to his own satisfaction, and Boydell paid him some more. When the sum reached £155 Boydell insisted that Woollett had been paid the limit. The engraving was finished. It was so popular that Boydell's income from the sales reached £2000. It did, of course, lead to Boydell requesting more work from Woollett, and the pair seem to have had a good working relationship. One of Woollett's most important historical engravings is the *Death of General Wolfe,* after Benjamin West, (see plate 52, page 79). The task of printing was not given to Woollett's customary printer because of the intervention of Benjamin West and Bartolozzi. The son of the chosen printer dropped a hammer onto the plate, exactly onto the face of General Wolfe. At this time there had been very few impressions taken from the plate. Woollett thought that his finest work had been destroyed and despite all efforts to restore the damage, the plate was never the same. Nevertheless, Woollett persevered, and thereafter oversaw the printing. The print was extremely popular. Less well-known is West's *Battle of the Hogue,* which was also engraved by Woollett. When West saw a proof he suggested adding some more engraving to certain places and more light to a few others. Woollett readily agreed to the alterations. West asked how long the alterations would take. After some thought, Woollett nonchalantly said, 'Oh, about three or four months'. And that was how long the alteration work took to complete.

Woollett excelled in the art of line engraving, and, like most engravers, he kept to one technique. During the date span of this book, various printing techniques evolved, line engraving being just one of them. Some of these techniques lasted for many years, others were superseded by improved, perhaps less time-consuming methods. Progress, as in all things, was much slower than the development of printing today, but it is remarkable that most engravers kept to one technique. Branching into any other technique was for experimental purposes, which is an indication that engravers were constantly striving to master the art of their chosen technique.

Returning to Martin Hardie's comment on printing, he mentions that a printer could take 50 or more prints from a plate, a remark that needs to be expanded upon. There is a popular misconception that, once a plate or a block has been made, an unlimited number of prints could be taken from it. Some materials were suited to making considerable numbers, but that number was never limitless. The etchings that Hardie enjoyed were rarely printed in numbers of more than 50, and some of the most delicately detailed etchings were made in smaller numbers than that, simply because the plate began to wear, losing the fine detail. Limited editions did not come into use until the second half of the 19th century, after our period, and before that there was no reliable way of knowing how many prints were made from any one plate. There have been calculated guesses. Amongst the highest are the maps of John Speed, Britain's most famous mapmaker, which were published over a period of 160 years, using the same plates, except for a few that had to be replaced. Early editions are excellent examples of engraving and printing; the last editions were for practical purposes only, and could not be described as fine works of art (see plates 3 & 4, pages 18–19). It is estimated that about 3000 of each of Speed's county maps were printed. It is not possible to estimate the number that have been destroyed over the years (but perhaps as many as half of them), because once the geographical content became redundant, the maps had little or no practical use until they began to be collected. That means that, although the 'print run' was high in terms of old prints, there is not a large number available on the market today, and they are considered relatively rare.

Leaving aside the life of a plate, there is another important factor which dictated the number of prints that were made. Engraving, printing and publishing a print was an expensive exercise, which meant that publishers would only print a number that they were able to sell, that led to demand, a matter that has always been a problem to assess. Prints were made of all subjects that are appropriate to the date, and obviously some subjects were more popular than others. Two hundred years ago many of the same subjects were as popular then as they are now. The main difference is that 200 years ago, artists and engravers produced realistic likenesses, unlike the artist's impressions that are popular today. Portraits and topical subjects were a means of communicating with the public.

Queen Victoria was the first monarch to be photographed; before that the majority of the population would have only seen the monarch's likeness by seeing prints and paintings. The first time that photography was used to record action in war was during the Crimean War (1854–6), but the only way the pictures could be reproduced in newspapers was by engraving woodcuts – a lengthy procedure. A large number of prints were made for the sole purpose of providing the public with pictorial records of events – the only means of communication. The Great Exhibition of 1851 drew the attention of printmakers, mainly to provide cheap keepsakes for the many thousands of visitors, a greater number than visited the Festival of Britain 100 years later. Though prints were made for tourist markets long before 1851, there was no other event which was quite so commercially exploited. There were annual events which are still happening today and which provided a steady market for printmakers. Horse racing is one example. Printed portraits of the winners of the Derby and the St Leger, with the jockey on board, have always been extremely popular. The difference is that anyone wanting a picture of the winner in, say, 1840, bought a print, not a photograph.

Topographical prints have always enjoyed a reliable demand. They were, perhaps, late to start in Britain. Before the start of the 18th century, nearly all the prints of British scenery were made by engravers from European countries, the first being a series of bird's-eye views engraved by Frans Hoefnagle, a German, published in 1572. Wencelaus Hollar (plate 60, page 87) was brought to England by the Earl of Arundel and made some of the finest views of London. The English brothers Samuel and Nathaniel Buck (plate 73, page 101) rectified the situation with a comprehensive series of prospects of cities and major towns in England and Wales, which they started in 1721 and completed almost 30 years later. As well as the 80 prospects, there were over 400 smaller prints of castles, monasteries, palaces and 'venerable remains'. The brothers were the catalyst that set many other artists and engravers to work, and from then onwards there was rapid progression; the output of topographical prints grew. The demand for such things was reliant on the buyer having some association with the subject, a requisite that still exists. Small and inexpensive prints have always held a great interest for the tourist. The pity is that idyllic scenes of picturesque village streets, thatched cottages and wonderful countryside were not considered to be commercial subjects unless the artist or the occupant of the house was famous, sponsoring the print himself. Nor was there much demand for prints of industrial scenery and factories, and the few that were made were highly sanitised.

The other kind of demand was for prints that were fashionable. Fashions came and went, just as they still do, some lasting longer than others. Often these fashions were created by a famous artist, and this applies particularly to some of the best cartoon and caricature artists, like Hogarth, Rowlandson and Gillray, whose prints have always been highly collectable. John Wootton commissioned engravings of his sporting paintings and began the craze for collecting sporting prints in the early part of the 18th century, and the subject remains equally popular today. There were many important painters whose work was made popular by the print. Gainsborough and Turner come to mind. Joshua Reynolds, the society painter, commanded large fees from publishers, who found his work highly collected. There are, of course, many more painters in the same league as Reynolds, but few commanded the prices that Reynolds did.

Generally speaking, most prints were the joint work of several people: an artist, an engraver, a printer and a publisher. An engraver copied the work of an artist, and once the engraver had completed his work, the printer took over before the print was finally marketed by the publisher. Most prints have 'credits' in the bottom margin, beneath the image. On the left side is the name of the artist; on the right side is the name of the engraver. The publisher's name appears in the middle, either above or below the title. The printer is the poor relation of the group, rarely receiving any credit for his craft. It should be pointed out that not all prints have these credits; this is purely a guide to what they mean when they do appear. It is also quite common for a print to have some kind of dedication to someone, sometimes the sponsor or the owner of the original painting.

From the commercial point of view it was generally the publishers who took the financial risks, and they were not always successful entrepreneurs. One of the most prominent publishers in Britain was John Boydell (plate 86, page 118), who worked during the latter half of the 18th century. He was so successful that he became Lord Mayor of London. Up to this point in his life, he could be compared to Dick Whittington, as having made his own way to London, he became apprentice to William Toms, learned how to engrave with varying success, set up his own business, which did succeed, and became Lord Mayor in 1790. A volume of his prints in the British Library is inscribed by Boydell to the effect that this is the only book that made a Lord Mayor. Unlike Whittington, Boydell died in penury, partly because he had huge faith in publishing a collection of prints of scenes from Shakespeare, the sales of which did not come up to his expectations, and partly because he was overgenerous in paying large sums to leading artists of the time for the right to make prints of their paintings. He paid Rubens £1000 in order to make prints of one painting, a huge sum at the time. Boydell is also unusual in that he was an artist and an engraver, as well a publisher. Very few people were accomplished in all three professions, though there is justifiable doubt about his engraving ability; he never reached the heights of Woollett. He will be remembered as an influential publisher.

There are various permutations of the ways that prints came into being. Certainly most came from the acknowledged publishers. Many prints were published by the artist or the engraver, especially etchings. Many were published privately for proud owners of houses, yachts, favourite pets, prize cattle and so on, examples being endless. There are prints that were published by architects of their design work, often proposals for construction, which they used to promote the adoption of their design and to advertise their skills. There were prints made on practically any subject you can mention, which is in keeping with the period. Any subject that had a large demand, such as sports, yachting, professions, trades and industry, is very difficult to obtain today.

The illustrations of houses at Sidmouth (plates 96 & 97, pages 134–5) are an interesting case. Sidmouth is a most unusual town, in the south-west of England on the Devon coast. It became an extremely fashionable place to live in about 1800, having previously been a fishing village. It has been said that the town developed because the Napoleonic war prevented European grand tours, but it is more likely that it grew because of the influential people who lived there, among them being Edward, Duke of Kent, the brother of George IV and of William IV and the father of Queen Victoria. Unlike Brighton, there are no particular tourist attractions such as the Pier and the Pavilion.

The Sidmouth houses built at the time were a unique mixture of Strawberry Hill gothic and ornate dwellings of thatch and bay windows. The two illustrations are typical of many houses like them in Sidmouth. The prints are after Henry Haseler, an art master in Sidmouth, aquatinted by Daniell Havell, one of a large family of printmakers, and published as a series titled *Sidmouth Scenery* by John Wallis at the Marine Library, Sidmouth from 1817. Wallis had worked in London, where he was known for publishing children's books, games and puzzles. He left the London business to his son, Edward, and began publishing in Sidmouth, working from two prominent buildings fronting directly onto the sea. The Marine Library was the first building, known affectionately as 'the Shed' – it is now the Moccha Restaurant – and the second was an imposing building, where the Bedford Hotel now stands, and that building, too, was known as 'the Shed'. Apparently, 'the Shed', apart from being a very successful books and prints shop, became a social meeting place. London newspapers were available, as well as some magazines, there was a billiards table and refreshments were provided. There is a commemorative plaque on the wall outside the Bedford Hotel, which reads, 'Formerly the Royal Library of John Wallis, Bookseller by appointment to the Duke and Duchess of Wales. Established here c.1813. Publisher, bookseller and business associate of R. Ackermann of Strand, London. Much knowledge of early $19^{th}$ C. Sidmouth comes from Wallis's publications and topographical prints. The Library was badly damaged in the great storm of $22^{nd}$ Nov. 1824, the Wallis family only just escaping.

Devon makes a good comparison for the purpose of explaining the variety of topographical prints available. John Somers Cocks spent many years compiling a very complete bibliography, which the Devon Library Services published in 1977, titled, *Devon Topographical Prints, 1660–1870, a Catalogue and Guide.* The number he amassed was 3502, the majority being 19th century, and he says that one sixth of the total are small vignettes, which were made for a tourist market, interesting from the topographical point of view but not quite coming into the realms of fine prints. Unfortunately, no one else seems to have had the stamina of Somers Cocks, so it is difficult to know how Devon compares with other counties. There is a clue if we compare Somers Cocks's section on Sidmouth, which numbers 222 prints, and the bibliography of *Images of Brighton*, by John and Jill Ford, which numbers 1200 prints including some portraits of local characters. Brighton is at least ten times larger than Sidmouth, and since the majority of Sidmouth prints were published by Wallis, he was obviously an extremely successful man.

The strange thing is that Wallis was able to publish so many prints of this most unusual small seaside town. No doubt there was considerable wealth and pride among the inhabitants, or perhaps John Wallis inspired his own success. There is certainly no other town which while lacking a 'tourist' feature attraction, has had so many prints made of it. John Wallis was not unusual in that he worked in conjunction with other publishers, and the series of *Sidmouth Scenery* was sold by Ackerman and by Fuller in London. The illustrations of Ackermann's (plate 19, page 28) and Fuller's shops (plate 100, page 139) are similar to Wallis's Shed, typical of the shops where prints and art materials were sold.

A great many prints were made to illustrate books.

Many publishers sold their prints in any way that they could, either loose, bound or in wrappers, which are thin paper covers with sets of prints stitched into them. William Daniell produced an amazing series of views round the coast of Britain, which took him eleven years; he made drawings in the summer, engraved the aquatint plates during the winter months and sold the prints to finance the next section of his tour. When it was completed, he sold all 308 prints in volume form or in small groups by geographical location. Bound sets of prints, like those of Buck, Boydell and Daniell were obviously popular, and encouraged buyers to buy more than perhaps they would have if the prints were loose. Most maps were made for atlases and most of the large series of topographical prints were published in book form or in wrappers. If prints were not intended for binding they are known as 'separate publications'. Removing prints from books is known as 'breaking', a subject which is contentious to put it mildly, and a matter which is not always fully understood. A few years ago there were no illustrated books that were safe from being broken because the books were so seriously undervalued. Fortunately, the situation has changed so that the value of the prints is often less than the value of a good complete book, or at least it is not worthwhile for a dealer to sell prints separately. However, the cost of restoring an imperfect book is not often economically viable, so these are usually still being broken.

Hand-colouring is another underrated craft. In the 17th and 18th centuries, colourists were generally freelance, but some of the European publishers, the Dutch and the Flemish in particular, employed their own teams. In Britain and France it was not until the early 19th century that it became the common practice to hand-colour prints at the publishers. Ackermann was one of the leaders in the field, producing some of the finest colour-plate books and prints. The majority of prints made before 1850 were printed in black and white, and any colour was added by hand. Prints are still being coloured today because so many people want coloured prints in preference to something which is in its original state. Dealers are led by public demand, but they always get the blame for breaking books and for adding colour. I am not in favour of the practice of adding colour, though there is a case, of course, for touching up faded colour or other restoration activities, as you would do with a piece of furniture. Modern addition of colour to a black and white print is usually detrimental to the value of the print no matter how well it is applied. Any hand-colouring, regardless of the date of application, obscures the craft of the engraver. Naturally, a purist will want to acquire prints that are in their original condition. If a print of poor quality, which is not of interest to a purist in any case, is 'improved' with modern colour, there is no harm in it.

This brings us to considering the condition of prints when they are found on the market. Being made of paper they are vulnerable to damage. Tears, creases, scratches, frail paper, ingrained dirt and stains are the main problems. Like any form of antique, prints can be cleaned and restored – a job for a specialist restorer. All things considered, there are a large number of prints that can be found in mint condition, even those made three or four hundred years ago. Many dealers will tell you that they have had difficulty in persuading potential customers that an original print is not a modern re-strike or reproduction. Naturally, it is good advice to suggest to potential buyers that they should look out for good examples. This is why it is important for collectors to have an understanding of the kind of prints that are likely to be found on the market, and a beginner is advised to explore the stocks of some of the specialist dealers in old prints, as opposed to the growing number of shops that have re-strikes, which are new prints made from old plates, in their stocks without making the difference abundantly clear. With a little practice, a new collector will soon begin to know whether a print is good value or not (and be able to judge whether any restoration is acceptable): rare enough or desirable enough to justify buying it. I have a print in my own collection which I acquired because of its rarity, a subject which has significance to my family; it is the only copy that I have ever seen. The condition is absolutely appalling, so bad that I wonder why it was not relegated to the wastepaper basket long before I discovered it. I would, of course, prefer to own a perfect example; I have not given up my efforts at finding one.

It is quite likely that a wide disparity of prices will be found around the trade for apparently identical prints. This is not necessarily because one dealer is more expensive than another, but because it is actually unlikely that the two prints are identical when examined more closely. Apart from condition, there are many other factors to be taken into account. For example, it has to be remembered that a date that appears on a print can be very misleading; it really only serves as a guide to the date at which the print was engraved, and not the date it was printed. Many prints were issued over unspecified periods of time, still with the original date on them. To carry the point to absurdity, if a photograph or a photocopy is made of an original dated print, the date will obviously occur on the copy. As I have mentioned already, the life of printing plates was limited, and early impressions are generally more desirable than late ones. However, the most important factor is that prints taken from the same plate can be vastly different. Remarkable differences, both in the appearance of the pictures and also in value, can be seen in the three illustrations of Cymbeline (plates 80 and 81, pages 112–113), and the variant prints of Brighton Chain Pier (plates 103 to 105, pages 142–4). Much depended on the ability of the underrated printers, especially when producing colour prints like these. See chapter on *Intaglio Colour Printing*, page 150.

Printers made their own inks on a more or less daily basis to keep them fresh. They had to be the correct consistency and free from any impurities. The smallest piece of grit in an ink could easily cause some damage to a copper plate, enough even to make it useless. Inferior ink would not provide the required richness to the finished print. The inks were made from various pigments and compounds, ground together with linseed oil – a lengthy and tedious task. Inking the plate, as already mentioned, was a skilled and also tedious operation. The printer had to ensure that the paper was correctly dampened, which made it more receptive to the ink when the plate was in the printing press. If the paper was too dry the transference of ink was not as good and the impression would be weak; if the paper was too wet the ink would smudge, giving a feathery appearance to a line which should be clearly defined. Again, if the paper was too wet, it would distort, causing it to crease under the pressure in the printing press, forming a pleat, known as a 'printer's crease'. If you should encounter a print with a crease in it, it is best to leave it well alone because if the paper is stretched out again, the blank unprinted piece will be even more obvious.

The essential piece of equipment missing from the illustration *The Art of Etching and Engraving* by Benjamin Cole (plate 2, page 17) is, of course, the printing press. The illustration of *Dutch Printers in the Seventeenth Century* (plate 28), shows a large robust wooden press that relied on vertical pressure. This type of press was in use for many years, and, even now, small etching presses work on the same principle, but are made of iron instead of wood. The disadvantage of these presses was that it was difficult for the printer to see into the press enough to ensure that everything was in the correct position, and that the paper was flat, without the slightest crease in it (the printer's crease). An improved press was like a domestic mangle with a moving bed on which the plate was prepared outside the press, with the printer being able to ensure that all was well. The mangle action of the rollers propelled the flat bed through the press, the rollers being low-geared and turned very slowly to ensure maximum pressure was exerted onto the plate.

Papermaking was another specialist craft. During the date span of this book, all paper was made by hand. There were two kinds, known as 'laid' and 'wove'. Laid paper was made in a flat rectangular mould, a wooden frame supporting fine wires stretched across it, very close together in one direction and about two centimetres apart on the transverse, the wires acting as a sieve. These wires make a mark in the finished paper which can be seen when the sheet is held up to light, because the paper is fractionally thinner where the lines occur. Watermarks were put into paper in the same way; any thin wire design could be transferred onto the paper. Watermarks are either a symbol, initials or the full name of the papermaker, sometimes with a date, which is very useful. The trouble was that a full-sized sheet of paper would be cut down, so that, even if there was a watermark in the paper, it might not appear on a particular print. If a sheet was, say, cut into four, there would be one sheet of the four that shows the watermark.

Wove paper was made in a similar way, using a sieve, the difference being that the mesh was much finer, so there are no apparent lines in the paper. The two types of paper have very different textures, wove paper being much smoother. Wove paper was first made in about 1770; the smoother surface suited the finer-quality prints that began to be made at that time.

It is thought that paper was being made in China in the early part of the second century. It was made from silk rag which was soaked in water and then beaten with sticks to separate the fibres. The pulp was put into a large vat and mixed with water. The mould was dipped into the vat and a small amount of the mix, which was a little like a cheese sauce, was taken into the mould and rocked to ensure the mix is evenly spread over the wires of the mould. Water dripped through the wires, leaving a sheet of paper. When the sheet was nearly dry, the mould was inverted and the paper fell onto a thin felt blanket, covered with another piece of felt, followed by another sheet of paper, and so on, until the pile consisted of about 12 sheets. The pile was then pressed and left to dry. At that stage the page had little body to it, and it was coated with 'size' which is a gelatine – a weak glue – that was painted onto the paper to give it the necessary strength. Size also makes the paper less absorbent of printing ink, which is required to stay on the surface of the paper and not sink into it. After printing, the sheets had to be dried without buckling, and this was done by suspending them. The paper could only be pressed when the ink was completely dry.

This system slowly travelled westwards. Italians were making paper in this way in the 13th century, and the first mill in England began at the end of the 15th century – slow progress indeed.

In Europe, early papers were made with rag pulp. Strangely, it was the shortage of rag that caused research into other materials. Wood began to be used in the middle of the 19th century after a German, Friedrich Keller, discovered how to make wood into a pulp, but the quality of the paper was never as good as rag.

The book trade has a useful method of describing book sizes, sometimes adopted by print sellers. It is not at all precise, but is a rough guide. Paper sizes were not at all standard, but the sheets made in the mould were about 40 x 54 cm (15.7 x 21.3 in.). For the purpose of a book, the sheets were folded in half, so they then measure 27 x 40 cm (10.6 x 15.7 in.), and that is known as *folio.* If the sheet is not folded it is known as *large folio.* If a folio sheet is folded again it becomes 20 x 27 cm (7.8 x 10.6 in.), and is known as *quarto* or 4to. Folded once more and it becomes roughly 13 x 20 cm (5 x 7.8 in.), known as *octavo* or 8vo.

If you are not good with centimetres, it is useful to know the measurement of the span of your hand, which will help you to judge the sizes of prints given here. Most men's hands have a span of 9 in., which is equal to 23 cm.

So, that is some background history behind prints. Now all that needs to be done is to explain how the printmakers managed to put ink onto the paper – the most important part of all.

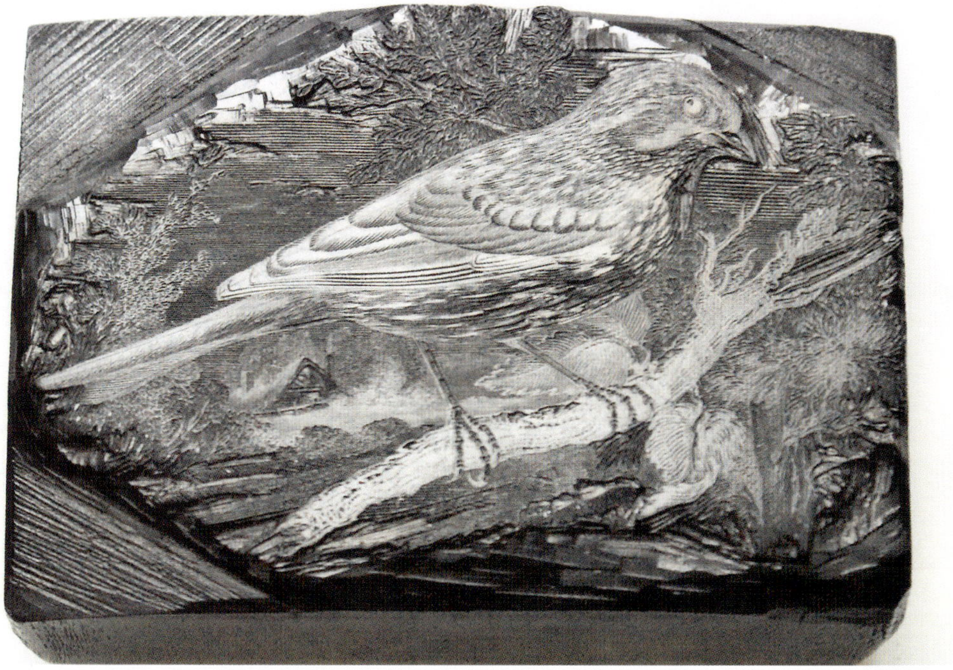

PLATE 1
*Corn Bunting,*
engraved by one of the Dalziel brothers, *c.*1860.
Wood engraving.

The aim with my potato was to produce detail as fine as this; impossible, of course, but the principle is the same. This is a wood engraving made in about 1860 by one of the Dalziel brothers. The bird is a corn bunting. See also plates 25 & 26 (pages 40 & 41) for other Dalziel bird prints and a full explanation of the process.

There can be few artists' studios that are as tidy as the one in this copper engraving by Benjamin Cole, from 1754. See plate 32 (page 50) for more details.

PLATE 2
*The Art of Engraving and Etching,*
Benjamin Cole, 1754.
Line engraving.

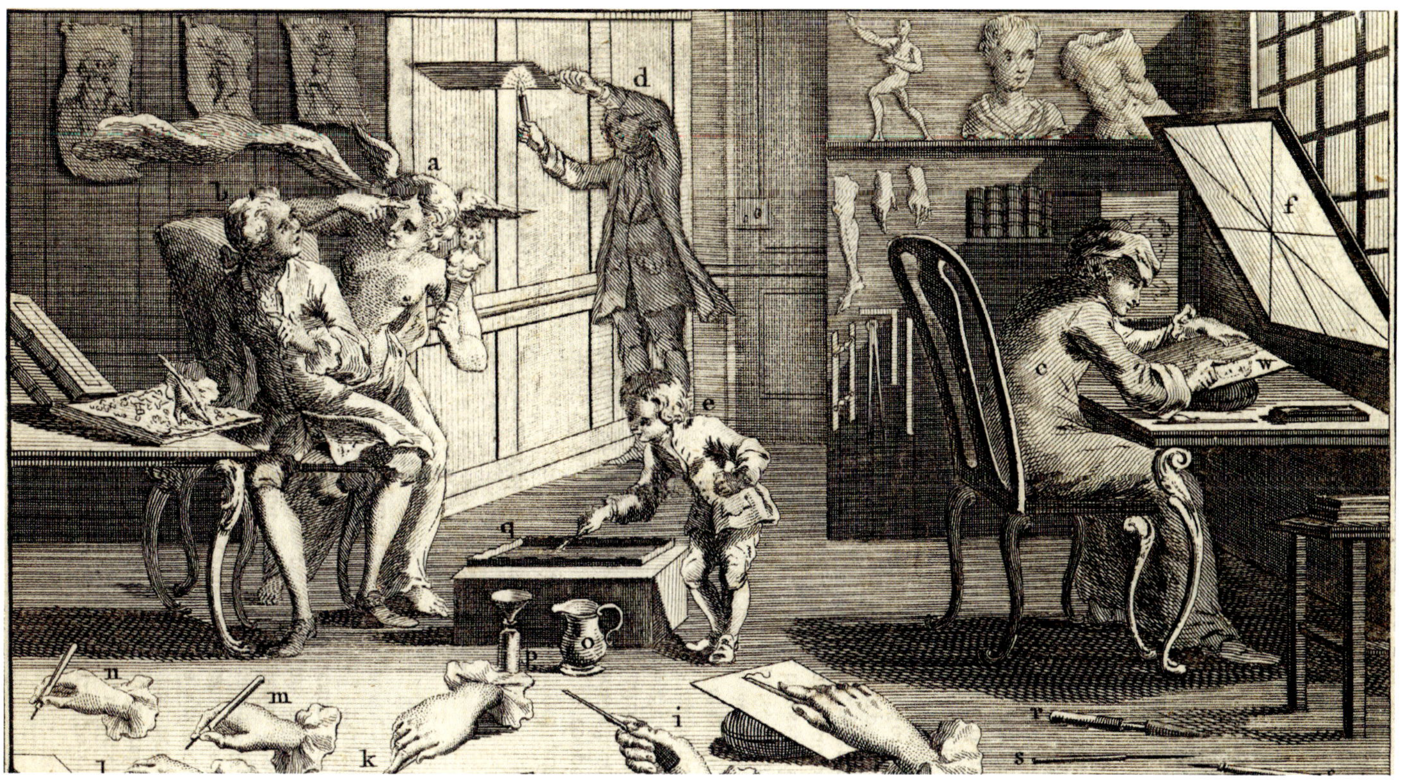

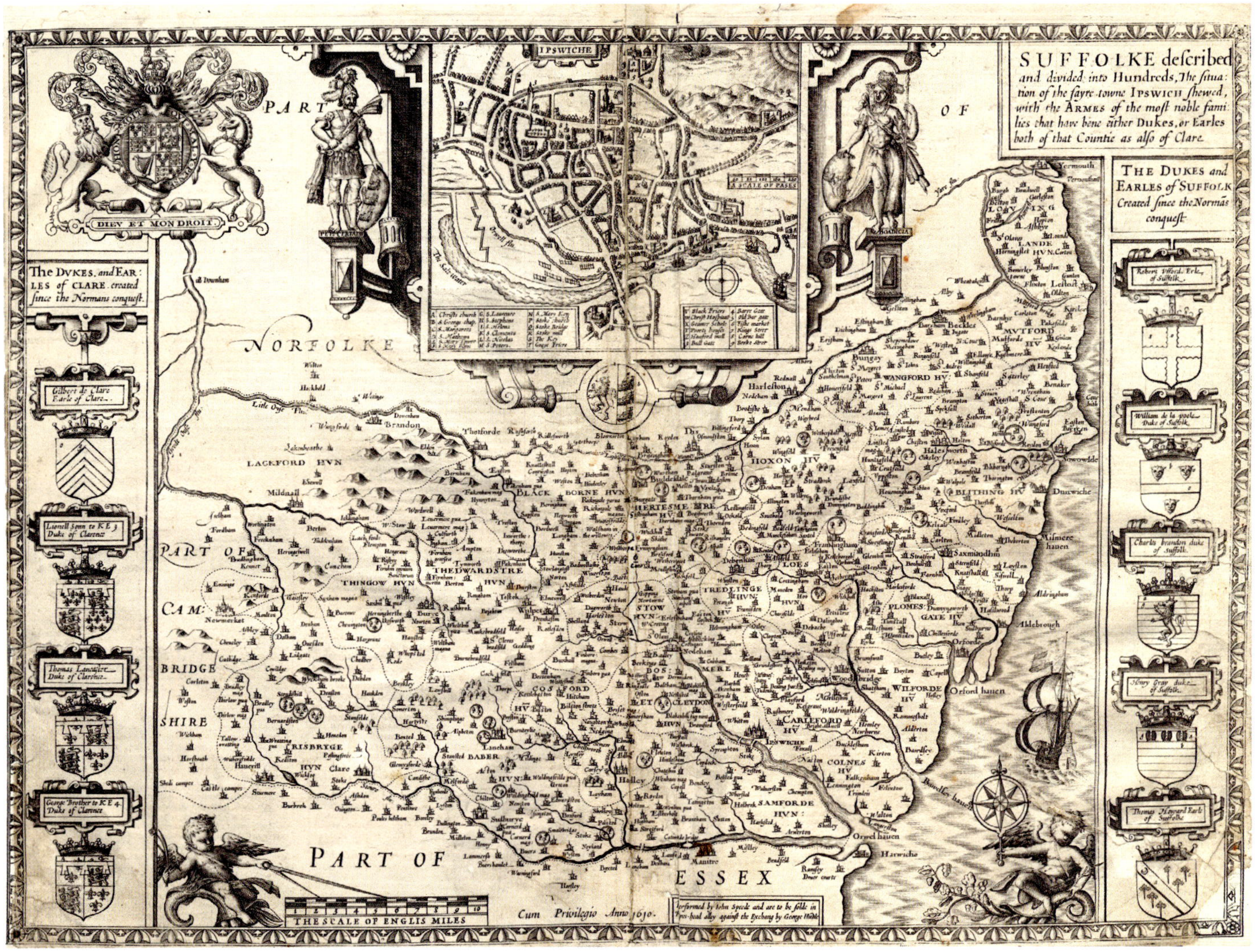


PLATE 3
*Suffolk*, John Speed's map, engraved by Jodocus Hondius.
First edition, 1611.
Line engraving,
38 x 51 cm (15 x 20 in.).

*Suffolke described and divided into hundreds …*

This is the map by John Speed, the best-known of the English mapmakers. It was engraved by Jodocus Hondius, who included his name on most of the other county maps. Two editions are illustrated, 1611 and 1676. The prints are both dated 1610, which is the date of the engraving. There are changes to the imprint and to the text on the reverse, and that enables us to date them accurately. The first edition of 1611 has the imprint, 'Performed by John Speed and are to be solde in Popes-head alley against the exchange by George Hu[m]ble'. The square brackets used here are something that a cataloguer would use to show a word or a letter that is not actually present on the print. The letter 'm' is omitted, so it reads incorrectly as 'Huble'. The edition of 1676 has the imprint, 'Performed by John Speed and are to be solde by Thomas Bassett in Fleetstreet and by Richard Chiswell in St Pauls Churchyard'. The only other alteration is the addition of the arms of John Holles. The reason for showing two examples is because of the serious wear to the plate. The fine detail seen in the Royal arms

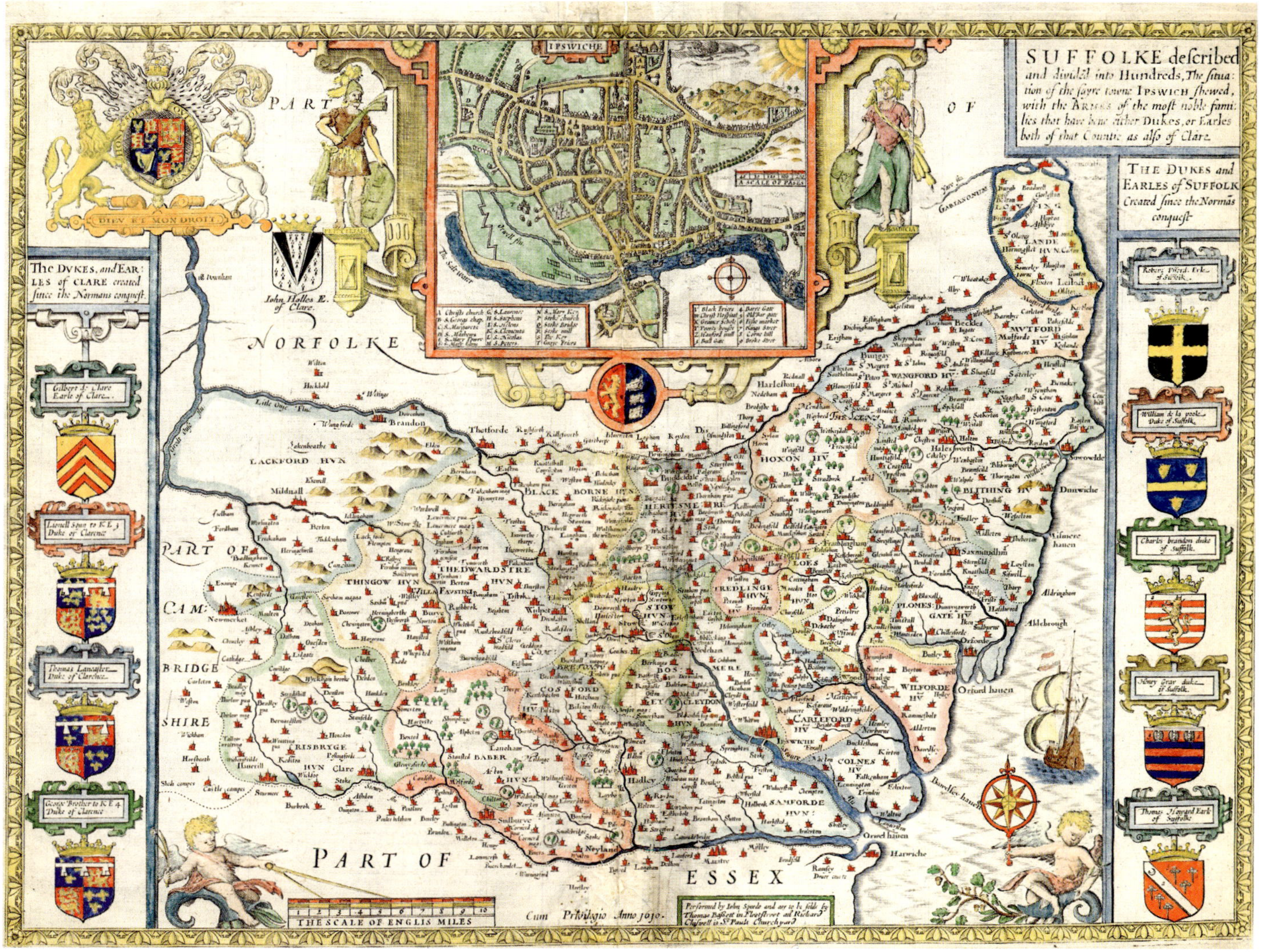


of the 1611 map is lost in that of 1676. The colouring of the later map was probably added in the second part of the 20th century, and if the map had not been coloured the arms would hardly show at all. This is an excellent example of the importance of an early edition.

PLATE 4

*Suffolk,* John Speed's map, engraved by Jodocus Hondius, 1676.
Line engraving,
38 x 51 cm (15 x 20 in.).

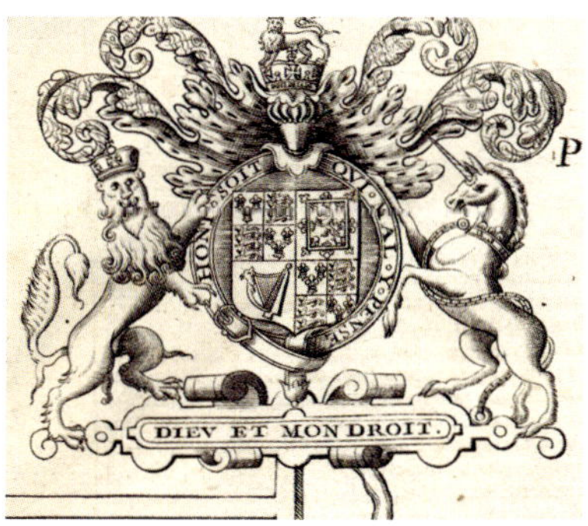


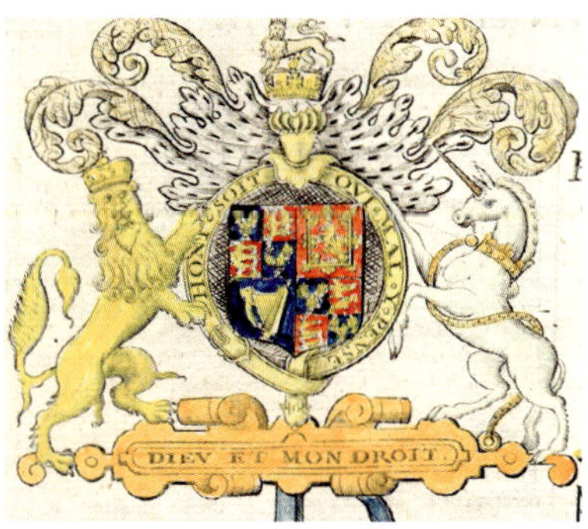

PLATE 5

*William Caxton, the first Printer in England,*
Hopwood (probably James), 1813.
Mixed method.
Including the border,
the size is 15 x 9 cm (5.9 x 3.5 in.).

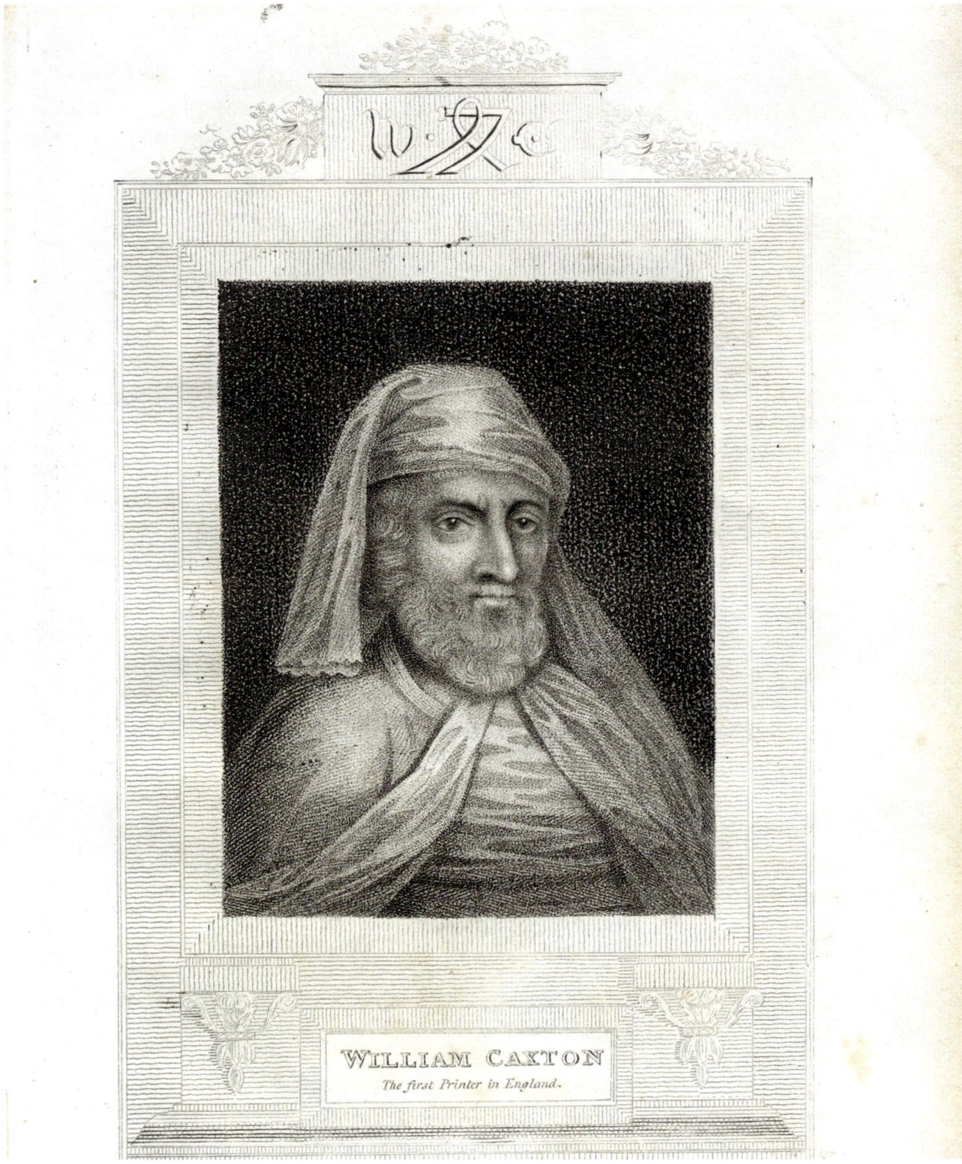


William Caxton was not only the first, but certainly the most famous printer in England. He produced books with letterpress, single letters of movable type made from cast metal to his own designs, the letters printing in the same way as relief. The art of printing letterpress is known as 'typography'. Some of his books were illustrated with woodcuts. He lived from 1422–91, and worked as a merchant and a translator before becoming a printer, only 20 years before he died. His output in that short time was amazing: he published nearly a hundred works.

This is a simple book illustration, signed 'Hopwood sc.', probably James Hopwood, and published in 1813. To be technical, the print is described as 'mixed method', because there is more than one engraving method used, in this case stipple and etching. This is explained later in the section on mixed methods (page 146).

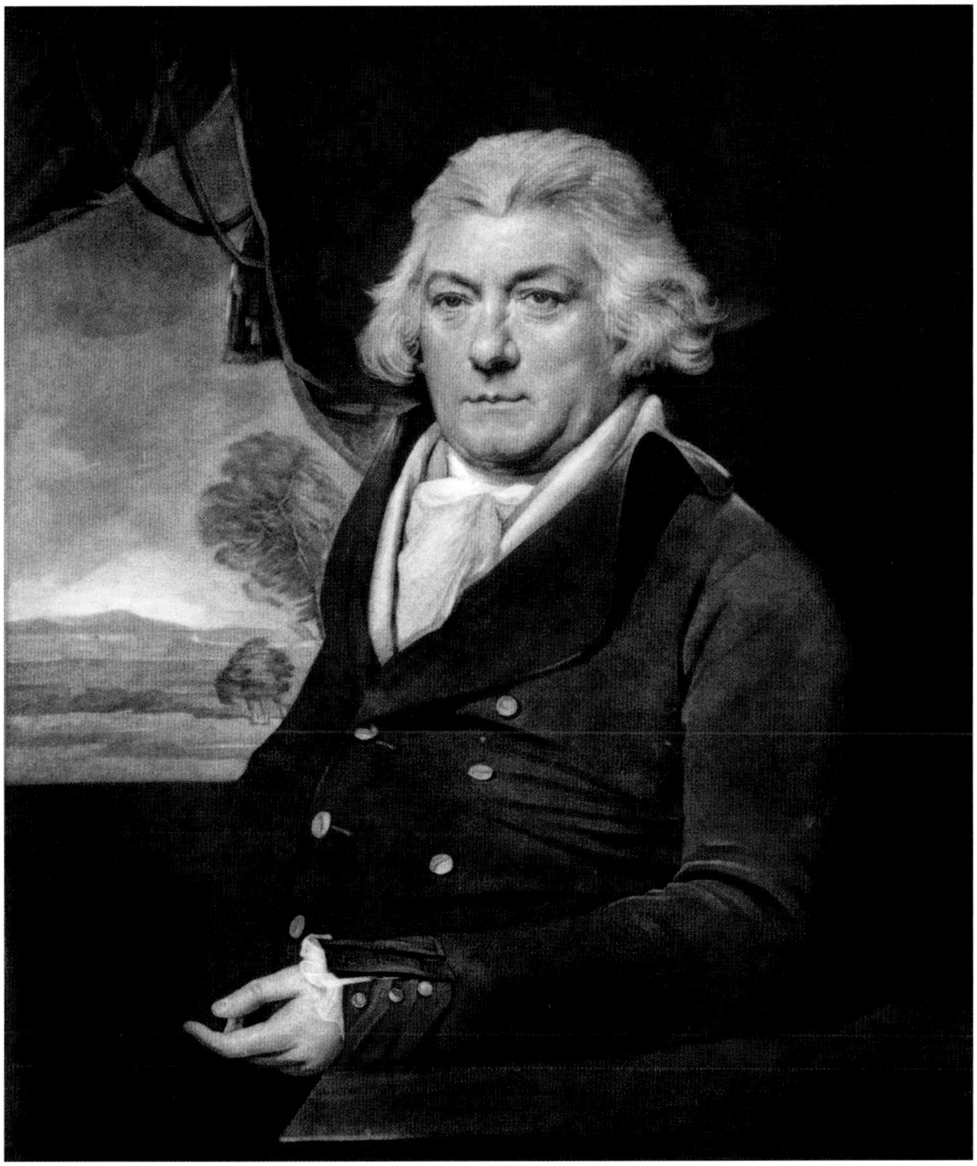

PLATE 6

John Mitchell. Engraved by Valentine Green. ND. *c.*1780. Mezzotint, 48.5 x 35.5 cm (19 x 14 in.).

This is a portrait of John Mitchell, the British botanist who published an important map of America in 1755.

Mezzotint copper plate and a modern print from it. The plate size is 48.5 x 35.5 cm (19 x 14 in.), about the average size for an 18th-century mezzotint portrait, and it is also average from the point of view that the mezzotinting is quite dense; there are large areas of heavy shading. The heavier the shading, the longer it takes to ink the plate. Susanne Smith made the print from the plate. From the time she started to ink the plate to the time she produced the print was a little over an hour. The process has to be repeated to produce a second print. In the 18th century the printer needed to mix his own inks before starting work. The print and the plate are described at length with plates 71 and 72 (pages 100–1).

PLATE 7

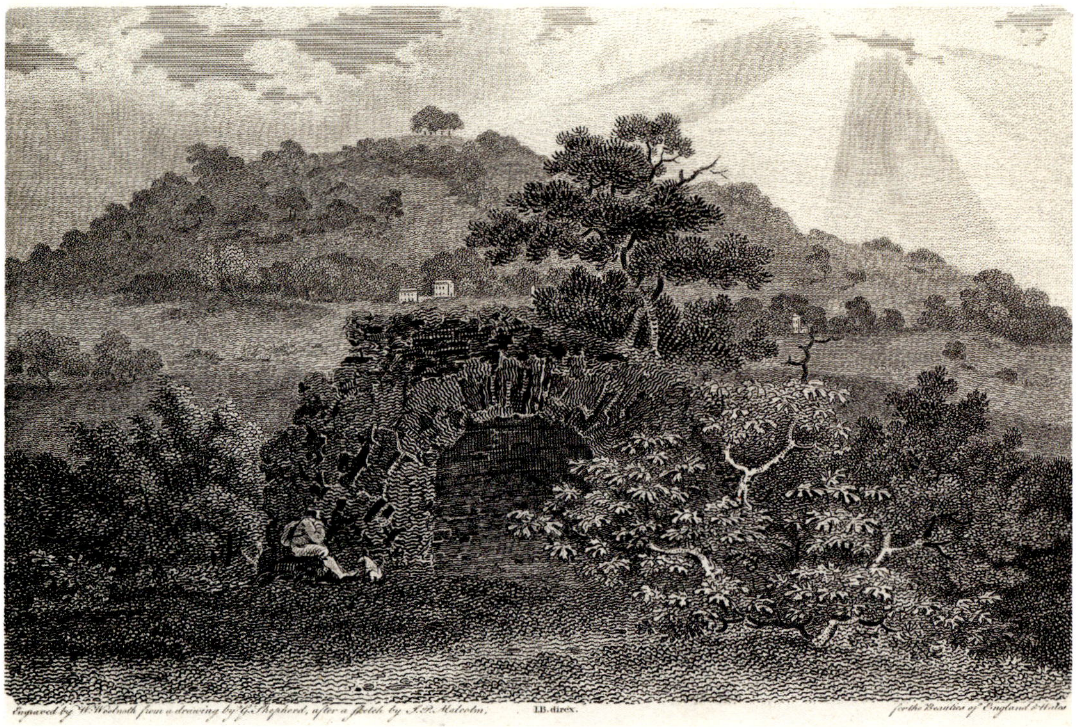


PLATE 8

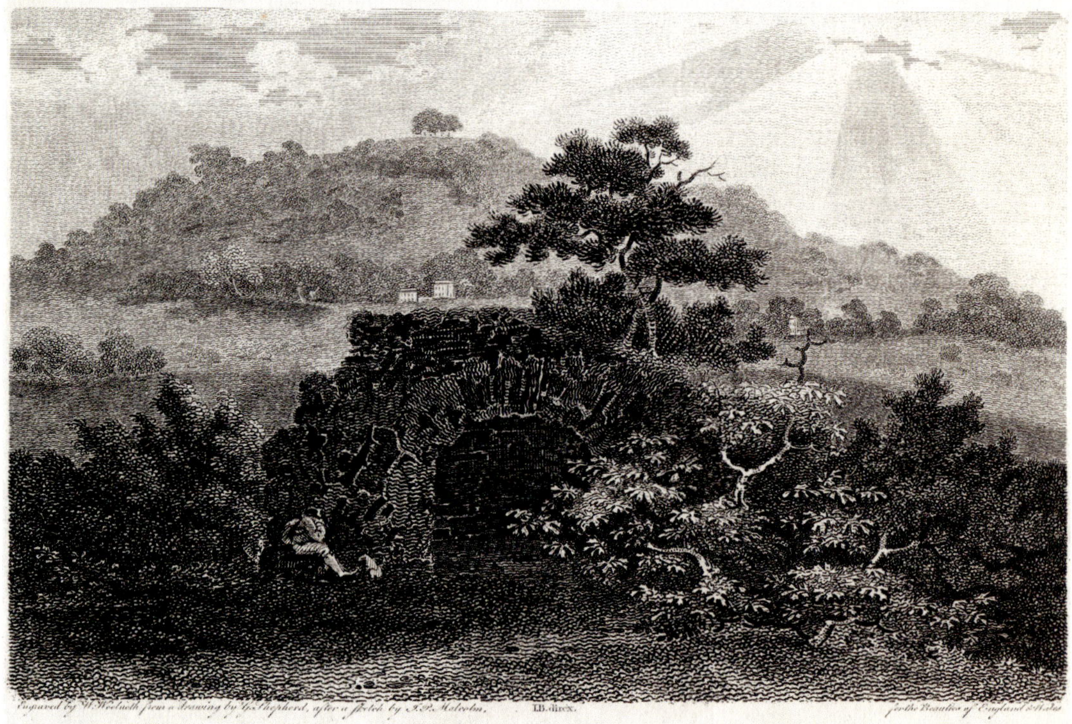

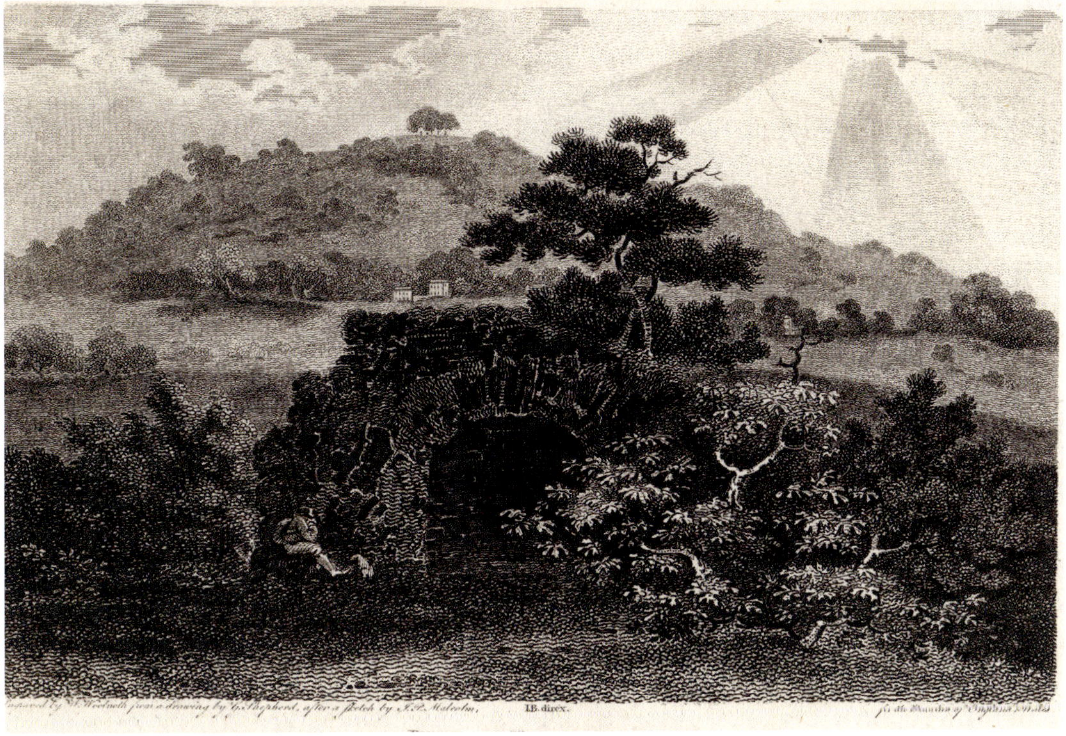

PLATE 9

Three differing examples of the same print, which provide a good example of the skill required in the inking of a plate. The prints are cheaply produced book illustrations. With prints of better quality, the printer would take more care to ensure the inking was correct. The plate itself is not worn, which might explain the differences in the prints. If it was worn, the fine detail in the sky, the clouds and the sun's rays, would vary a lot more in clarity from one print to another, whereas they are very similar and equally good impressions. Plate 7 print appears to be slightly misty; there was not enough ink on the plate. Plate 8 has the right balance; there is good sharpness and dimension to the picture. Plate 9 is overinked, meaning that there is too much ink in the incisions, making it too black, and the detail lacks definition.

PLATES 7, 8 AND 9
*Ruins at Kenchester, Herefordshire,*
engraved by William Woolnorth
after George Shepherd, 1806.
Line engraving,
10 x 15.8 cm (4 x 6.2 in.).

PLATE 10

*A View of the Canal and of the Gothick Tower in the Garden of His Grace the Duke of Argyl at Whitton,* engraved by William Woollett, *c.*1765.
Line engraving.

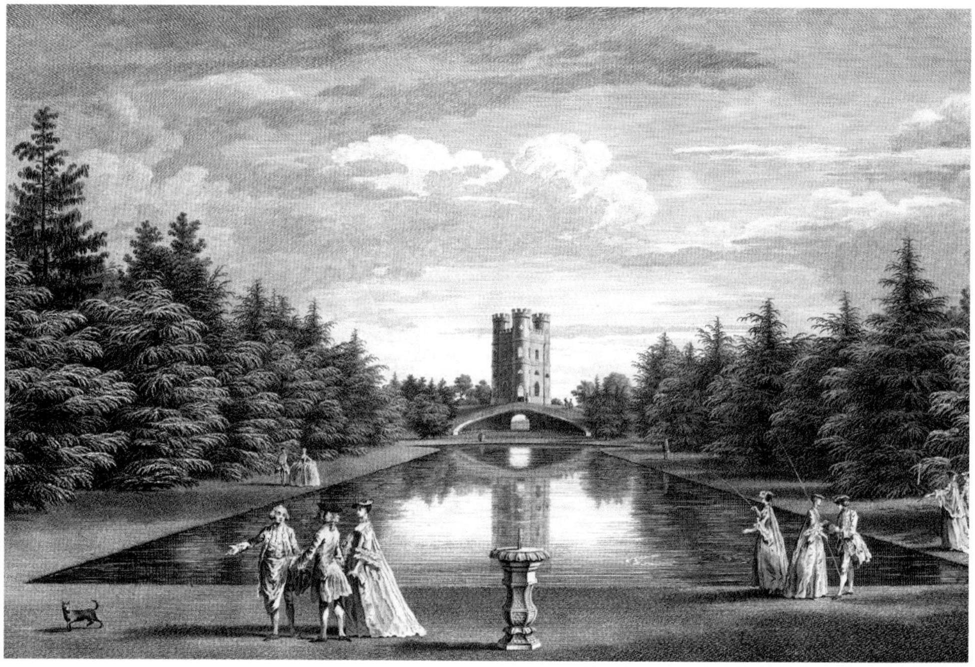

This line engraving by William Woollett, the artist and the engraver, *c.*1765, is an excellent example of how varying textures could be achieved. It is fully described at plate 40 (page 62).

PLATES 11–17

Title page of *At Home and Abroad* from Harding's *Sketches at Home and Abroad.* After J.D. Harding, 1836.
Lithograph.

These small views surround the title of the book. They illustrate the trials of a travelling artist. Two show lack of privacy, two show modes of transport, with Harding still drawing while on the move, and two show contrasts of weather, stifling heat and pouring rain. The last shows Harding in the comfort of his own home (see plate 123, page 164, for full description).

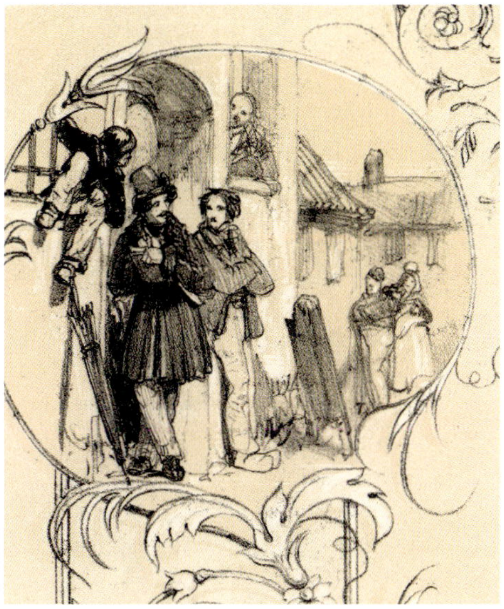
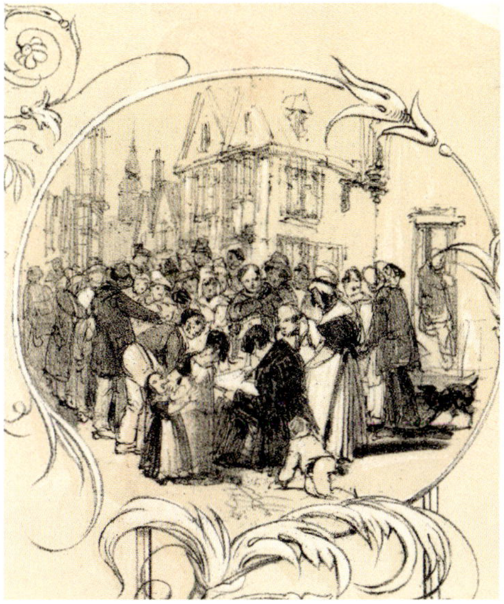
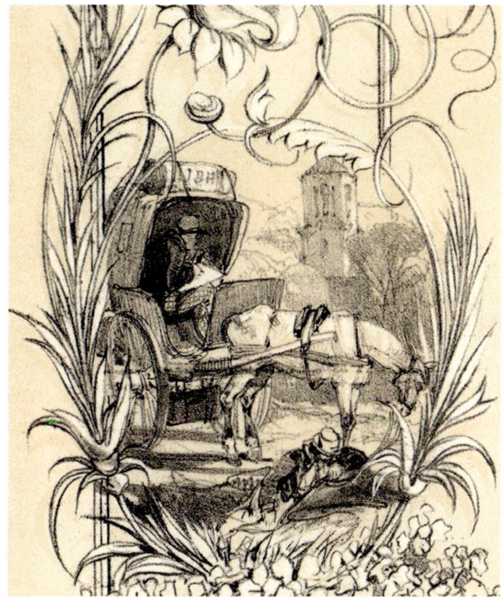
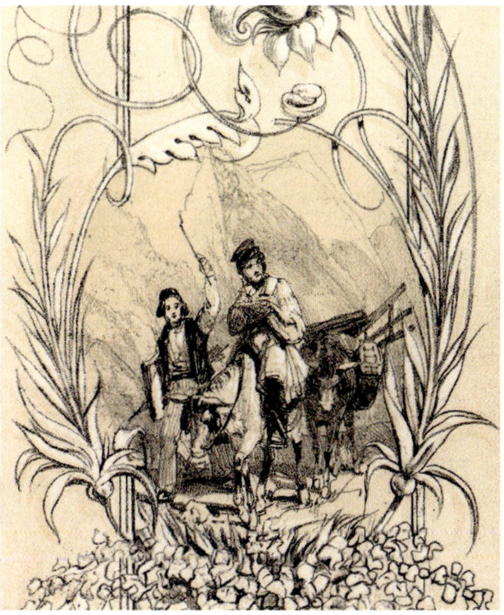
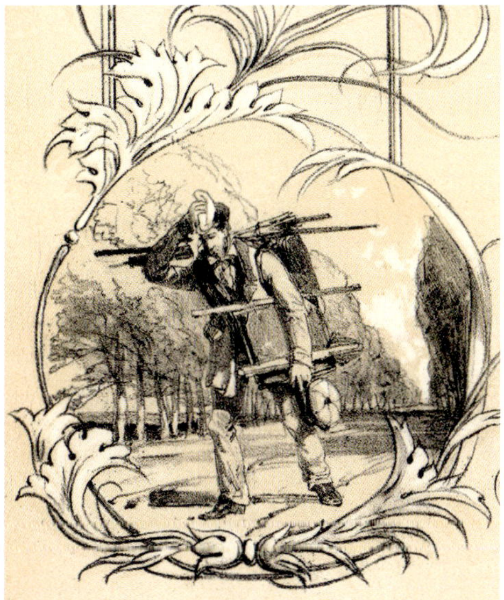
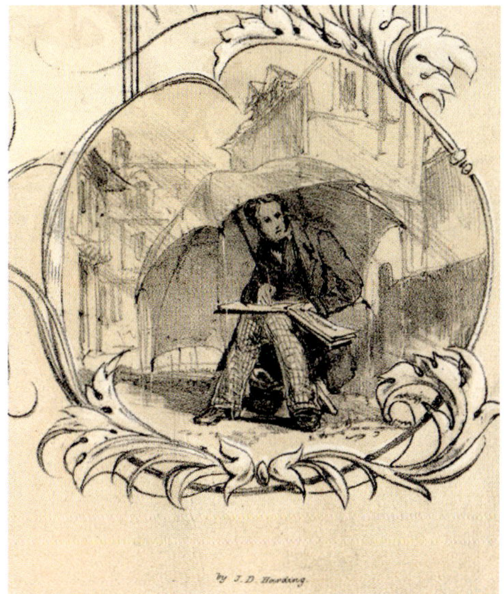
by J. D. Harding
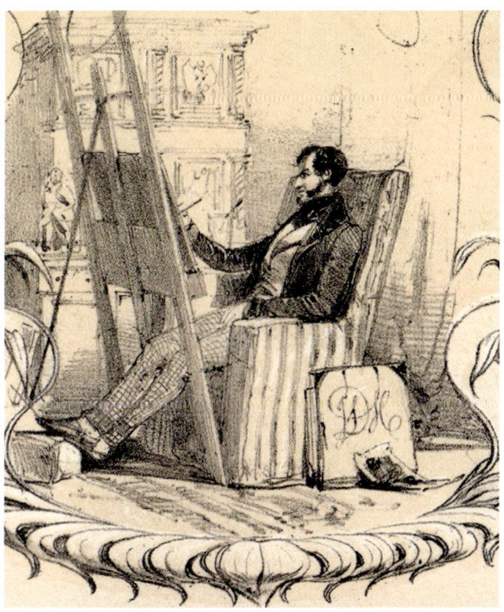

PLATE 18
*William Hogarth,* from the original picture in the collection of John and Josiah Boydell engraved by Benjamin Smith after William Hogarth. Published 4 June 1795 by J. & J. Boydell, No. 90 Cheapside, & at the Shakspeare [sic] Gallery, Pall Mall. Stipple engraving, 39.5 x 30 cm (15.5 x 11.8 in.).

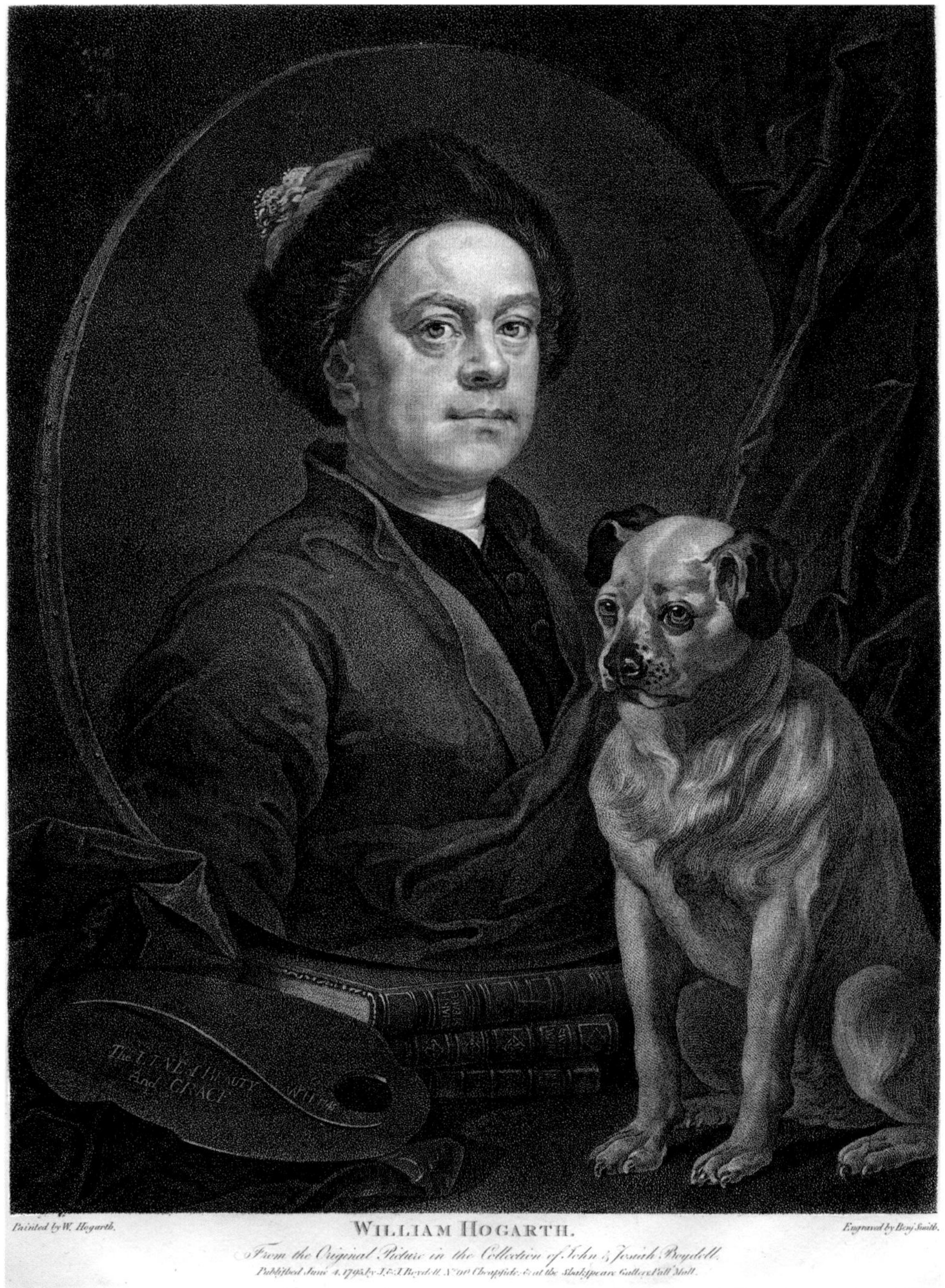


In fact, the print is one that was published by Baldwin, Cradock & Joy in 1822, and the detail is not as clear as an earlier impression because the plate had worn a little. In the notes which accompany bound sets of the prints, with the title *The Works of William Hogarth,* written by John Nichols, there is a short description. On the palette at the left corner can be seen 'W.H. 1745', the date of the Hogarth painting. Also on the palette is Hogarth's trademark, The Line of Beauty and Grace. Early impressions have the title in Latin: *Gulielmus Hogarth, seipse pinxit et sculpsit,* 1749 (the date of the first issue). Also in early impressions, the titles of the books in front of Hogarth are legible. In the illustrated print they are a little obscured: *Shakspeare* (again spelt that way), *Swift* and *Milton's Paradise Lost*, the latter being totally illegible. The original picture was in the collection of J.J. Angerstein, not the Boydells.

Hogarth is pictured with his dog Trump. Apparently Trump was a pug dog, though there is no similarity with the modern variety. Most early prints of breeds of dogs are equally unrecognisable.

Technically, the print is interesting because it is very densely engraved with stipple, and there is minimal use of line engraving, which is confined to Hogarth's cap and the upper parts of the dog.

Beneath the list of plates in Boydell's edition of the works of Hogarth is a note:

> Messrs Boydell & Co. think it their duty from the miserable copies of the Works of Hogarth that are published in this and other countries, to inform the Public that they are the sole Proprietors of the ORIGINAL WORKS of that celebrated Artist; for which they have long paid his family a large annuity:- That the Original Plates, engraved by the hand of that inimitable Artist, or under his eye, are in very good preservation, and produce good impressions. They also beg to inform the public, that since the Plates have been in their possession, they have never allowed any artist to profane them with a single touch, being very sensible that Hogarth's style of etching and engraving was so masterly, and expressed what he meant to convey so forcibly, that it shows all the imitators, and pretended restorers, at a great distance, as may be seen by comparing these miserable copies with the originals.

Much of the point of this is that Hogarth fought long and hard to achieve some sort of copyright to protect artists' work, not only his own. Hogarth led a group of prominent artists in the appeal to Parliament, and the appeal became known informally as Hogarth's Act. Such was the popularity of Hogarth's *Harlot's Progress* that the prints were quickly pirated, and, at the time, there was nothing that artists could do about it. Worse still, Hogarth's next set of prints, *The Rake's Progress*, was copied and on the market before Hogarth had completed his own engravings. Finally, a copyright act came into force in June 1735. From that date on, many prints have the imprint 'Published as the Act directs'. The Act went a long way towards protecting artists' work. Boydell's protestation in 1795, above, is an indication that he thought the Act was not working as it had been planned.

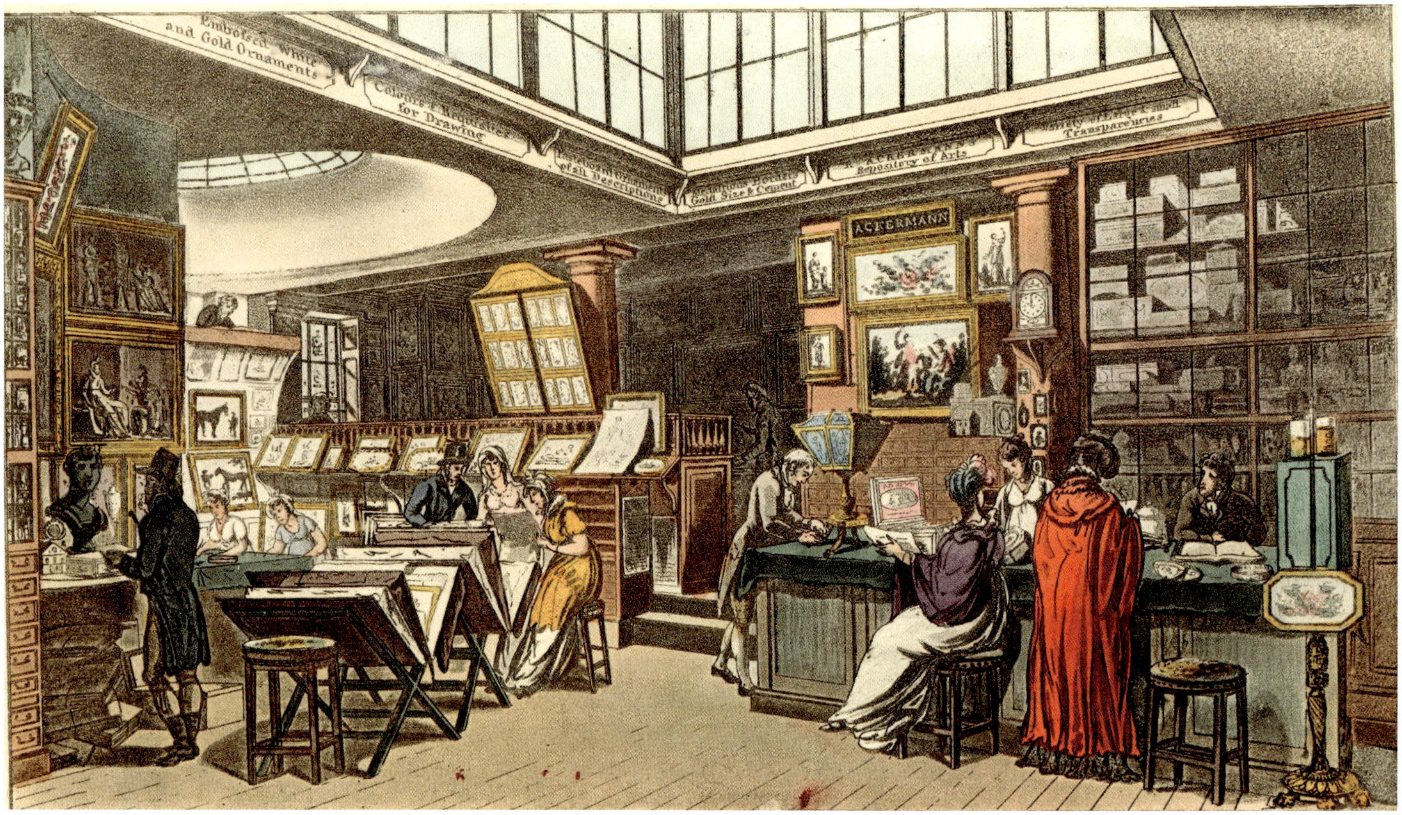


PLATE 19
*Ackermann's Repository of Arts. 101 Strand,* 1809.
Pugin & Rowlandson delt.
[No engraver's name.]
Aquatint, Image size: 13 x 22 cm (5 x 8.6 in.).

This print was published in January 1809 for the first issue of the monumental monthly magazine, named after Rudolph Ackermann's shop, but lengthened to *The Repository of Arts, Literature, Commerce, Manufactures, Fashions and Politics,* known as the *Repository*, or *Repository of Arts.* The publication continued until 1829, three months short of 30 years. It was such a success that there were 3,000 subscribers before the end of the first year. This was just one of many fine book productions that made Ackermann's name famous.

Lighting a shop like this was a problem. Here we see a large lantern light and a smaller domed roof light, to get as much daylight in as possible, though they might not have been good at keeping water out. Ackermann patented a method of making paper and cloth waterproof, so he probably had some scheme to keep his roof watertight as well. He was one of the first to have gas lighting in a London shop, made from his own design, but there is no sign of it in the picture. Ackermann's father was a coach builder; Rudolph's first career was in his father's footsteps, designing coaches himself. He was entrusted with the building of Nelson's funeral carriage. The carriage is shown in the print of Greenwich Hospital, published in Ackermann's *Microcosm of London.* Greenwich Hospital is now the Maritime Museum, and they still have the carriage. He also patented a system of movable carriage axles, a spare-time occupation, in about 1820, when he was still publishing fine works of art.

The signs around the edge of the lantern light are to do with artists' materials and not the wealth of prints that were available.

What about the print? It was certainly aquatinted by a competent engraver, probably one of the team who worked on the *Microcosm.* Many of the illustrations in the *Repository* are not credited with the names of artist or engraver. The colouring is excellent. It would have been done by a colourist using a master as a guide, so the colouring of the same print tends to be very similar. In the top margin can be seen two stitch marks, which held the print and the rest of that month's magazine into the original wrapper. Often these 'parts' were grouped together and put into a full binding. The left side of the print has been severely shaved, actually cutting into the image, a problem caused by the clumsiness of the binder, and something that happens too often.

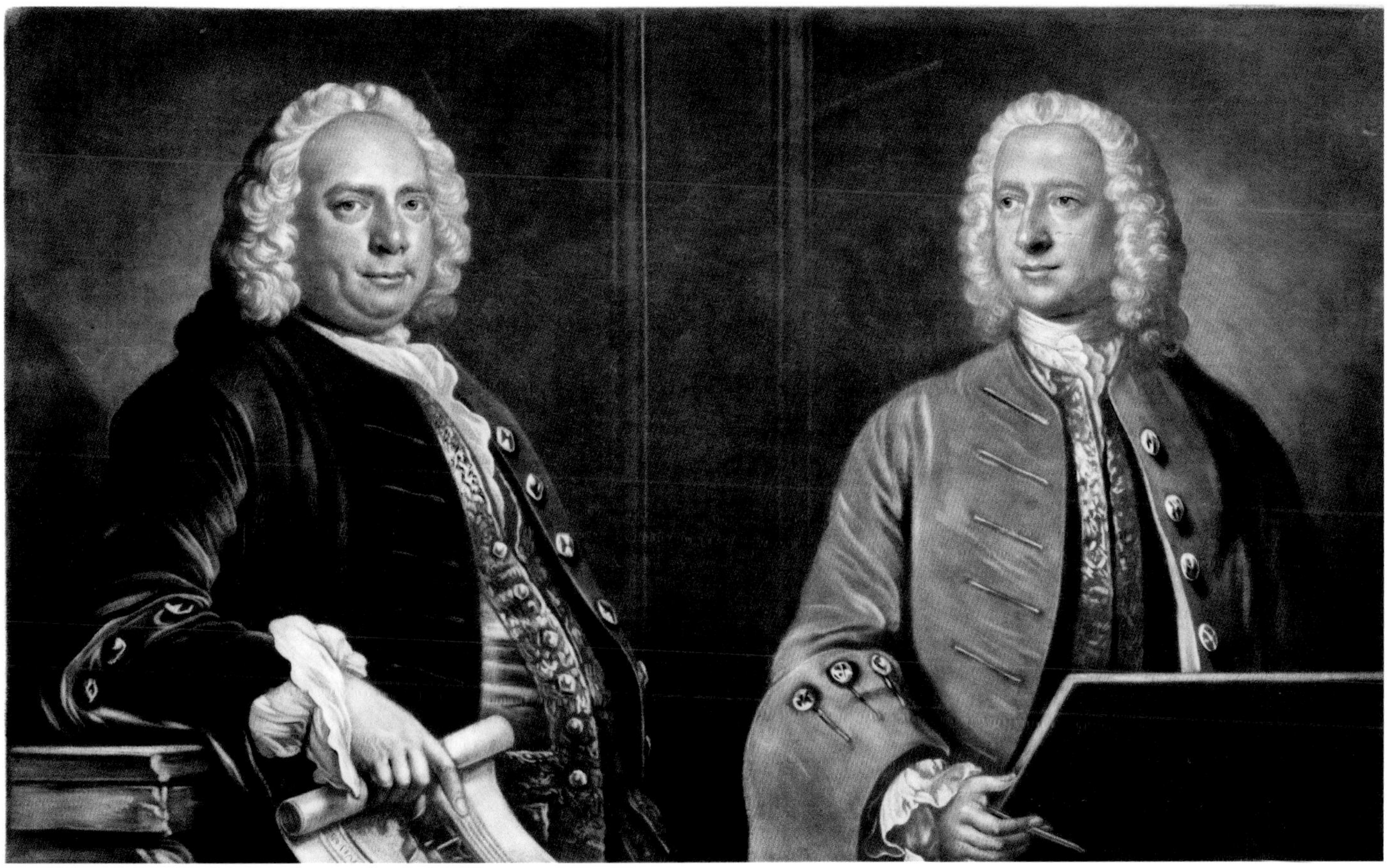

PLATE 20
*Samuel Buck – Nathaniel Buck,* engraved by Richard Houston, 1774. Mezzotint.

The Buck brothers were prolific topographical artists and engravers in the early part of the 18th century. Many of their town views are the earliest prints of the places depicted. The print is a mezzotint, fully described at plate 73 (page 101). Before moving on, notice the subtle textures, particularly in the clothing. The buttons on their jackets are made to look highly polished by contrasting black and white, which I totally failed to achieve when I tried to make a print of a polished van with my potato.

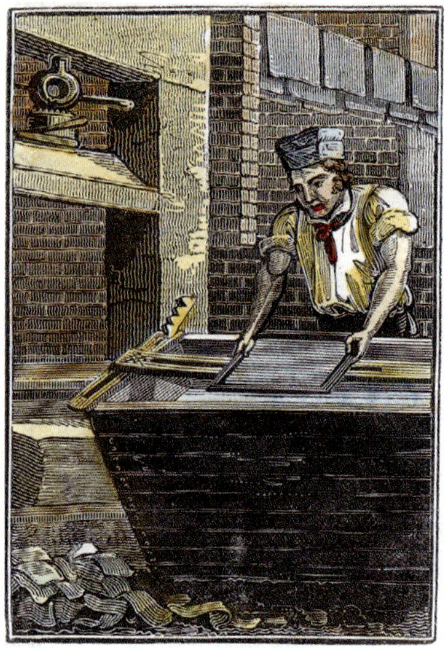

PLATE 21
*Papermaker,*
Anon, *c.*1800.
Copper engraving,
Image size: 9 x 6 cm (3.5 x 2.4 in.).

This is an anonymous print made in about 1800 for a series titled *The Book of Trades*. It was a popular publication, running into several editions over a period of at least 50 years. Here the papermaker is shown with a vat of pulp and a tray, which acted like a sieve, the surplus water draining through the wires. Behind him, sheets of paper are hanging up to dry, and to the left of the print is a large press, which was used to flatten the paper before it was completely dry. At the bottom of the press is a pile of paper ready to be pressed.

The following is the text from an edition of the book, volume III, 1807, *The Paper-Maker*:

> The manufacture of paper is so curious, and so well worth the attention of young persons, that we recommend them to take some pains to get a sight of the whole process, which may easily be done wherever there are paper-mills.
>
> Linen, such as our shirts are made of, is spun from flax that grows in the fields; and from linen rags, that is, from shirts and other articles of dress when worn thread-bare, fine white paper is manufactured: of course every piece of rag, however small, should be preserved, and not thrown into the fire.
>
> The first thing to be done towards the formation of the paper, is to put the rags into a machine, or cylinder, formed of wire, which is made to turn round with great velocity to whirl out the dust; they are then sorted according to their different qualities; after which they are put into a large cistern or trough perforated with holes, through which a stream of clear water constantly flows. In this cistern is placed a cylinder about two feet long, set thick with rows of iron spikes. At the bottom of the trough there are corresponding rows of spikes. The cylinder is made to whirl round with inconceivable rapidity, and, with the iron teeth, rends and tears the cloth to atoms, till with the assistance of the water it is reduced to thin pulp. By the same process all the impurities are cleared away, and it is restored to its original whiteness. This fine pulp is next put into a copper of warm water, and here it becomes the substance of paper, and ready for the mould; for which purpose it is conveyed to the vat. The vat, of which we have a representation in the plate, is made of wood, generally about five feet broad, and two or three feet in depth. It is kept to a proper temperature by means of a charcoal fire.
>
> The mould, which the paper-maker has in his hand, is composed of many wires set in a frame close together, and of another moveable frame equal in size to the sheet of paper to be made. These wires are disposed in the shape of a figure, which is discovered in a sheet of paper when we hold it to the light.
>
> The workman holds the frame in both hands, plunges it horizontally into the tub, and takes it up quickly; the water runs away between the

wires, and there remains nothing on the mould but the beaten pulp, in a thin coat, which forms the sheet of paper.

Another person, called a coucher, receives the mould, and places the sheet of paper on a felt or woollen cloth, during which [time] the workman makes another sheet. They proceed in the manner, laying alternately a sheet and a felt, till they have made six quires of paper, which is called a post: such is the heap on the right hand of the vat. When the last sheet of the post is covered with the last felt, the workmen employed about the vat unite, and submit the whole heap to the action of the press, which is on the paper-maker's right hand. After the operation, another person separates the sheets of paper from the felts, laying them in a heap: and several of these heaps, collected together, are again put under the press. They are turned and pressed several times, and then the sheets are hung up, three or four together, on lines to dry.

The paper is now to be sized, because in its present state it will not bear the ink. The size is made of shreds and parings, collected from the tanners, curriers, and parchment-makers; and immediately before the operation, a certain amount of alum is added to the size. The workman takes a handful of the sheets, smoothed and rendered as supple as possible, and dips them into the vessel containing the size, and when he has finished ten or a dozen of these handfuls, they are submitted to the action of the press; the superfluous size is carried back to the vessel by means of a small pipe. The paper is now hung, sheet by sheet, on lines to dry.

When the paper is sufficiently dry, it is carried to the finishing room, where it is pressed, selected, examined, folded, made up into quires, and finally into reams. It is here submitted twice to the press; first when it is full of size, and secondly, after it is folded.

Every quire of paper consists of twenty-four or twenty-five sheets; that is, the larger numbers refer to paper made for the use in printing: and each ream contains twenty quires.

In the manufacture many sheets are damaged; these, in the sorting room are put together, and two of the worst quires are placed on the outsides of the ream, called outside quires. The reams are tied up in wrappers made of the settling of the vat, and then they are fit for sale. Some paper is made smooth and glossy like satin, by means of hot plates; this is called hot-pressing. The process of paper-making takes about three weeks.

Paste-board is made in a similar way to that of paper.

Blotting-paper, and paper used for filtering fluids is paper not sized, in which the ink rapidly sinks or spreads. Brown and other coloured papers are made of coarse or coloured rags.

Wove or woven paper is made in moulds, the wires of which are exceedingly fine, of equal thickness, and woven or latticed one with another. The marks, therefore, of these are easily pressed out, so as to be scarcely visible.

# THE PRINTING PROCESSES

There are three basic materials that were used in the making of the plates and blocks that printed pictures. These are wood, metal and stone.

There are three distinctive ways in which these materials were used. Wood and metal required some sort of engraving – cutting into the material in various ways to produce the image that could be transferred to paper with a printing press. These engravings are either 'relief' or 'intaglio'. Printing from a stone required a flat surface, without any engraving, and is known as 'lithography'.

With all three processes, work begins on a perfectly flat surface. If there are any blemishes, especially with metal plates, they will be seen on the eventual prints, so the engraver had to ensure that the surface was perfect before starting work.

Printing in relief is the most straightforward of the three, and, for the record, is the same process as working on my potato or, perhaps more common in schools now, the linocut. The customary material was wood, though copper and zinc were also used. The method was to cut away all the areas of the block that did not print any part of the design, or, in other words, the white areas, leaving the design standing up in relief.

Intaglio is the opposite of relief. Metal plates were used, and it is the incisions into the metal that will print onto paper. It differs from relief because there are many ways that these incisions can be made into the plate, either with a wide variety of special tools or with the controlled use of acid.

Lithography is different from relief or intaglio, and does not require any incising of the surface. It is the most modern of the three, and by far the most exploited, for the simple reason that slight variations in printing on a flat surface are always called lithography. The earliest lithographs were made with stone. Metals were used in the later period.

The words 'relief' and 'intaglio' are not in common use, being words to describe collective forms of printing. Instead, the usual words are those which are more descriptive of the method, and are the headings for each of the sections on the printing processes. These are:

- ❖ Woodcuts and Wood Engraving
- ❖ Intaglio
- ❖ Line Engraving
- ❖ Etching
- ❖ Drypoint etching
- ❖ Mezzotint
- ❖ Stipple Engraving
- ❖ Soft Ground Etching
- ❖ Aquatint
- ❖ Mixed methods
- ❖ Lithography
- ❖ Transfer Lithographs
- ❖ Multi-block Colour Printing.

# WOODCUTS AND WOOD ENGRAVING

The difference between a woodcut and a wood engraving is simply in the way that the wood is used. When a piece of wood is prepared from a tree trunk or branch, it has two surface textures, one that is smooth, with the grain, and the other that is quite rough, cut across the grain. Woodcuts are made from the plank, cut with the grain, on the smooth surface. Wood engravings are made from wood cut across the grain, and, surprisingly, the rough end grain is capable of making finer detailed prints than can be achieved with a smooth plank. The wood for engravings had to be hard and fine grained and the most commonly used was box wood and fruit woods. Any wood cut from those trees tends to be small, and that limited the size of wood engravings. However, for larger works, it was possible to join pieces of wood together, which is the way that very large prints were made for *The Illustrated London News* supplements, published from 1842 onwards. Being a newspaper, these illustrations had to be produced rapidly, and the engraving was often done by several engravers, each engraver working on a separate block, which needs some very careful co-ordinating. In the circumstances, the results are amazing.

Woodcut was the first method used to print images onto paper. The earliest record of its use was not for printing onto paper, but for printing designs onto fabric. It was used in the East for 200 years before it was introduced into Europe, in about 1200. The earliest known picture printed onto paper dates from a little before 1400. Obviously, woodcut played an extremely important part in the history of printing illustrations, and even with such crude materials, the first printmakers managed to produce wonderful work. Wood engraving emerged considerably later, perfected by Thomas Bewick and his followers during the revival of the use of wood in the late 18th century.

To prepare a woodblock, the wood was finished to an even thickness of about 2 or 3 cm. The working surface needed to be perfectly flat, but the rest of it – the edges and the back – were often left in a rough state, and were not always cut to be rectangular. Once the block was prepared, the outline of the image was traced onto the block, and then the engraver began the task of cutting away all of the wood that was not required to print onto the paper. In the case of relief, this means the parts of the image that show white on the paper. The engraving was done with a variety of knives and finely tipped chisels, which obviously had to be kept as sharp as possible. All that was required was that the engraver cut into the wood enough to leave the printing parts standing up in relief, a millimetre or so, but engravers chose to reduce the level by more than that to ensure that there was no chance of the white parts touching the paper during the printing stage. For that reason, a printing block is a crude-looking thing, probably not rectangular, and certainly not looking capable of making a fine print. All that mattered to the engraver was the accuracy of the detail of the parts left standing in relief which produce the eventual print – hopefully a perfect one.

The main difficulty was to produce fine lines of an even width, cutting the wood away until the finest possible line remained. A slip of the hand was sometimes unavoidable, but the wood at each side of the line was cut at an angle to keep the maximum strength in the wood, the line being on top of the pyramid, which reduced the risk of a mistake. When a mistake was made, a correction could be done by cutting out the area of the mistake, inserting another piece of wood, and then re-engraving – a time-consuming job.

Because of the difficulty of producing fine lines, woodcut was suited to simple designs in which fine detail is not crucial to the picture. The earliest printed maps were made with woodcut, although they look crude in comparison to those printed from metal plates. In many cases, the lettering was added by the use of typeset let into the woodblock, the letters set at the same height as the relief, so that a print could be made in one pull, which was obviously easier and more economical than printing text and illustrations separately.

Woodcuts could be printed using a small amount of pressure. Presses were used, but many were printed by laying paper over the block and applying pressure with the hand. Some were printed by pressing the handheld block down onto paper, like the illustrations on printed wallpaper and fabrics.

Metal cuts were produced in the same way, cutting away the areas which were not required to print the image, but the method never became popular. There were a few prints made this way in the middle of the 15th century, but these are rare indeed.

Despite their limitations woodcuts and wood engraving kept their popularity over a long period, from the early days of printed fabrics to far beyond the date limit of this book.

Many aquatints were printed in two or three colours with the rest of the colour added by hand, and this, of course, speeded up the operation. Fox's *Brighton Suspension Pier* (plates 103 to 105, pages 142–4) provides a good example.

The customary manner of description is to use 'colour' when a print is printed in colour, and 'coloured' when a print is hand-coloured. So 'colour stipple' means that it was printed in several colours; 'coloured stipple' means it was printed in one colour and the additional colour was added by hand.

There is, sometimes, some difficulty in detecting whether a print is colour-printed or hand-coloured. For the purpose of explanation, it is easiest to describe stipple engraving. Close examination of a particular detail – usually a face is the best – will show a multiplicity of dots. If the print was made in black ink only, these dots are obviously still going to show black if the print is hand-coloured, whereas a colour print will show the dots as skin-coloured. As well as the two examples of Boydell's *Cymbeline* (see plates 80 & 81, pages 112–13), see what happens when a black and white print is hand-coloured in the illustration of *Emma Dolben* (plate 82, page 113), stressing the point about black dots.

All of this may seem complicated, a finer point for print connoisseurs, but the colour-printed *Cymbeline* has a value of five times the black and white example, so it is worth understanding the difference.

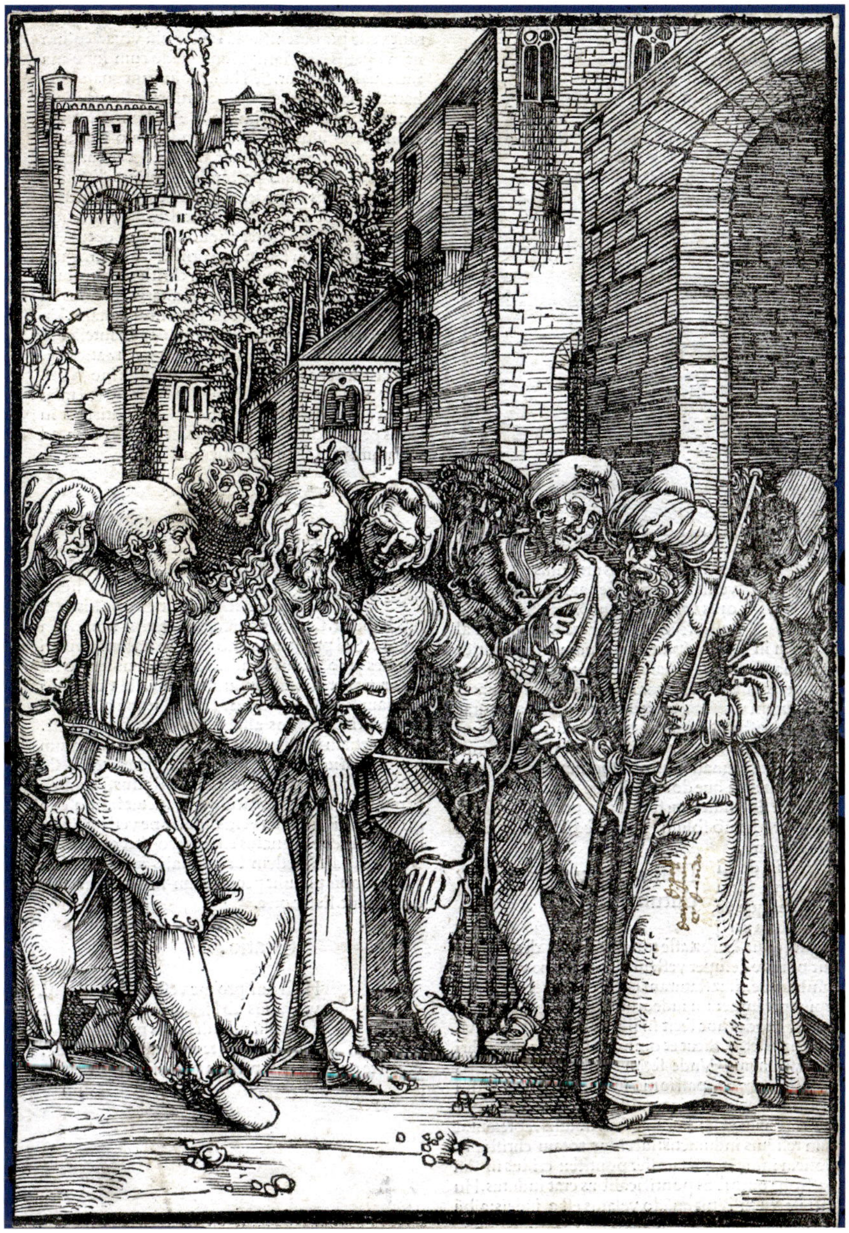

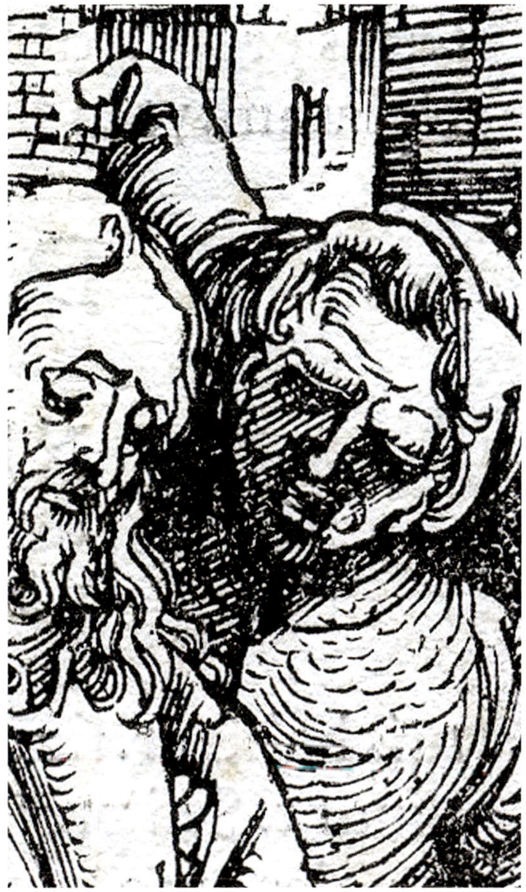

PLATE 22 AND DETAIL
*Christ before Pilate*, engraved by Hans Leonard Schenflein, 1507.
Wood engraving,
23.5 x 15.5 cm (9.2 x. 6.1 in.)

Printed to illustrate Pindar's Speculum Passionis. Schenflein is thought to have been a pupil of Albrecht Dürer, and this print is very much in Dürer's style, a typical wood engraving of the period, produced with bold, definite lines which print the same density of black, without any grey tones. This example has some very fine lines in it, very difficult for the engraver to achieve. If you look at the enlarged illustration you can see the fineness of the lines of the detail. Imagine the difficulty of cutting away the wood so that the parts required to print onto paper are left standing in relief. The remaining lines of wood are no thicker than you would produce with a sharp pencil on paper.

Early editions of the print, such as this one, have text on the back which shows through the paper slightly, and the lines of text have made ridges in the paper.

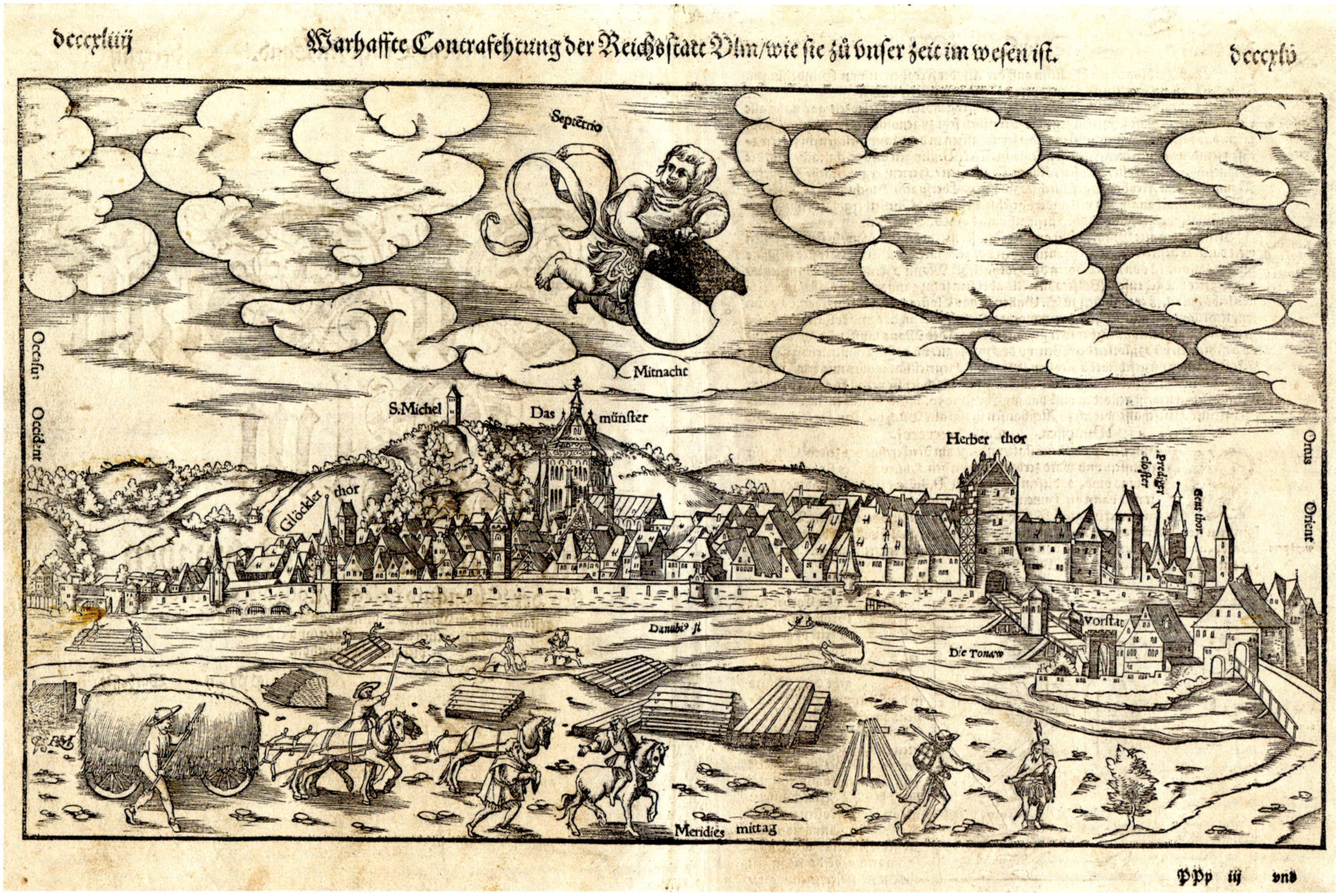


PLATE 23 & DETAIL.
*Ulm,* published in Sebastian Munster's *Cosmography*, *c.*1550.
Woodcut,
22 x 28 cm (8.6 x 11 in.).

Notice how the lines in the background are just as black as those in the foreground, because all lines are printed with the same density, making perspective difficult with wood engraving. Also, the top section of the shield is a dense black, as dense as is possible with woodcut. The lettering was done by typeset, let into the wood block. There is also typeset on the back of the print, which shows through the paper. At the time, Ulm was a major centre of printing.

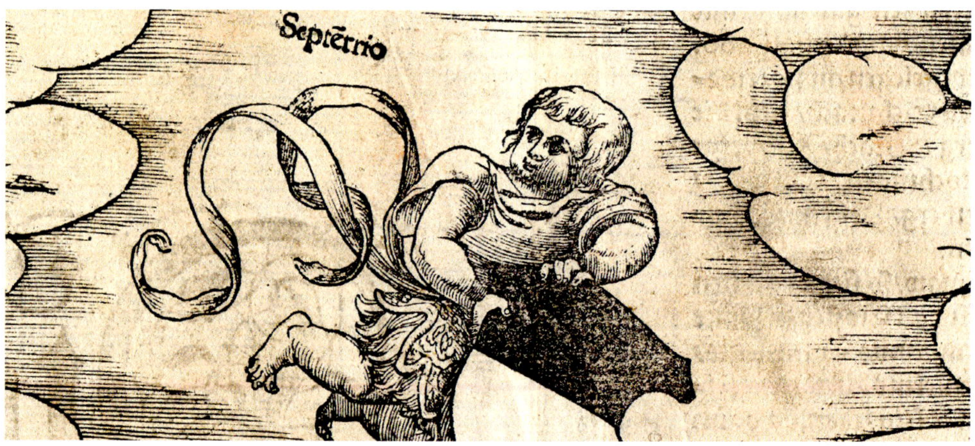

PLATE 24.

*Wilhelm Tell,* another illustration from *Cosmography, c.*1550. Woodcut, 13 x 12 cm (5 x 4.7 in.).

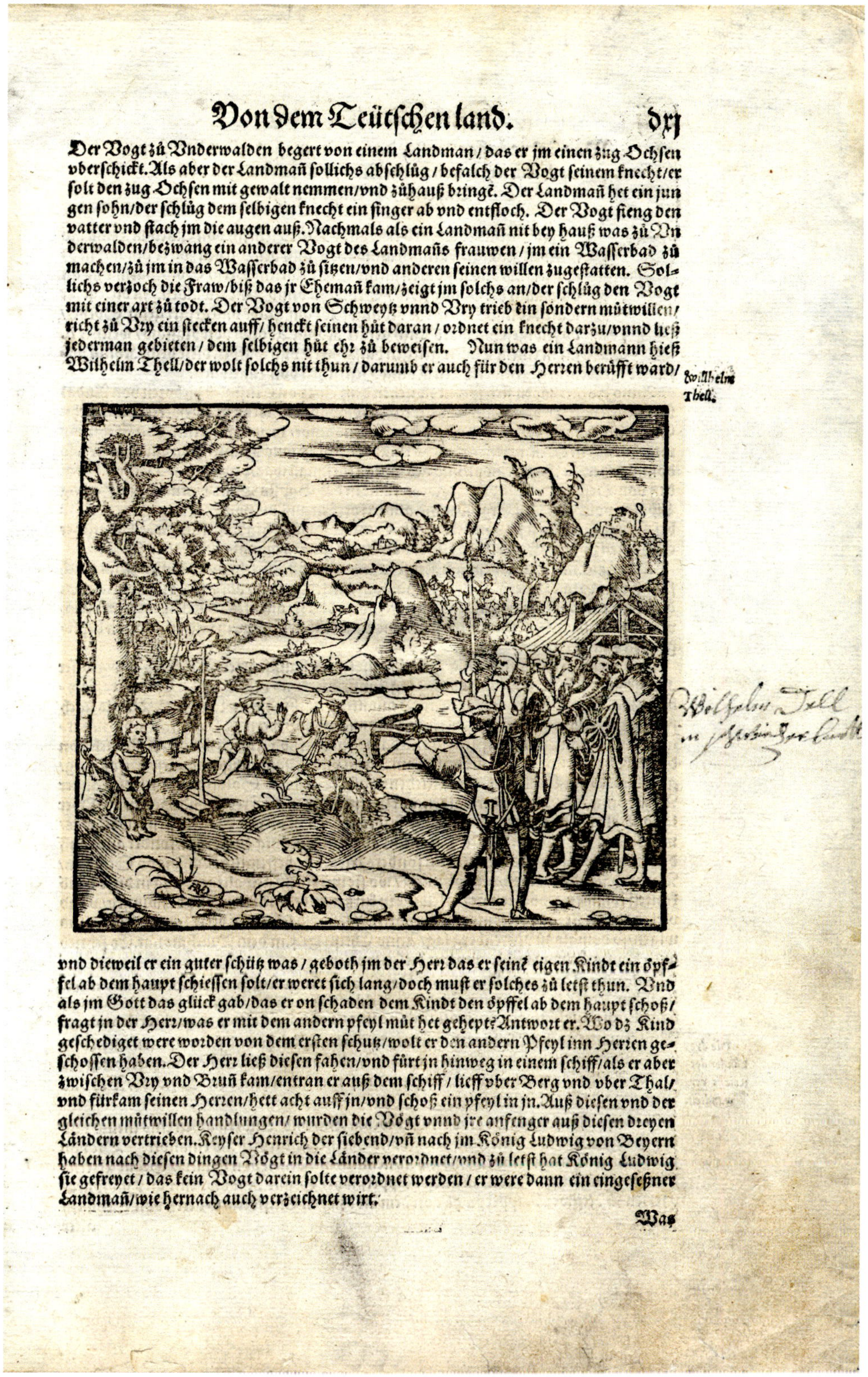

Von dem Teütschen land. xxj

Der Vogt zů Vnderwalden begert von einem Landman / das er jm einen zug Ochsen vberschickt. Als aber der Landmañ sollichs abschlůg / befalch der Vogt seinem knecht/er solt den zug Ochsen mit gewalt nemmen/vnd zůhauß bringẽ. Der Landmañ het ein jungen sohn/der schlůg dem selbigen knecht ein finger ab vnd entfloch. Der Vogt fieng den vatter vnd stach jm die augen auß. Nachmals als ein Landmañ nit bey hauß was zů Vnderwalden/bezwang ein anderer Vogt des Landmañs frauwen / jm ein Wasserbad zů machen/zů jm in das Wasserbad zů sitzen/vnd anderen seinen willen zugestatten. Solichs verzoch die Fraw/biß das jr Ehemañ kam/zeigt jm solchs an/der schlůg den Vogt mit einer axt zů todt. Der Vogt von Schweytz vnnd Vry trieb ein sondern můtwillen/ richt zů Vry ein stecken auff/ henckt seinen hůt daran / ordnet ein knecht darzu/vnnd ließ jederman gebieten / dem selbigen hůt ehr zů beweisen. Nun was ein Landmann hieß Wilhelm Thell/der wolt solchs nit thun / darumb er auch für den Herren berůfft ward/ Wilhelm Thell.

vnd dieweil er ein guter schütz was / geboth jm der Herr das er seinẽ eigen Kindt ein öpffel ab dem haupt schiessen solt/er weret sich lang/doch must er solches zů letst thun. Vnd als jm Gott das glück gab/das er on schaden dem Kindt den öpffel ab dem haupt schoß/ fragt jn der Herr/was er mit dem andern pfeyl můt het gehept? Antwort er. Wo dz Kind geschediget were worden von dem ersten schutz/wolt er den andern Pfeyl inn Herren geschossen haben. Der Herr ließ diesen fahen/vnd fürt jn hinweg in einem schiff/als er aber zwischen Vry vnd Bruñ kam/entran er auß dem schiff / lieff vber Berg vnd vber Thal/ vnd fürkam seinen Herren/hett acht auff jn/vnd schoß ein pfeyl in jn. Auß diesen vnd der gleichen můtwillen handlungen/ wurden die Vögt vnnd jre anfenger auß diesen dreyen Ländern vertrieben. Keyser Henrich der siebend/vñ nach jm König Ludwig von Beyern haben nach diesen dingen Vögt in die Länder verordnet/vnd zů letst hat König Ludwig sie gefreyet / das kein Vogt darein solte verordnet werden / er were dann ein eingeseßner Landmañ/wie hernach auch verzeichnet wirt.

Was

The engraving shows William Tell about to shoot the apple from his son's head, another illustration from Sebastian Munster's *Cosmography*, published in about 1550. The smaller illustrations, like this one, were integrated into the typeset text.

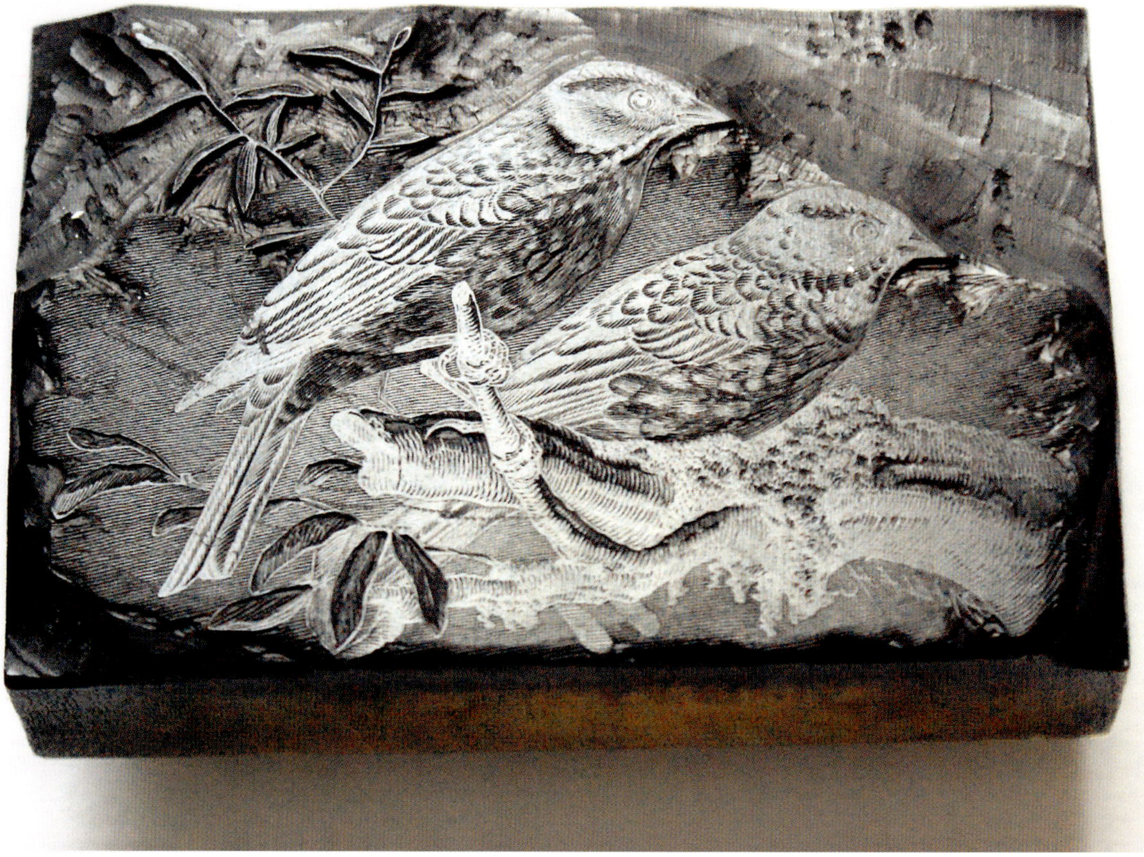

PLATE 25
*Rustic Bunting, Summer Plumage.*
Wood engraving. Blocks and prints.
AND PLATE 26
*[Hooded Crow]*
Size: about 6.5 x 9 cm
(2.5 x 3.5 in.).

The Dalziel brothers were followers of Thomas Bewick, the great wood engraver, also from Northumberland, who revived the art in the late eighteenth century. You can see here that Bewick greatly influenced the work of the brothers. The effect of their work is very different from their early hard style; there are some tones and degrees of blackness in the print. The block is box wood, their preferred wood because of its hardness and fine grain. Although quite small, there were many wood engravings of about this size, because of the limitations of the size of the wood. It is well preserved, and the surface is smooth and polished. The extremities of the block are crudely cut away; there was no need for symmetry. The illustrations were recently printed from the woodblocks by John Land at the Printing Workshop at Amberley Museum.

Plate 26

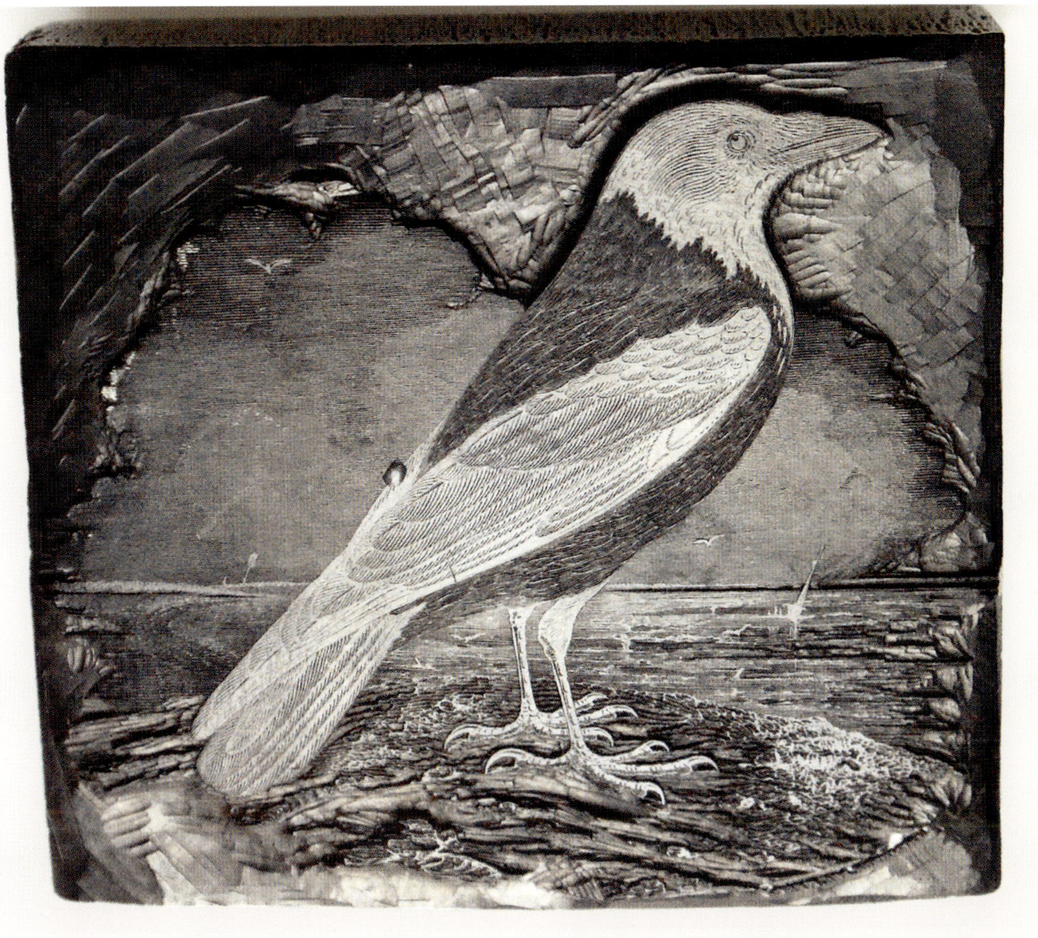

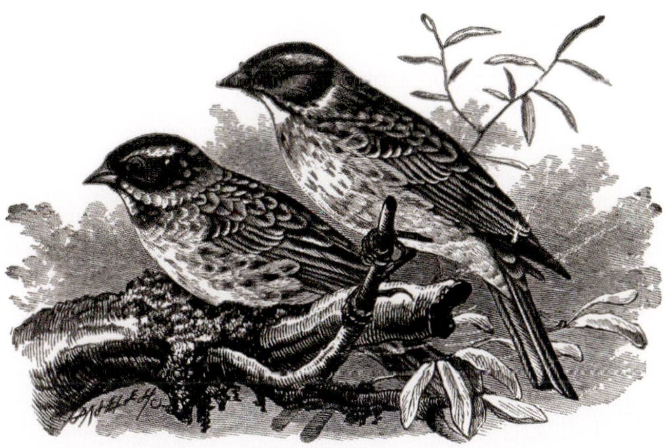

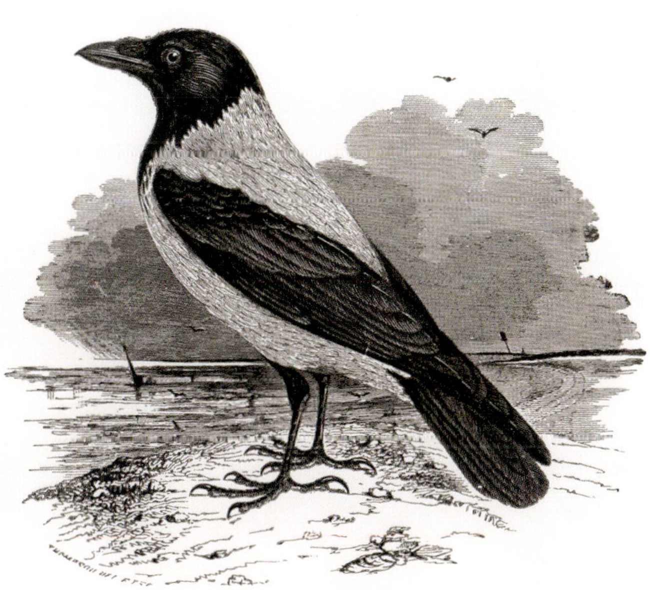

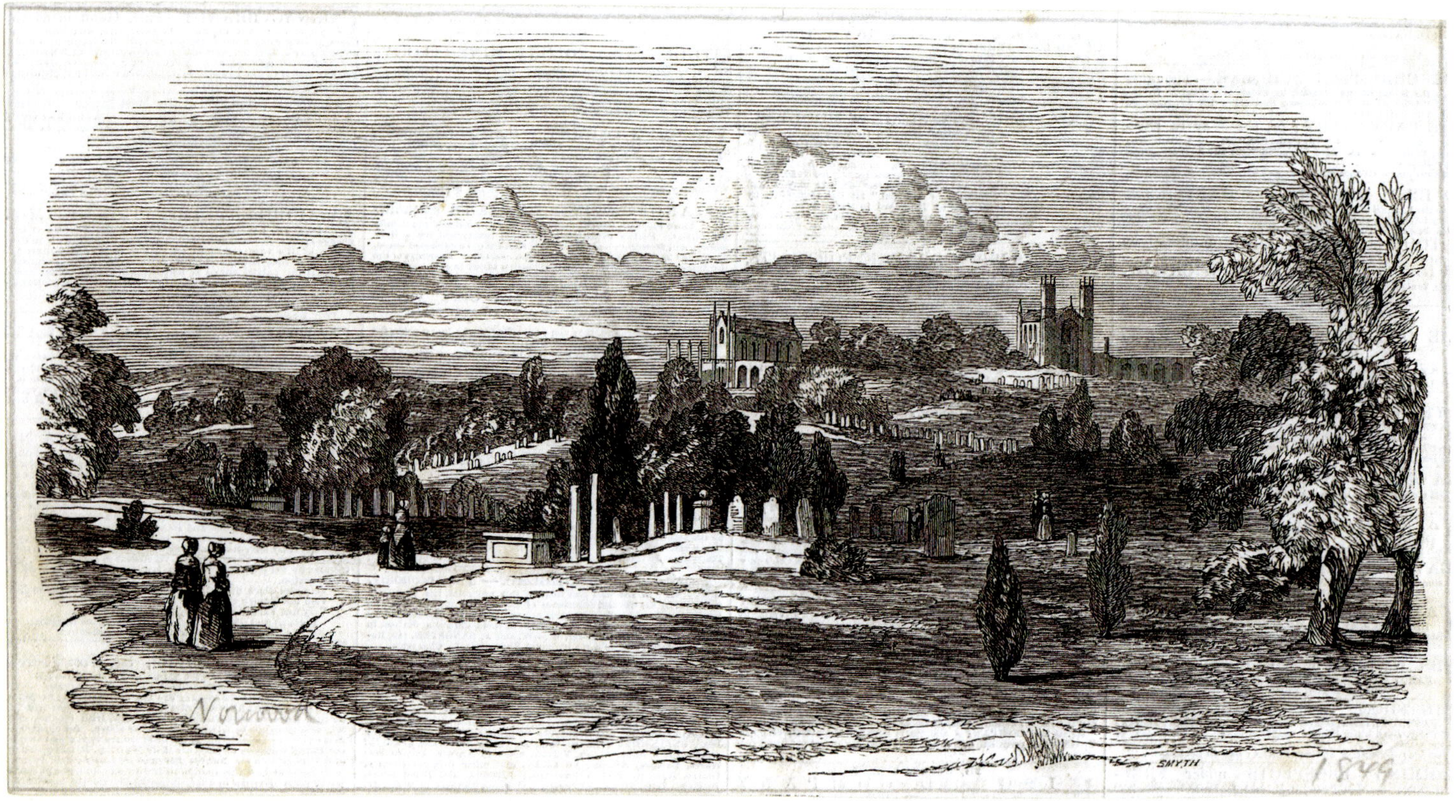


PLATE 27
*Norwood.* Engraved by Smyth.
1849.
Published in the *Illustrated London News*, 1849.
Wood engraving,
12 x 22.5 cm (4.7 x 9 in.).

The 'ILN' employed numerous engravers, who were required to produce illustrations like this as quickly as possible, due to the fleeting nature of a daily newspaper. All things considered, the results were good. On the reverse are some advertisements which are fascinating to read, covering many subjects. One is for bottles of brandy sold by the dozen for 54 shillings (£2.70). Another reads, 'Deane's registered postal alarum [alarm] letter-box. Her Majesty's Postmaster – General having commended to the public the adoption of letter-box in houses and office doors, G. and J. Deane have introduced a new Letter-box and Alarum, so constructed that notice is given whenever a letter or newspaper is inserted. For public offices and chambers this invention is most valuable, as without it, communications of the utmost importance often remain for hours unnoticed.'

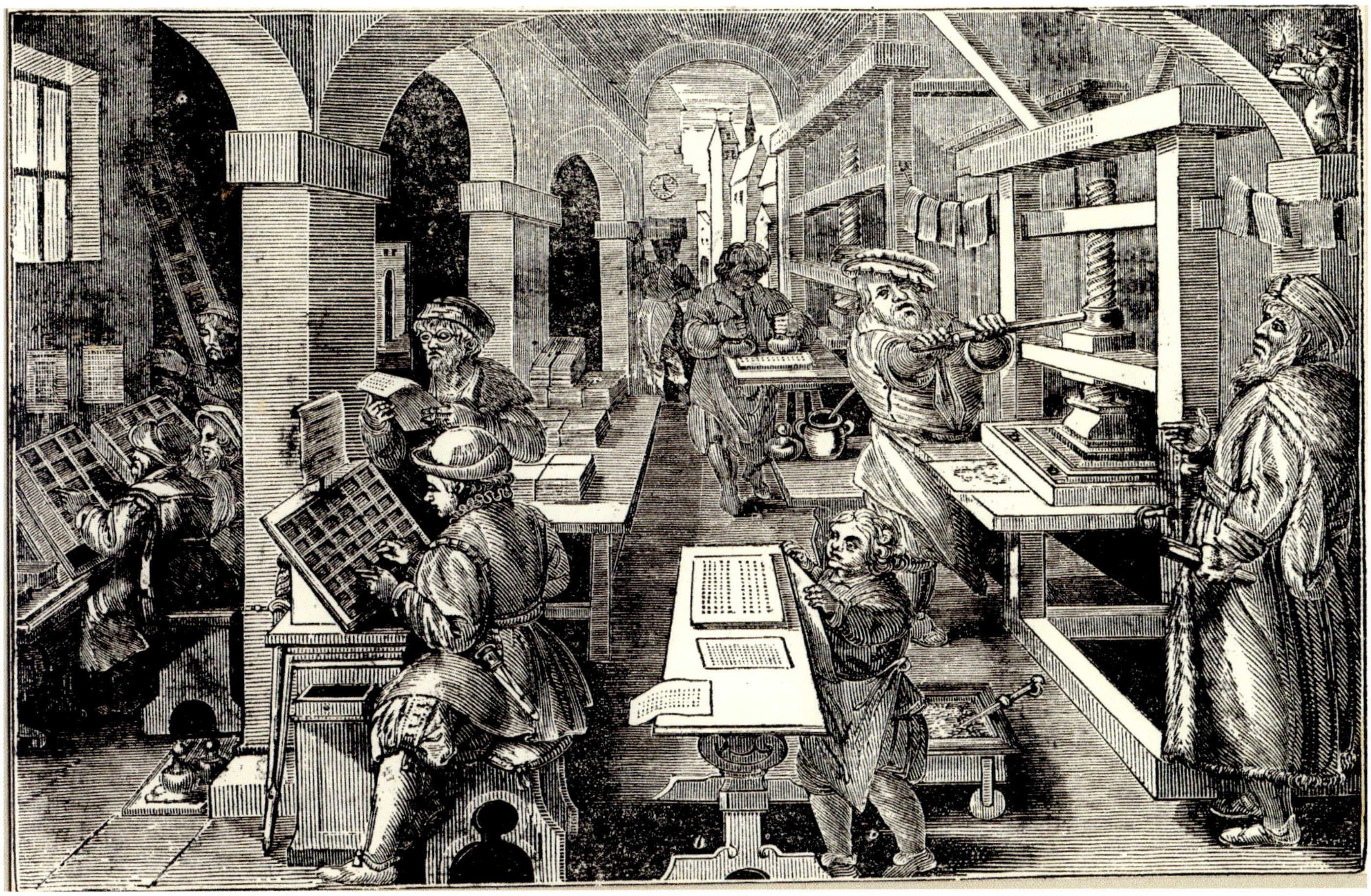

An anonymous print, produced for a magazine or a periodical during the late 19th century, probably *The Illustrated London News*. The scene is set in the early 17th century. The printers are using typeset for text, and do not appear to be printing illustrations. The men on the left are setting type, and the letters are kept in the divisions of the boxes in front of them. In the centre of the background a man is inking a galley of text. On the right is a large and robust printing press.

On the reverse is some text explaining the work of a 19th-century compositor and the speed at which they worked, which seems ridiculously slow to us. Nominated is a government report of an inquiry into factories, published by Messrs Hansard, who still publish government reports. The report contains about 1200 pages. Each page contains an average of 72 lines of 80 letters. To quote, 'A good compositor can pick up about 15,000 letters in a day, so it would take one compositor 460 days to produce the text for this volume. But, in addition to this, there are side notes of the Report, which would occupy at least a fourth more of the time; making a total time that it would occupy one compositor to produce this book, 600 days, or two working years.' Since such a report would have had to be published in two weeks, there were some 50 compositors involved.

PLATE 28
*Ancient View of a Dutch Printing Office,* anon, *c.* 1860.
Woodcut,
10 x 14.5 cm (4 x 5.7 in.).

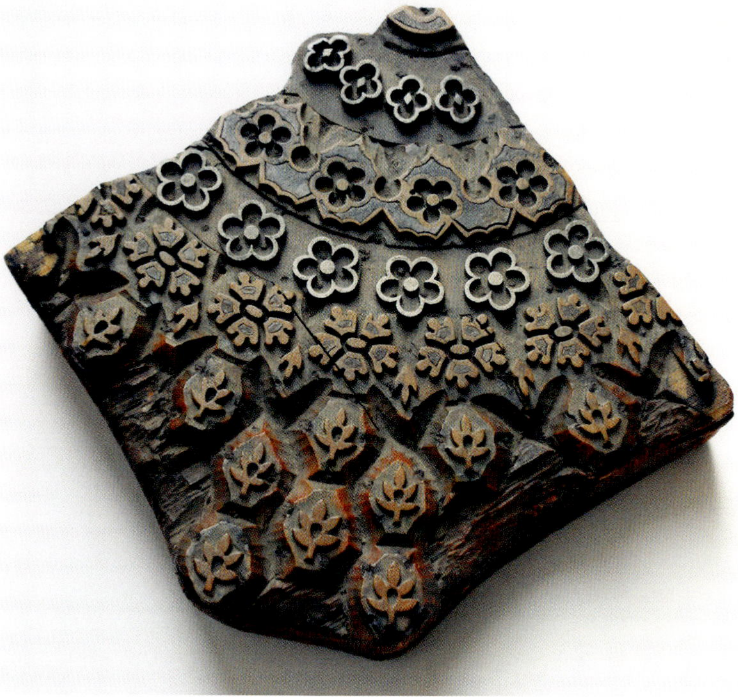

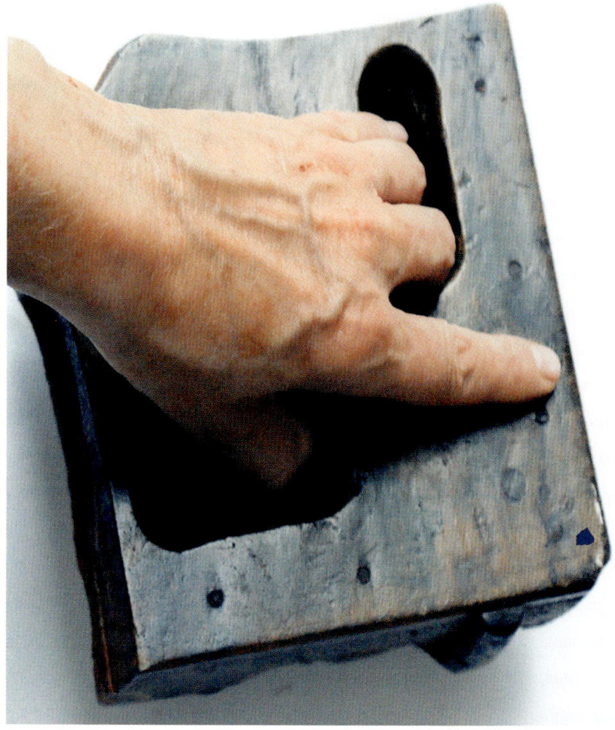

PLATE 29
Fabric printing block.
16 x 16 cm (6 x 6 in.).

This block was used to print fabrics without the use of a printing press, placing the block in precisely the correct position on the fabric and sharply tapping the back of it with a mallet, as shown in plate 31, a method which is in total contrast with the pressure required to print an intaglio plate. The block-maker simplified his job and made the block more durable by using metal inserts for the second and fourth ring of the design.

On the back are two wide slots that enabled the block to be gripped with the fingers and thumb. The block is a quarter of the complete pattern, so the printer had to carefully position the block four times for each section of the design, applying more dye each time.

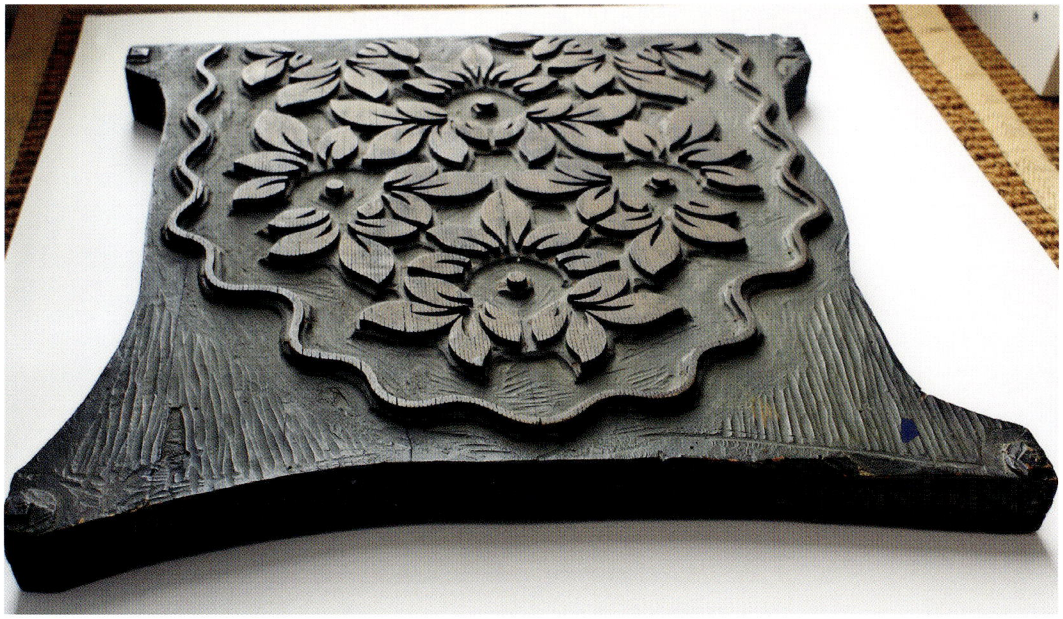

PLATE 30

Wallpaper printing block.
46 x 48 cm (18 x 18.9 in.).
Made between 1850 and 1880.

The wood is oak, which is a much rougher grain than fruitwoods, and not suited to printing fine detail. The block is made up of five layers of wood laminated together, with the grain running in alternate directions for each layer, which helped to prevent warping. The block is still completely flat. The thickness of the block is 5 cm. For added strength, there are nails along the edges of the relief; there are 63 in the outer border alone.

The block is half of the design. At the four corners are pinholes to 'register' the block, making it easier to ensure that the block was in exactly the right position when turned to print the other half of the design. Notice the depth to which the wood has been cut away. This was done to ensure that only the design touched the paper during the actual printing. Notice also that the sides of the relief are steeply cut near to the surface and are bevelled lower down; this was done for added strength.

On the back is a strap for handling the block. It is made of canvas, which is folded over twice and then glued together, making it immensely strong. The block would have been used in a similar manner to those used to printing fabrics.

# INTAGLIO

'Intaglio' is an Italian word meaning to cut into, so the word is used to describe many things other than prints. In the context of printing, it is a generic word used to describe the types of prints which are made by cutting into metal. It is the opposite of relief; the incisions in the plate are what produce detail on the print. There are several ways that the incisions can be made in the plate, and each method has its own title. These are: line engraving, etching, drypoint etching, mezzotint, stipple engraving, soft-ground etching and aquatint, listed here in chronological order.

With all the intaglio methods, there were actually only two ways that the metal was incised: either with a tool or by acid. The object with each method is the same. The slightest incision in the copper will show on the print. The deeper the incision the darker it will show on the print. Later on, when the plate was completed and ready for the press, it had to be inked, which was a craft. The entire surface of the plate was covered with ink, and using a pad of rags covered with fine silk, called a 'dauber', the ink is rubbed into the plate in circular movements to ensure that the ink is forced into all the engraved incisions. Then the surface is wiped clean, completely free of any excess ink, leaving the ink in the engraved incisions. Overcleaning would take too much ink out of the engraving, resulting in a poor impression, while undercleaning meant there was too much ink, creating dense areas of black on the print, or leaving a grey hue in the parts of the print or the margins that should be white. The illustrations (plates 7, 8 & 9 (pages 22–3) and 56 & 57 (page 82))make the point. The process was quite time-consuming; even small plates like those take about 20 minutes to ink and print.

Once the plate was ready for the printing press, it was placed in the press with paper over it and then a felt blanket was placed over the paper, which helped to press the paper down evenly and hard into the plate. Great pressure was required to force the ink onto the paper, which had been previously dampened to make it more receptive to the ink. The pressure is indicated by the 'plate mark', an obvious ridge in the paper where the extreme edges of the plate make an indentation in the paper because of the pressure exerted by the printing press. This pressure is enough to gradually flatten out the fine detail of a copper plate when the plate is used to print large numbers. This is seen in the illustrations of John Speed's map (plates 3 & 4, pages 18–19).

The illustrations of Baker's canal map (plates 35, 36 & 37, pages 54–7) are clear examples of how an engraver made light and shade. This is one of the most simple prints, the detail and the variation of shading being minimal.

# LINE ENGRAVING

The most widely adopted intaglio method was line engraving. Prints were made in this method from about 1430, about 50 years earlier than woodcuts, and lasted right through the whole period of printing covered by this book, with hardly any changes or technical improvements. Copper was the favoured metal, which was used until the early part of the 19th century, when steel was introduced because it was harder, could print finer detail, and print in larger quantities because there was less wear to the plate.

It might seem that a print comprised of lines is nothing short of being mundane. It is true that there are lot of prints which have little importance as works of art, being often made for simple illustration purposes, but a competent engraver could produce effective pictures with his craft, creating light and shade, tones and textures by the subtle variance of the engraving technique.

The engraver used a variety of v-shaped chisels, known as 'burins' or 'gravers', which were used to cut tiny channels into the plate. The tools have wooden handles, shaped like mushrooms. The domed part fitted into the palm of the hand, the fingers pressed to the underside of the dome to keep the tool steady, the stalk protruding between the fingers, the index finger used to guide the tip of the tool, detail of which is shown in plate 39 (page 61), the portrait of Tanje. Although the incisions into the plate were small, the process of engraving required firm control and even pressure, which was critical because the slightest variance in the depth of the incision would show on the print. It is interesting that many engravers actually used the method of etching to put the initial outline design onto the plate.

While engraving, the engraver always pushed the graver away from himself so that the maximum even control could be achieved. Generally, a line is the same width from end to end, but a good engraver could vary the width with very effective results. A number of the illustrations show this, particularly Wille's *Bonne Femme*, plates 42 and 43 (pages 66–7), Sherwin's portrait of Woollett, plate 41 (page 64), and Bickham's *Universal Penman*, plate 38 (pages 58–9).

In order that the engraver could keep pushing the graver away from his body while he worked, the plate was laid on a cushion filled with sand, so that the engraver could easily turn the plate while he worked on a line with a curve in it. Several of the illustrated portraits of engravers show the cushion beneath the plate.

Line engravers worked directly onto polished copper, which meant that there was a lot of reflection on the surface of the plate. Artificial light was not quite of the standard that we enjoy today, and daylight was the best option. Again, several of the illustrations show a screen between the engraver and the window to help reduce reflection. Usually tissue paper was used for the screen, as it was lightweight and evenly translucent.

With all intaglio methods, light and shade depended on the depth of the engraving – the deeper the incision, the blacker the detail on the finished print. Beyond that there were no set rules, and engravers found their own ways of showing detail, whether a polished button, a fold in a dress, or recognisable foliage.

Line engraving was used for all kinds of subjects. When it started, there was, of course, no other option, but by the 18th century other methods were widely used, though line engraving continued with great success. The advantage over wood was mainly in the fine detail and variance of tones. Additions were simply a matter of engraving the extra detail onto the plate. Corrections and alterations were more difficult. The plate had to be knocked up from the back, smoothed over, and then re-engraved, which was a laborious process, not to be recommended, although much easier than replacing an area of a woodblock. Printing maps from a copper plate was a great improvement over wood with typeset lettering. Maps needed additions made regularly. Early 17th-century maps of British counties did not show roads. Later editions of Speed's maps had them added simply by engraving the extra detail onto the plate. Some maps were altered beyond all recognition during the life of the plate.

Steel plates were used from about 1820. The main advantages were that the metal is so much harder than copper, enabling more prints to be made, and it was possible to engrave in much finer detail. A good example of this can be seen in the two almost identical prints of the death of General Wolfe, (plates 51 and 52, pages 76 & 79). Steel plates were ideal for producing large numbers of small, detailed pictures, especially for book illustrations.

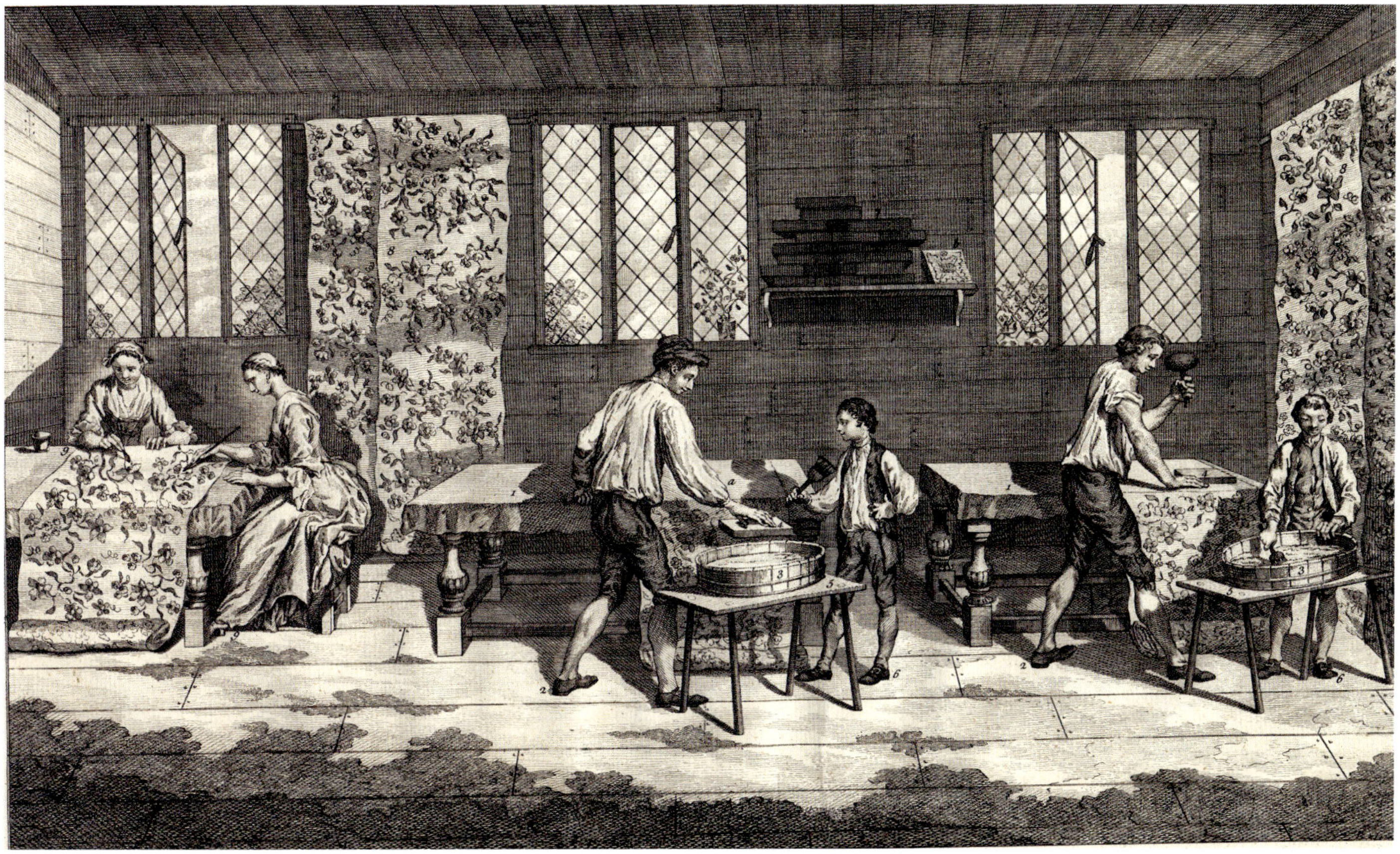

This is another typical book illustration, without any acknowledgment to the artist or the engraver. It can be seen that the fabric printing method was quite different to printing on paper. On the right, a printer is shown striking a thick woodblock with a mallet instead of using a press. Also, the two women on the left of the picture are doing the finishing detail by hand, which is similar to early colour printing.

An interesting feature of calico printing is that green was produced by first printing blue and then overprinting in yellow – probably the first use of colour separation.

The key, extracted from the text: 1. Tables covered with blankets on which calico is printed. a. Calico on the tables. 2. Two printers at work, the first of whom is going to dip his print (i.e. the block) in the colour, and the second of whom has just placed his print on the calico. 3. Tubs containing the colour. 4. Blocks on which the pattern is cut. 5. Stools that support the tubs of colour. 6. Boys who stir the colour in the tubs, and keep the proper quantity in them. 7. Blocks or prints placed on a shelf in the printing room, one of which, marked b, is placed with the face downwards. 8. Pieces of calico printed and hung up to set the colour. 9. Woman pencilling in the yellow and blue colours.

PLATE 31

Calico printing. Anon. Published by Hinton, 1754.
20 x 33 cm (7.8 x 13 in.).

An idealised print of a studio, showing an etched plate being immersed in an acid bath, and an engraver at work. On the print are letters, which form a key:

a 'A genius' inspiring b.
b A draughtsman.
c An engraver.
d The method of using a candle to blacken the 'ground' on a plate before etching begins.
e A boy pouring acid onto a plate, part of the method of etching a plate. The plate has a rim round the edge to form a container for the acid (the wall method, explained later).
f A thin paper blind which allows even light and cuts out any disturbing reflections on the highly polished copper plate.
g A selection of tools for line engraving.
i Methods of holding a graver. Handles of gravers were made of hard wood and shaped like a mushroom. The domed part fits into the palm of the hand the stalk, with a blade at the end, protrudes between the fingers.
k & l
Methods of sharpening gravers on an oil stone.
m & n
Methods of holding etching needles.
o Jug (probably containing water for rinsing the plate to wash away any remaining acid).
p Bottle of acid.
q A scraper.
r Etching needles.
s A pencil.
t A polisher.
w A plate resting on a cushion.
Another cushion is seen under the plate in fig. h. in this print, and similar cushions will be seen in the illustrated prints of engravers at work in this book. The purpose was to make it easier to turn the plate.

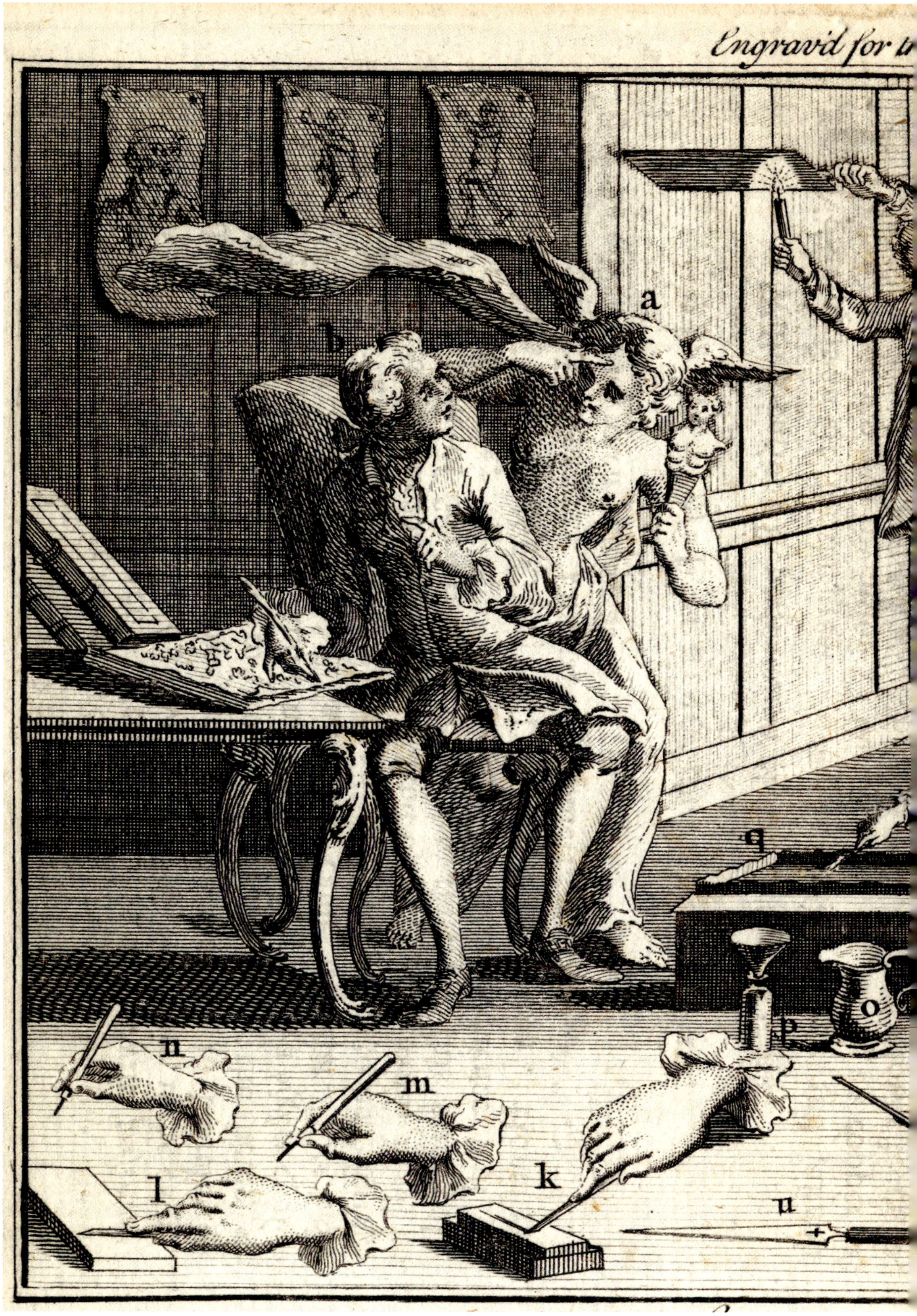


PLATE 32
*Art of Engraving,*
engraved by Benjamin Cole for *The Universal Magazine*, 1754.
Copper engraving, 11 x 18 cm (4.3 x 7 in.).

Also on the engraver's elegant table is another graver and an oil stone which was regularly needed to keep the graver sharp. Behind the back of his chair, hanging on the wall, is a parallel ruler used as a guide for parallel lines,

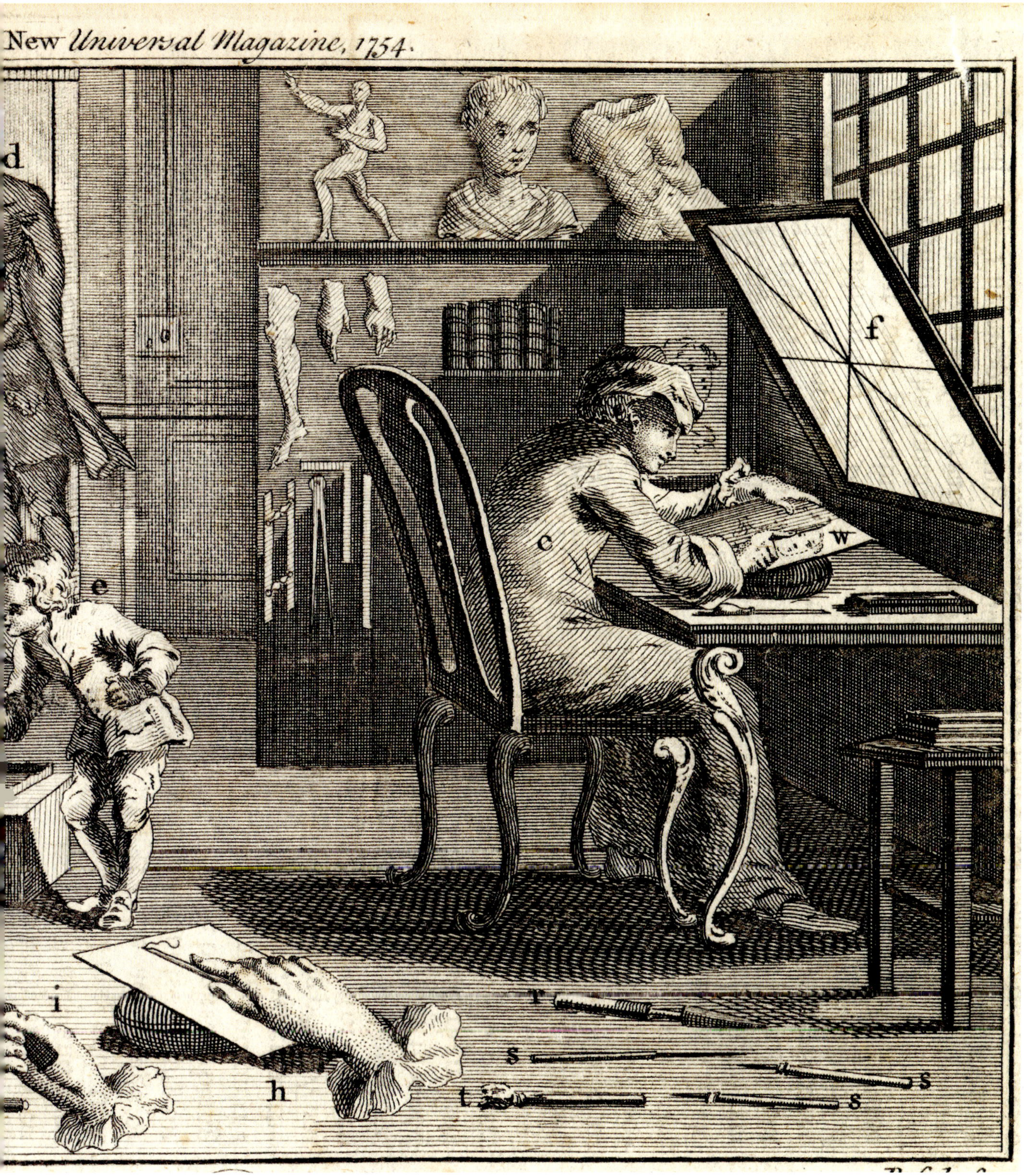


compasses for scribing circles and marking distances, a set square and an ordinary ruler. Printing workshops were never as clinically clean and tidy as this picture would have us believe. The essential equipment and functions are shown very well. Many of the features are described in more detail in the text.

Extract from the *The Universal Magazine*, May 1754.

*The Art of Etching and Engraving.*
Engraving is an art, for the greatest part, a modern invention; the antients, [ancients] it is true, practiced engraving on precious stones and crystals, with good success; and there are still some of their works remaining, equal to any production of later ages. But the art of engraving on plates to afford prints or impressions, was not known until after the invention of painting in oil.

Engraving is derived from the Latin word, which signifies to cut hollow; and from thence all devices cut in metal or wood, are called engravings. And some assert, that cutting in wood, though not the most beautiful operation of that kind, was the first invented, I shall begin with it. This sort of engraving which is used for various purposes, as for initial or figured letters, head and tail pieces of books, and even for schemes, and figures, to save expense of engraving on copper, and for prints and stamps for paper, linen, &c, as well as that in copper, was invented by a goldsmith of Florence.

The secret soon got abroad; and at last coming to the hands of Albert Dürer and Lucas, they greatly improved it. The art of cutting in wood was certainly carried on to a very great pitch about 150 years ago, [i.e. 1600] and might even vye, for beauty and justness with that of engraving on copper: at present it is in a very low esteem, as having been long neglected; and the application of artists wholly employed on copper, as the most easy and promising province; tho' I may add, that wooden cuts have the advantage of copper on many counts, chiefly for figures and devices in books, as being printed at the same time, and on the same press as the letters, whereas the other is work'd by a rolling press. What I say here in commendation of wooden cuts, must be understood of those done by good artists.

PLATES 33 AND 34
*Diane and Acteon,* two plates engraved by Jean Le Potre, *c.*1670. *La Chaste Diane se baignant avec ses compagnes, sut veue par Acteon dequoi la déesse iritée le changea en cerf. Ovid Im X Fab XIII. [sic] Le Potre Invent et Fecit. Avec privilege de Roy.*
Engraved in about 1670 from a series of mythological subjects.
Plate size: 22.5 x 32.5 cm (8.9 x 12.8 in.).

This plate is very heavily engraved, the incisions being deeper than normal, and most of the surface is engraved because of the darkness of the wooded scene. The crude appearance of the plate would suppose that it was not possible to create such a clear print from it. The accompanying print was made recently by John Land at the Printing Works, Amberley Museum, West Sussex. The ink at the darkest parts of the print is quite rough to touch.

Also of interest is the name of the artist and engraver. He used several spellings, either le Paultre, Le Pautre or Le Potre. The first name, Jean, was consistent. It is not an unusual occurrence for artists to use variations of their names, but it does, of course, make for confusion.

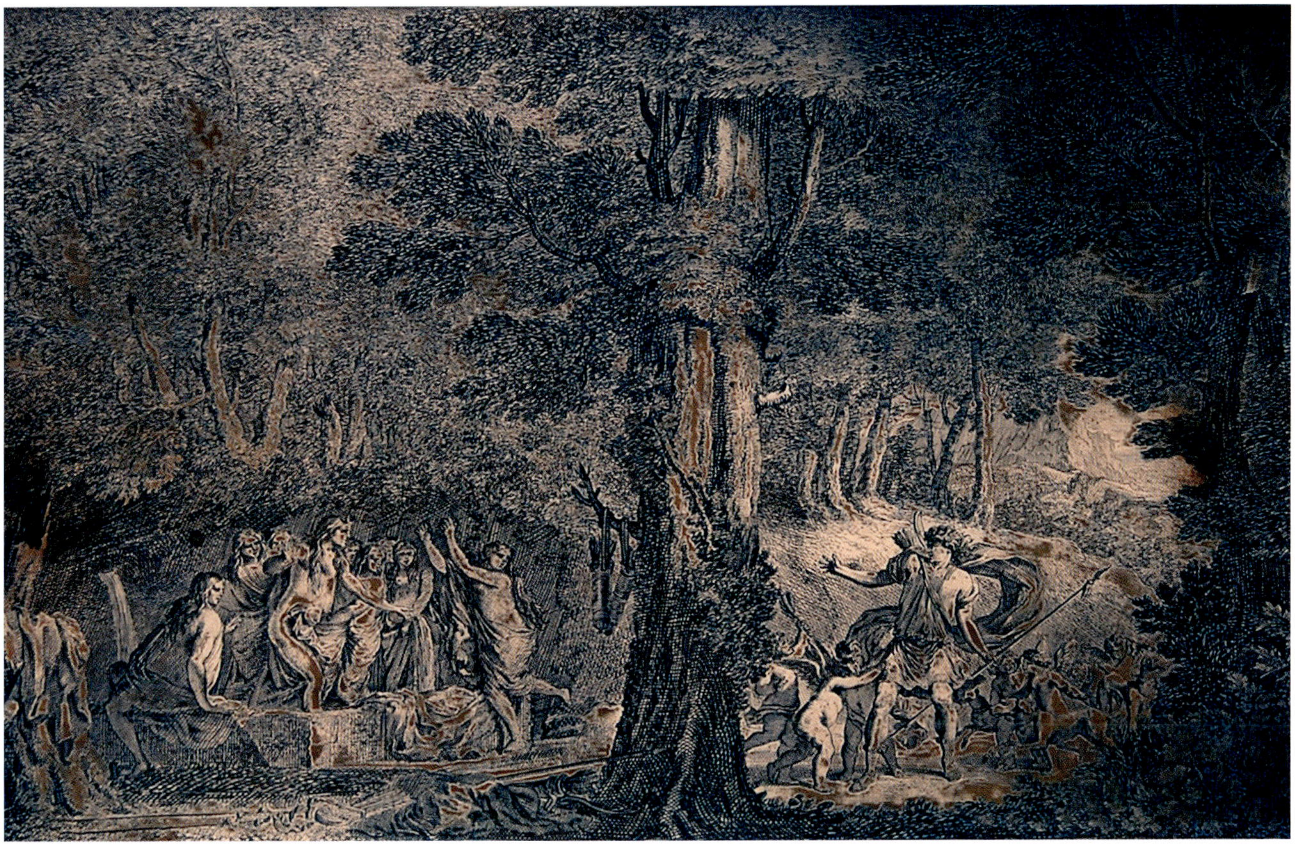

PLATE 33
The copper printing plate.

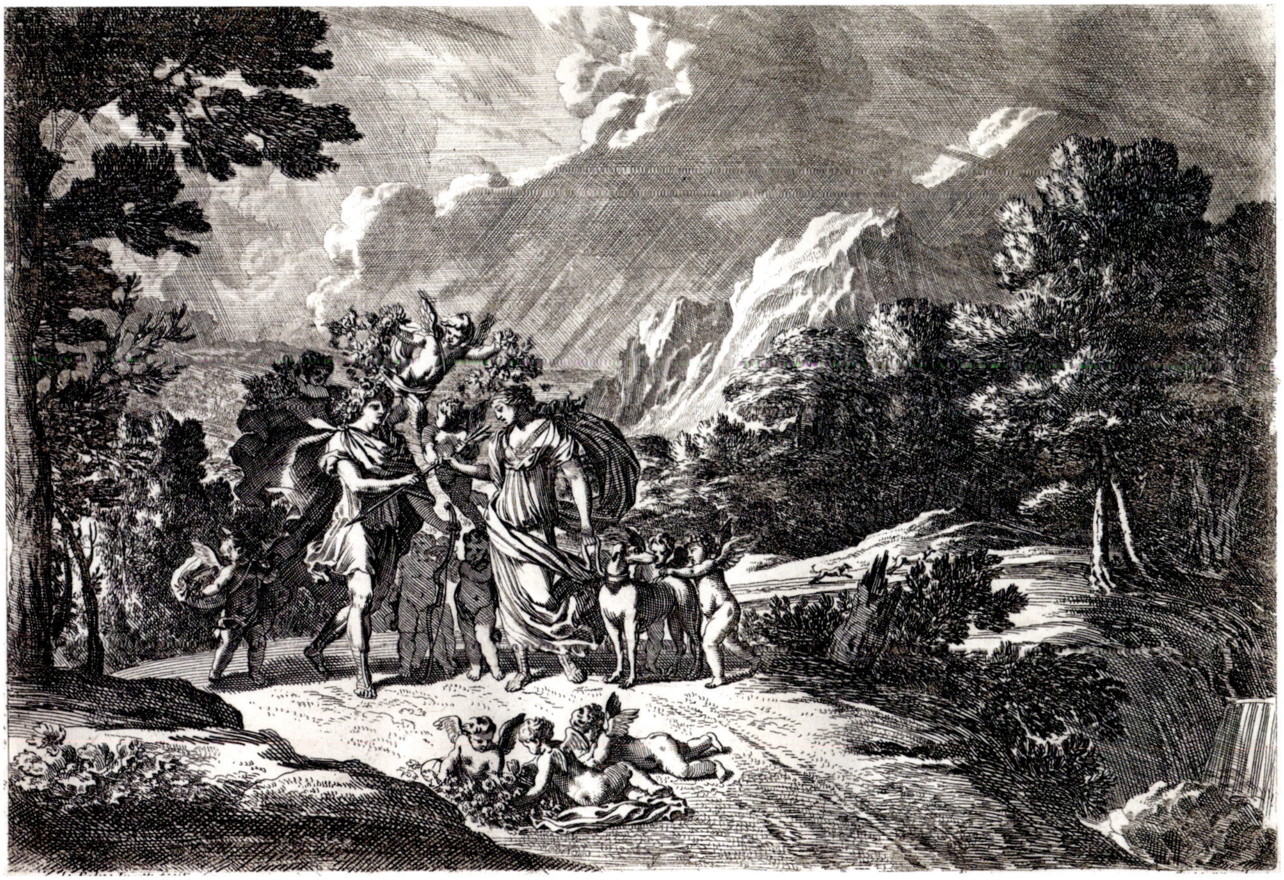

PLATE 34
A print.

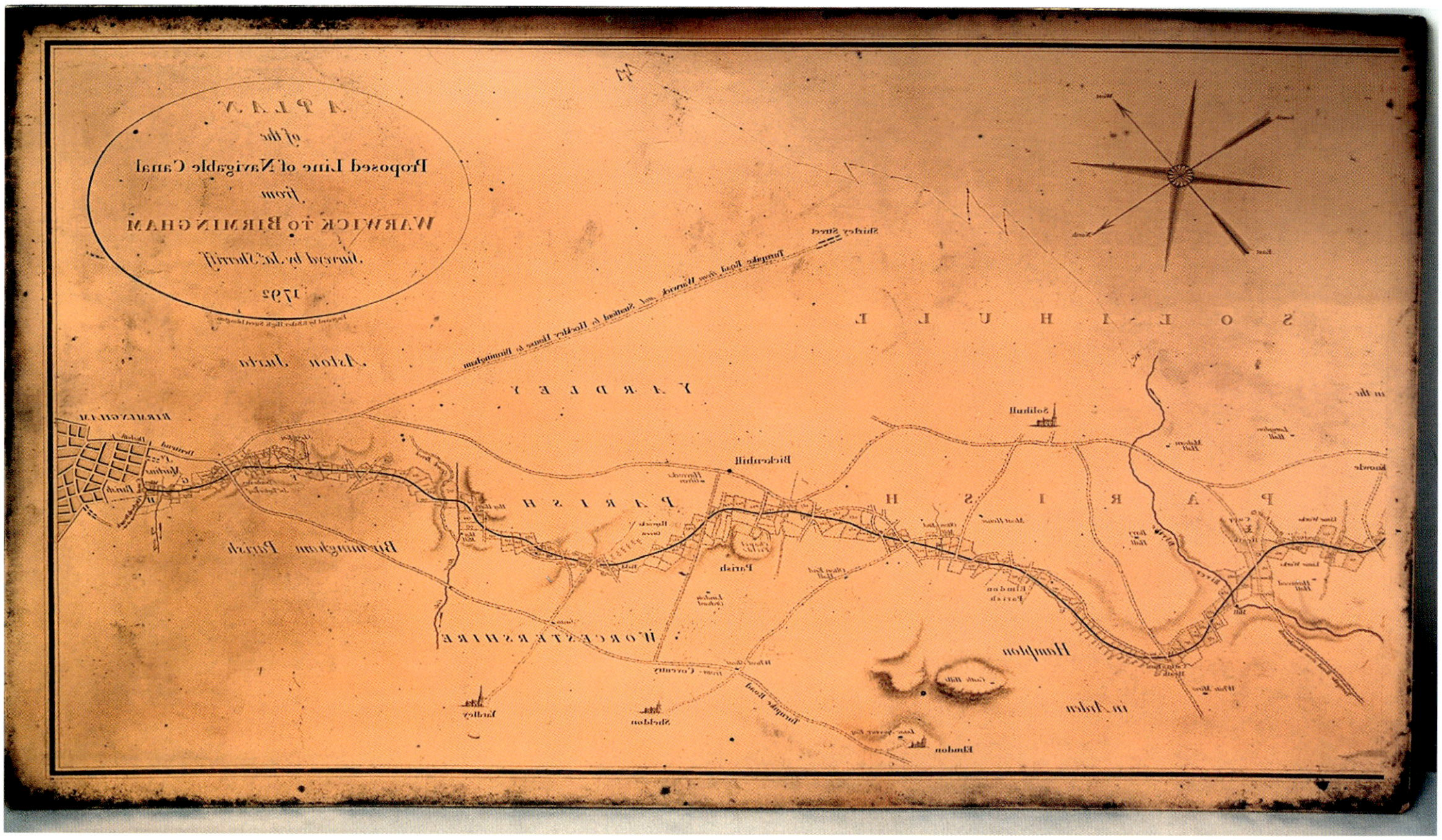

PLATE 35
The plates and modern prints of them.

PLATES 35 AND 36
*A Plan of the Proposed Line of the Navigable Canal from Warwick to Birmingham.* Surveyed by Jas. Sherriff. Engraved by Benjamin Baker, High Street, Islington, 1792. 30 x 48 cm (11.8 x 18.9 in.).

There are a number of interesting features about this. There are two printing plates, and prints were taken from both, to be joined, if required. Each copper plate measures 32 x 50 cm, and the overall width of the joined sheets is 97 cm. The two plates were essential simply because of the limitations of size. In the middle of the 18th century, there were single-sheet maps made from plates measuring about 50 x 70 cm – considered to be big, but not big enough to print a map of this width in one piece. There were size restrictions for all the technical reasons: sizes of paper, of plates and of printing presses.

The plate, which is only 3 mm thick, is typical of the finely engraved maps of the period. The scale is 2 in. to one mile, allowing great detail. It might appear to be relatively simple to engrave such a plate. Each of the plots of land through which the canal was routed was given a number, which was keyed to a separate list of owners' names. The land was also delicately shaded to aid clarity.

Notice the depth of the incisions that printed the border and the canal. You can see that the deeper the incision, the blacker the line is on the paper, and this is the basis of all intaglio printing. Just below the title, to the left of Birmingham, is some light hachuring, indicating hills, which appears on the plate as hardly more than a fingerprint. The contrast of the black between the canal and the hachuring is done by the depth of incisions made by the engraver into the

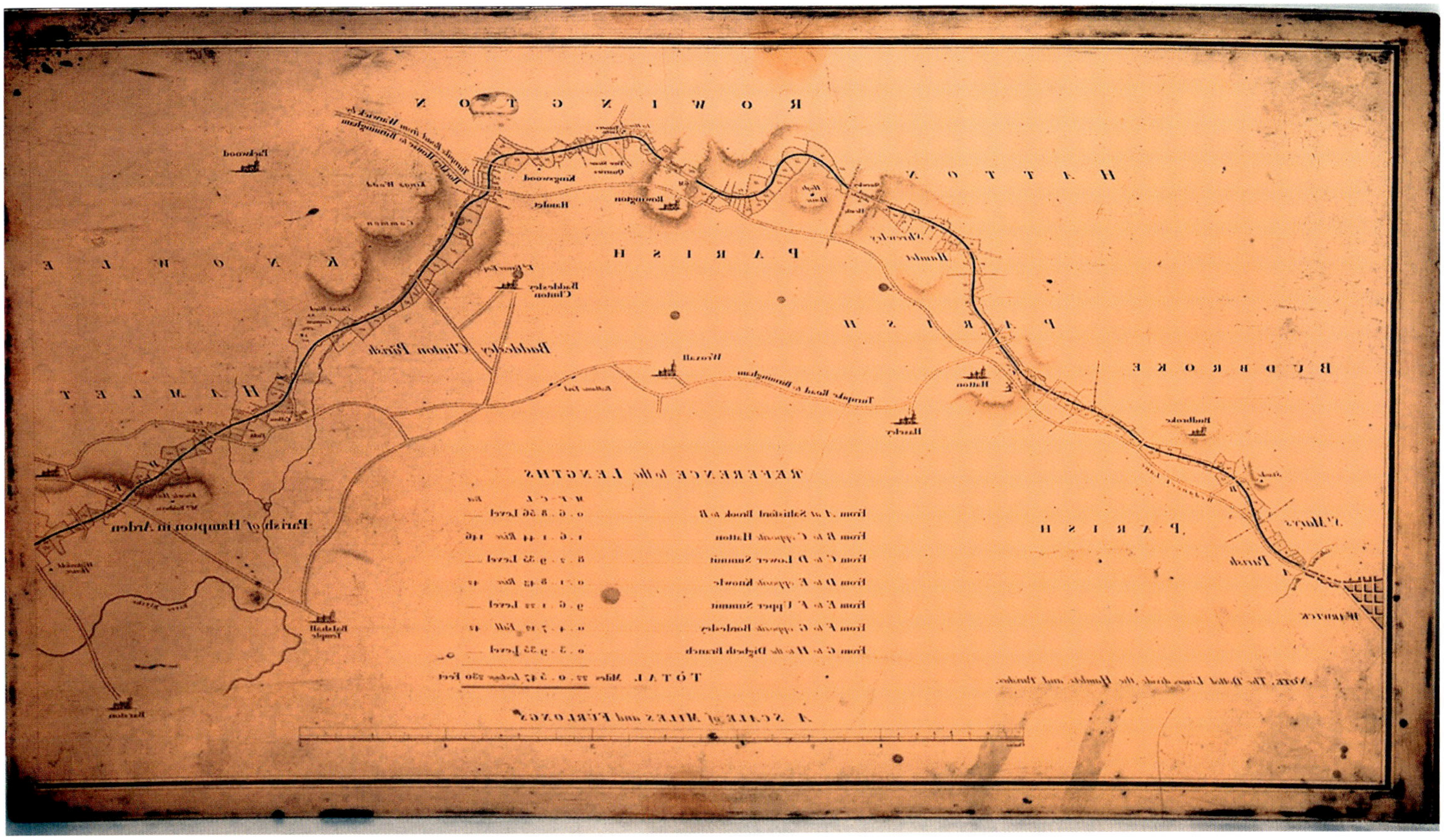

PLATE 36

copper. A minimal incision will print something onto paper. This is one of the most simple types of engraving. Imagine the complications of engraving a more detailed subject, like *Woollett's Whitton*, plate 10 (page 24), or *Wille's Le Concert de Famille*, plate 44 (page 68).

There are features that are worthy of note. Look at the oval surround of the title; there is no trace of where the engraver started or stopped. See how the engraver slightly varied the width of the oval border. Notice, too, the way the compass is engraved, simply using lines to make it appear three-dimensional. Also, note the uniformity of the numbers of the properties beside the canal. The engraver, Benjamin Baker, began to engrave maps of the Ordnance Survey shortly after he made this.

To the right of the compass can be seen a bad scratch, a jagged line, looking like wilful damage. In fact, it was probably caused by nothing more sinister than a small piece of grit which rubbed into the copper when the plates were carelessly stored together, an indication of the softness of the copper and how easily damage could occur.

Work on the canal commenced in 1793, the year after this plan was printed; rapid progress indeed, as planning applications take a lot longer now. The canal is now part of the Grand Union.

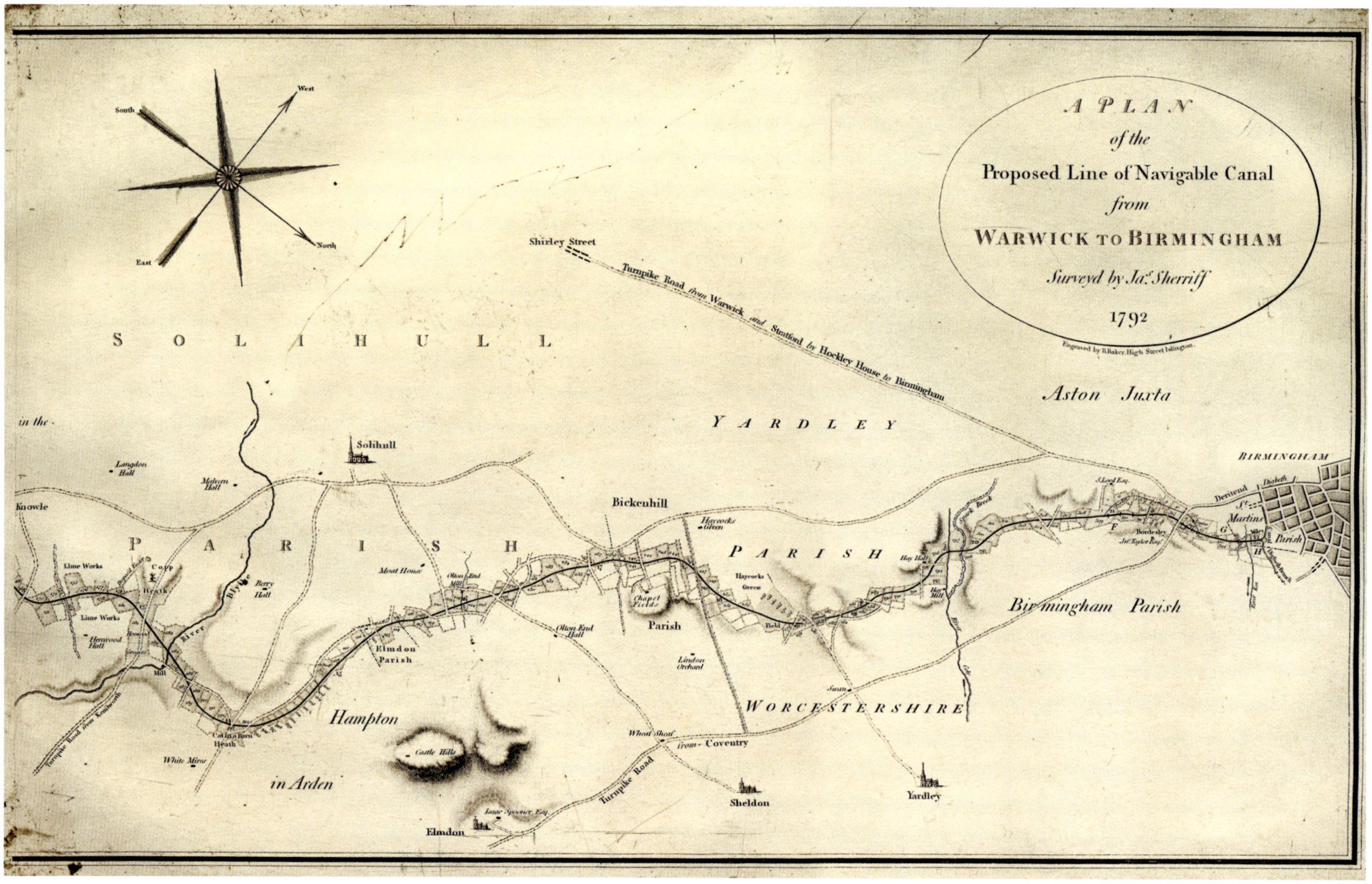


PLATES 37 A & B The print was made in 1972, shortly after I acquired the plate. I found the plate at a printer's in Islington High Street that was closing down. The plate had probably been there since 1792: Baker's address was Islington High Street. I have been hoping to find an original print ever since. There were probably very few prints made from the plates in 1793, and these were probably made for the people whose land was affected by the route of the canal; therefore, the prints were ephemeral.

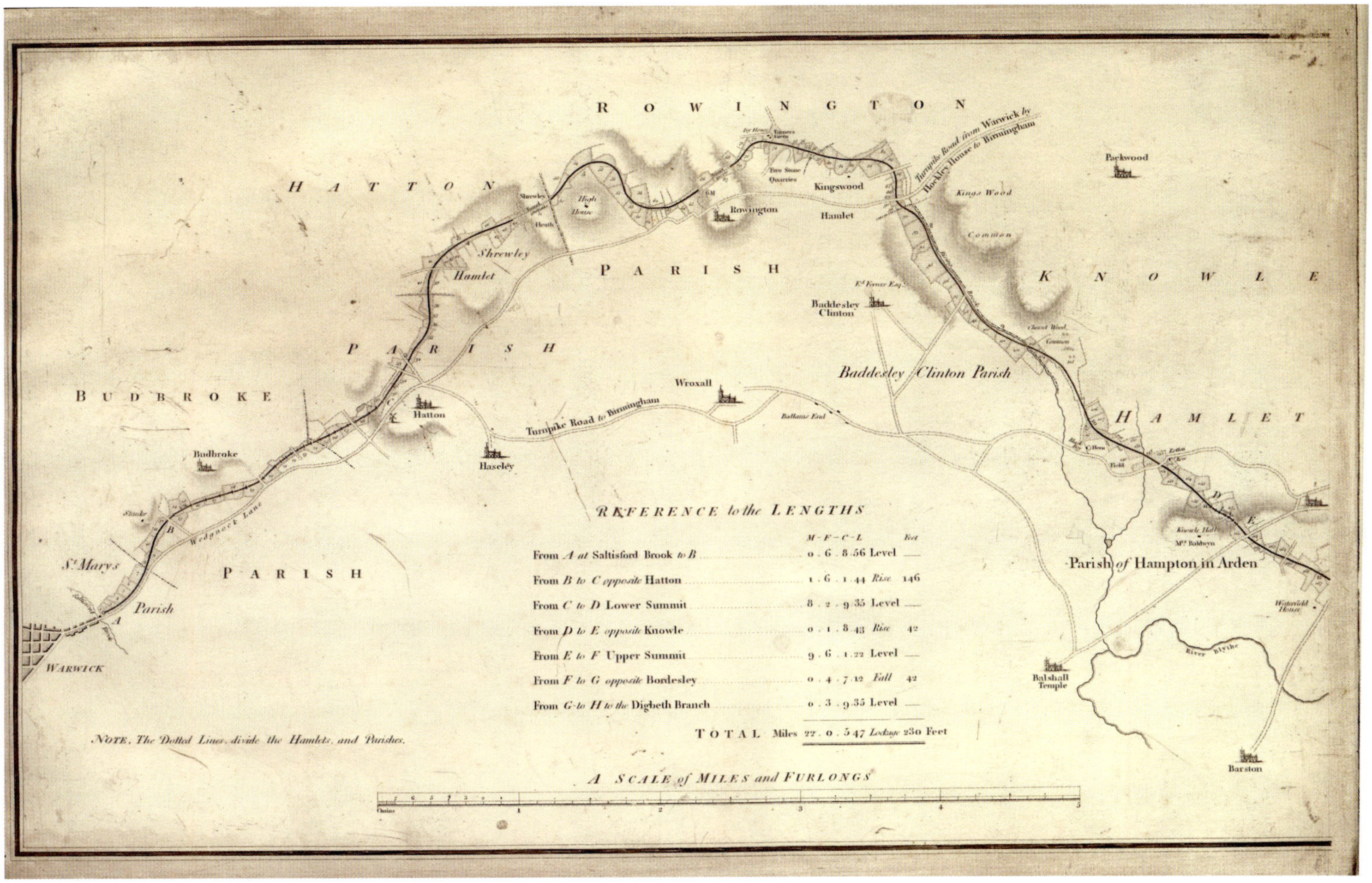
ROWINGTON
HATTON
PARISH
BUDBROKE
PARISH
KNOWLE
HAMLET
Turnpike Road from Warwick by Hockley House to Birmingham
Packwood
Kingswood
Hamlet
Rowington
Shrewley
Hamlet
Baddesley Clinton
Baddesley Clinton Parish
Wroxall
Turnpike Road to Birmingham
Hatton
Haseley
Budbroke
St. Marys
Parish
PARISH
Wedgnock Lane
WARWICK
Parish of Hampton in Arden
Balsall Temple
Barston
River Blythe
REFERENCE to the LENGTHS
M - F - C - L Feet
From A at Saltisford Brook to B 0 . 6 . 8 .56 Level —
From B to C opposite Hatton 1 . 6 . 1 .44 Rise 146
From C to D Lower Summit 8 . 2 . 9 .35 Level —
From D to E opposite Knowle 0 . 1 . 8 .43 Rise 42
From E to F Upper Summit 9 . 6 . 1 .22 Level —
From F to G opposite Bordesley 0 . 4 . 7 .12 Fall 42
From G to H to the Digbeth Branch 0 . 3 . 9 .35 Level —
TOTAL Miles 22 . 0 . 5 47 Lockage 230 Feet
NOTE. The Dotted Lines divide the Hamlets and Parishes.
A SCALE of MILES and FURLONGS

PLATE 38
A page from George Bickham's *The Universal Penman*, printed in 1750. Copper engraving, 33 x 20 cm (13 x 7.8 in.).

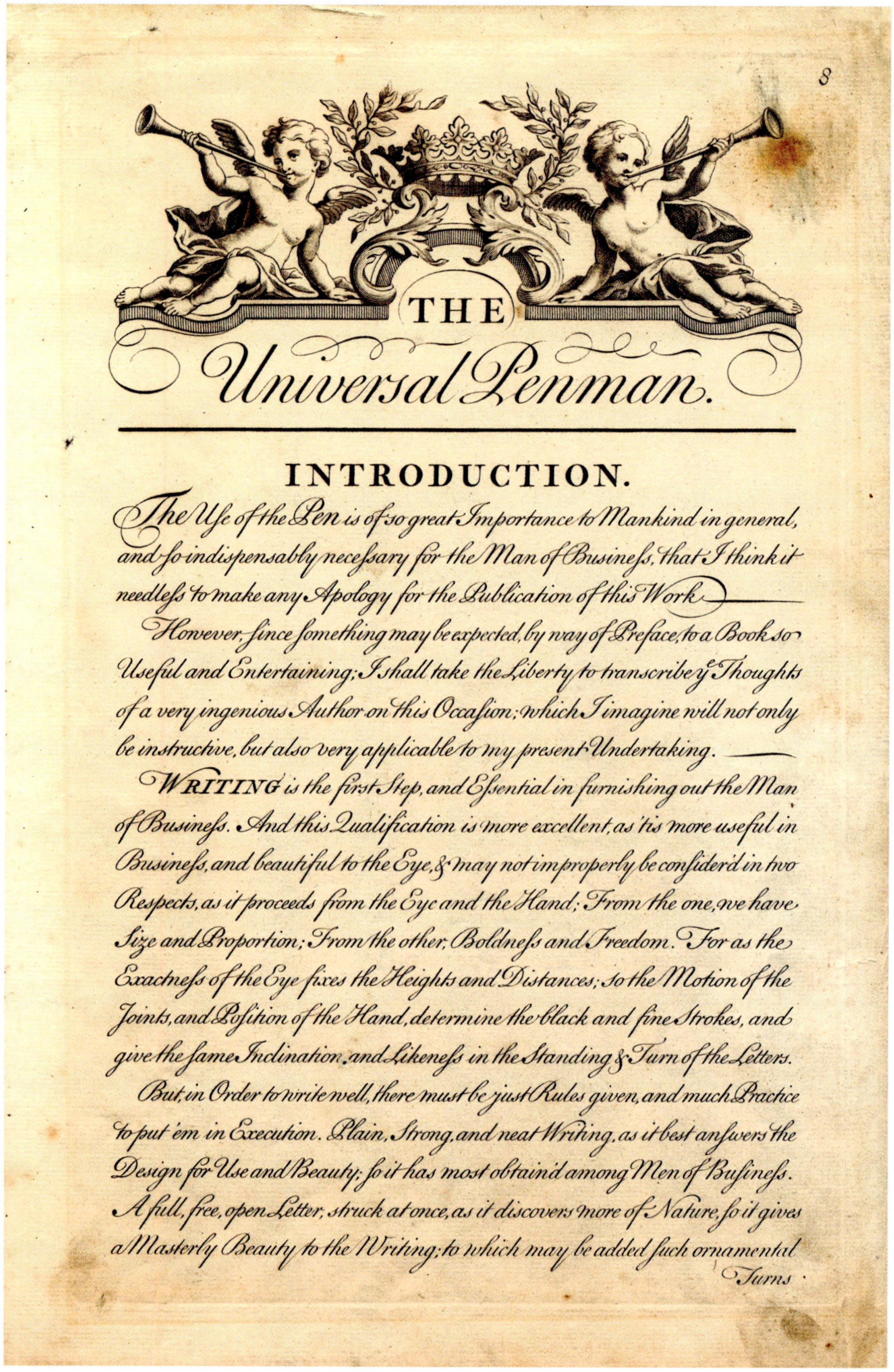

8

THE
Universal Penman.

INTRODUCTION.

The Use of the Pen is of so great Importance to Mankind in general, and so indispensably necessary for the Man of Business, that I think it needless to make any Apology for the Publication of this Work.

However, since something may be expected, by way of Preface, to a Book so Useful and Entertaining; I shall take the Liberty to transcribe ye Thoughts of a very ingenious Author on this Occasion; which I imagine will not only be instructive, but also very applicable to my present Undertaking.

WRITING is the first Step, and Essential in furnishing out the Man of Business. And this Qualification is more excellent, as 'tis more useful in Business, and beautiful to the Eye, & may not improperly be consider'd in two Respects, as it proceeds from the Eye and the Hand; From the one, we have Size and Proportion; From the other, Boldness and Freedom. For as the Exactness of the Eye fixes the Heights and Distances; so the Motion of the Joints, and Position of the Hand, determine the black and fine Strokes, and give the same Inclination, and Likeness in the Standing & Turn of the Letters.

But in Order to write well, there must be just Rules given, and much Practice to put 'em in Execution. Plain, Strong, and neat Writing, as it best answers the Design for Use and Beauty; so it has most obtain'd among Men of Business. A full, free, open Letter, struck at once, as it discovers more of Nature, so it gives a Masterly Beauty to the Writing; to which may be added such ornamental

Turns

*The Universal Penman* is a highly regarded book on calligraphy. Bickham excelled in the art of copperplate lettering, as the illustration shows. To be able to write as well as this is one thing; to be able to engrave as accurately and evenly, in reverse, requires a different skill. Notice that the page is justified. The word 'eye' appears three times in the middle of the page – identically – each time (see lines 10–13).

# INTRODUCTION.

Turns of the Pen, as seem rather design'd to fill up Vacancies on the Paper, than studiously compos'd to adorn the Piece. In Flourishing the Fancy would be so Luxuriant, was it not corrected by the Judgment, as almost to destroy the End of Writing; as Airs in Musick, when too often repeated, or too long or too variously performed, disorder the Harmony of a just Composure. ——

But, as above, if Usefulness and Beauty are the Excellencies of Writing; that which will, with the greatest Facility, contribute to these, is the best Method of Teaching. Supposing, therefore, the Make and Proportion of the Letters and Joinings to be once well fixed and understood, and then if the Learner is us'd to copy the great Variety of Examples which are here produc'd, his Hand will grow confirm'd in an Aptitude and Readiness, which will insensibly arrive at Perfection and Dispatch; and give in Writing, what we admire in fine Gentlemen; an Easiness of Gesture, and disengag'd Air, which is imperceptibly caught from frequently conversing with the Polite and Well-bred. ——

DRAWING is another necessary Qualification, and therefore I have attempted to make the Decorations of this Work fit for the imitation of those, whose Genius prompts them to the Study of that Art. ——

But as **Writing** is the most Useful Accomplishment of y^e two, I have given a larger Number of Specimens for that purpose; Exhibited in Precepts Divine and Moral, with many Examples in Trade and Business. ——

And as the **Whole** is compleated, through y^e friendly Assistance of several Eminent Penmen, and Engrav'd with the greatest Care and Exactness; I make no doubt but it will meet with a favourable Reception from the Publick; & that I my Self shall be excus'd for attempting so Universal a Performance.

G. Bickham.

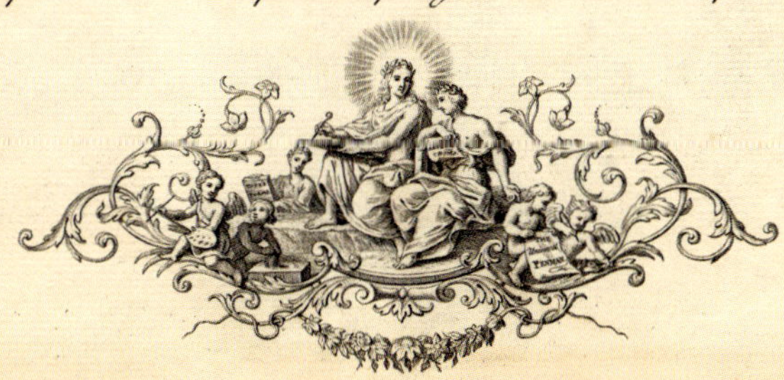

No. II.

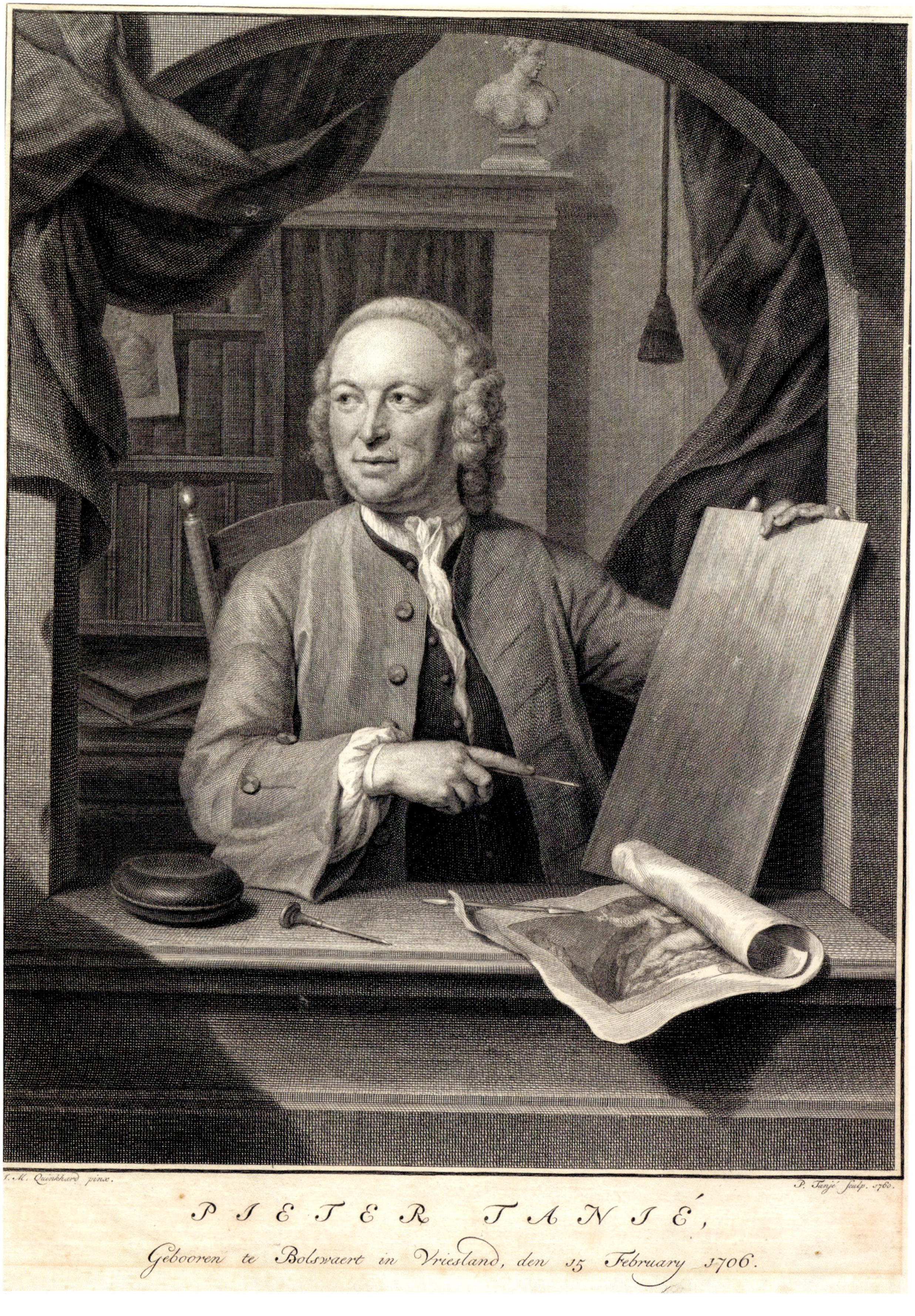
J. M. Quinkhard pinx.
P. Tanjé sculp. 1760.
PIETER TANJÉ,
Gebooren te Bolswaert in Vriesland, den 15 February 1706.

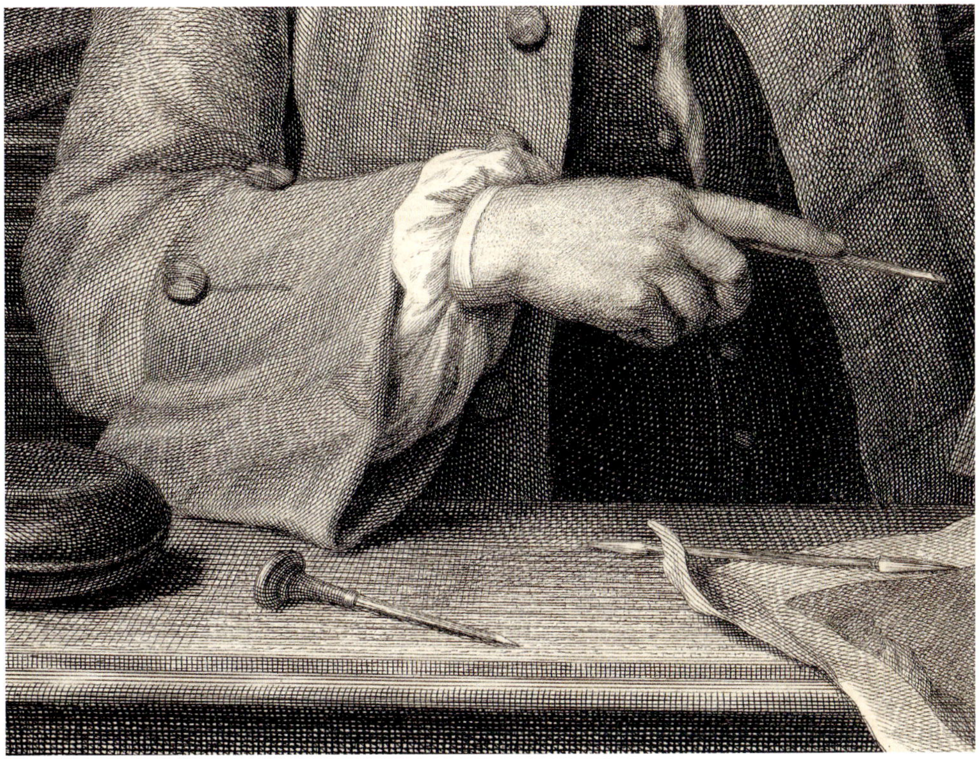

PLATE 39 AND DETAIL

*Pieter Tanje* (portrait of the engraver)
P. Tanje (1706–66), after J.H. Quinkhard, engraved in 1760.
Copper engraving, 30.5 x 27 cm (12 x 10.6 in.).

The engraver is shown with engraving tools and a copper plate in his left hand. Left of centre is a typical graver, with a long steel shaft and a wooden, mushroom-shaped handle, which sat comfortably in the palm of the hand as the engraver pushed the point of the graver into the plate, away from himself. He is holding another graver, and the picture gives an idea of the way the tip is firmly controlled with the index finger, the wooden handle buried into the palm of his hand. The other tool in the picture is pointed at each end, and was used for engraving fine finishing detail, when little pressure was required. On the left is a familiar cushion, on which the plate was rested.

The quality of the engraving is excellent, and shows how cleverly the engraver varied light and shade by densities of lines. In this case, there is nothing that is left white: every part of the plate is engraved in some form or another. He could have made the copper plate look more polished by reducing the amount of engraving in it. Notice how he engraved the cushion, to the left of him, giving it a reflected shine.

Tanje was Dutch, born in Bolsward, and worked in Amsterdam. Most of his engravings are portraits, but few are as large as this.

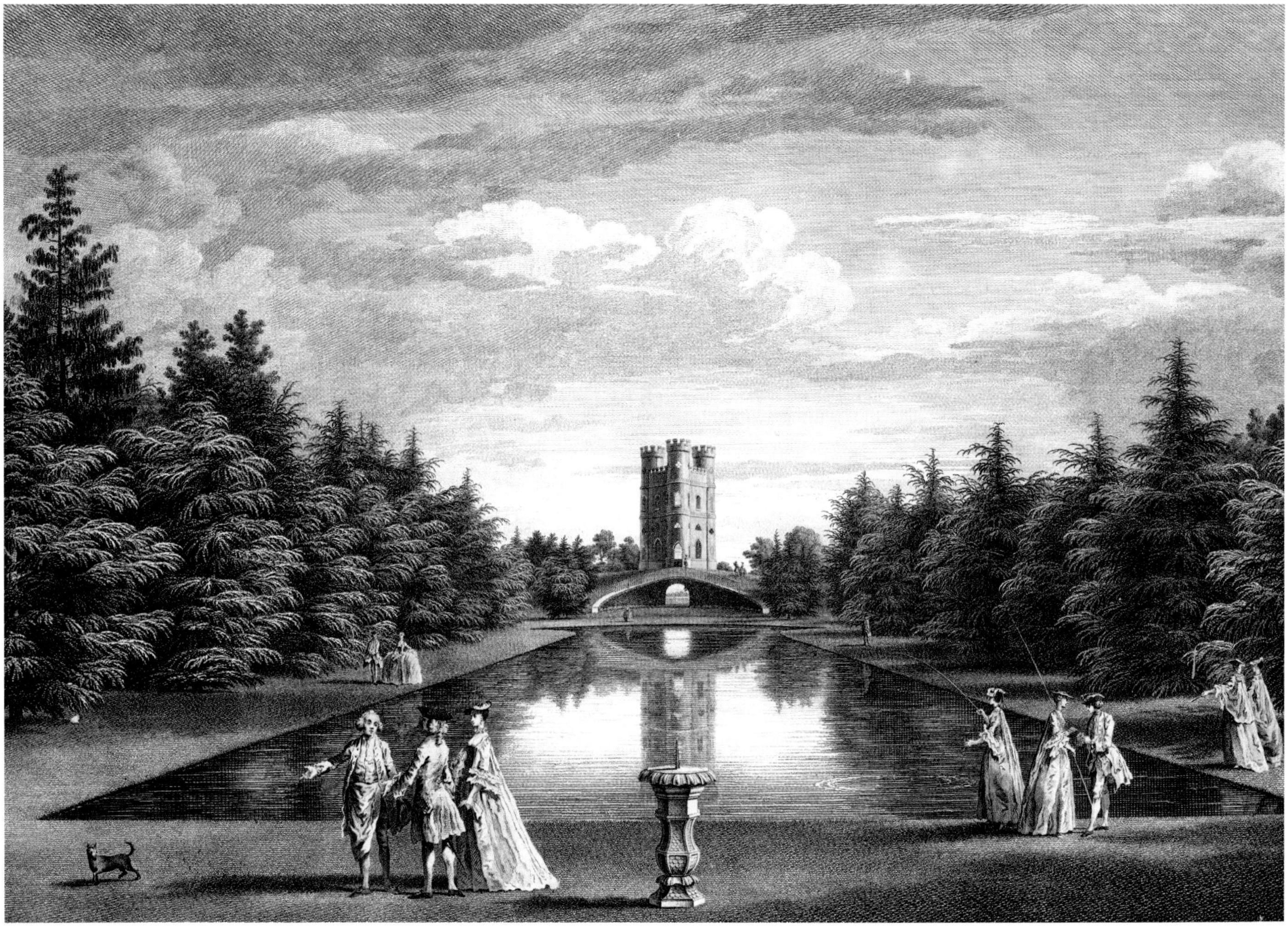

PLATE 40 AND DETAIL
*A View of the Canal and Gothick Tower in the Garden of His Grace the Duke of Argyl at Whitton.*
William Woollett, artist and engraver, *c.*1765.
Copper engraving,
33 x 51 cm (13 x 20 in.).
Beneath is the title in French, the fashionable 18th-century language, and, in this case, a direct translation with just a slight addition: *Veue du Canal, et de la Tour Gothique, dans le Jardin de Monsgr le Duc d'Argyl a Whitton, a 4 lieues a l'ouest de Londres.*

This is the second published state, which simply means that a change has been made since the print was first published. In this case it is a change of publishers. The first state has the imprint of John Tinney and is dated 1757. In the second, Woollett's name, which was previously within the image, is added beneath the image in the right corner: *W. Woollett del et sculp.* The imprint reads: 'Printed for Robt Sayer in Fleet Street, John Boydell in Cheapside, Henry Parker in Cornhil, Carington Bowles in St Pauls Church Yard'.

The print is a very fine example of copper engraving and an excellent impression. There were certainly not enough of them printed in the first state to cause any significant wear to the plate. Woollett's perspective and depth in the picture is obvious, but the charm of the scene lies in the brilliantly engraved variety of textures, widely contrasting, including the architecture, men's and women's clothes, the reflections on the lake, and the soft foliage of the cedar trees. The print was used to decorate a piece of the Green Frog Service, commissioned by Catherine the Great. The service was made by Josiah Wedgwood in 1774, consisting of 952 pieces all decorated with British scenery, and is now in the State Hermitage, St. Petersburg.

In topographical prints at this time it was customary to show groups of gentry

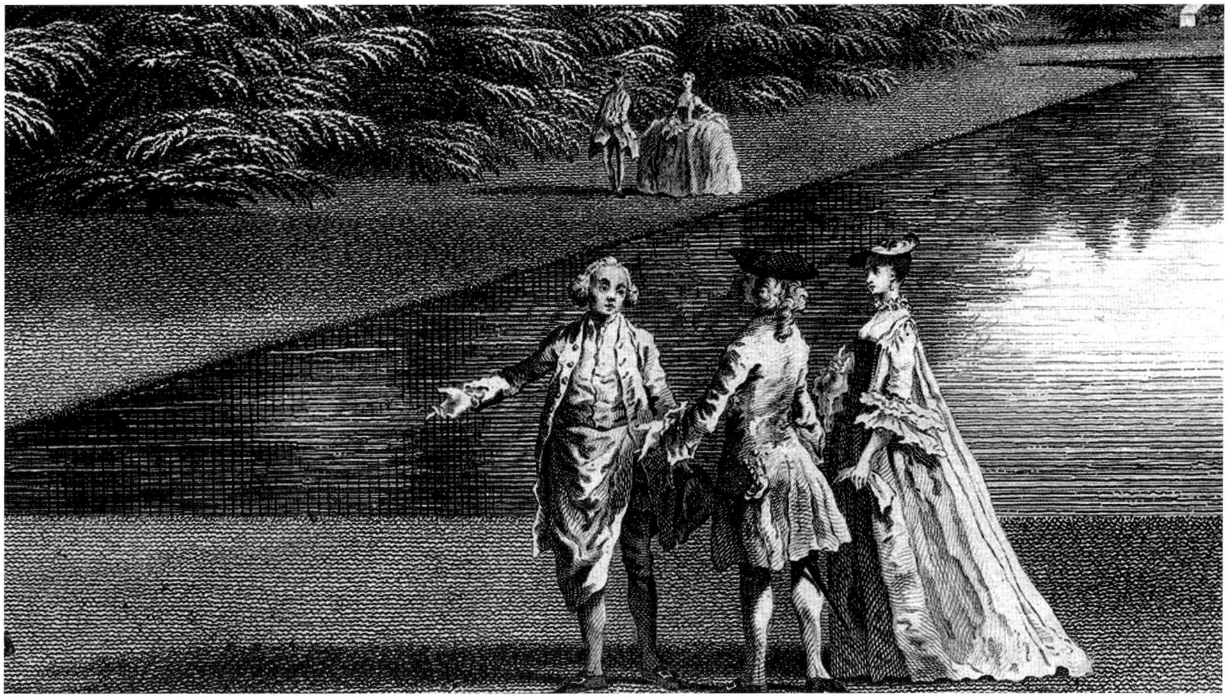

in their finery promenading in the scene. Not long afterwards, scenes began to be more realistic, and, for example, in a print like this there might be a gardener or someone felling trees or building something. Slightly later than Woollett was the influential artist and printmaker Paul Sandby, who managed to fill his landscapes with people going about everyday activities.

The house stood to the right of this picture, a relatively modest Palladian building, which is shown in a matching print by Woollett. Although there is no mention of it, the Duke of Argyle (the third duke) probably sponsored the publication because there would only have been a small demand for the prints. However, such was the popularity of Woollett's work that prints were sold because of his name, hence the reason that so many publishers were involved.

The house, which was called Whitton Place, was demolished in 1847, and the land is now part of Whitton Park. The Duke's land was about one third of a mile square. He was a keen horticulturalist and grew many cedar trees from seed. The mature trees are seen in the print on each side of the canal. Some of them were transported to nearby Kew Gardens. William Chambers, the designer of Kew Gardens, was a later owner of the house. The area around Whitton was highly suited to growing plants, and the local market gardens supplied vegetables to London. The house is a short distance from Twickenham Rugby Ground, which is still affectionately known as 'the Cabbage Patch' because the land was a market garden. Also of interest in the area is Kneller Hall, named after Sir Godfrey Kneller, who painted the portraits of ten reigning monarchs during his lifetime. Kneller had the house built for him as a country residence early in the 18th century. At the time Kneller lived there it was known as Whitton House. Now, in a much altered form, the building is the home to the Royal Military School of Music.

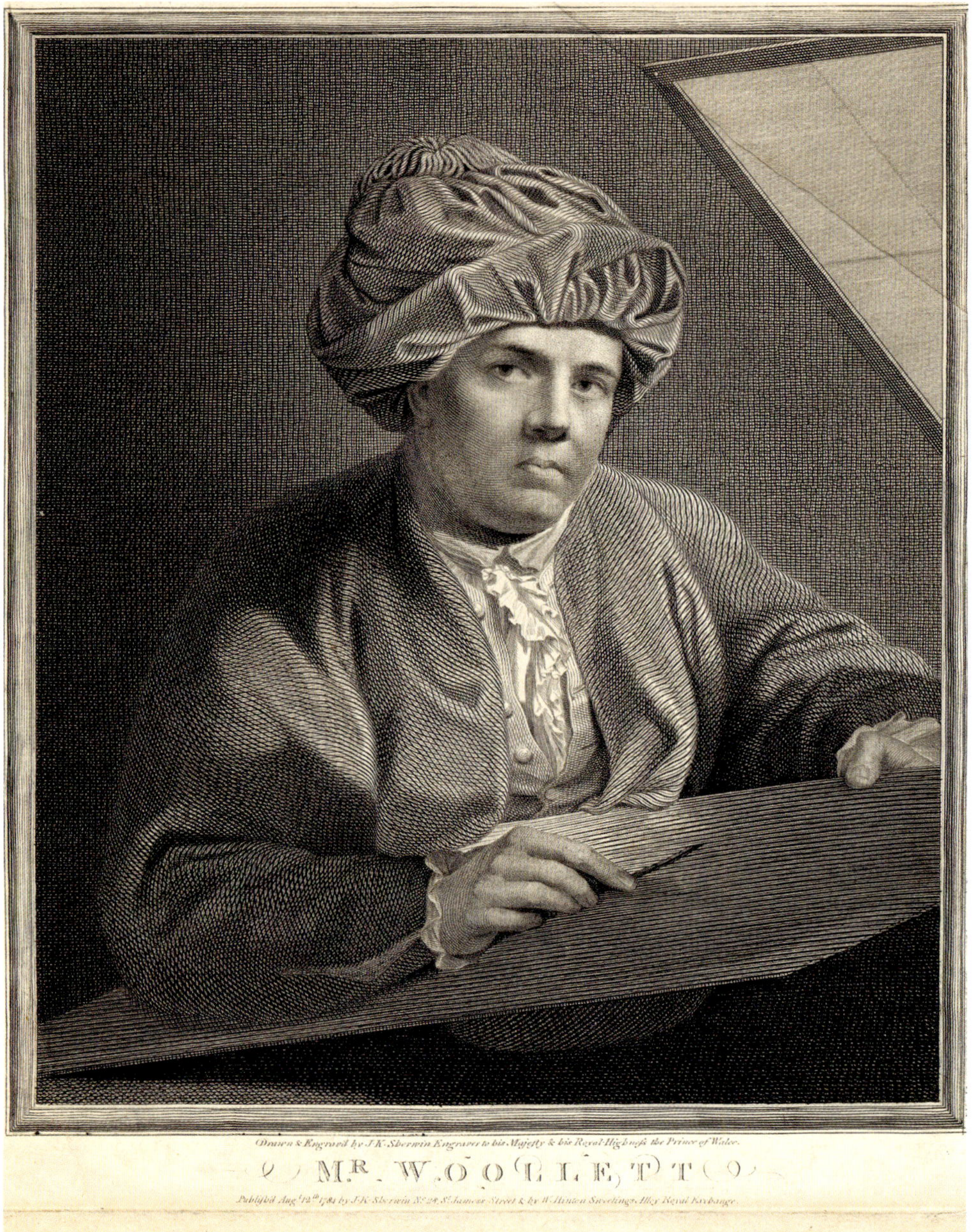


PLATE 41 AND DETAIL
*Mr Woollett,* John Keyse Sherwin, artist and engraver, 1784. Copper engraving, 27 x 23 cm (10.6 x 9 in.).

This is a portrait of William Woollett made in the year before he died at the age of 50. Sherwin did not quite make the age of 40, but he managed to earn himself a good reputation for his portraits, either engraved in line or in stipple, and this print shows just how capable he was. Notice the intricate patterns of lines used. Similar to the portraits by Wille (plates 42 & 43, pages 66–7) the same technique of varying the width of lines is used, this time in the folds of Woollet's jacket.

Engraving the background would have been a very tedious job, but notice how it is cleverly shaded, gradually darkening to the lower left corner of the picture.

Of particular interest is that Woollett is shown working on quite a large plate, one of his largest prints. In his hand is a graver. Beneath the plate is another

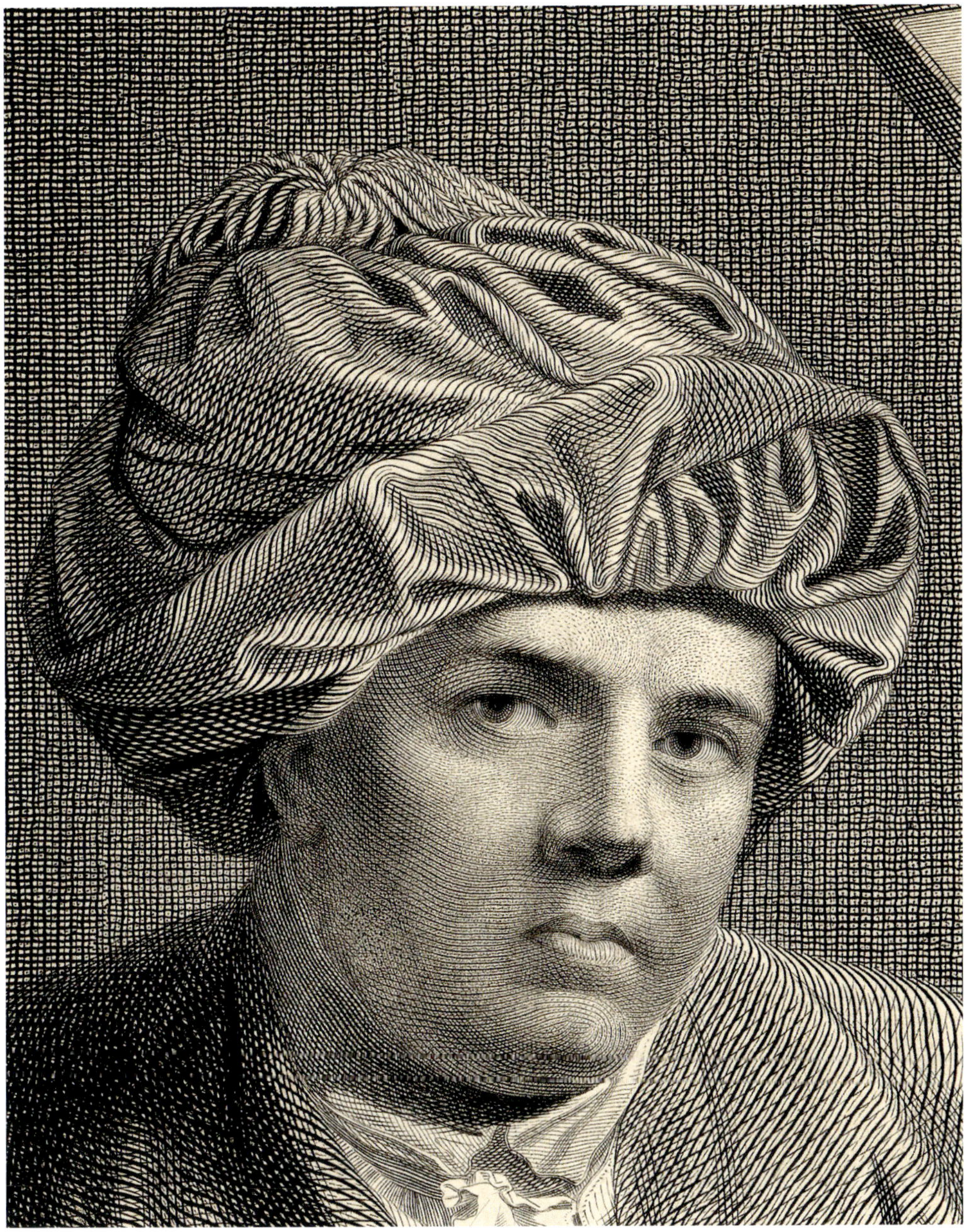

cushion for turning the plate. Also, there is a screen, on Woollett's left side, between him and the window to reduce reflection on the plate. Similar to the portrait of Tanje, plate 39 (page 60), Sherwin has chosen not to make the plate look too polished, and it is, in fact, darker than in the Tanje print.

Plate 83 (page 114) is another portrait of Woollett.

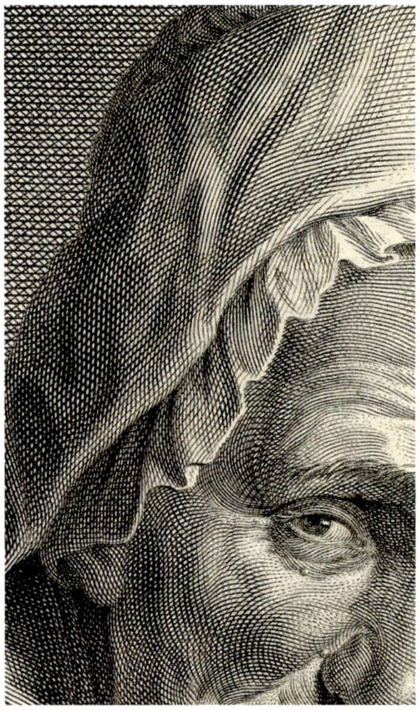

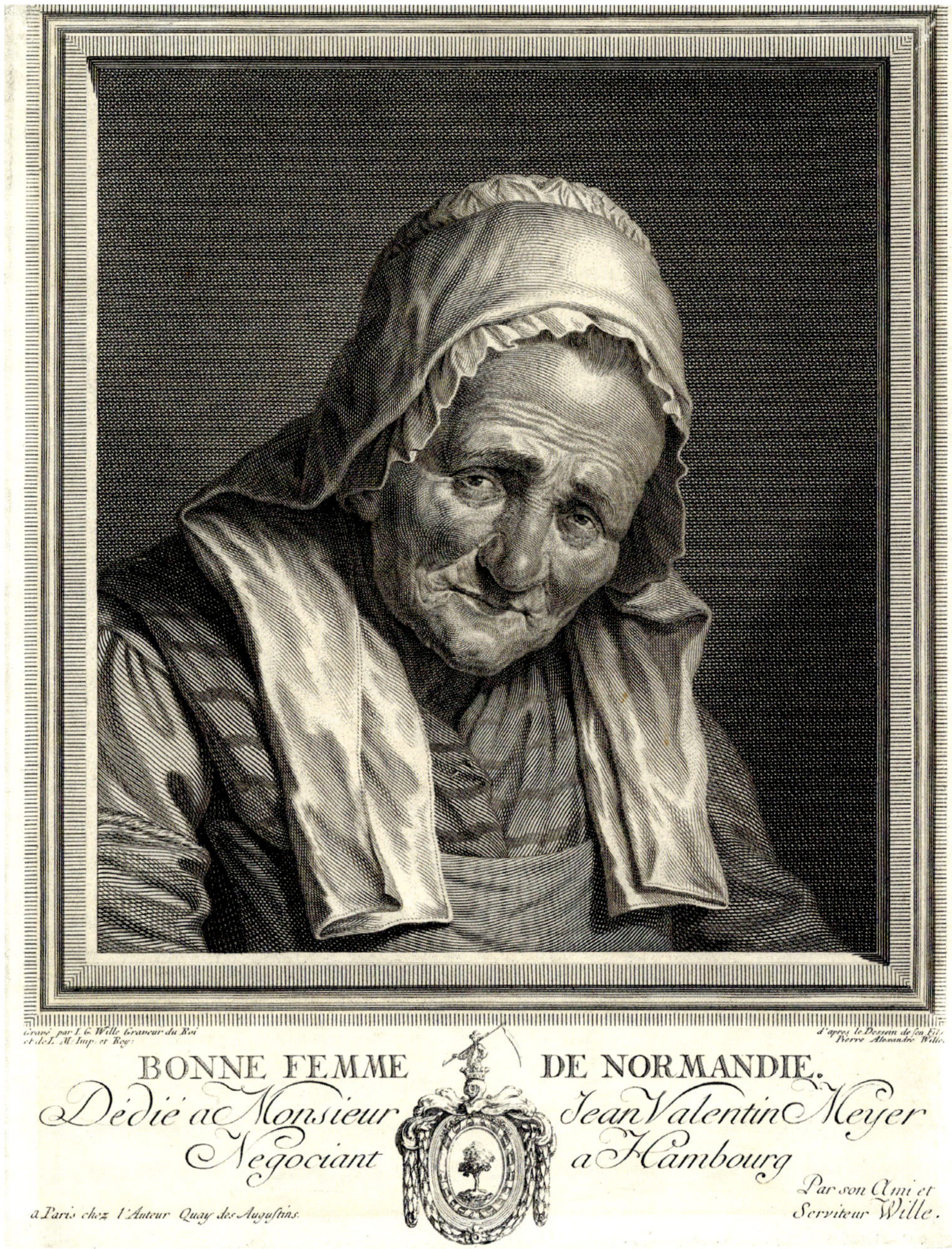


PLATE 42 AND DETAIL
*Bonne Femme de Normandie,*
engraving by J.G. Wille, 1774.
Copper engraving.

Johan Wille excelled in engraving portraits like these, and there were few engravers able to convey such lifelike characters in their prints. The delicacy with which he used his graver is apparent here. The faces are engraved entirely with lines and some dots. Notice how he created curves, particularly in the nose and the cheeks, simply by varying the width of the lines. By contrast, the backgrounds are heavily engraved with horizontal, vertical and diagonal lines, but notice, in *Soeur de la Bonne Femme*, how Wille achieved a subtle variation in the light, the background gradually turning darker from left to right, in a similar way to the portrait of Woollett, plate 41 (page 64). The effect of the clothing is good, too; he is renowned for his skill in engraving silks and satins. It is interesting to compare this technique with the work of Tanje, illustrated in plate 39 (page 60).

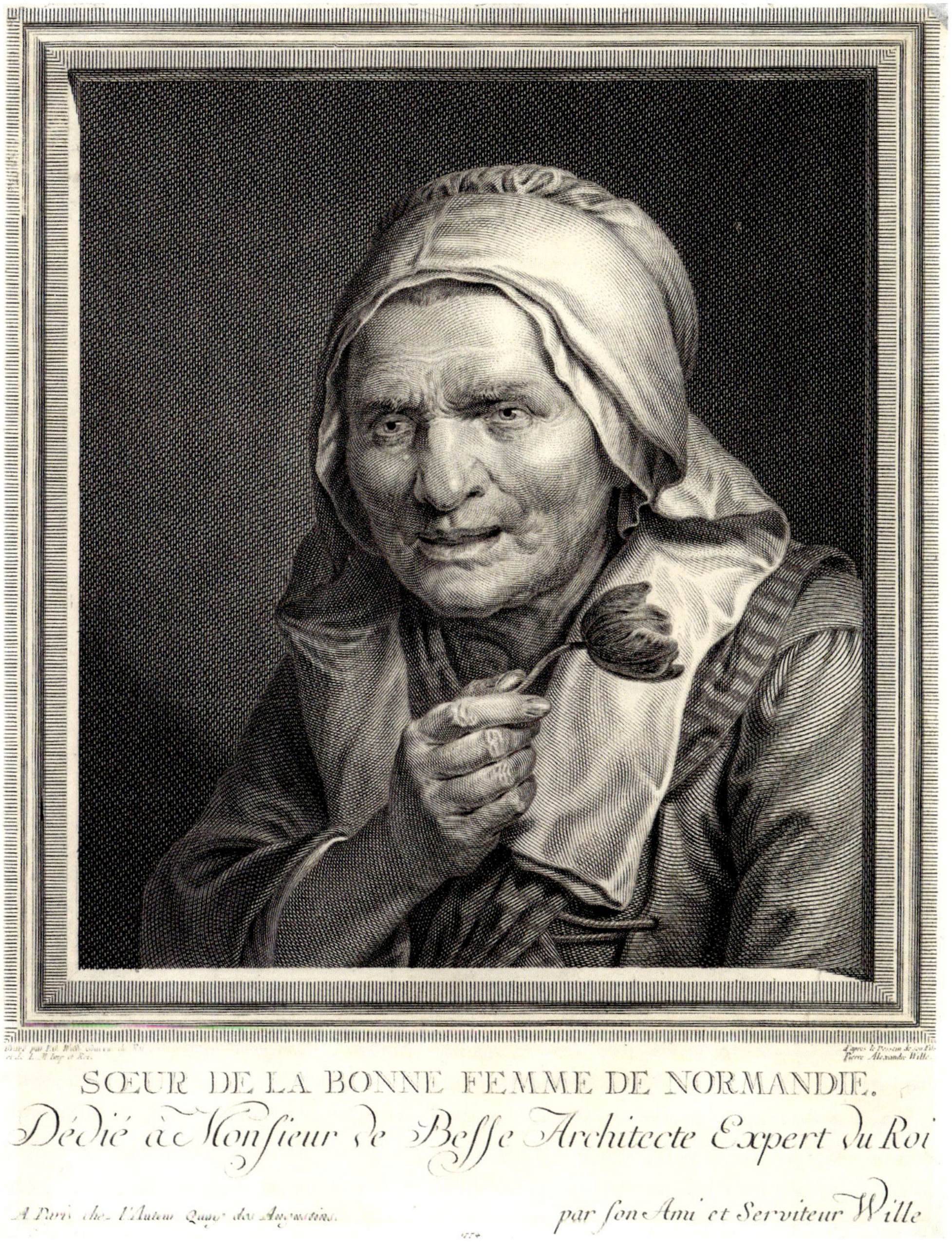


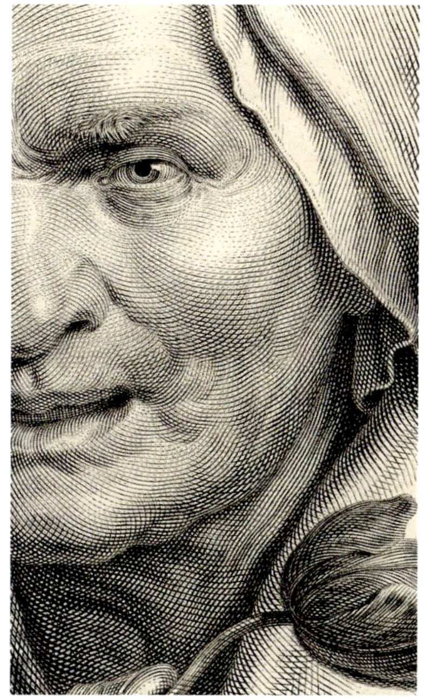

Also, the prints make an interesting contrast with *Le Concert de Famille*, plate 44 (page 68), where Wille had greater scope because of the varied group of people.

Wille was born at Königsberg in 1715, and started his career working for a gunsmith, engraving steel and silver. In 1736 he went to Paris and engraved some plates after Rigaud. He continued to engrave until 1790, when his eyesight began to fail, an occupational hazard for his trade, but he was fortunate to have worked that long, especially considering he engraved in such minute detail.

PLATE 43 AND DETAIL
*Sœur de la Bonne Femme de Normandie,* engraved by Johan Georg Wille, after Pierre Alexander Wille, his son, 1774. Copper engraving. 18 x 20.5 cm (7 x 8 in.).

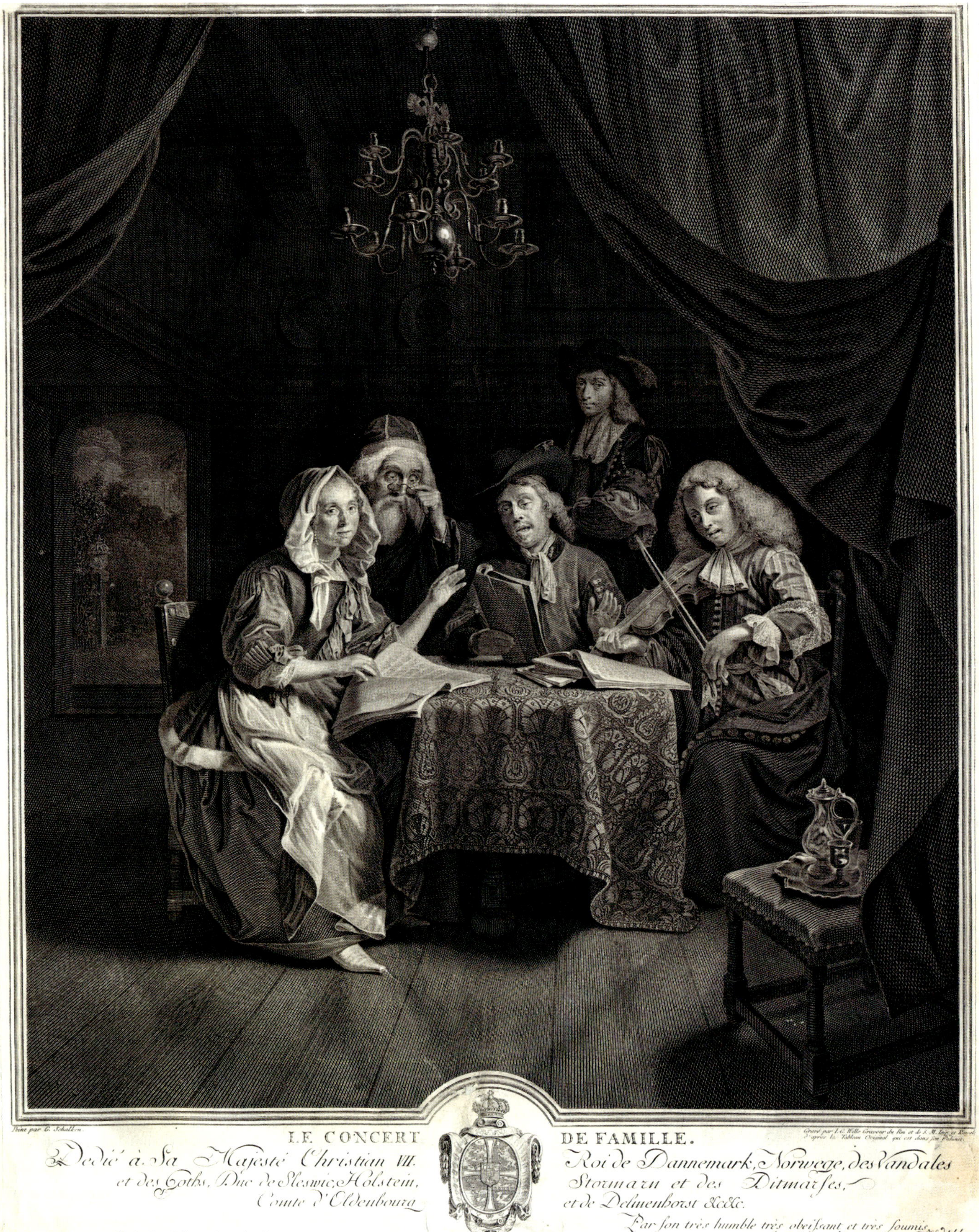
Peint par G. Schalken.
LE CONCERT DE FAMILLE.
Gravé par I.G. Wille Graveur du Roi et de S. M. Imp. et Royale d'après le Tableau Original qui est dans son Cabinet.
Dedié à Sa Majesté Christian VII. Roi de Dannemark, Norwege, des Vandales
et des Goths, Duc de Sleswic, Holstein, Stormarn et des Ditmarses,
Comte d'Oldenbourg et de Delmenhorst &c.&c.
Par son très humble très obeissant et très soumis
Serviteur, Jean George Wille.
a Paris chez l'Auteur Quai des Augustins.

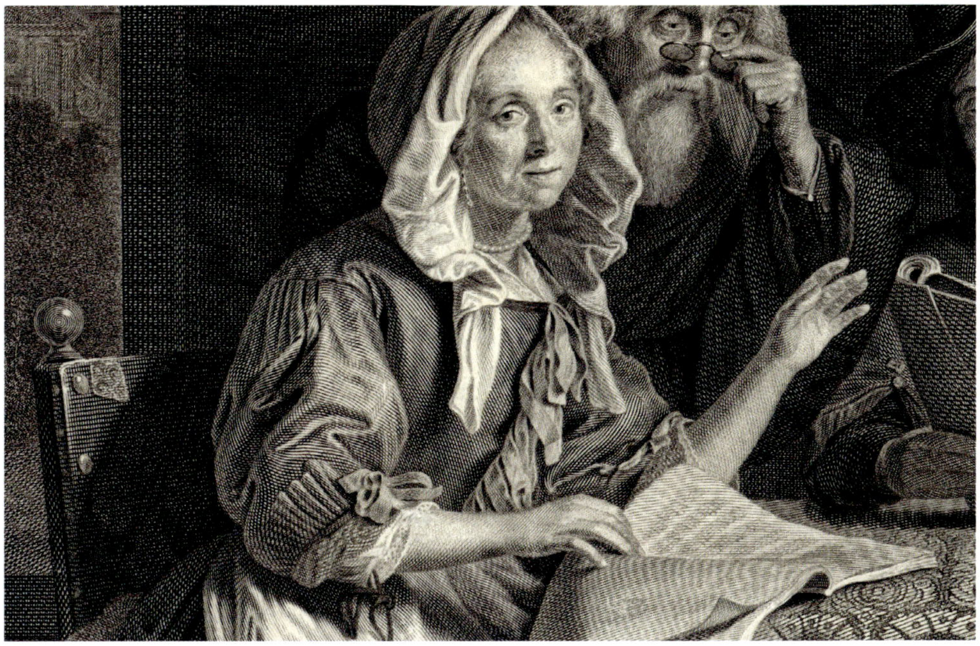

PLATE 44 AND DETAIL

*Le Concert de Famille,* engraving by Wille, n.d., *c.*1780. Peint par G. Schalken. Grave par I.G. Wille. Copper engraving, Plate size: 48.5 x 37.5 cm (19 x 14.7 in.).

This print is dedicated to the King of Denmark, who also owned the painting. Wille was engraver to the King of France and the Emperor of Germany. At the end of the dedication, Wille signs himself Jean George Wille. It is quite normal for spelling of names to vary. 'I', as an initial, was commonly used for 'J', but the spelling of a name does not often vary on the same print.

The textures in this print are again amazingly clearly defined, in a different style to the previous portraits by Wille. Every part of the image is engraved. Each of the floorboards has about 100 almost parallel lines in it, without counting any hatching. The lines are not exactly parallel because of the perspective. The floor, after all, is a comparatively unimportant part of the picture, but Wille even shows the grain in it. More importantly, notice that the hair of each person varies in texture, as, of course, does their clothing. Look at the way the folds are engraved, particularly in the tablecloth.

Perhaps the most extraordinary feature is the knob on the top corner of the chair on which the girl on the left is sitting. Tiny and insignificant it might be; the actual size of it in the print is 7mm. It was engraved in one line, a continuous spiral stopping only to create a highlight of the reflection on it. This was a tremendously complicated thing to do. Remember that the point of the burin is kept in the same position, pointing in the same direction, away from the engraver, and he had to keep turning the plate to create the spiral. It is beautifully done. Wille must have given himself huge satisfaction in the challenge of engraving a minor detail that would go unnoticed by most people looking at the print.

Although Wille has not used the method in this picture, at about this date he developed a method which has become known as 'dot and lozenge', in which the lines of hatching cross to create a tiny diamond or lozenge shape. Wille added a dot to the centre of the lozenge, which added subtlety to the effect. It also meant that a tone of more dense black was possible.

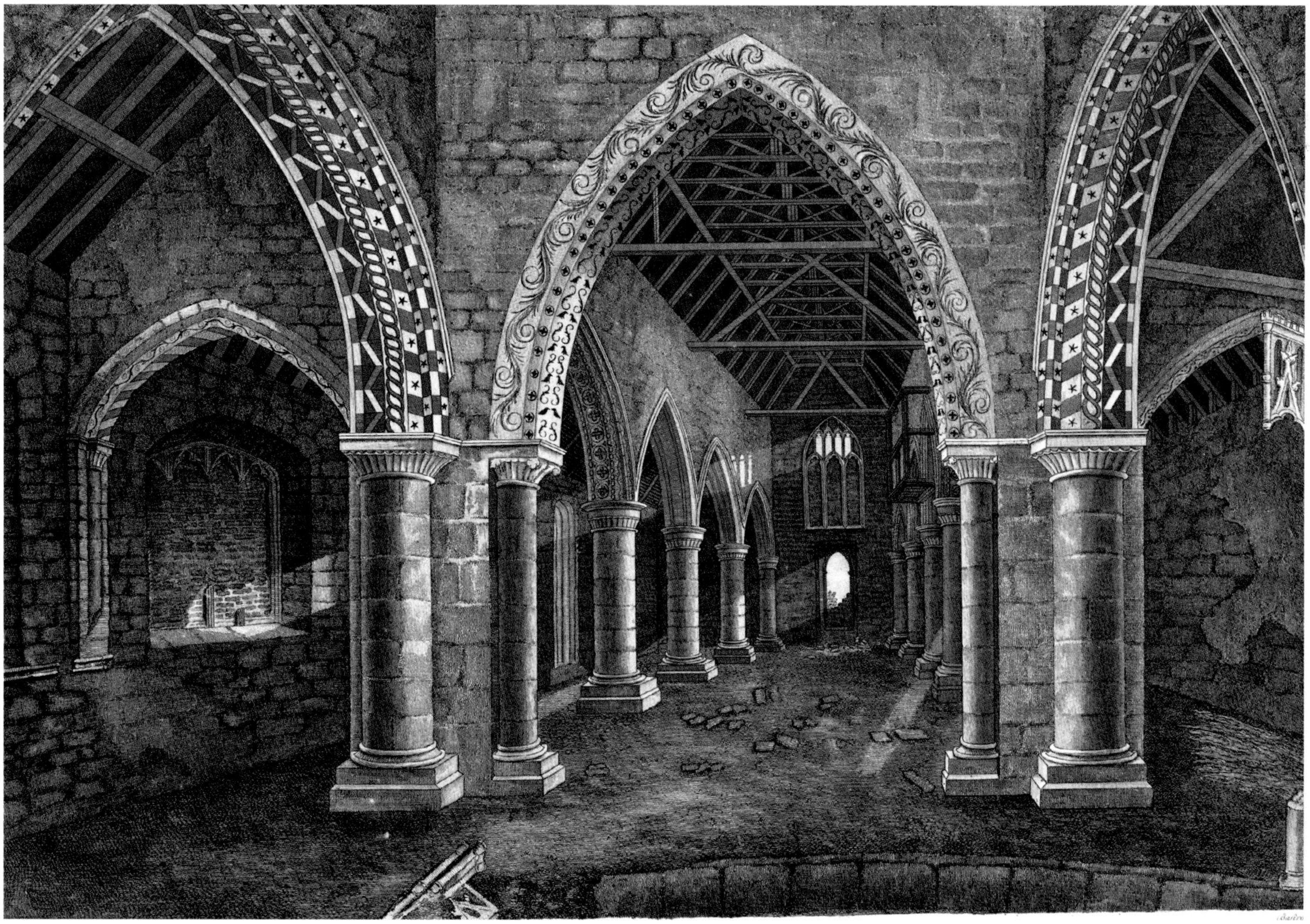

PLATE 45
*Magdalen Chapel, near Winchester,*
engraving by James Basire, 1790.
Inside View of Magdalen Chapel
near Winchester, taken from the
Chancel
looking to the West.
Engraved by James Basire after
Schnebbelie, and published by the
Society of Antiquaries.
Copper engraving,
34 x 48 cm (13.4 x 18.9 in.).

There were three generations of Basires, all called James and all engravers for the Society of Antiquaries. This could be the work of the elder: the second would have been 21 years old in 1790, so the older James is the more likely. Jacob Schnebblie was born in London in 1760 and was given art instruction by Paul Sandby, but it is unlikely that Sandby would have influenced Schebblie to produce this work in which Jacob seems to try to create as many textures as possible in one picture. It would have been an interesting test in the art of engraving.

Schnebblie became a draughtsman for the Society of Antiquaries, and made architectural drawings for *Gentleman's Magazine* and Morris's *Monastic Ruins.* Magdalen Chapel was pulled down in about 1790, the date that the print was made. The site was a short way to the east of Winchester, close to the road to Alresford. To the south of Winchester is the famous church of St Cross Hospital, which is quite similar internally to Magdalen Chapel, but is a lot larger and more robust, with a similar zigzag design in the stone. Apparently, the two churches were built by the same person.

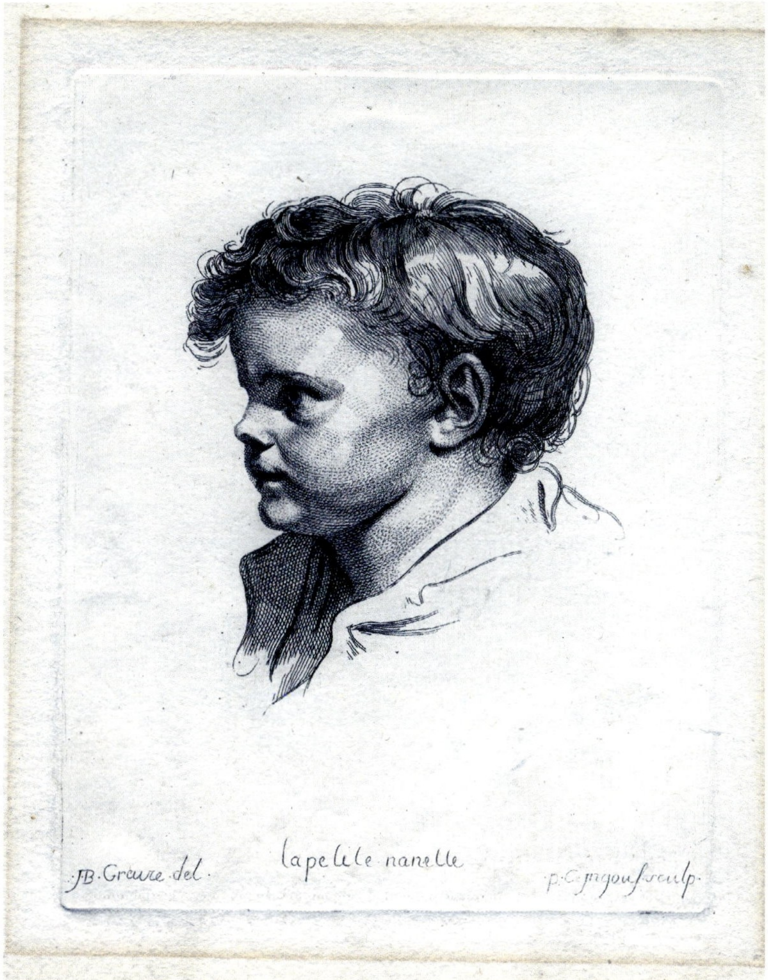


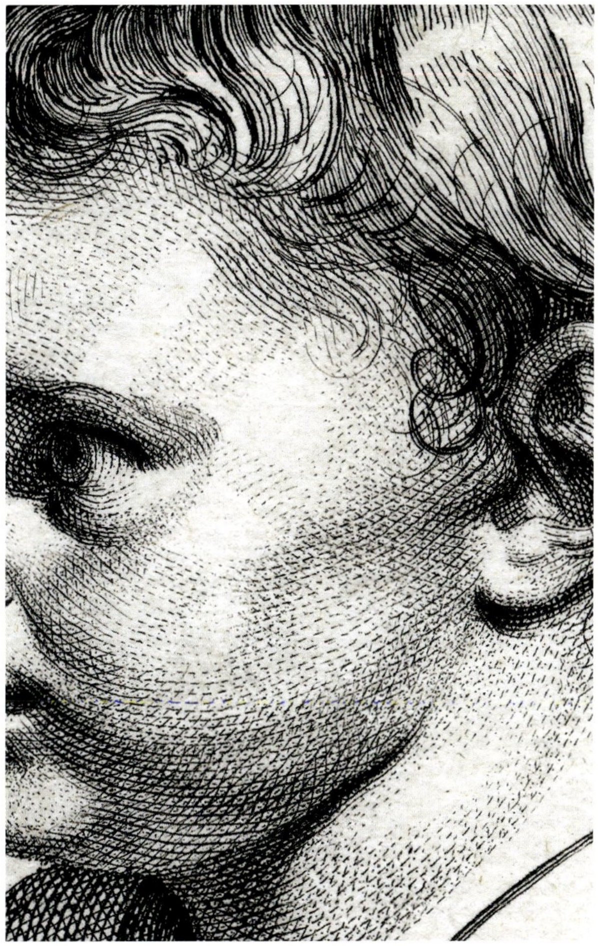

At first sight the face could be taken to be stipple engraving, but in fact the engraver has used the burin to make tiny elongated incisions in the plate, not dots as a stipple engraving would be. To complicate matters further, the lines are extremely delicate, and could be taken for etching, particularly in the hair and the lines of the shirt on the closest shoulder. The title and the credits are etched.

The portrait is of Anne-Marie Javouhey (1779–1851) who practised as a nun during the French Revolution, and survived. This determination is shown in the youthful face in the print.

This print and the two portraits of women by Wille (plates 42 & 43, pages 66–7) were printed at a very similar date. They make an interesting comparison. Wille's work is very detailed, most of the print being covered by engraving. Ingouf has left a large proportion of the plate untouched.

PLATE 46 AND DETAIL.
*La Petite Nanelle,* engraved by Pierre Charles Ingouf, after Jean Baptiste Greuze. No date, published *c.*1780.
Copper engraving,
Plate: 15 x 11.5 cm (6 x 4.5 in.).

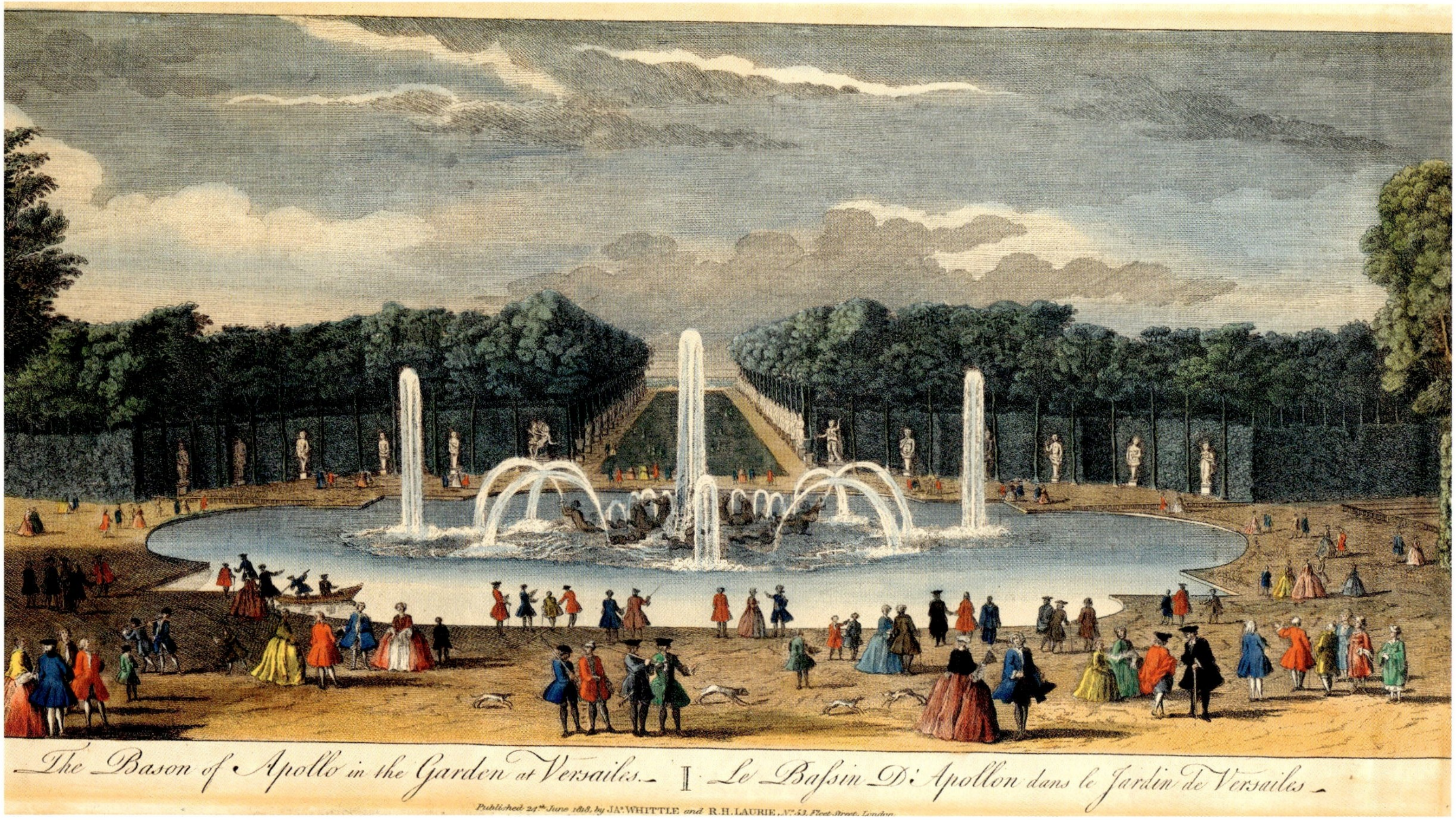


PLATE 47
*The Bason of Apollo in the Garden of Versailes,* anonymous engraving after J. Rigaud.
Published by Whittle and Laurie in 1818.
Copper engraving.
22 x 46 cm (8.6 x 18 in.).

Typical of this period, the title is repeated in French: *Le Bassin D'Apollon dans le Jardin de Versailles.* The scene has not changed, apart from the costumes, of course. The date of this publication is quite important. The print has the appearance of being 60 years earlier. It was published first by Robert Sayer sometime about 1750, so this is a reissue. Laurie & Whittle took over the firm of Robert Sayer in 1794. There is some retouching of the engraving in the sky, which was heavily done, and that is the sign of a late impression, even without the date in the publisher's imprint. The colouring is contemporary, i.e. 1818, and, again, is in the style of the mid-18th century. Very few colours have been used, and the clothing of the people in the foreground is coloured by using only six colours, which was the customary manner of colouring engravings at this time.

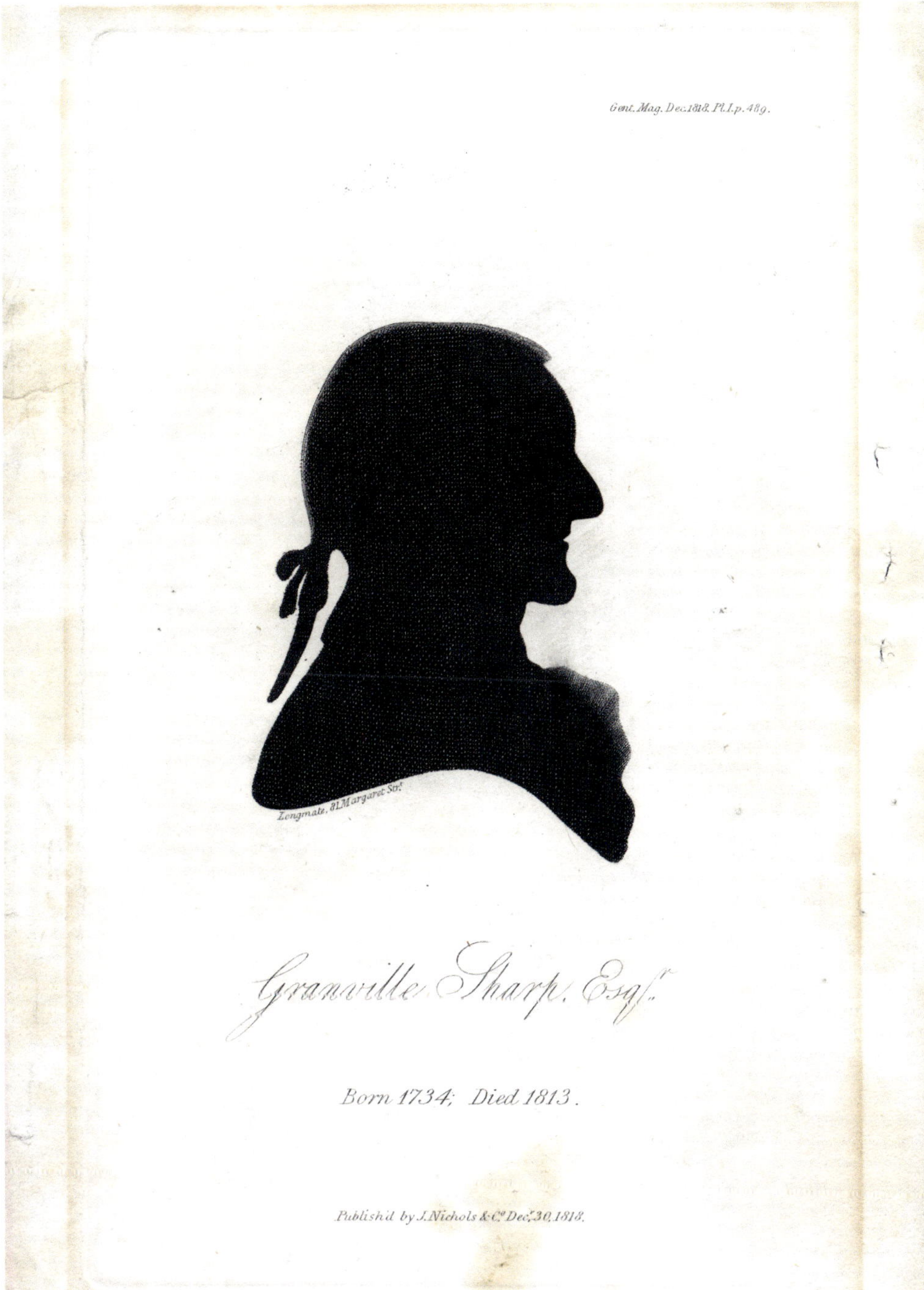

PLATE 48 AND DETAIL

*Granville Sharp Esqr.*, engraved by Barak Longmate, published in the *Gentleman's Magazine*, 1818. Copper engraving, 19 x 11 cm (7.5 x 4.3 in.).

This is a very unusual style of engraving, selected as an illustration because it is the blackest line engraving one is likely to find. It is not entirely black because there have to be grooves in the copper to hold the ink in place. The engraver has worked the plate with fine lines vertically, horizontally and on the diagonals to achieve this texture, but at first glance the print has the blackness of a silhouette. Notice how the engraver has lightened the stock and the hair on the top of the head.

Granville Sharp was a philanthropist, deeply involved with the freedom of slaves, and crusaded against press gangs. He produced many pamphlets on the movements in which he was interested, including history and religion.

PLATES 49 AND 50
Sleeping girl. Engraving by H. Platt. 1823.
Copper printing plate.
17 x 12.5 cm (6.7 x 5 in.).

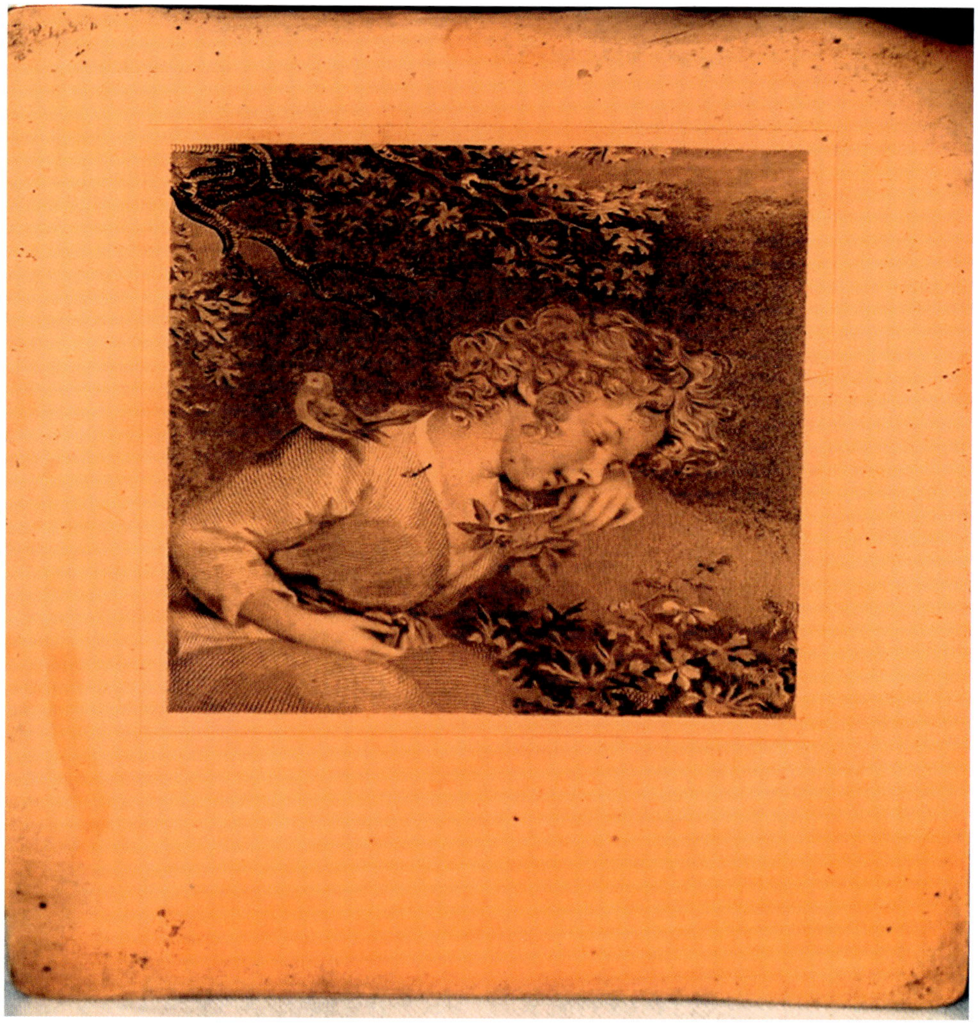

Variant of sleeping girl. Engraving by H. Platt.

There is no lettering on the plate. The name of the engraver and the date have been roughly scratched onto the back.

Platt is obviously a competent engraver, but he has not been traced. At first glance, it would be reasonable to suppose that the plate was stippled, especially in the face and the background. In fact the whole plate is engraved in line, and is extremely finely detailed.

Also of interest is how the plate prints. The two prints are new, printed by Susanne Smith. The pale one was a first attempt. The darker, and more successful, was expected to be too dark when the plate was inked.

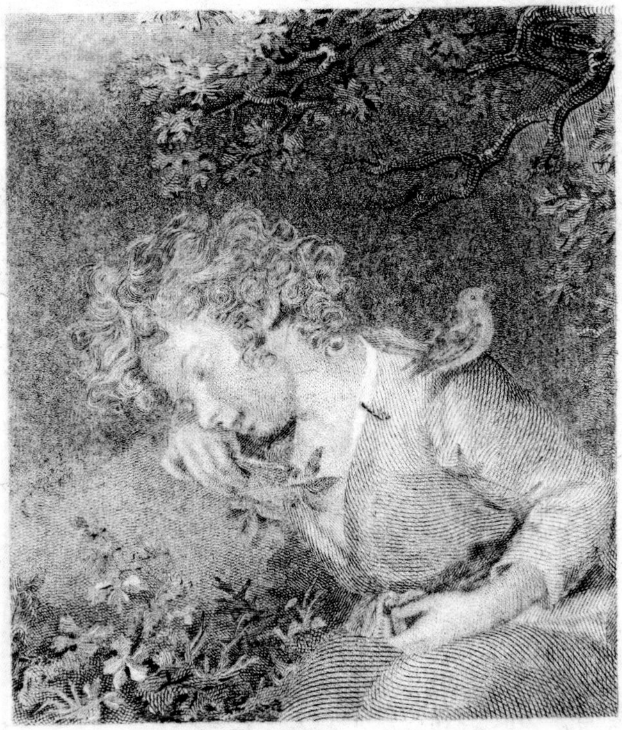

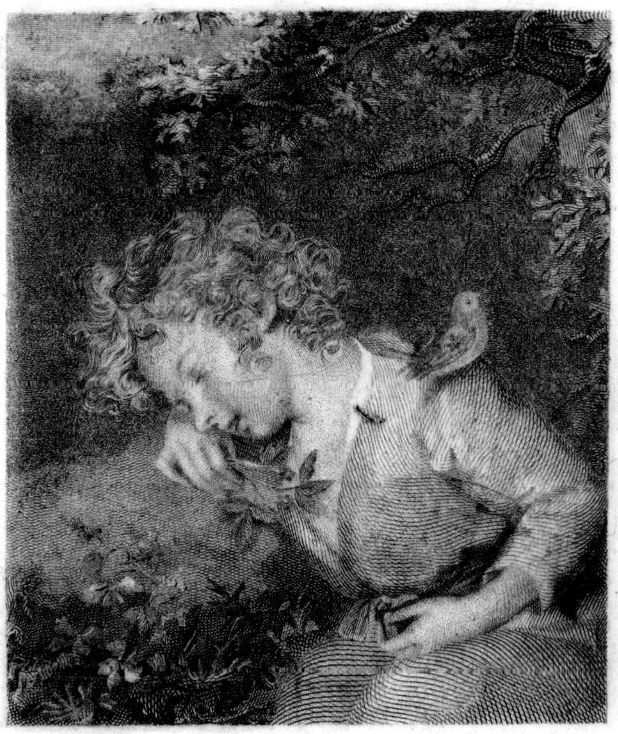

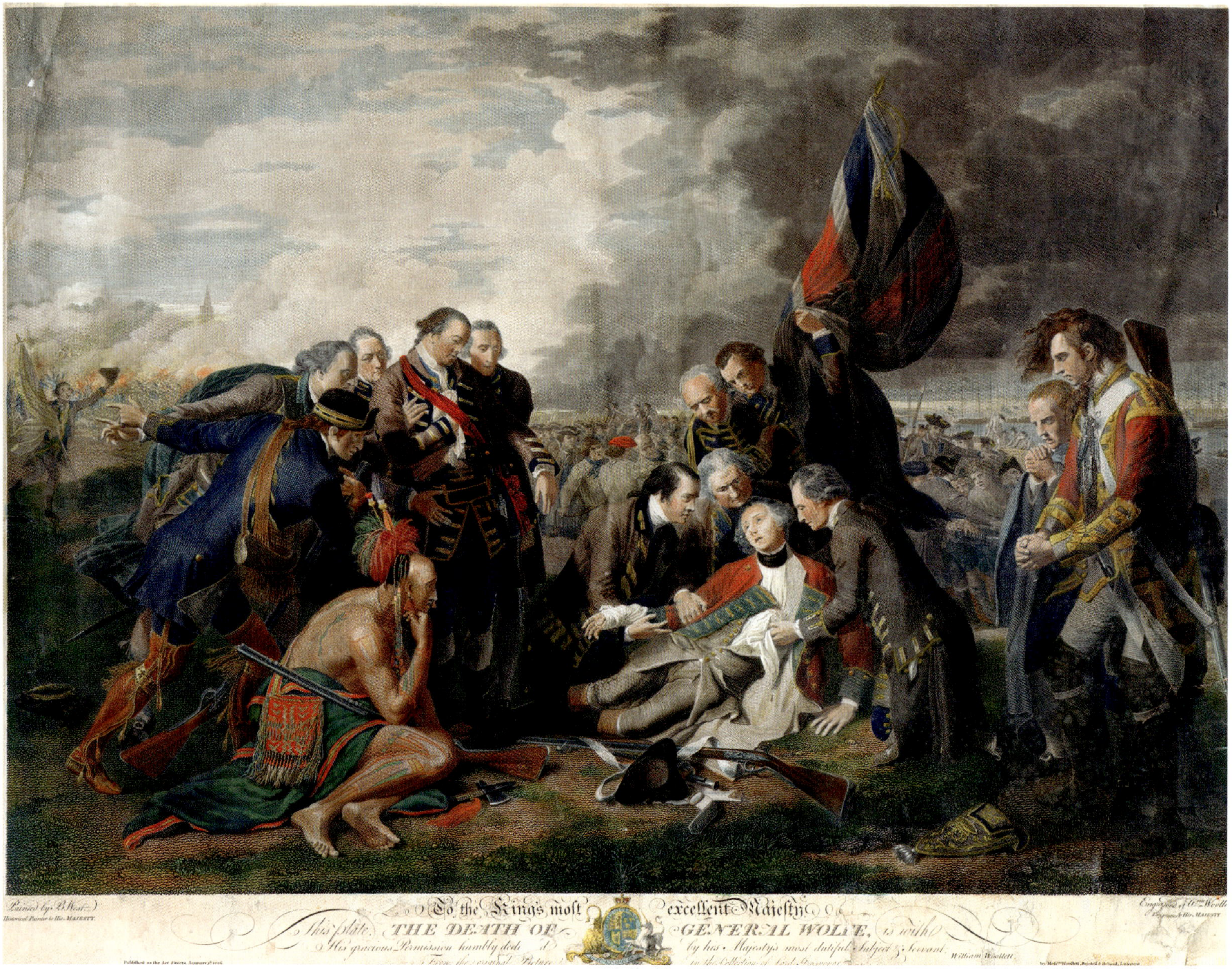


PLATE 51 AND DETAIL

*Death of General Wolfe*, engraved by William Woollett after Benjamin West. Published by Messrs Woollett, Boydell and Ryland, 1776. Copper engraving, 42.5 x 58.5 cm (16.7 x 23 in.).

In the centre of the title imprint is the Royal Arms, because the print is dedicated to the king. The date of publication of the print is significant: Wolfe died in 1759. Benjamin West exhibited the painting shortly after the completion of it in 1771. It was another five years before the print was published. In modern times, the demand for a picture of a major event 17 years afterwards would be extremely limited, yet this print enjoyed huge success. The subject was a major historical event and both West and Woollett were at the heights of their careers. The painting is quite large, 152 x 214 cm, nearly four times larger than the print; at the time, the print was considered to be too large.

In the Catalogue Raisonné of the Engraved Works of William Woollett by Louis Fagan, the print is listed as XCIII. To confuse the issue, Fagan lists seven proof states, which are in the British Museum, beginning with the etched outline, before arriving at the eighth state, which is the first published state. But then Fagan fails to list the published states, which, of course, are the most important to most people, since unfinished proofs are unlikely to come onto the market.

The first published state has the title in open letters. Interestingly, Fagan says that after about 30 impressions of the print had been taken, Woollett was appointed Engraver to the King, on 27th November 1775, before the print was due to be published. The plate was immediately altered. Historical Painter to His Majesty was added beneath West's name, and Engraver to His Majesty was added beneath the name of Woollett. The first 30 impressions had the additions made in pen and ink. The example illustrated here has the printed additions, and is therefore at least the second published state. The subsequent editions are something of a grey area. It would simplify things if states were described at proof state or published state.

The painting was exhibited at the Royal Academy in 1771. It created a sensation there. West had rejected the convention of representing heroes in out-of-period armour or clothing. He was meticulous in the detail of the uniforms and the native costumes. The scene, however, is somewhat contrived. The people who are featured in West's painting were not necessarily at Wolfe's death, mainly because they were fighting elsewhere or because they were injured. To the left can be seen a messenger bringing news of victory, which heightens the poignancy of the picture. The accuracy of the subject is not at all reliable, and that is typical of historical pictures of the period.

The painting was bought by Lord Grosvenor for his collection, as we see from the title on the print. The painting remained in the family until 1918, when the 2nd Duke of Westminster gave the picture to the Canadian War Memorials. It is now at the National Gallery of Canada. There is a second version of the painting in the Royal Collection.

The example illustrated is a good impression, particularly noticeable in the detail of the faces and the distance; later impressions would not be as clear as this. The condition of it is dreadful. Although the colour is meticulously applied, it is relatively modern and further reduces the value of the print. Compare this engraving with the steel plate by Smith, plate 52 (page 79). Also of allied interest is plate 83 (page 114).

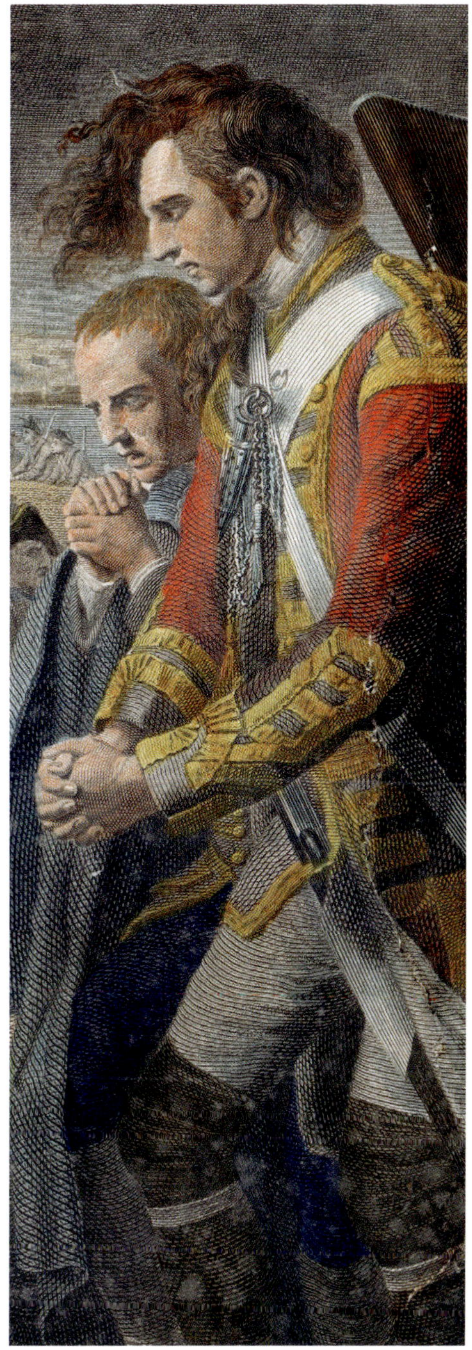

# COMPARISON OF COPPER AND STEEL ENGRAVING

These two prints, plates 51 & 52, were made about 70 years apart. The copper engraving was published in 1776, and measures 42.5 x 58.5 cm (16.7 x 23 in.); the steel engraving was published in about 1850, and measures 12 x 18 cm (4.7 x 7 in.). Despite the disparity in sizes, the engravers have faithfully copied the original painting by Benjamin West; the central figures are virtually identical, down to the folds in the clothing and the expressions on the faces. There are some slight variances to the right of the Union Jack. Most of the reason for the similarity is that a steel plate was capable of printing finer detail than copper, and prints could be made on a much smaller scale without losing detail. It would not be possible to produce such fine detail by using a copper plate of the same size as the steel plate.

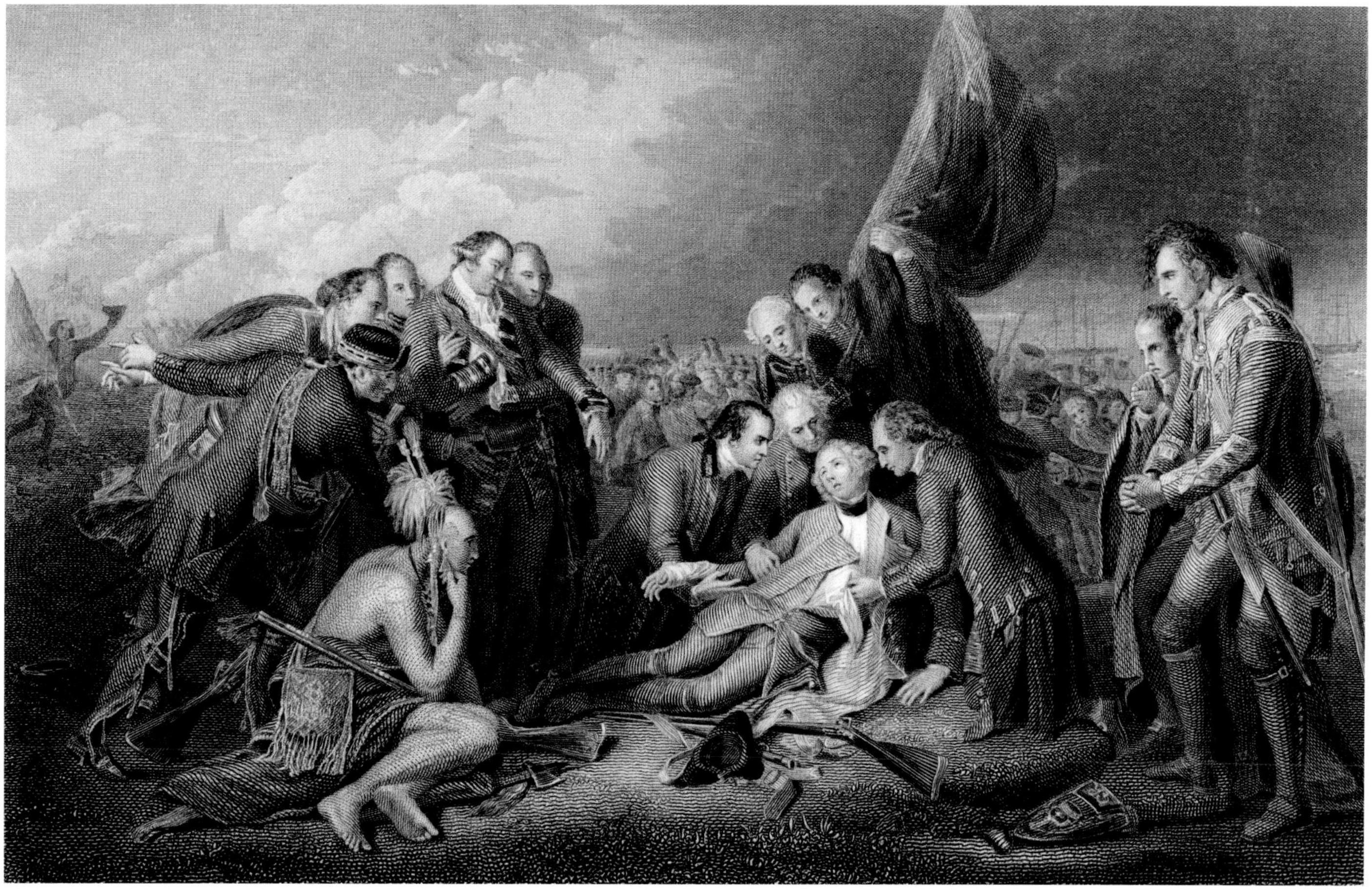

Despite the big reduction in size, this print manages to include the same detail as that of Woollett, even the same expressions on the faces. You might think that both Woollett and Smith faithfully followed the original painting. It is possible, but it is more likely that Smith copied his work from Woollett's print, which was more accessible.

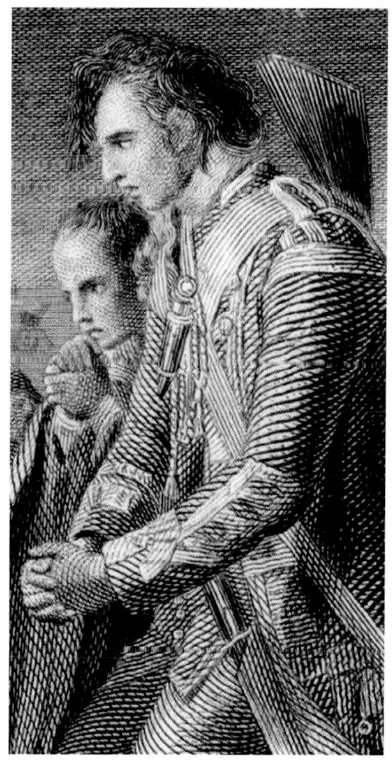

PLATE 52 AND DETAIL
*The Death of General Wolfe,*
Samuel Smith, after Benjamin West, *c.*1850.
Steel engraving,
12 x 18 cm (4.7 x 7 in.).

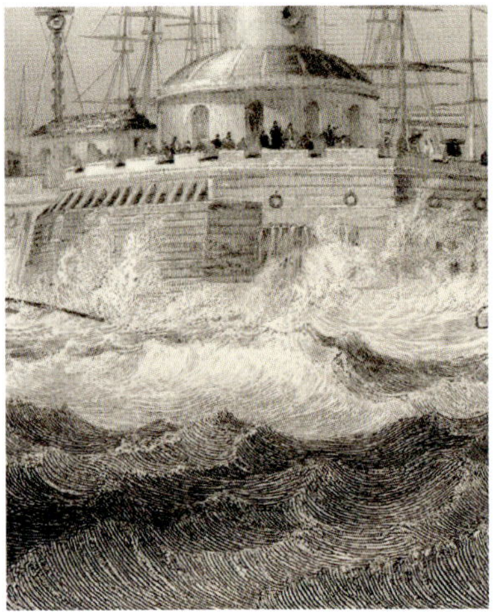

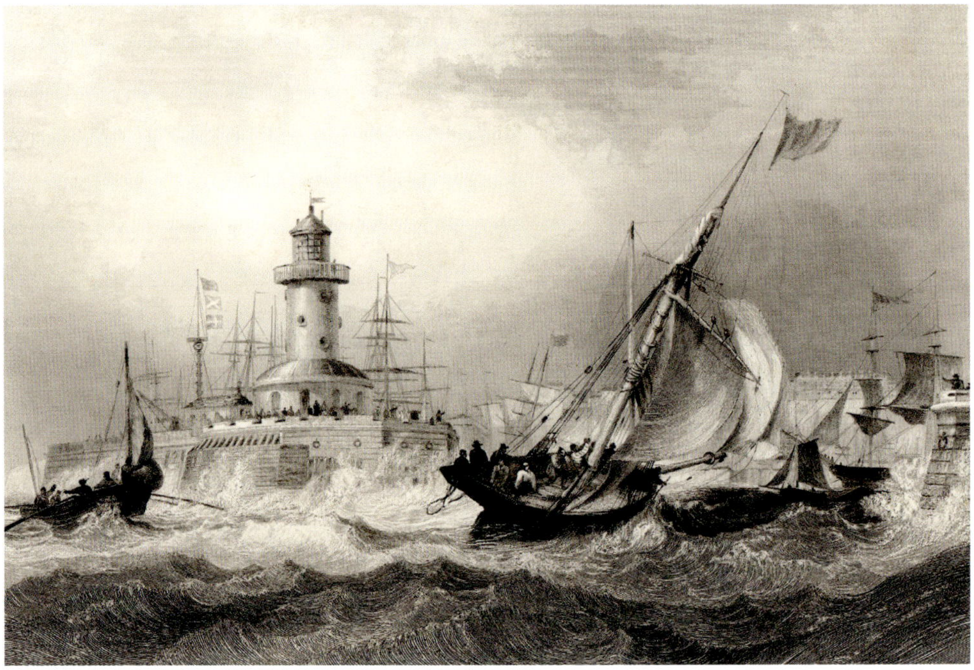

PLATE 53 AND DETAIL
*Ramsgate*, engraved by W. Finden, 1837.
Steel engraving,
12.5 x 18 cm (5 x 7 in.)
From the painting by E.W. Cooke, now in the Ramsgate Public Library.

This is an illustration for Finden's *Ports and Harbours*, published in 1837, and is a good example of the extremely fine detail that was possible with a steel plate. The sky is engraved with a multitude of lines, mainly engraved horizontally in perfect parallel, with some added diagonally to create darker cloud effects. The white crests of waves hitting the harbour walls are engraved with extreme delicacy.

E.W. Cooke is a famous shipping artist and etcher. He etched some very good plates from his own drawings for his *Shipping and Craft*, published in 1829.

PLATE 54
Advertisement. Steel engraving by Isaac Slater, a well-known engraver and printer from Manchester, *c.*1840.
10 x 18.5 cm (4 x 7.3 in.).

Below is a splendid piece of ephemera, printed for advertising Slater's business, including all possible printing requirements, and, at the same time, providing a variety of lettering and decorating styles. The scene of the cherubim in the centre is a 'vignette', which is a picture without a border, usually oval.

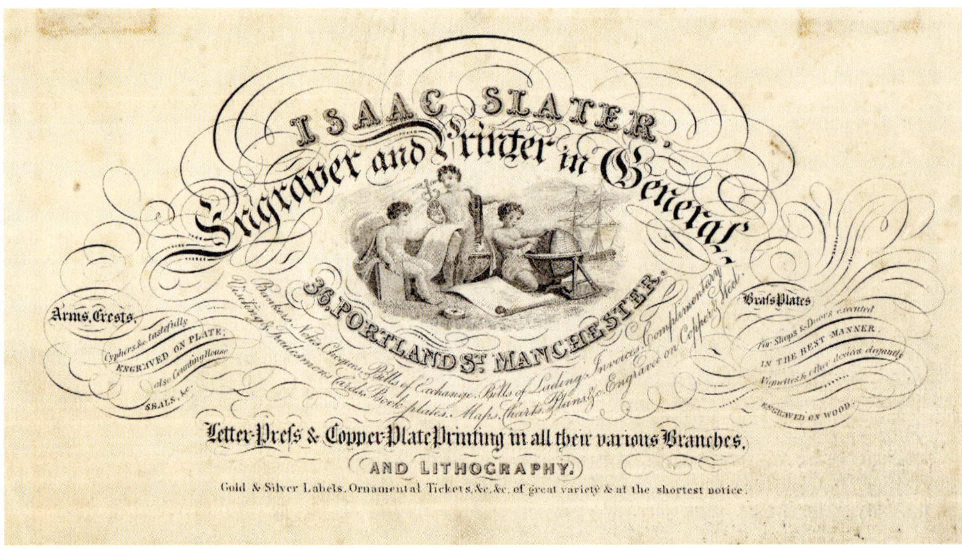

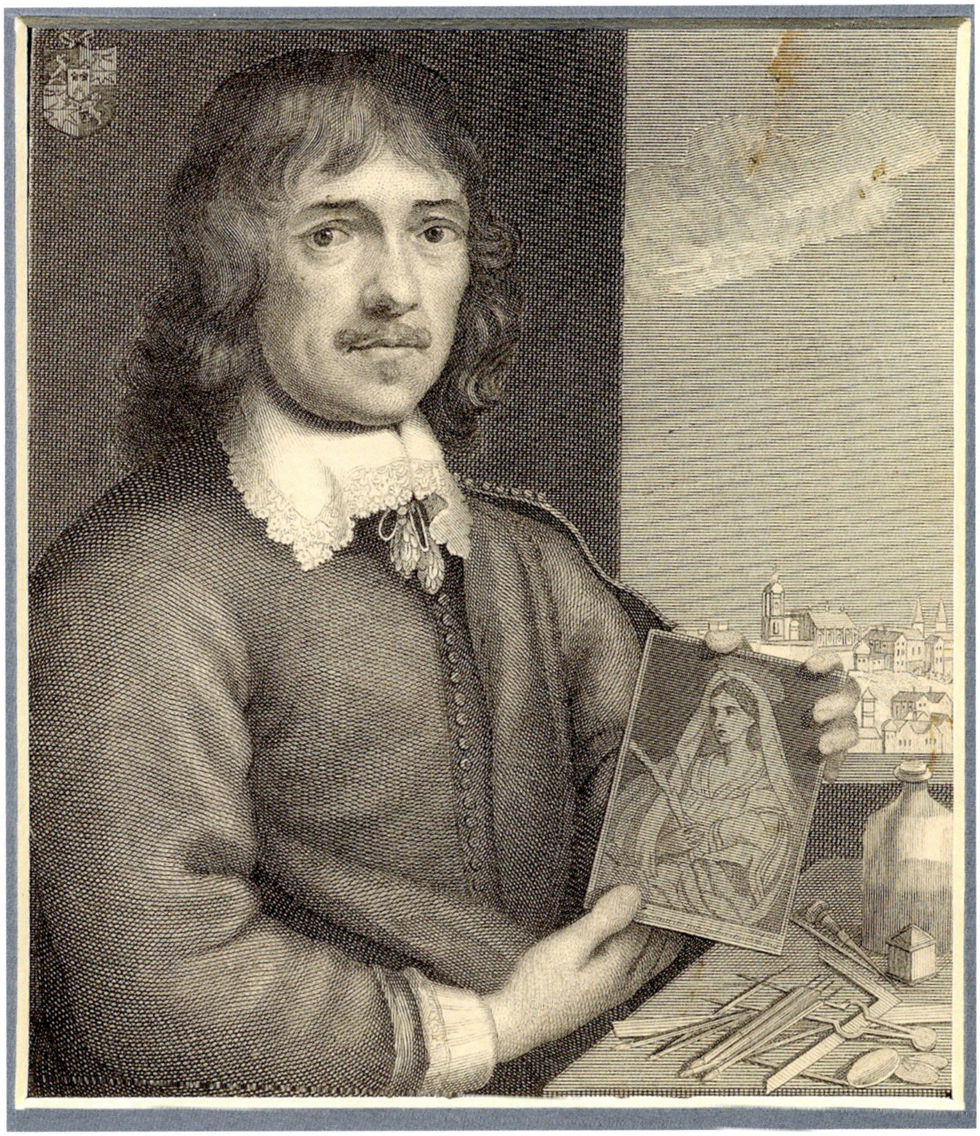

PLATE 55

*Wencelaus Hollar,* engraved by William Skelton about 200 years after the Jan Meyssons etching, plate 60 (page 87), published in 1837 for H. Walpole's *Anecdotes of Painting.*
Steel engraving.
Trimmed within the image, and now measures 11 x 9 cm (4.3 x 3.5 in.).

William Skelton (1763–1848) was a portrait engraver. He was over 60 years old when he made this engraving, which is probably his only engraving on steel. It makes an interesting comparison of the techniques of steel engraving and etching. In this steel engraving there is no attempt to make the wording legible beneath the plate in Hollar's hand.

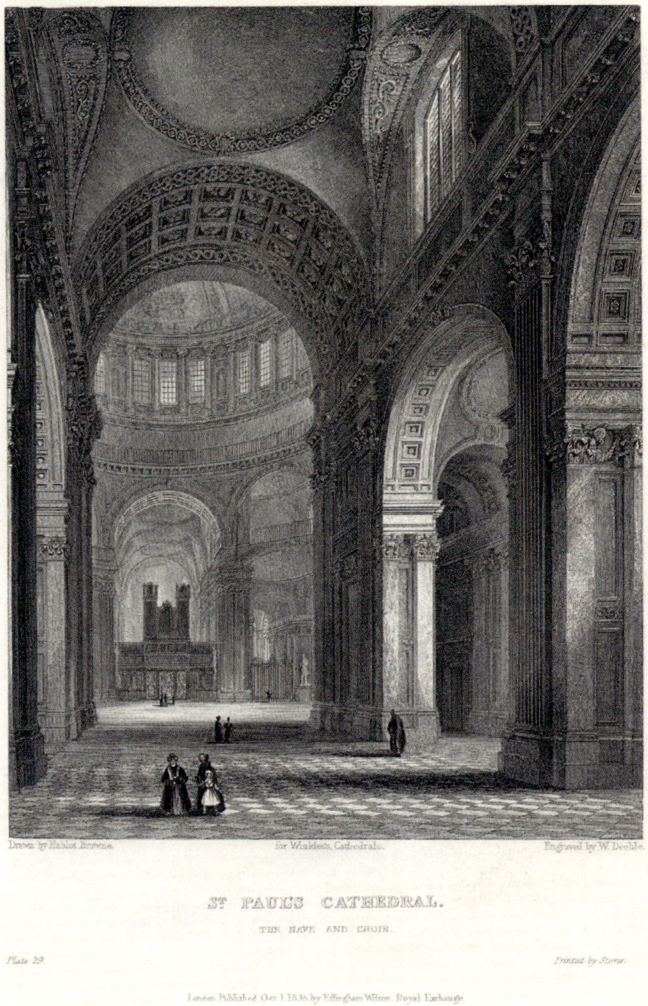


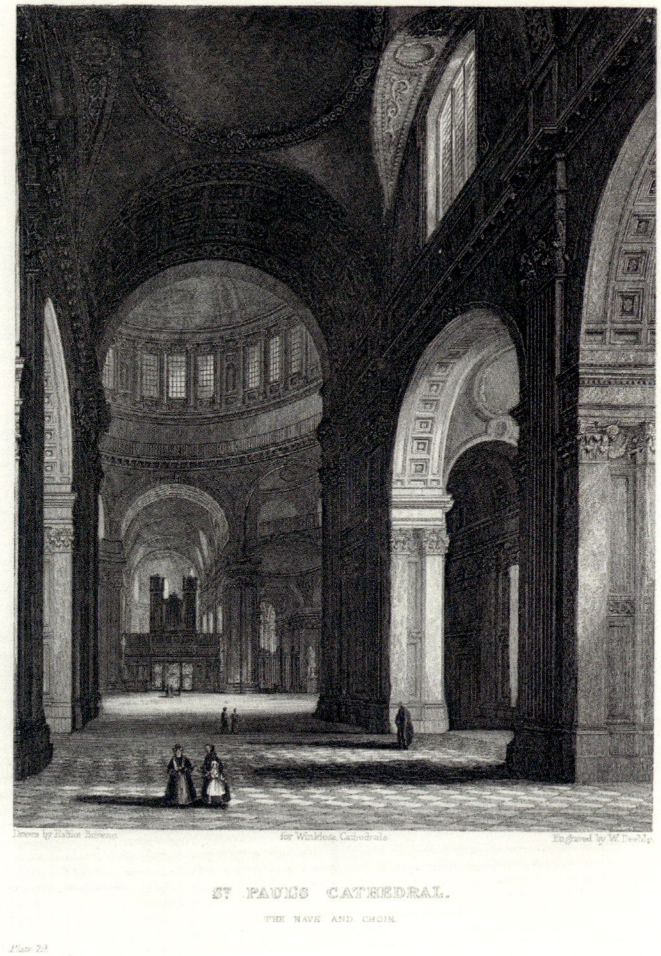


PLATES 56 & 57
*St Paul's Cathedral, The Nave and Choir,* engraving by W. Deeble after Hablot Browne, for Winkle's *Cathedral Churches of England,* published by Effingham Wilson, Royal Exchange, London, 1835.
Steel engraving, 14.5 x 11 cm (5.7 x 4.3 in.).

William Deeble was a painter and engraver of architectural subjects. Early in his career he did some copperplate engraving, but steel suited his style better, and he worked on several of the famous topographical series during the second quarter of the 19th century.

The print shows a total contrast with the work in Hablot Browne's etchings (plates 68 & 69, pages 96–7). Browne was 20 years old when he drew this St Paul's scene. He later became better known by the pseudonym of 'Phiz'. Pseudonyms were quite common. Phiz did a lot of illustrations for the books of Charles Dickens who used 'Boz' as his pseudonym.

Also of note is that the name of the printer appears on the print: 'Printed by Storer'. The second example of the print has had the publisher's imprint and the name of Storer removed. The plate has been overinked, so that the fine detail of the architectural features is lost. However, viewed from a distance, the effect of the second print is actually more dramatic, and gives a greater sense of perspective.

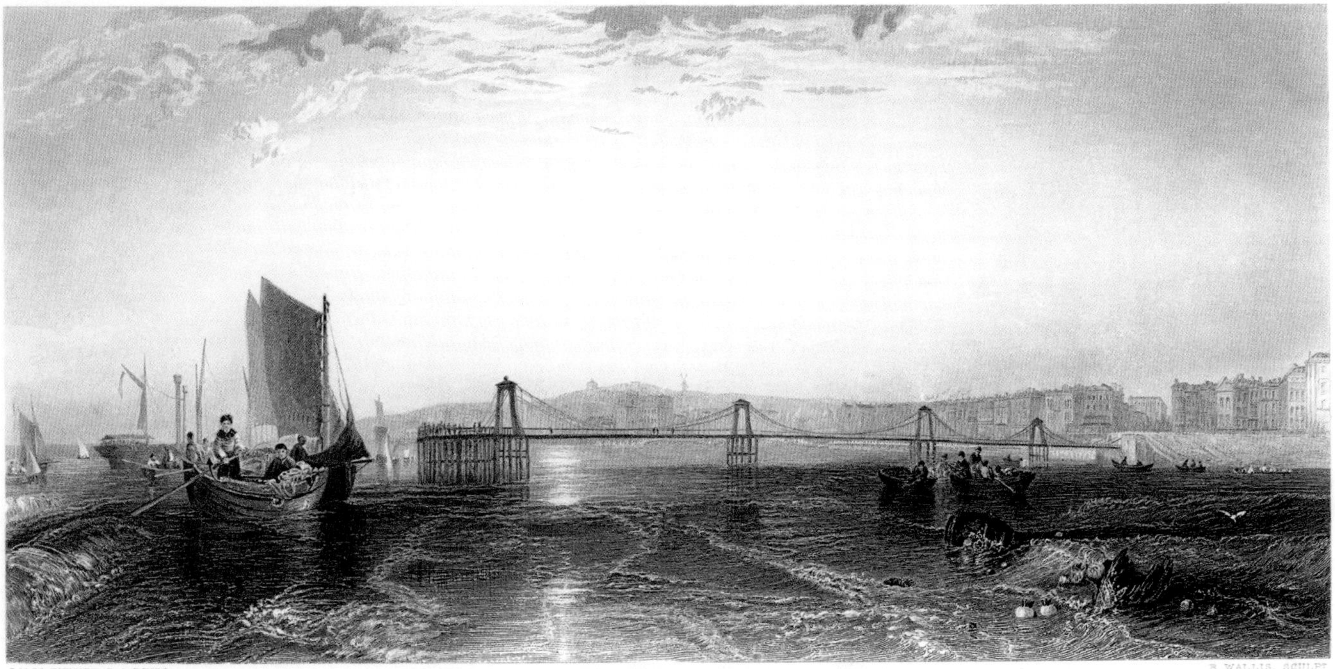

J.M.W. TURNER, R.A. PINXT  R. WALLIS, SCULPT

BRIGHTON CHAIN PIER.

This print is an interesting contrast to the scene by Fox (plate 103, page 142). This one is viewed from the east and shows more of the Brighton buildings in the background. Turner includes boats of all sizes, more fishing boats than pleasure boats, with a steam ship to the left. The rolling sea is not quite as lifelike as some of Turner's prints or as good as Finden's view of Ramsgate (plate 53, page 80).

PLATE 58

*Brighton Chain Pier*, engraving by Robert Wallis after J.M.W. Turner, R.A. Dated 1859 but later.
The print was first published in the Turner Gallery in 1859. This is a late edition, published by Virtue & Co, *c.*1878.
Steel engraving.
Image: 14 x 28 cm (5.5 x 11 in.).
The print has minimum margins of more than 3 cm (1 in.), and there is no sign of the plate mark, so the plate must have been quite large.

# ETCHING

The earliest known etching is dated 1513, and is by Urs Graf, and rare enough for only one copy to exist. It is possible that there were etchings made at the end of the previous century, but, in any event, the beginning of etching was a little later than line engraving. The system of etching metals for decorative purposes, like armour and silver, was being used long before the 15th century, and before any line-engraved pictures appeared.

Etching is an intaglio method, also producing lines on the paper, but instead of complicated engraving tools being used to cut into the metal, the incisions can be made with carefully controlled use of acid. At the start, the whole surface of the plate is coated with a very thin layer of resin, which is acid-resistant. This is known as 'laying a ground'. The resin has to be heated to melt it before it is spread over the plate. Once the ground cools it will harden again and is blackened with lampblack to make it easier for the etcher to see his progress; resin is transparent, so the black makes a contrast to the copper plate. The etcher traces his design or image onto the resin, and then uses a needle to scrape through the ground just enough to expose the plate. Unlike line engraving, the needle is not used to cut into the copper. The incision, known as 'bite', is done by the acid eating into the plate.

Once the etcher completes his design on the ground, the acid process starts. There were two ways of doing this. The most common is to immerse the plate in an acid bath. The first is to varnish the back of the plate to protect it. The second is to form a wall of wax around the edge of the plate, forming a tank to hold the acid. The wall method was used in late 19th-century etching, though I am told that it was used by goldsmiths and armourers from very early etching times. It makes sense. It would be much easier than trying to protect all other parts of a suit of armour from acid, which would have had to be done when using an acid bath.

The acid 'bites' into the copper wherever the etcher has scraped through the resin. In this way, the etcher can achieve an incision similar to the engraver's burin, although the acid makes a 'u' shape, whereas the burin makes a 'v' shape, and this does have a different effect in the prints. The immersion in acid would create an equal 'bite' to all the exposed metal. That means that all the lines on the print would be the same, which is not the object, of course. There has to be some variance to make the print interesting. So, once the etcher has achieved the right amount of 'bite' on the feintest parts of the print, these parts are 'stopped out', which means that more resin is used to cover these parts and protect them against any further bite. Then the plate is subjected to acid again, and further 'bite' to the exposed copper takes place. The etcher repeats this procedure, gradually adding the required variety of tones; the more 'bite', the darker the effect on the print will be.

Fine lines need very little 'bite', and the slightest incision in the plate will create an impression on the paper, just the same as line engraving. The darkest lines require considerable 'bite'. The length of time that the plate is subjected to the acid depends on several factors, the main one being the strength of the acid and the amount by which it has been diluted, a matter which has to be decided by the etcher. Also, acid works faster in warm conditions, another matter to considered. Furthermore, it is not possible to judge the progress of the etching 'bite' when the plate is submerged in acid.

The acid used was usually nitric or nitrous. Hydrochloric acid mixed with chlorate of potash was a third option, though this was considered to be unpredictable in its performance. The submersion time is crucial, especially for the finest detail of the print; usually a few minutes will suffice. To achieve the blackest lines, the plate will take several hours of submersion. Like engraving, there is an optimum width to any etched line: if it is too wide, it will not print clearly. When subjected to acid, the 'bite' is not only downwards into the plate, but sideways as well, beneath the resin, so when the etcher is using his needle, allowance has to be made to ensure the lines do not become too wide. Some acid bites downwards more than across, for some weird chemical reason that I do not begin to understand.

If the etcher needed to see how his work progressed, the resin had to be removed from the plate before a 'proof' could be taken. If he decided that more bite was required, it was necessary to lay another ground before any further etching could take place. This was complicated. A clear resin was used in order that the etcher could see the etched detail beneath the resin, and see which of the etched lines needed more 'bite'. He could then open up the lines again, using a needle. There was also a technique of relaying the ground with a roller, in which the roller would fill the fine lines and leave the bolder ones exposed.

Some etchers used a slightly different method, dispensing with 'stopping out'. By using the needle on the dark parts of the print first, the detail became darker as the etching progressed, finishing with the finest detail.

The difference between a line engraving and an etching may be difficult to detect sometimes. Generally, an etching is much more freehand, like a pen-and-ink drawing, less formal than a line engraving.

Although the explanation of the method might not make etching seem simple, it was considerably easier than line engraving. Many artists etched their own plates, whereas there are few artists who did any line engraving. Certainly, many collectors like etchings because the prints are close to the original work of the artist.

## DRYPOINT ETCHING

The appearance is similar to etching but is achieved without acid. Or, in other words, it is more like engraving only the etcher, as he is called, uses a drypoint needle (much stronger than an etching needle), worked directly onto the plate, forcing the needle into the plate to make lines. The difference between a drypoint needle and the graver is that the needle does not cut a neat 'v' in the plate, and it also makes a jagged score in the plate, causing the metal to 'burr' at the sides of the incision, giving a rich effect to the print. When the plate is inked, the burr holds ink on the outer sides as well as in the incision, creating a characteristic all of its own. The burr meant that the number of prints taken from the plate was very limited. Just rubbing ink into the plate would remove some of the burr. The pressure in the printing press meant that the burr quickly wore away. As few as 20 prints was quite normal before the effect of the burr was lost.

The needle is pointed at each end, so the etcher did not have the benefit of the mushroom handle in his palm while he worked. Considerable force is needed to make the incisions in the plate, and for that reason, drypoint lines are generally quite short, especially the dark parts of the print. They are also irregular, as if they were made at random, with little attempt at trying to make parallel lines, unlike most line engravings, and that is the charm of drypoint.

PLATE 59

Etching copper plate with ground
Anonymous, unfinished. *c.*1880.

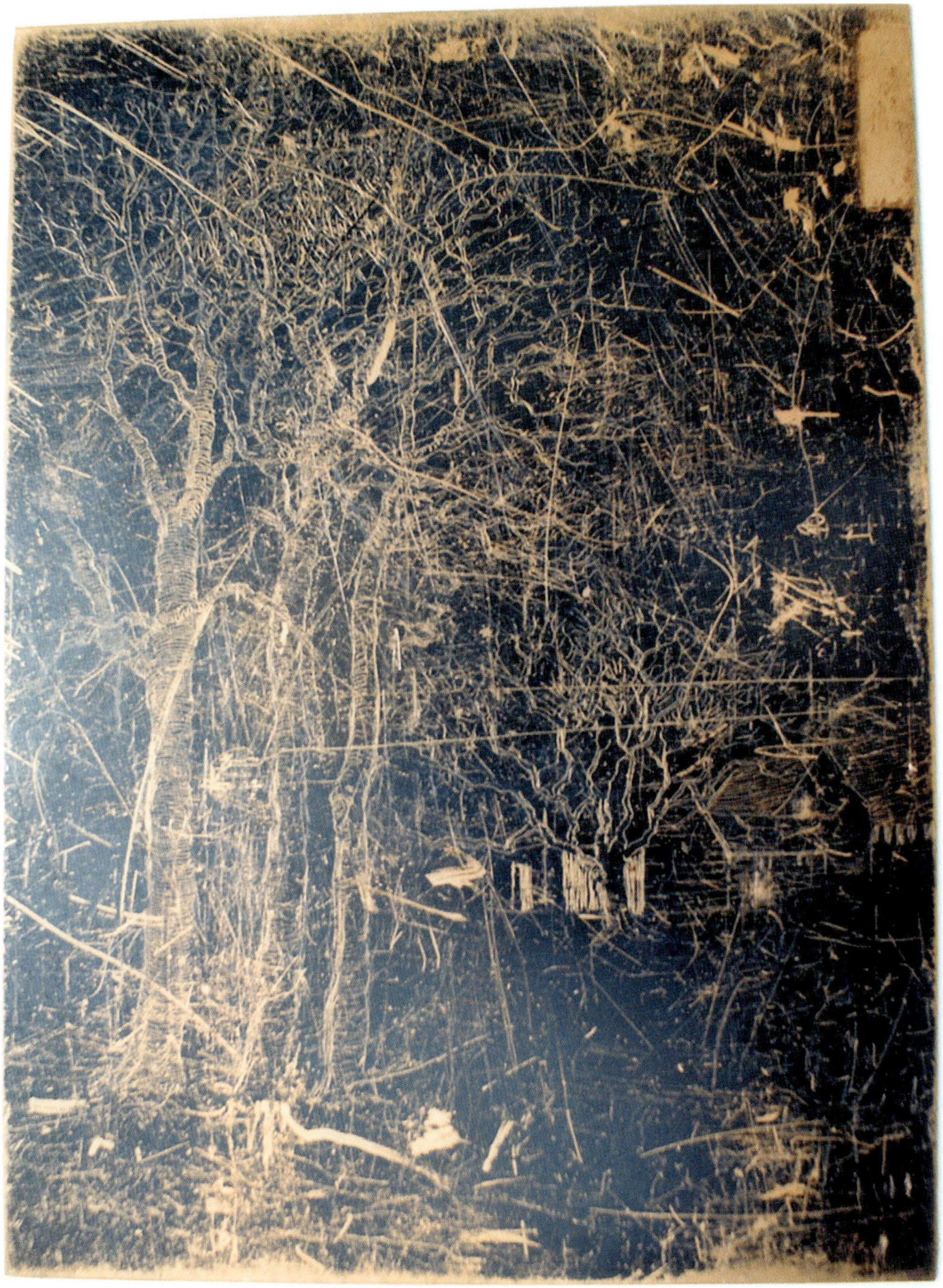

The plate is covered with a very thin ground, just enough to protect it from acid. Unfortunately, the ground is scratched and rubbed, but shows how the method worked, particularly the way that the etcher only had to use the needle very gently to expose the copper through the ground.

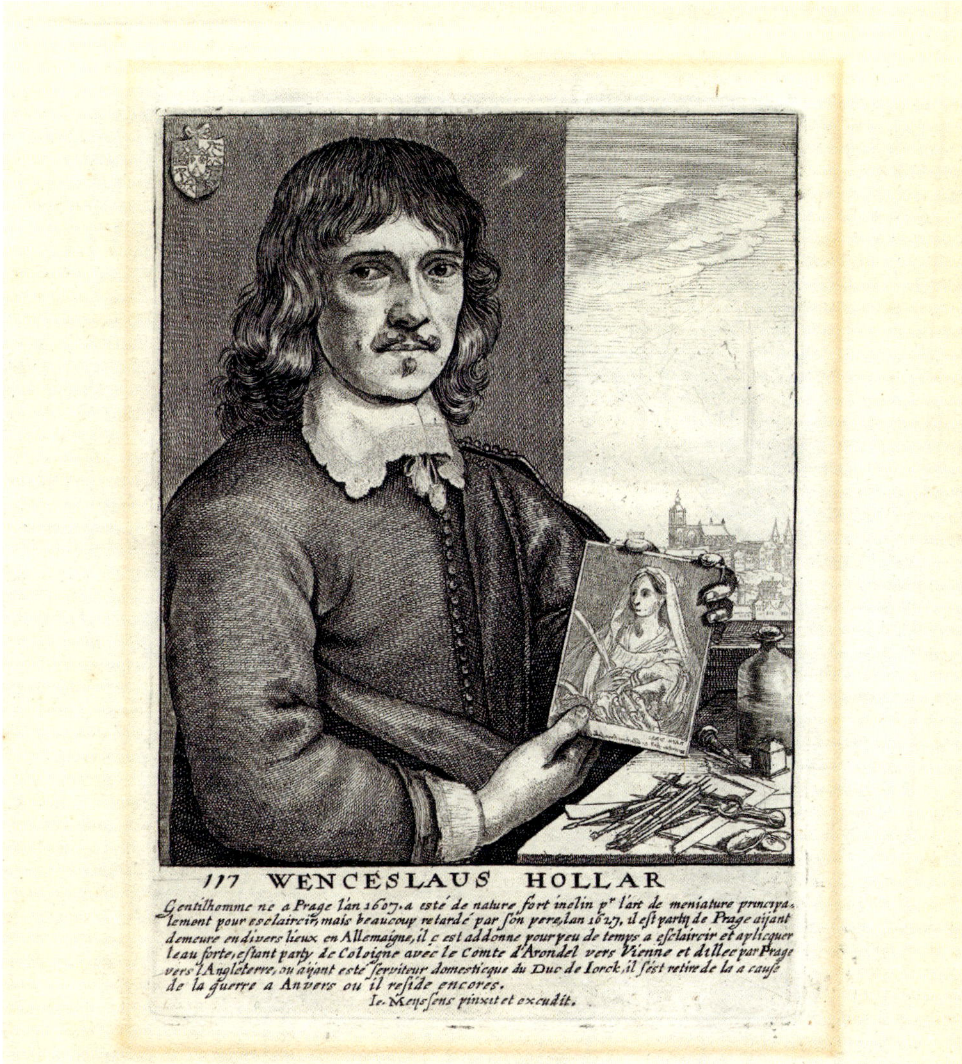


PLATE 60

*Wencelaus Hollar,* etched by Jan Meyssons (1612–70). *c.*1660.
The first state. The second showed drapery on the wall.
Etching,
13.3 x 11 cm (5.2 x 4.3 in.).

This print is typical of the etchings made from 1580 to 1750, but there is not always as much of the plate worked as we see here. There are many etched portraits which are no larger than this.

Hollar was born in Prague, 'discovered' by the 14th Earl of Arundel (a patron of the arts), and brought to England, spending most of his working life in London. Much of his work was sponsored by the Earl, but he did a lot of work for various publishers and produced a wide range subjects, including important views of London, and some maps for Richard Blome.

In the print, Hollar is seen with a view in the background which is typical of his own work. In his hand is an etched plate; the writing at the bottom can be clearly read, though in reverse: 'Raph Urb. W. Hollar fecit. Ex collection Arondelle', which means the portrait is after Raphael of Urbino, etched by Hollar, in the collection of the Earl of Arundel. On the table is a variety of etching tools and an acid bottle.

Meyssens was a prolific etcher and engraver. This print shows that he tried to emulate Hollar, but he never quite equalled the master (see also plate 55, page 81).

PLATE 61

Copy of Rembrandt's *Man in a Broad-brimmed Hat.*
Anon. *c.*1700.
Etching.
The plate and a modern print.
Plate size: 8 x 7.2 cm (3.1 x 2.8 in.).

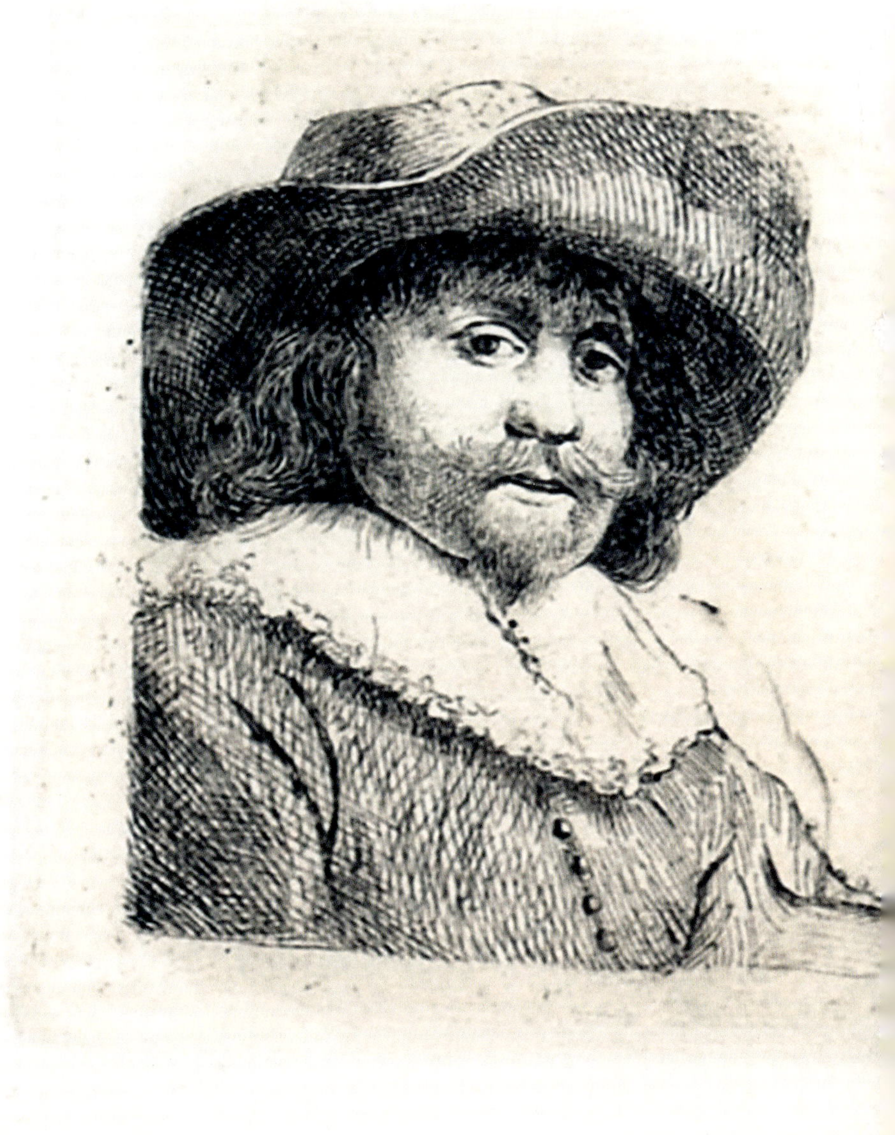

A poor attempt at copying Rembrandt. The etcher tried to make a correction to the man's left shoulder, the eyes are not quite correctly focused, and the print lacks the sparkle of the original Rembrandt print of 1638. The frills on the collar and the buttons are not clear. The whole is not set squarely on the plate (this is particularly noticeable at the bottom of the print), but, strangely, this has been carefully copied and is the same as Rembrandt's original.

The main interest here is the reason for this print to be made. During his lifetime Rembrandt was highly regarded and his work was being copied as much

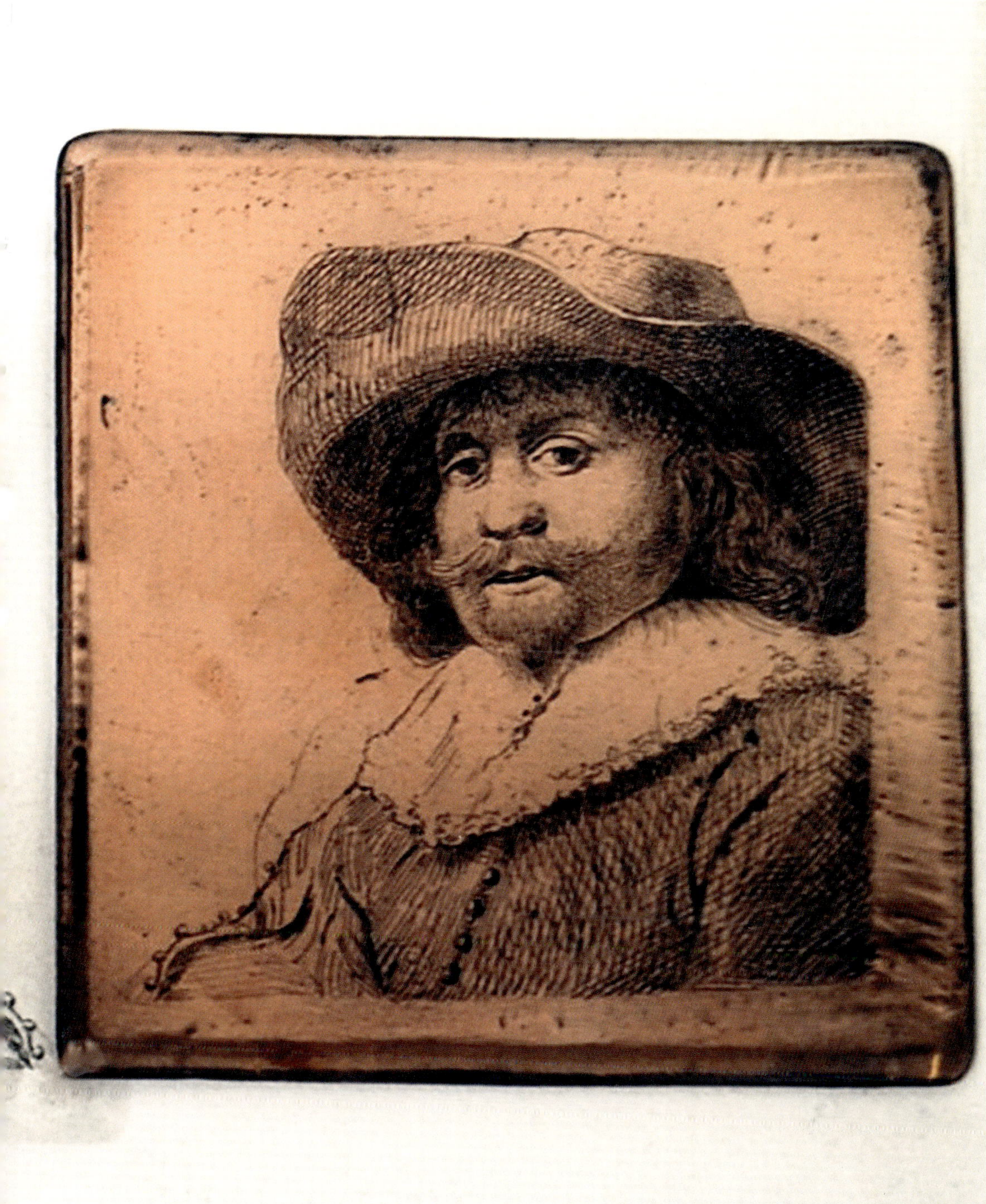

as there were people trying to emulate him. Was this print a fake, intended to deceive? Or was it an etcher doing his best to copy the master, learning the craft? It is in any case, an early etching plate and typical of the subjects that were being printed at the date.

The print is new, printed recently by John Land at the Printing Works, Amberley Museum.

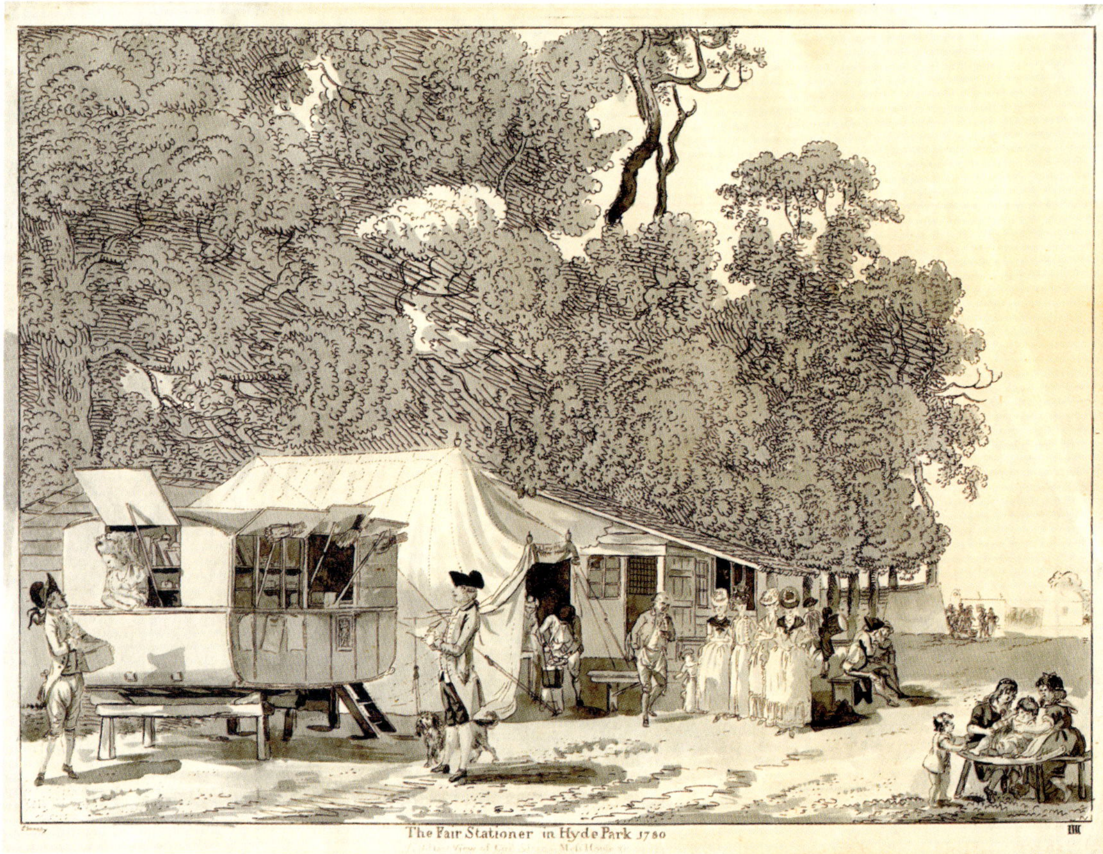


PLATE 62
*Fair Stationer,* etched by Paul Sandby, 1780.
Etching,
21.5 x 28.5 cm (8.5 x 11.2 in.).
From the collection of Sarah Baynton-Williams.

This is an unusual style, which could easily be confused with aquatint or even watercolour. The detail is etched in outline with no aquatint ground added. The soft tones are watercolour which Sandby probably added himself. He was largely responsible for introducing aquatint into Britain with a series of 12 views of South Wales, five years before this print was made, so it is surprising he did not use aquatint for the print. On the other hand, adding tones to the etching with watercolour was probably quicker than adding aquatint to the plate, particularly when the print run was expected to be small.

The figure with a drawing pad, just to the left of centre, is Sandby. It was common for artists to portray themselves in their pictures. At the time of the Gordon Riots, 1780, there were military encampments in Hyde Park, St James's Park and the garden of Montague House (the British Museum), and another at Blackheath. Sandby made prints of them, and these are a good record of the social history of the time. The camps were like small towns, mostly under canvas, providing essentials for the soldiers and their families. Stationers such as this were vendors of prints, but none appear to be on sale here.

The scene is typical of the lively scenes that Sandby produced. He liked to include a variety of people in his pictures, preferring to illustrate people at work instead of the customary promenading aristocracy, seen in the pictures of many of his contemporaries.

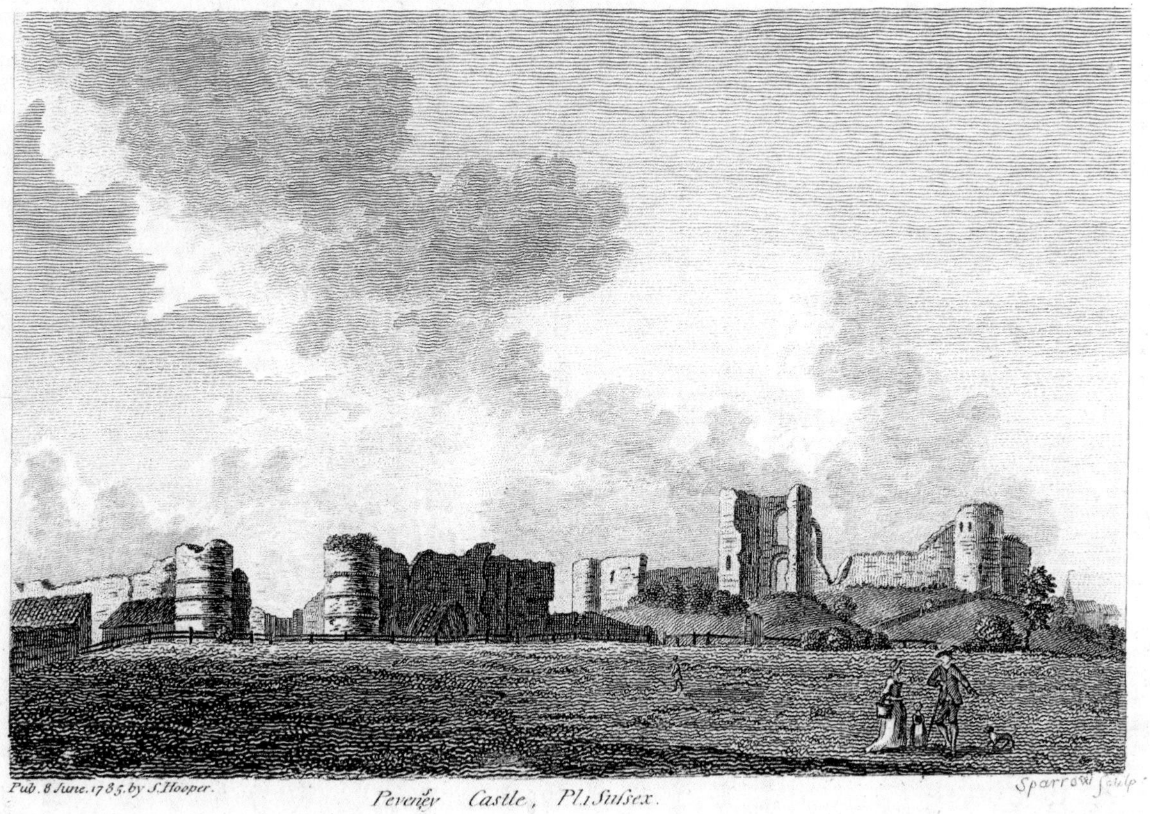


This print has very little merit, but there are some things worthy of note. Sparrow's name, beneath the image, appears in 'scratch letters', looking as though they were simply scratched onto the plate, as if it was not finished. 'Scratched letters' normally refers to a proof state. After his name are the letters 'sculp', which suggests that the plate was line engraved. At a glance, the print could easily be taken for a line-engraving, but none of the lines are straight, something that's particularly noticeable in the sky. The print has a slightly more freehand appearance than is typical of line engraving.

Lastly, of interest for an entirely different reason is that the title is misspelled, the 's' not included, but added above the original letters. It was possible for errors like this to be corrected by knocking up the plate from the back, smoothing the copper and re-engraving, a laborious procedure. Many engravers did not bother and so mistakes like this are quite common.

PLATE 63

*Pevensey Castle,* etched by S. Sparrow. Published by S. Hooper for Francis Grose's *Antiquities of England and Wales,* dated 1785. Etching, 10.5 x 15 cm (4 x 6 in.).

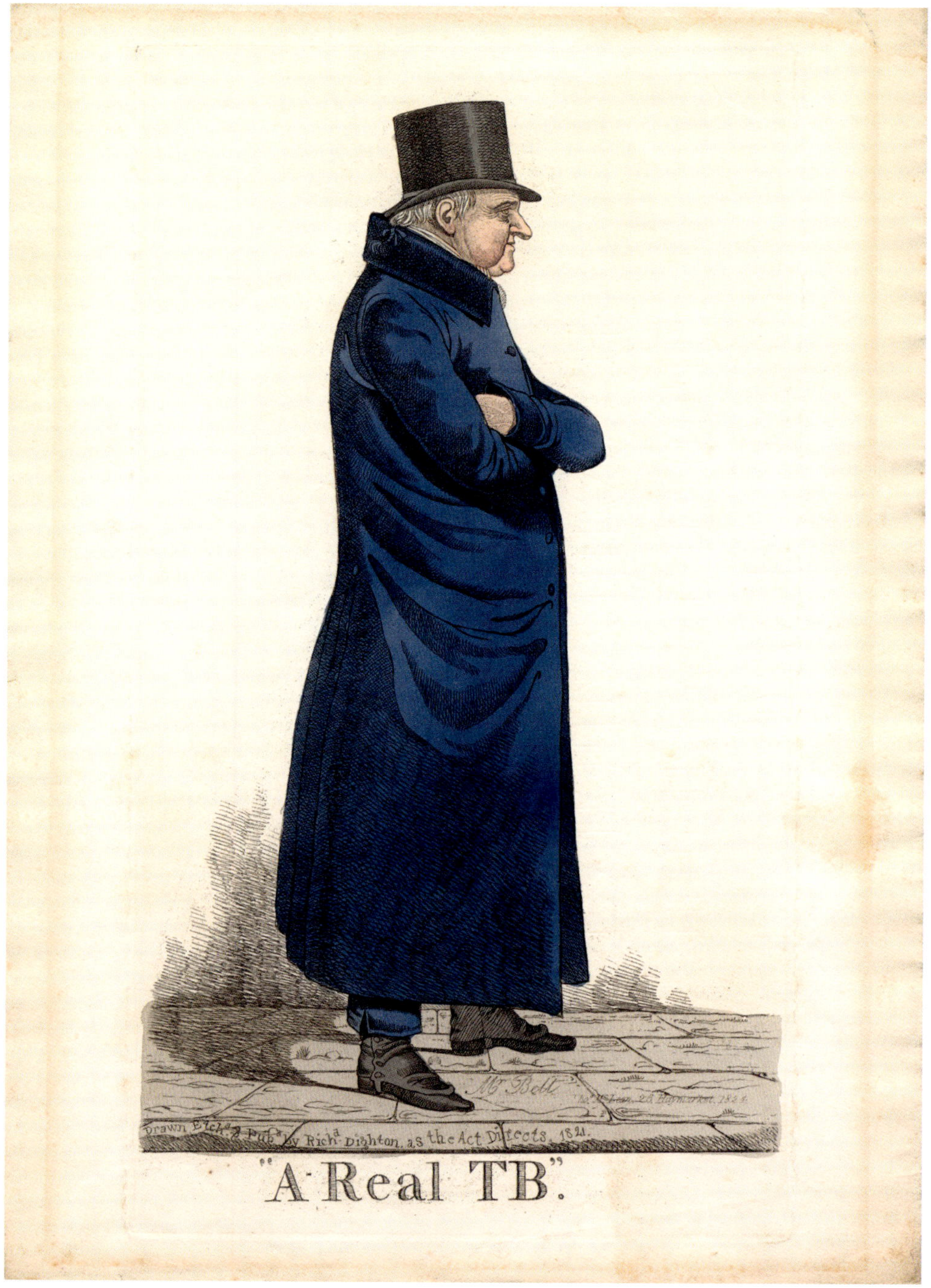


PLATE 64
*The Real TB.*
Drawn, etched and published by Richard Dighton, in 1821. This is a reissue, with the name Mr Bell added in the paving between the feet, published by Thomas McLean, dated 1824. There is a wonderfully clear watermark in the Whatman Turkey Mill paper, dated 1826, so this is likely to have been printed a year or two after that.
Etching.
Plate size: 32 x 17.5 cm (12.5 x 6.9 in.).

The portrait is of John Bell 1745–1831, a prominent book publisher, best known for his pocket edition of *The Poets of Great Britain complete from Chaucer to Churchill*, and for an edition of Shakespeare. He produced several periodicals, including a monthly *La Belle Assemblée*, illustrated with well-produced and colourful fashion prints. He was the first printer to stop the use of the long 's', which always looks more like an 'f'. Bell was bookseller to the Prince Regent. *The Real TB* is a reference to him being 'A Real True Blue'.

The hand-colouring is the original publisher's work. Just three colours are used; simple and effective.

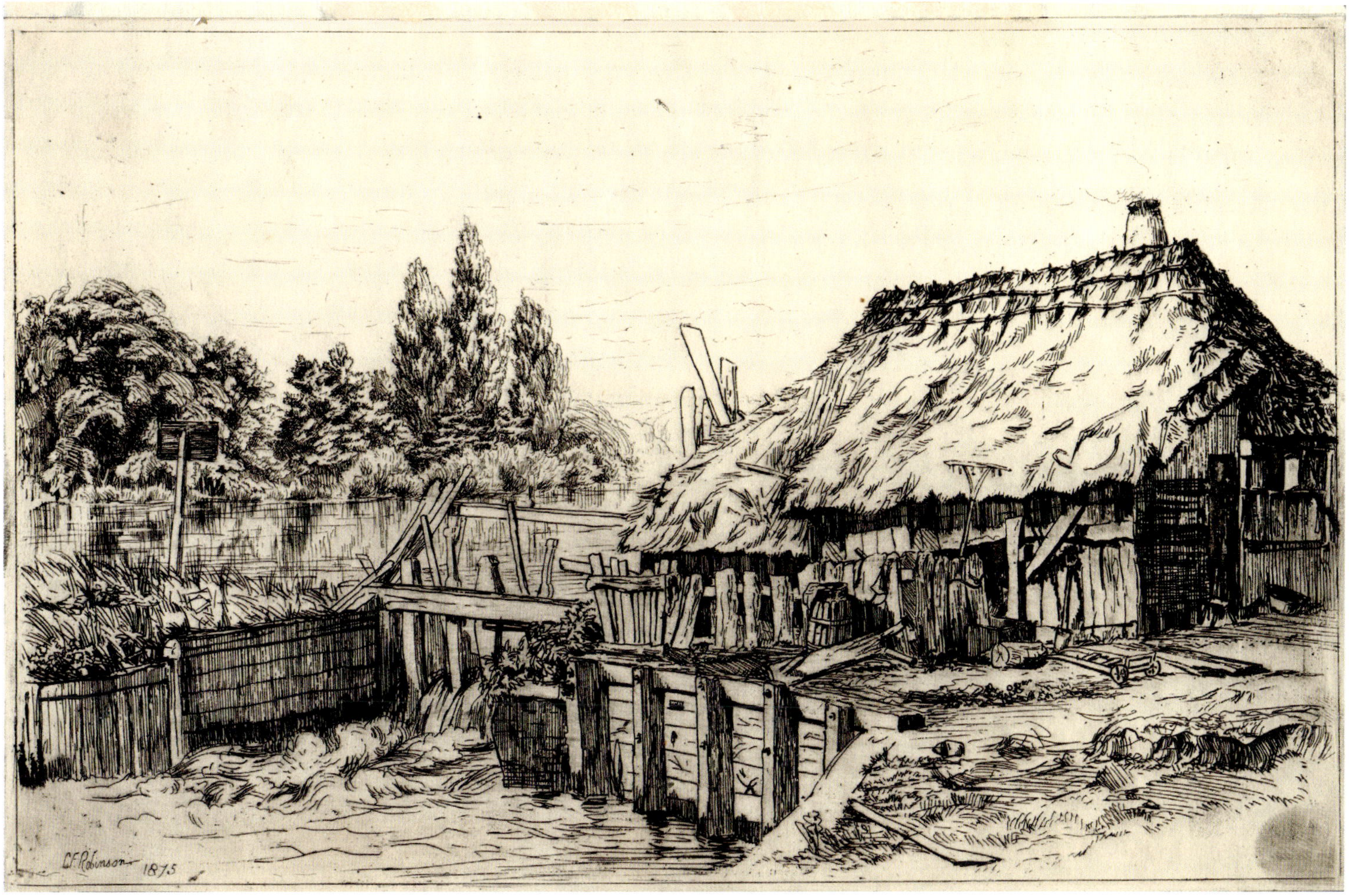


This is a good-quality etching with drypoint, worked with free-flowing lines, obviously by a good artist who is not well-known. A feature of it, which unfortunately cannot be demonstrated in the illustration, is the amount of burr on the plate which is a residue of copper at the edges of the incisions of drypoint, and which held more ink. The result is that the ink stands up on the paper and feels rough to the gentle touch.

PLATE 65
*The Weir.* Etched by Charles F. Robinson 1875.
Etching,
15 x 23 cm (6 x 9 in.) to border.

PLATE 66

[Jig and Dauber.] Etched by R.M.
c.1920.
Etching.
15.5 x 10 cm (6.1 x 4 in.).

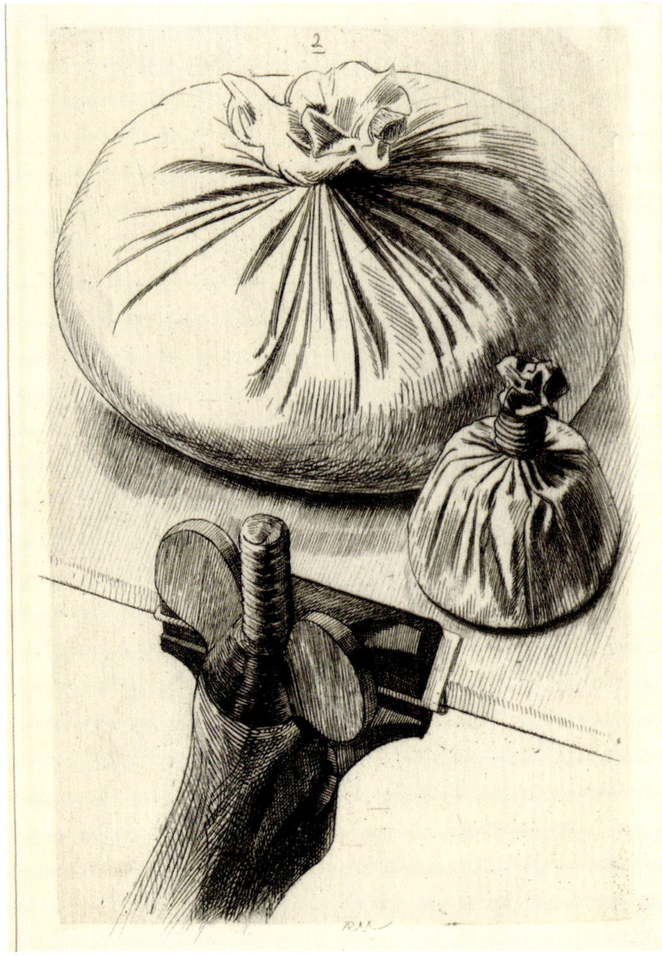

Another late etching, this has little consequence other than it shows more workings in the studio. A plate is held in a jigger, a kind of vice. On the bench are two cloth pads: the smaller one is a 'dauber' for applying ink to the plate; the larger is a polisher for cleaning the surface after the ink has been applied.

PLATE 67

*Rembrandt in his Studi,.* etched by P.A. Rajon, *c.*1860.
The print was taken from a picture by Rembrandt. The signature on the left reads 'J.L. Gerome pinxit' (pinxit means 'he drew it', but here it has to mean 'copied by'). It was etched by Paul Adolphe Rajon, a celebrated French etcher, mostly of portraiture, and this is typical of his extremely detailed work. The print was published by Virtue & Co., in London, in about 1860.
Etching,
22.5 x 19 cm (8.9 x 7.5 in.).

This is much more detailed than most etchings, using a steel plate, with contrasts of light and shade. Rembrandt's coat is particularly black. The print gives a good idea of working conditions. The source of light is natural, with the familiar screen of thin paper to reduce reflection on the polished plate. Similar screens will be seen in several prints of studio interiors. On the table are numerous etching tools and bottles of chemicals. The basin on the stand would have held acid; the larger one on the floor would have contained clean water for rinsing the plate.

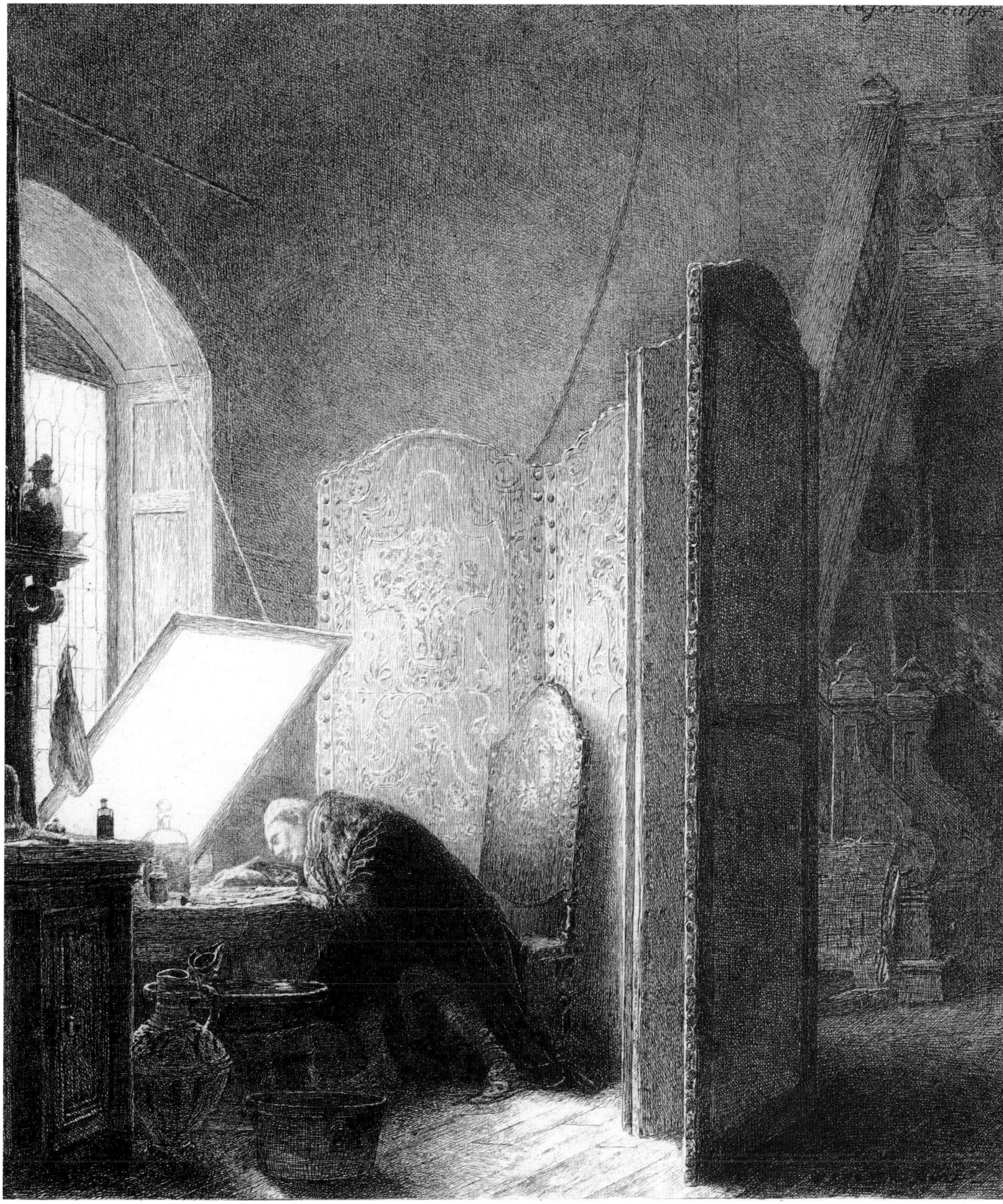

PLATE 67

PLATE 68

*Camanches*. Etching by Hablot K. Browne (Phiz) (1815–82), 1849.

PLATES 68 AND PLATE 69

Illustrations for Charles Lever's novel *Confessions of Con Cregan*, published by Williams Orr & Co. in 1849.

The illustrations were printed on one plate, overall size: 26 x 19.5 cm (10.2 x 7.7 in.). The plate is steel and is badly corroded, which is the main disadvantage of steel.

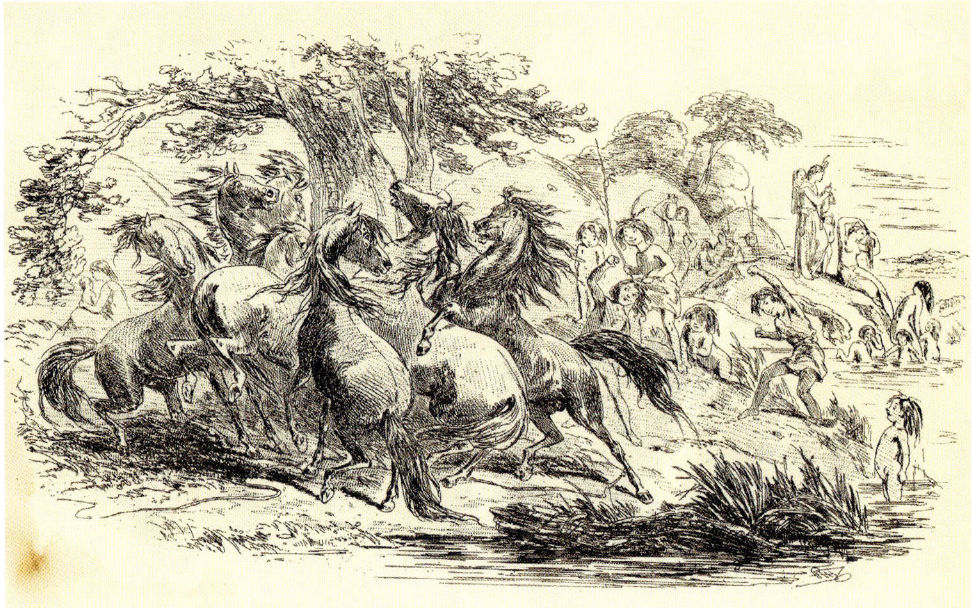

Phiz illustrated numerous books including some of those by Charles Dickens, who used the pseudonym Boz. Phiz had a particular liking for horses; John Leech is reputed to have envied Phiz's ability to draw them. Phiz's style had changed somewhat in the 14 years since he drew the print of St Paul's, plates 56 & 57 (page 82).

When I found the prints they were both in the same condition, some spotting and water-staining, which was enough to spoil them. One has had a gentle clean, just to show what a difference it makes.

Also, when I found the plate and the prints, I had no idea of their origin or purpose. The answer was rapidly established by Brian Lake and members of the firm of Jarndyce Antiquarian Booksellers, to whom I am very grateful.

PLATE 70

The title page of volume VI of the ornithology section of *Naturalist's Library*, which was edited by Sir William Jardine, c.1840. Steel-plate etching. The folded sheet measures 18 x 20 cm (7 x 7.8 in.) overall.

Most of the illustrations were engraved by W.H. Lizars, who also published the monumental work from 1833. In this case the parrots were drawn by J. Stewart, but the majority of the parrots in the series were drawn by Edward Lear. All of the illustrations were coloured like this, with the backgrounds left plain.

Facing the title page is a stipple engraving, also engraved by Lizars, who usually worked in line. The portrait is of Thomas Bewick, famous for his prints of natural history and for leading the resurgence of wood engraving during the latter quarter of the 18th century. His facsimile signature appears beneath the title.

The illustration is small, the image surface measuring 7 cm (2.8 in.) square, and might be dismissed as inconsequential. The engraving is almost pure stipple. There are a few etched lines in the hair, to the eyelids, and to the shading of his neck.

For some reason, Lizars signature appears as Lixars in both these prints, and many others in the series.

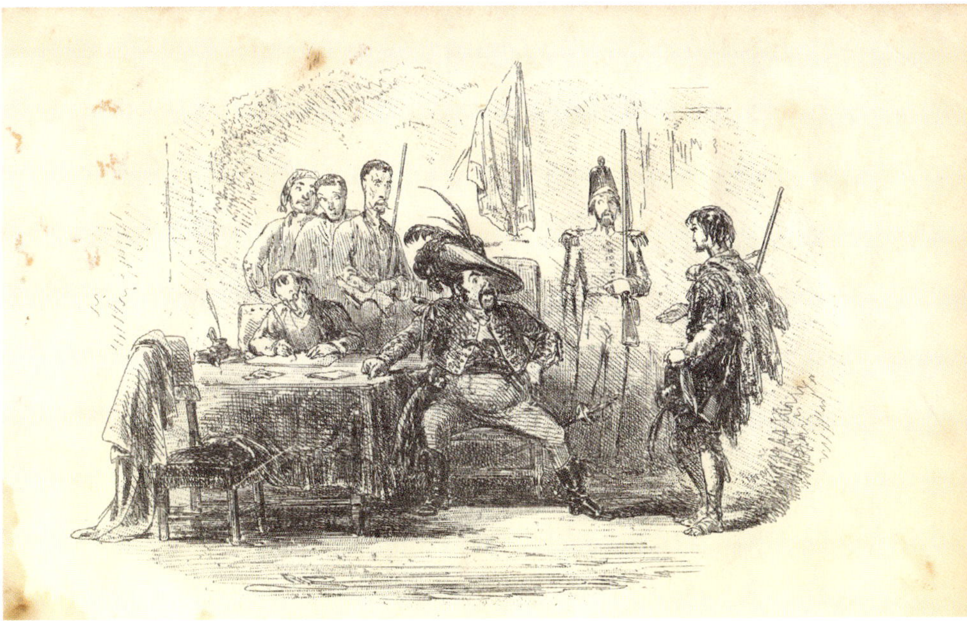

PLATE 69

*The Governor.* Another by Phiz (1815–82).

PLATE 70

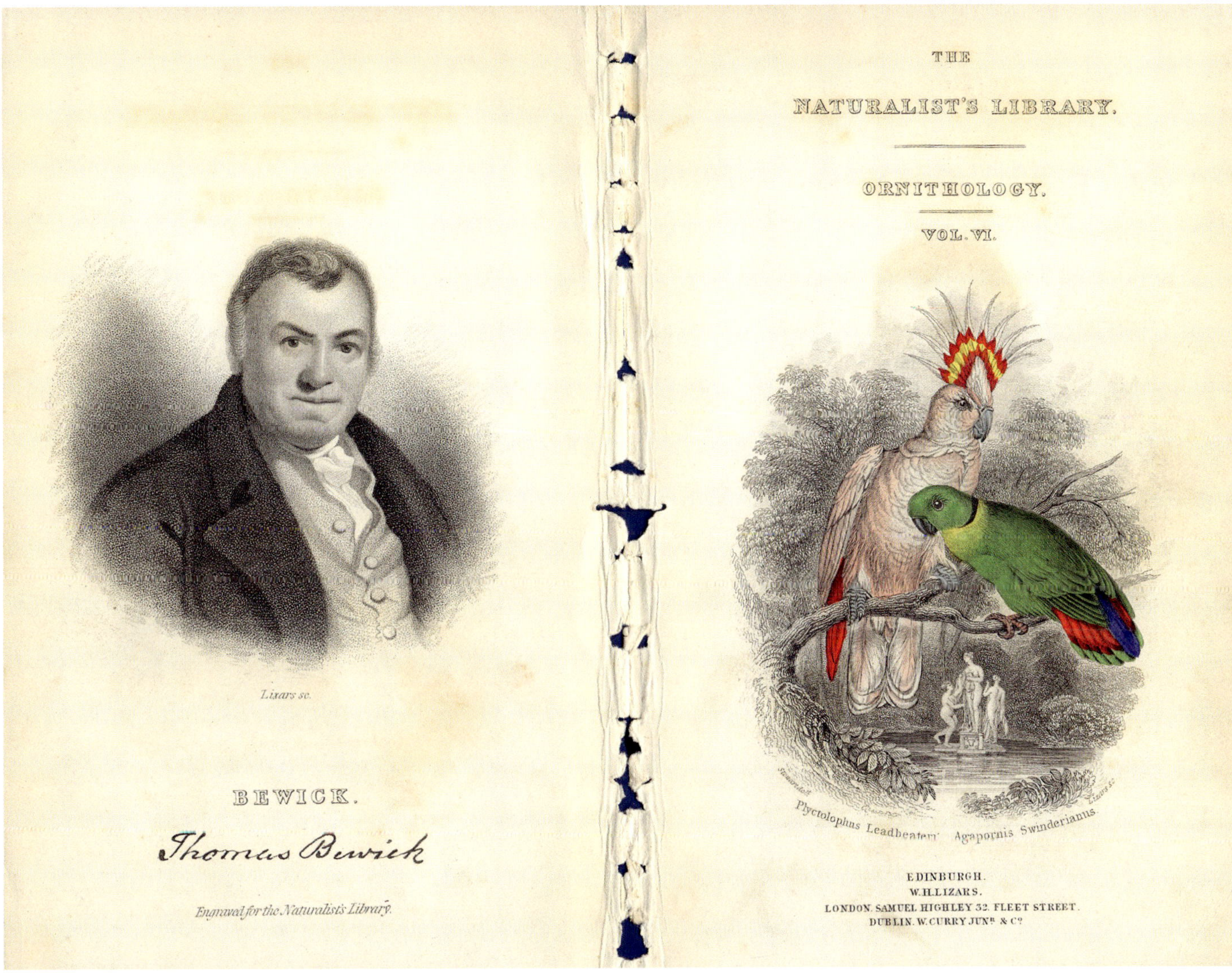

# MEZZOTINT

The intaglio printing processes described so far have all been variations of more or less the same theme – methods of making incisions in a perfectly smooth metal plate to create a picture. The main difference with mezzotint is that the engraver begins the serious business of creating a picture with a plate that would print almost entirely black if an impression was to be taken at this stage. The effect is a rich matt black that could be printed in large areas, quite unlike any other intaglio method.

Remember that all the other processes would effectively not print anything onto paper until the slightest score had been made in the surface of the plate. Mezzotint is the opposite way round. In order to achieve a surface that would print black, the engraver had to roughen the complete image surface of the plate. This was done with a 'rocker', which looks like a stubby chisel with a wooden handle, a blade about a centimetre wide, with a curved tip, the edge of which has a serrated surface. It is so named because the engraver rocks the implement from side to side over the plate, making hundreds of small incisions in the metal, producing burr at the edges of the incisions. Like drypoint etching, the burr provides the rich tone to the finished prints. If you look closely at a dark part of a mezzotint, you will see how many tiny incisions were made in the plate. Preparing the plate was a tedious business.

Once the plate was prepared, the engraver converted the design onto the plate using chalks, and then he began to introduce light into the engraving. This meant smoothing out the roughened surface again as required, working on the areas that he required to print in lighter shades or in white. To do this he used a tool like a chisel, called a 'scraper'. The more of the roughened surface he removed, the whiter would be the effect on the finished print. Naturally, areas that print completely white have to be completely smooth on the plate.

It might seem that it would take less time and much less effort if the engraver only roughened up the parts of the plate that he wanted to show dark, leaving the lighter areas. Some engravers did work in this way; the result was always crude and harsh and the method was frowned upon by the masters of the craft. It was considered that the whole of the plate had to be roughened in order to give the correct effect of one tone leading into another. Skilled engravers could create a gradual progression from an intense dark to bright light, a subtle change of tone without any visible demarcation.

Similarly, any reworking of the plate is a difficult undertaking without the work being obvious. A number of reissues can be found where the additional work does not fit into the original work at all well. Often any necessary reworking of worn plates with the addition of a line or two is done with a stipple-engraving roulette. Richard Earlom reworked Claude Lorraine's *Liber Veritas* plates several times because the demand for the prints was high and the plates quickly showed signs of wear. Even an engraver of his skill could not conceal re-engraving work.

The tones and textures achieved by mezzotint are very distinctive, quite unlike any other method, and it was perfect for portraits which required definite effects of clothing, from tweed to ermine, velvet, silks and satins.

There are some very fine mezzotints that were printed in colours, but the method is generally associated with black & white subjects.

Mezzotint was used for many different types of prints, not always successfully. It was the perfect medium for producing portraits, domestic scenes and rural scenes, which were made in the latter part of the 18th century and early in the 19th century. Success or failure depended on the ability of the engraver perhaps more than for any other method. Works by Joseph Wright of Derby are very dramatic. A remarkably fine pair are the *Fruit and Flower* pieces by Earlom after Van Huysum, included in The Houghton Gallery, published by Boydell. These are amazing examples of how monotone can provide lively realism, including dewdrops and insects. In my view, this pair is unsurpassed for the realism in a monotone picture, particularly as the subject is a still life. Some good topography was produced from the works of Gainsborough, Constable and Turner, but in the main, mezzotint was not the right method for topography. Turner used mezzotint for his *Liber Studiorum,* probably because he was influenced by Claude's *Liber Veritatis*, but the effect of the prints would have been better had he used aquatint.

The following is an extract written by Alexander Browne for *Ars Pictoria* in 1669.

> First take a very well polished plate of copper and ruffen it all over with your engin one way, then cross it over with the engin again, and if you find occasion then cross it over a third time, until it be ruffened all over alike (that is to say) if it were to be printed it would print black all over; this done take Charcole or black Chalk to rub over the plate and then draw you design in white chalk upon the plate, then take a sharp stift and trace out the outline of your design you draw with white chalk, and where you would have the light strike as clean as if was when it was first polished; where you would have the fainter light, you must not polish it so much, and this way you may make it either fainter or stronger, according to your fancy.

Browne makes it all sound easy.

PLATES 71 AND 72,
THE PRINTING PLATE

John Mitchell, painted by L.F. Abbott, engraved by V. Green, mezzotint engraver to his Majesty & the Elector Palatine, *c.*1780, though the print is modern.
Plate 71
Mezzotint plate.
Plate: 48.5 x 35.5 cm (19 x 14 in.).

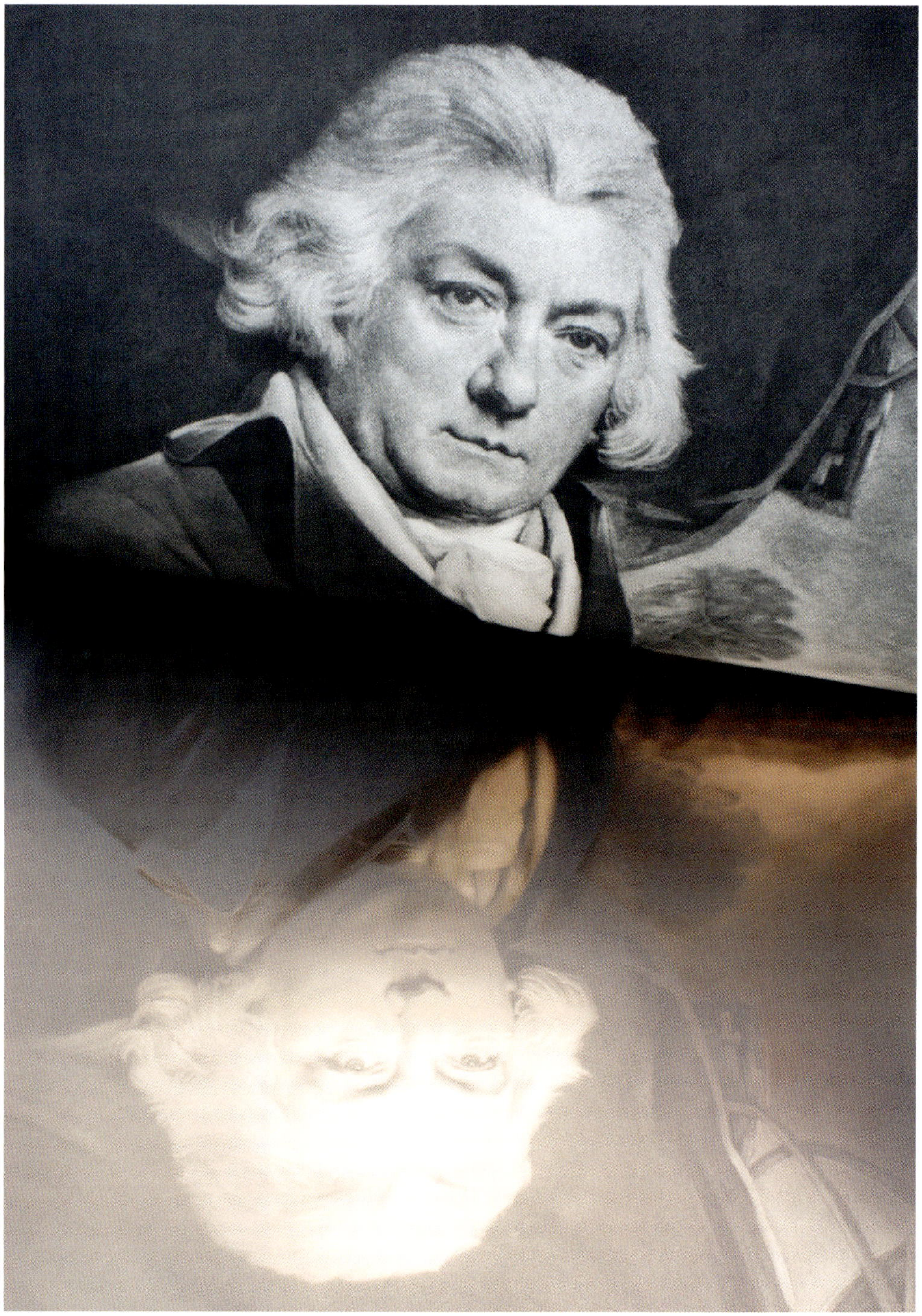

Valentine Green (1739–1813) was a leading British mezzotint engraver, specialising in portraits, of which there are some 160 subjects.

This plate is in the finished state, without the title, and without a publisher's imprint or date. It is interesting that Green engraved another print of Mitchell, identical to this, but slightly smaller, and again without Mitchell's name on it.

John Mitchell (d. 1768) was an English botanist who settled in Virginia, where he discovered several new species of plants, and published botanical works. He is principally famous for his *Map of the British and French Domin-*

*ions in North America*, a rare eight-sheet map, published in 1755, the best map of North America at that time, and often quoted in boundary negotiations.

The print is modern, printed by Susanne Smith of Arundel. This is the plate that took a little over an hour to ink and take one impression from. The first print which she made from the plate she thought insufficiently inked, and so she printed another, leaving a little more ink on the plate. The comparison is interesting. There is very little difference in the face, which is the main object of the picture, but the background is more effective when there is less ink on the plate.

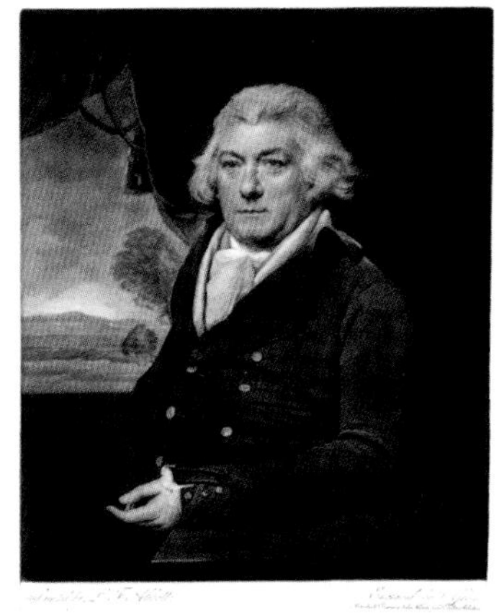

PLATE 72

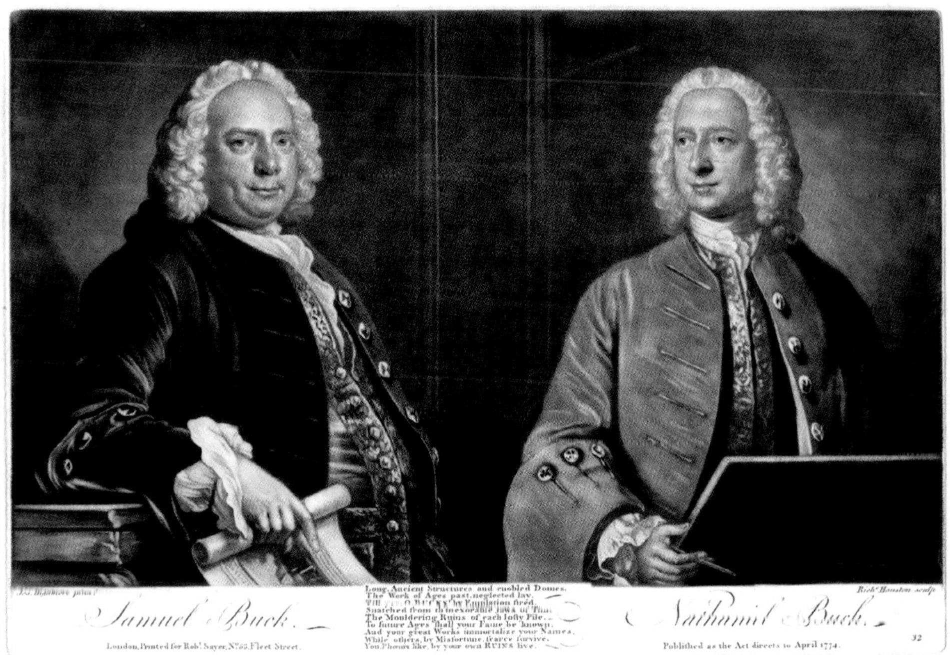


PLATE 73

*Samuel Buck – Nathaniel Buck,*
mezzotint by Richard Houston.
1774.
Engraved by Richard Houston after Joseph Highmore, published by Robert Sayer, 1774.
Mezzotint,
20.5 x 33 cm (8 x 13 in.).

The Buck brothers are famous for their series of 80 prospect views of cities and towns in England and Wales, which in many cases are the first views of the places depicted, and 400 views of castles, monasteries and ruins, smaller in size. Nathaniel is holding a pencil and a drawing pad. Judging by the number of prints they produced in 18 years, one supposes the equipment can hardly have left his side. Samuel is holding one of the small prints.

The print is an excellent example of the subtle variances of tone achievable with mezzotint. Samuel's coat is definitely velvet, rich in texture, with a glowing sheen, and his waistcoat is satin. Notice how the shading of the jacket is progressively worked from the shoulder to the waist. The buttons on his coat and the table on which he is leaning are highly polished. Backgrounds are usually more interesting than this, but it shows how a good engraver could gradually alter the shading of a flat surface. The even blackness of the pad in Nathaniel's hand shows the texture that the plate would print before the engraver started work on the image, putting in the lighter tones.

The ode beneath the print is most appropriate.

> Long, Ancient Structures and enobled Domes,
> The Work of Ages past, neglected lay,
> Till you, O BUCKS! by Emulation fired,
> Snatched from th[e] inexorable Jaws of Time.
> The Mouldering Ruins of each lofty Pile,
> To future Ages shall your Fame be known;
> And your great Works immortalise your Names.
> While others, by Misfortune, scarce survive;
> You, Phoenix like, by your own RUINS live.

The prophecy of fame has almost become true. Samuel is holding one of the prints of a ruin referred to in the verse, one of a series of 400 castles, ruins and monasteries in England and Wales.

Joeseph Highmore (1692–1780) was one of the best portrait painters of his time. He was accomplished at painting likenesses and his attention to detail was always good. This is typical of his work. In this case the engraver, Richard Houston, plays a big part with his ability to convert such detail onto paper.

PLATE 74
*Lord Chief Baron Wandesford,* mezzotint by James Watson, 1778. Beneath the image is a variety of credits. On the left is 'Van Dyke Pinxit.' Below that is 'G. Farington delint'. This means that Van Dyke did the original painting from which George Farington made a copy, which the engraver, James Watson (whose name appears on the right side) used to make his printing plate. In the centre is 'John Boydell excudit 1778'. *Excudit* is from the Latin meaning 'he beats out', but in this context it means that Boydell was the printer. Beneath the title is 'Published Decr. 1st. 1778 by John Boydell Engraver in Cheapside London'. Mezzotint, Plate size: 42 x 30 cm (16.5 x 11.8 in.).

A fine, rich impression, in excellent condition, is one of a large sized collection of 129 mezzotints which Boydell published for the Houghton Gallery, the collection of Horace Walpole, Earl of Orford. The collection was named because Robert Walpole, the first Earl of Orford, lived at Houghton Hall in Norfolk. Horace Walpole was buried there. The magnificent collection, which included 46 important Van Dyck paintings, caused a furore when it was sold to Catherine the Great to go to the Hermitage Museum in St Petersburg. It was the first major art collection to go abroad because of lack of funds to keep it in the country. Walpole may have endeavoured to keep the collection in Britain by producing the prints, which clearly did not achieve the right result if that was the case. Walpole wrote to George III in a last vain attempt to keep his inherited collection. The situation produced a huge public outcry, with Josiah Wedgwood stating that Russia was 'sacking our palaces and museums'.

Christopher Wandesford, 1592–1640, was Member of Parliament for Aldeburgh, Richmond (Yorkshire) and Thirsk before he went to Ireland, and

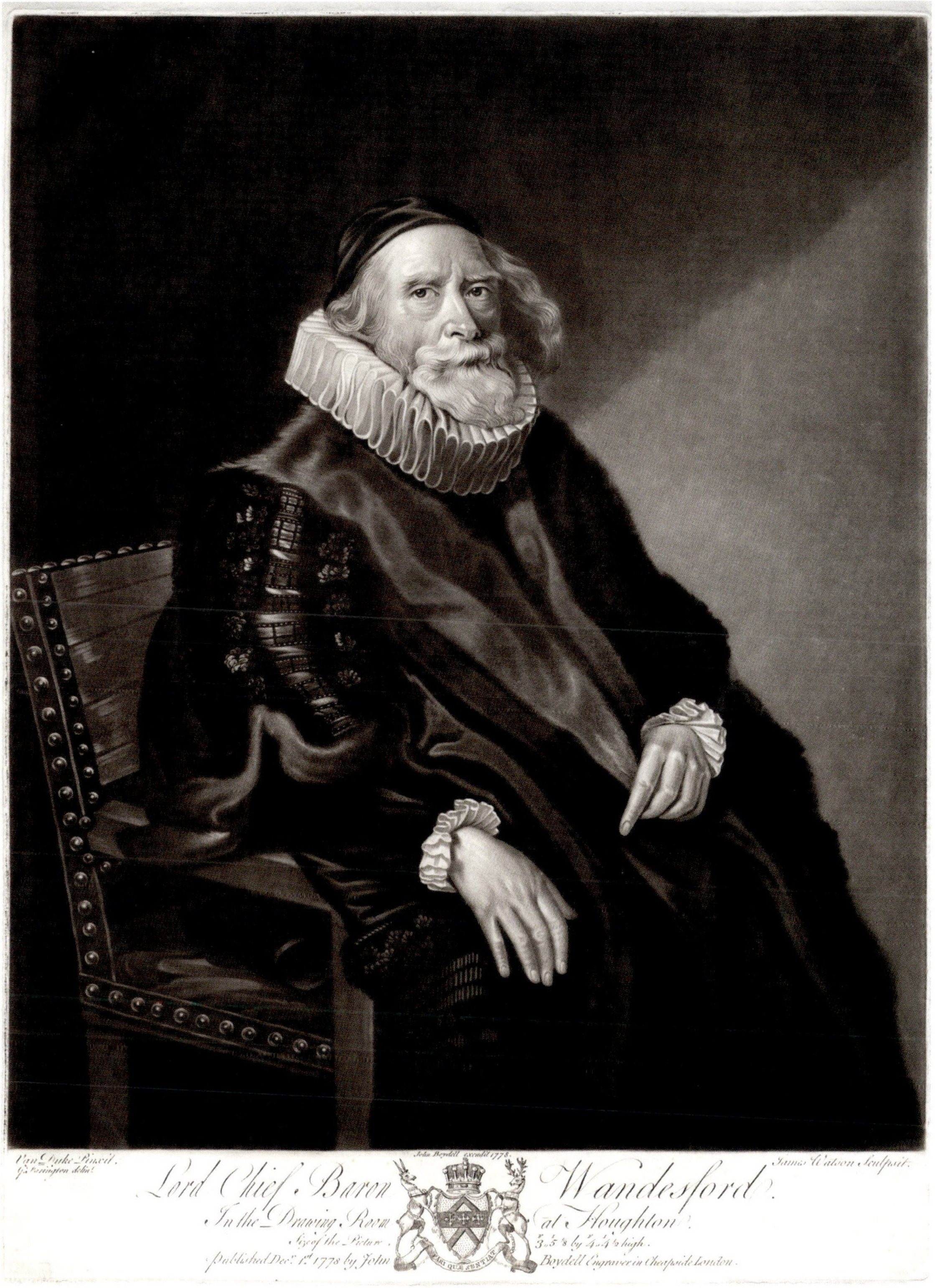


became Lord Deputy. He is described as having a sanguine complexion and auburn hair. The portrait might lack colour, but there is great strength and character in the face, which is superbly engraved.

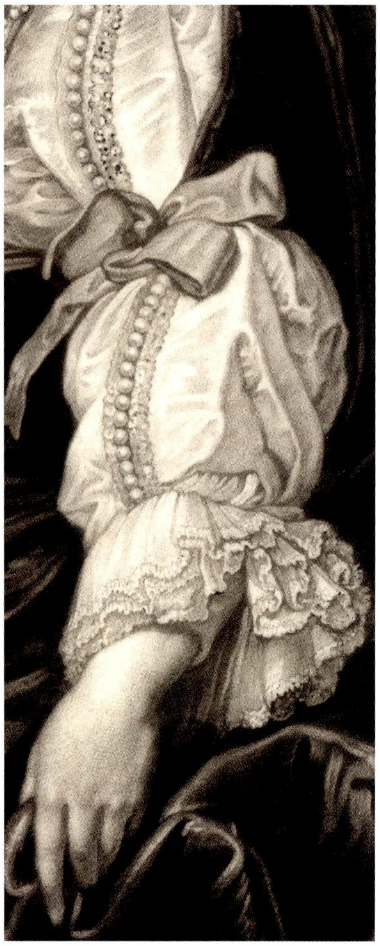

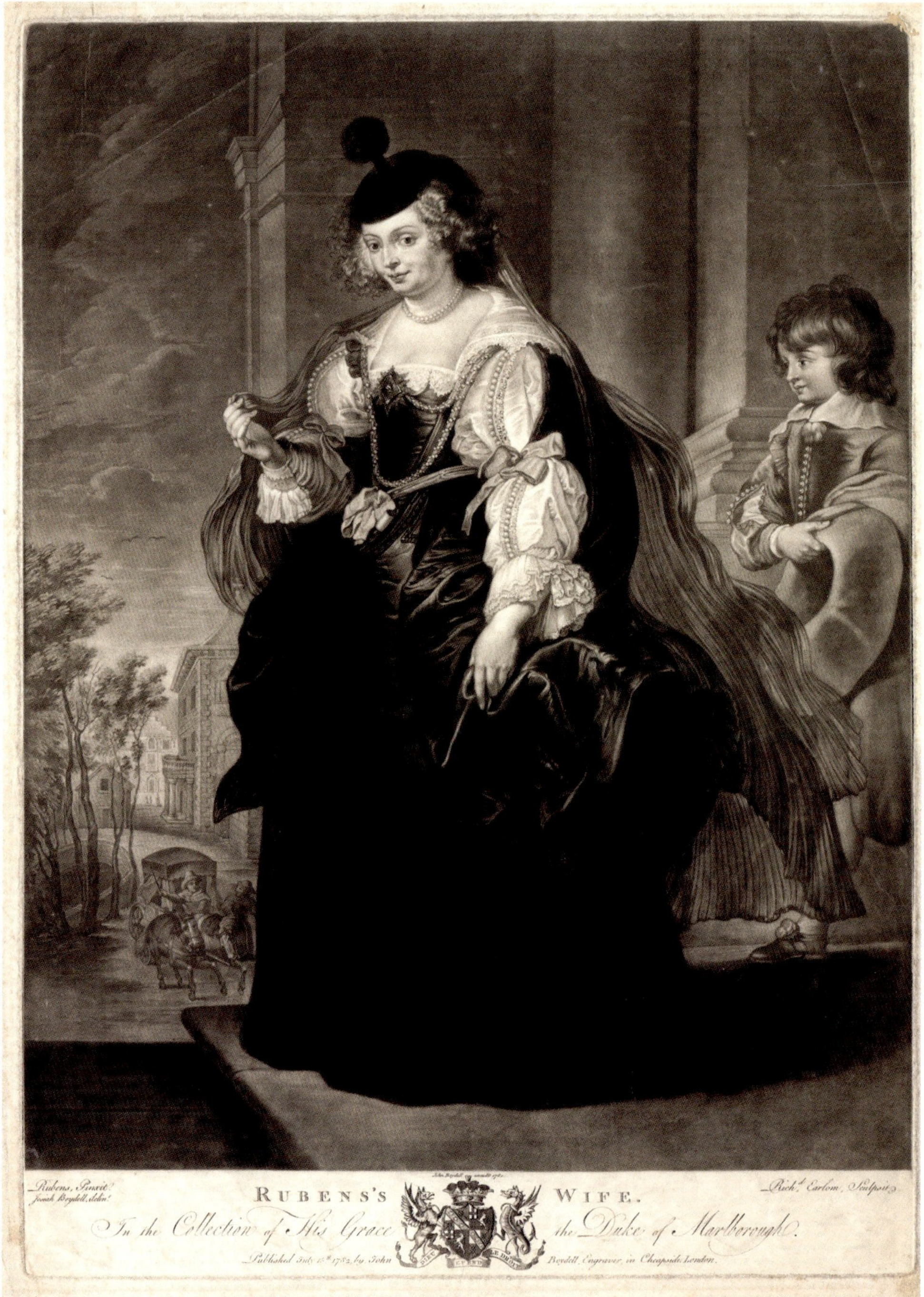


PLATE 75 & DETAIL

*Rubens' Wife* (detail), mezzotint by Richard Earlom, 1782. Engraved by Richard Earlom, from the painting by Rubens, copied by Josiah Boydell and published by John Boydell in 1782. Incorporated in the title is: 'In the Collection of His Grace the Duke of Marlborough'. It was common to credit owners of paintings from which prints were made. 40 x 35 cm (15.7 x 13.7 in.).

This is a fine example of the art of mezzotint. The bottom part of the wife's dress is a rich black, the upper part showing a realistic sheen to the material, contrasting with the white blouse, lace collar, the shawl, ribbons, beads and jewellery.

The portrait is Rubens's second wife, Helena Fourmen (Fourment or Forman), whom he married in 1630, and often portrayed by Rubens. At the time they lived in Antwerp, although the scene in the background of the print is fictitious.

Compare this with the stipple engraving, plate 85 (page 117).

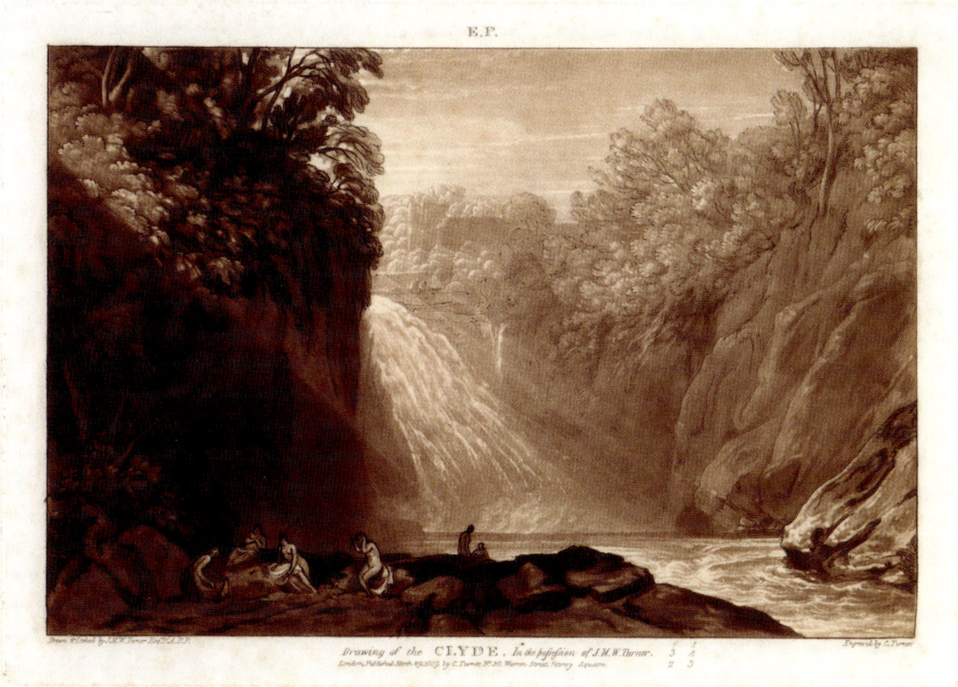


This print features the size of the original painting: 68.5 x 101.5 cm (2 ft 3 in. x 3 ft 4 in.). At the top, in the margin, are the letters 'EP'. Turner used a method of lettering his prints like this, to divide them into categories. Since the letters are few and subjects of the prints are obvious, it would seem to be a waste of time, but EP is perhaps not completely obvious. The scene is a known landscape with an unlikely group of naked female swimmers. The letters indicate the following: H for historical; M or Ms for mountain(s); P for pastoral; M (again) for marine; A for architecture. Finally, EP is for elegiac pastoral, which is not an apt description of this print.

There are very few mezzotint landscapes. Arguably, the method was not best suited to topography. This print is an interesting contrast of light and shade, especially the way the sun's rays light up the waterfall and the river in the right foreground.

Turner's relationships with his printmakers never ran smoothly. Maybe it is a comment on the difficulty of making prints; Turner expected engravers to be able to copy the effects of his paintbrush. His first separately published print is the *View of Oxford High Street*, engraved by J. Pye, Charles Heath and S. Middiman, published in 1812 after several years in the making. Turner's magnum opus, *Liber Studiorum*, never quite fulfilled its promise. After 12 years of spasmodic publication, and several engravers later, only 71 prints were published, and progress quietly came to a standstill.

*Liber Studiorum* was not the first of its kind: several artists' work had been published in a similar manner. *Liber Studiorum* was very similar to Claude Lorraine's *Liber Veritatis,* which was also engraved in mezzotint by Richard Earlom, published by John Boydell in 1777, and printed in sepia.

PLATE 76

*Drawing of the Clyde.* Mezzotint by Charles Turner after J.M.W. Turner. Drawn and etched by Turner, engraved by Charles Turner, (no relation) and published by Charles Turner in 1809. This is one of the early subjects in *Liber Studiorum,* which was J.M.W. Turner's major printed series.
18 x 26.5 cm (7 x 10.4 in.).
Printed in sepia.

PLATE 77

*Well! I can't help it,* mezzotint by [Robert Dighton], published by Bowles & Carver, *c.*1795. 14 x 11 cm (5.5 x 4.3 in.).

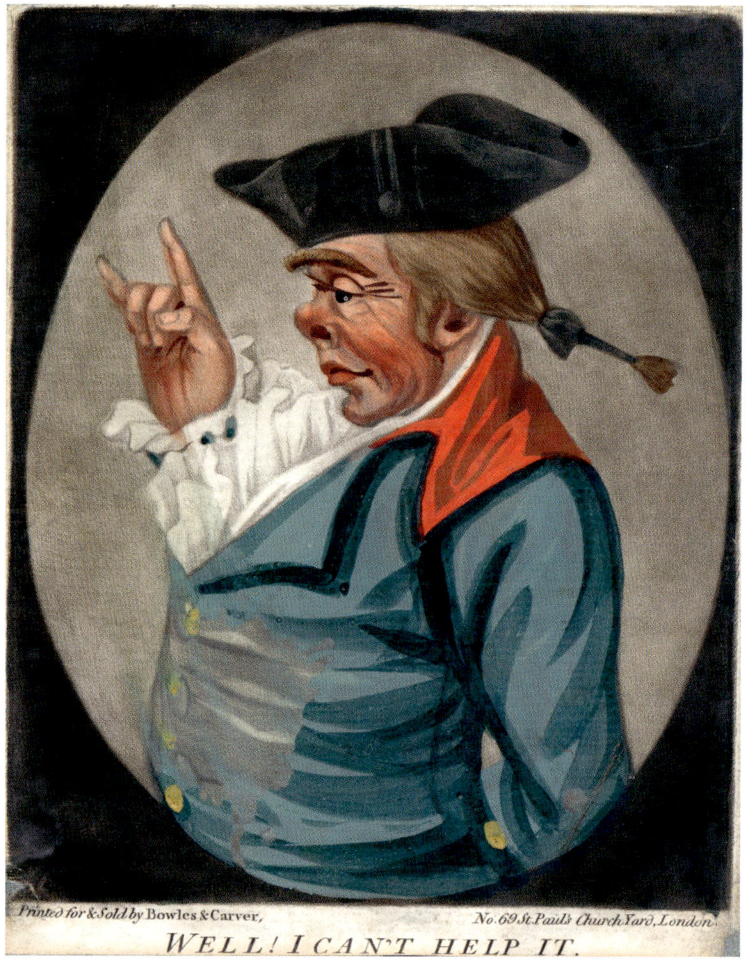


This is typical of late 18th-century hand-colouring that was applied to mezzotints, quite thick paint with enough body in it to obscure the detail of the engraving beneath. The colour often oxidises; this has kept its brilliance. The print was made in two colours, black and brown. The surround of the oval is black; inside it is brown. With so much colour on the print it is quite difficult to detect without a good magnifying glass. The overall effect of the colour is a richness that is characteristic of the style of the period from about 1750 to 1820.

There seems to be a popular conception that colouring of this kind was added to weak impressions to make them look as though there is more body in the picture. It is possible, but there are no real grounds for the argument. *Suffolk*, plate 4 (page 19), is greatly helped by the addition of colour. It is more likely that printers used less black ink when colour was to be added. Certainly, this was the case with original colouring on Sandby's early aquatints.

The use of square brackets round Dighton's name, above, is because the print is anonymous, aside from the names of the publishers. The reason for leaving his name out is not known. Robert Dighton was the father of a family of caricaturists. The picture is almost certainly a portrait. The title could be an indication of the reason why the print is anonymous. Dighton's work is usually more gentle than that of Hogarth and Gillray, though he was equally prolific.

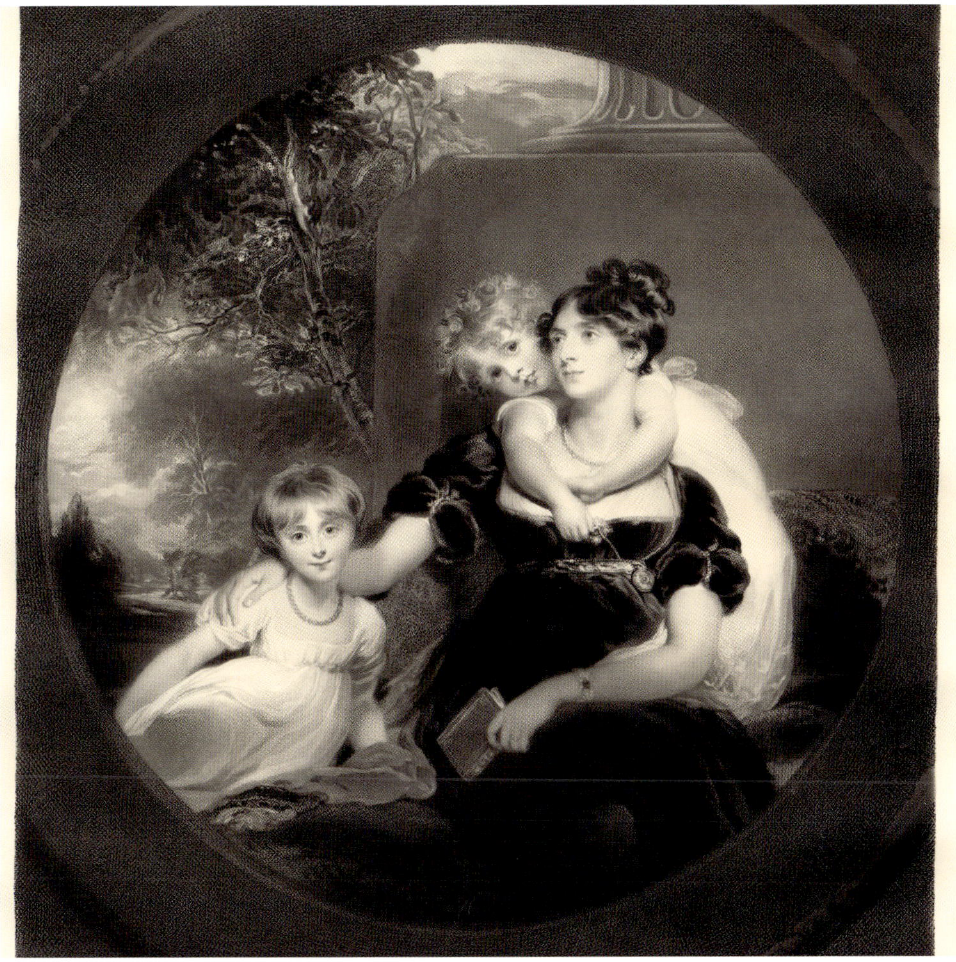

PLATE 78

*Lady Grey and Children,* mezzotint by Samuel Cousins, 1831.
Beneath the image is the imprint: 'Engraved by Samuel Cousins from the Original Picture by the late Sir Thomas Lawrence, P.R.A.'
32 x 27.5 cm (12.5 x 10.8 in.).

Proof state, after the addition of the imprint, above, but before another proof state, with the publisher's name added just inside the bottom edge of the plate: 'London, published May 2nd, 1831 by Colnaghi Senr Dominick Colnaghi & Co. Printsellers to their Majestics & the Royal Family, Pall Mall East'. Beneath the plate mark is a pencil title, and then 'Private Plate', suggesting that the print was not sold to the public.

It is not often that the date in the publisher's imprint is quite as helpful as it is in this example. Without it, it would be difficult to date the print within about 25 years. Lawrence died in 1830; Cousins became an R.A. in 1855, which is not mentioned in the imprint, so the print is likely to be have been made between 1830 and 1855. Usually prints can be dated more accurately than this. Strangely, Cousins is the only mezzotint engraver to become an R.A. While on the subject, the initials P.R.A. after Lawrence's name stand for President of the Royal Academy.

Interestingly, the print is much more lively than Cousins's self-portrait, but this is mainly to do with the content of the picture. The tones and textures in the faces, the clothing and the wooded background are excellent.

Lady Grey was married to the second Earl Grey, who gave his name to the blend of tea.

PLATE 79

*Samuel Cousins,* mezzotint engraved by Samuel Cousins, showing the engraver at work, 1884. Published by the Fine Art Society, in 1884. 43 x 33 cm (17 x 13 in.).

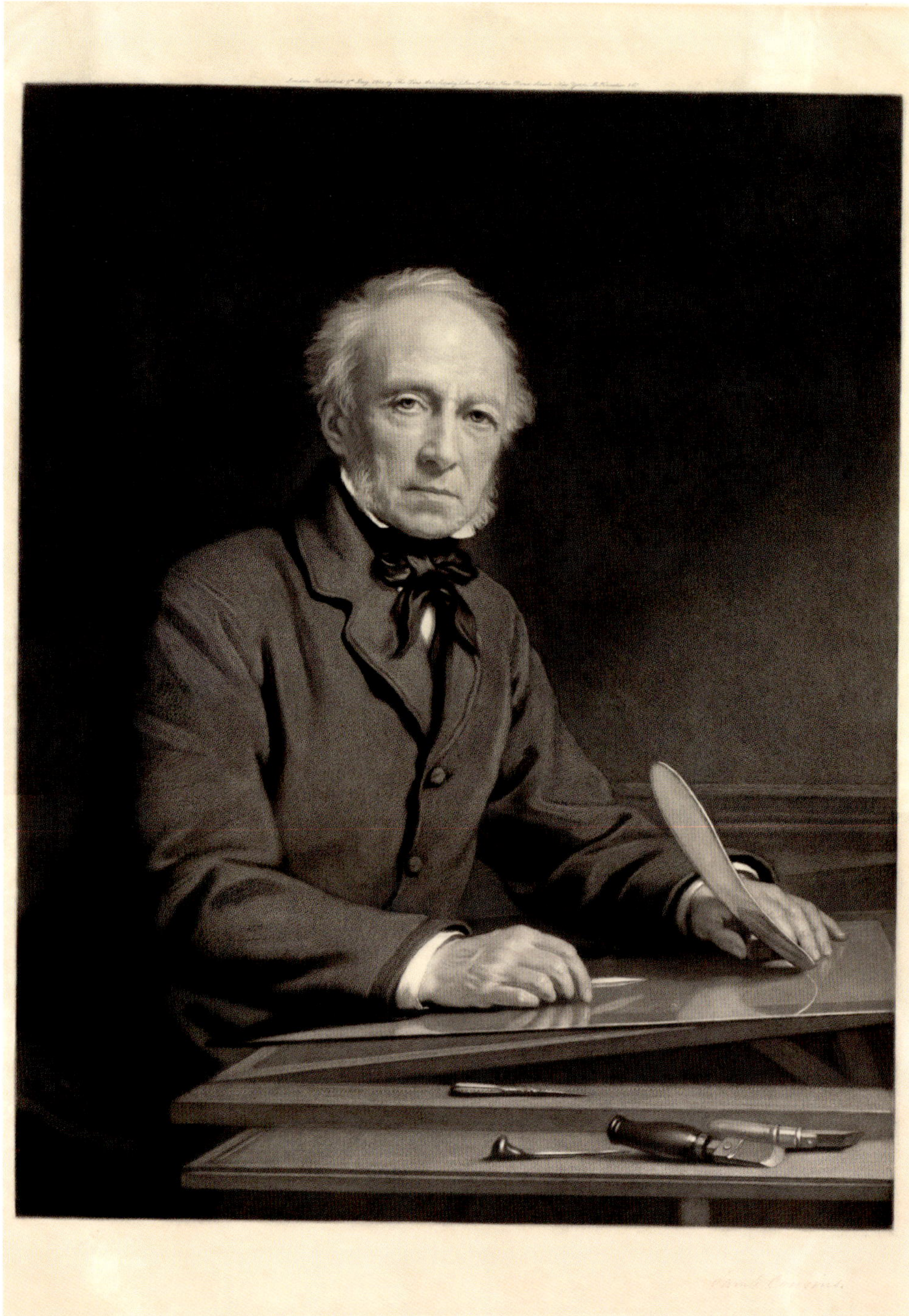

A portrait of Cousins, engraved by him, after Edwin Long. It was engraved on a steel plate, and this metal never provided the rich quality of a copper plate. The content of the picture again shows an engraver at work on a plate, with a variety of mezzotint tools. In his left hand is a piece of cardboard which was used to reduce reflection, perhaps more efficiently than the screens seen in other illustrations. In his right hand is a point for adding fine detail. On the table is another point, and also a burin, rocker and scraper.

The time span between this print and Cousins's portrait of Lady Grey is 53 years, and by this time Cousins was 83 years old. The print lacks the texture of earlier mezzotints, the detail being a little crude, and more typical of the mechanical Victorian mezzotints. The head, the cravat and the tools are well engraved; the way reflections are shown on the plate is particularly good. The background and the jacket are disappointing.

By this date it had become the custom for artists and engravers to sign their prints in pencil. It was also the custom to put an embossed stamp, a 'blind-stamp', somewhere in the margin. In this case the blind-stamp, hardly visible beneath the left corner of the image, is the sign of approval of the Printsellers' Association.

# STIPPLE ENGRAVING

As the title suggests, stipple engravings are comprised of printed dots. It is another laborious method, but in the right hands the results are splendid. Like mezzotint, some of the most typical prints are portraits and domestic scenes, rarely seen in topographical prints. It was occasionally used to show relief on maps; one of the earliest, and best, examples of this is the amazing four-sheet 2-inches to-the-mile map of the southern part of Sussex by Thomas Yeakell and William Gardner, 1778–83.

The method dates back to about 1500, and was used by Dürer for facial detail in some portraits, but generally speaking the method was used in the latter half of the 18th century and the first part of the 19th. The earliest method was literally to laboriously hammer dots onto the plate and was used mainly to add fine detail to a line engraving. Next came a method of using an engraving point to flick the dots into the plate, but these dots are not rounded, more oval or lozenge-shaped. Certainly, this method was quicker than using a punch and a hammer.

In the middle of the 18th century, stipple engraving was done by using the basic etching method: coating the plate in a resin ground, making dots in the ground and subjecting the plate to acid – a quicker and easier method. Again, these dots could be made by a needle or by a 'roulette' or a 'rocker'. A roulette was a wheel with teeth on the edge of it, mounted on a handle, which could be wheeled across the ground. The rocker, similar to that used in mezzotint, achieved the same result. Even though this speeded up the operation, the engraver still did the finishing work to the plate, after etching was done, with a stipple engraver. There was never a quick way of producing a stipple engraving.

Stipple engraving was introduced into England by William Wynne Ryland, one of the most celebrated English engravers, becoming engraver to George III, of whom Ryland engraved a fine portrait as the new king in his coronation robes. Many of his works were after Angelica Kaufmann, and these are immensely popular. Ryland's career was chequered, as he managed to squander his large earnings, regularly lurching from wealth to poverty and back again. He was hanged for forgery after a court case where the evidence against him was unsound, but it seems that there were a number of his acquaintances who were very unsympathetic.

By far the most famous exponent of the technique was Francesco Bartolozzi, who was born in Florence, but spent most of his working life in England, also becoming engraver to George III. He was a founder member of the Royal Academy. His output of portraits alone was immense, although this was only one of the subjects in which he excelled. His prints that were printed in colours are obviously the most desirable, but Bartolozzi used a wide variety of other methods, printing in monotone, not just black. Other single colours, like bistre and sepia, or sometimes red or blue, make his prints particularly appealing. His series of royalty, his most famous work, was printed in a flesh colour with either one or two other colours.

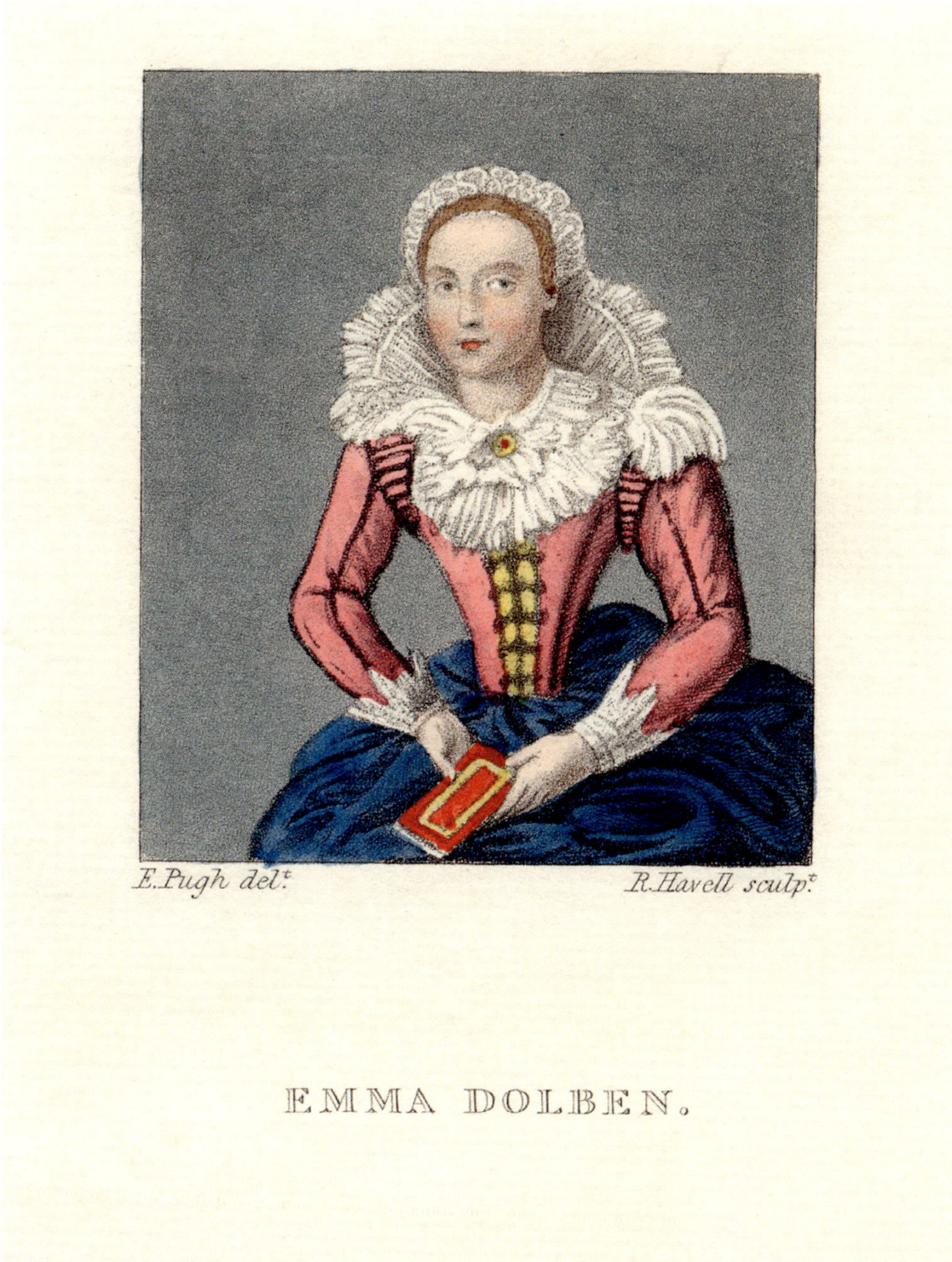


PLATE 80

*Emma Dolben,* engraved by Robert Havell after E. Pugh.
Published in 1816 for Pugh's *Cambria Depicta: a Tour through North Wales.*
Stipple engraving,
Image: 7 x 6 cm (2.7 x 2.4 in.). The plate measures 25 x 20 cm (9.8 x 7.8 in.), so the print has wide margins. The publisher's imprint reads 'Published 15 February 1815, by E. Williams, Strand'. The imprint is 7 cm below the image, the same measurement as the height of the print, which means that the print is likely to be cut down. It is quite common for a date on a print to be different from the actual publication date, if only by a year. In this case, the paper has a watermark dated 1821, so the print would not have been published before then.

This example is hand-coloured, as published, and carefully executed. The dots in the face are black and there is a pink wash over that, the dark cheeks being unflattering. The print consequently lacks the brilliance of the colour *Cymbeline* print. If the black & white *Cymbeline* print had been coloured, the effect would be similar to this, the black dots showing through the colour.

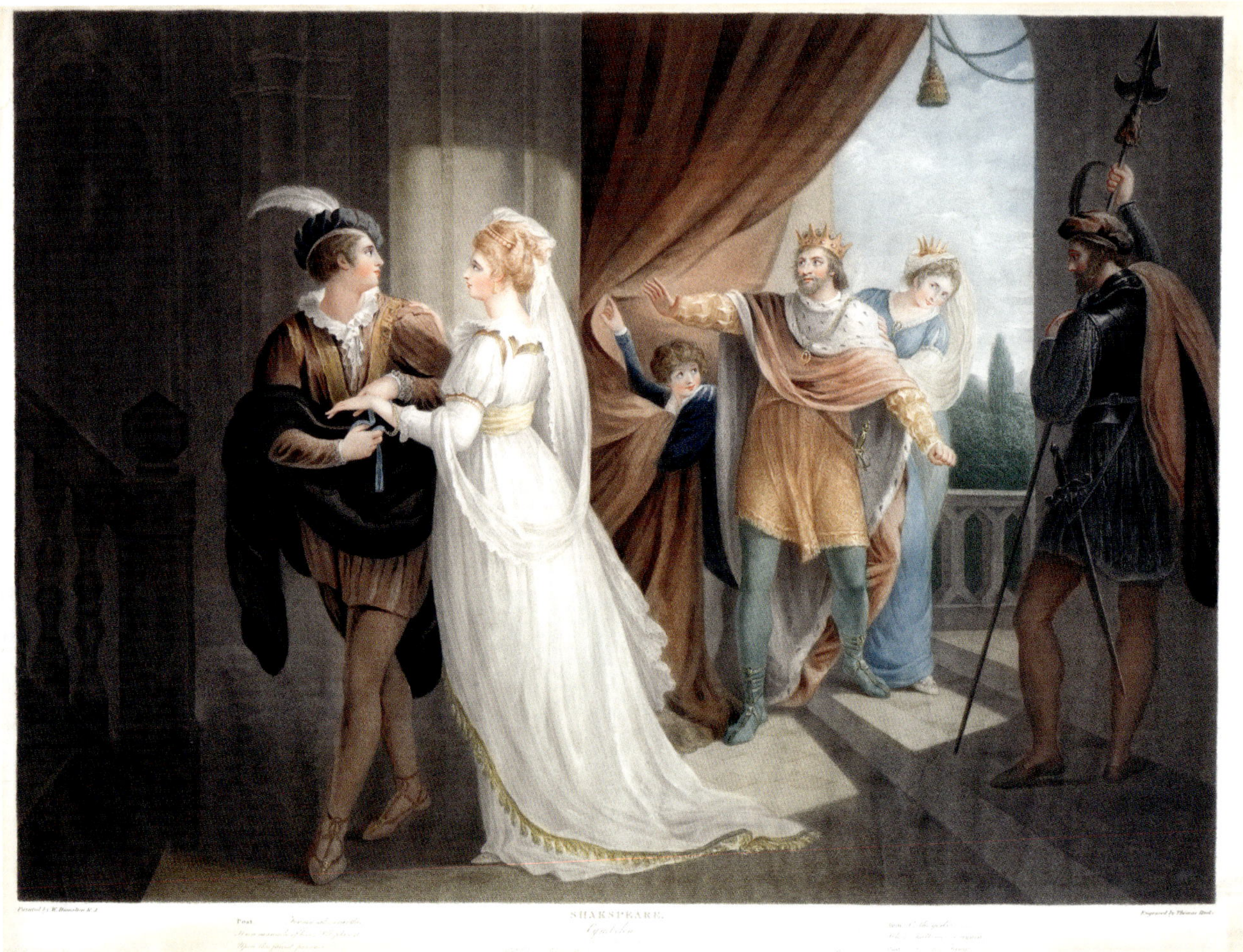

PLATE 81

*Cymbeline* (detail shown on page 113), engraved by Thomas Burke after W. Hamilton. Printed in colour. Published by John and Josiah Boydell in 1795 for *Scenes from Shakespeare.* Stipple engraving, 45 x 59 cm (17.7 x 23.2 in.).

These two prints were made from the same plate. There is such a striking contrast between them that, at first glance, they might appear to be different subjects. The colour version is almost entirely printed in colour with minimal hand-finishing. Each colour of ink had to be carefully applied to the appropriate part of the plate and carefully rubbed into the engraving, just as the printer would do with a monotone print, except that he had to be meticulously precise in ensuring the ink did not touch the wrong area, a painstaking job. The inks were thick oily substances which took a long time to dry. A plate of this size and detail would take a day to print, but the ink which was applied to the plate first would not have dried by the time the last had been added, so the printer was not in a rush from the point of view of the ink drying. Once all the inks were in place, the plate passed through the printing press only once to produce a completed print.

In this example there is a slight trace of blue on the hand of the man in the centre, where the ink has smudged from his jacket.

If the black & white example was to be hand-coloured, it would never acquire the brilliance of the colour print. This would be particularly noticeable in the faces; the black dots would still be obvious. The pageboy in the background is hidden in the shadows, whereas he is an integral part of the colour print. Black & white prints are relatively common. Naturally, because of the difficulty in printing them, colour prints are much rarer.

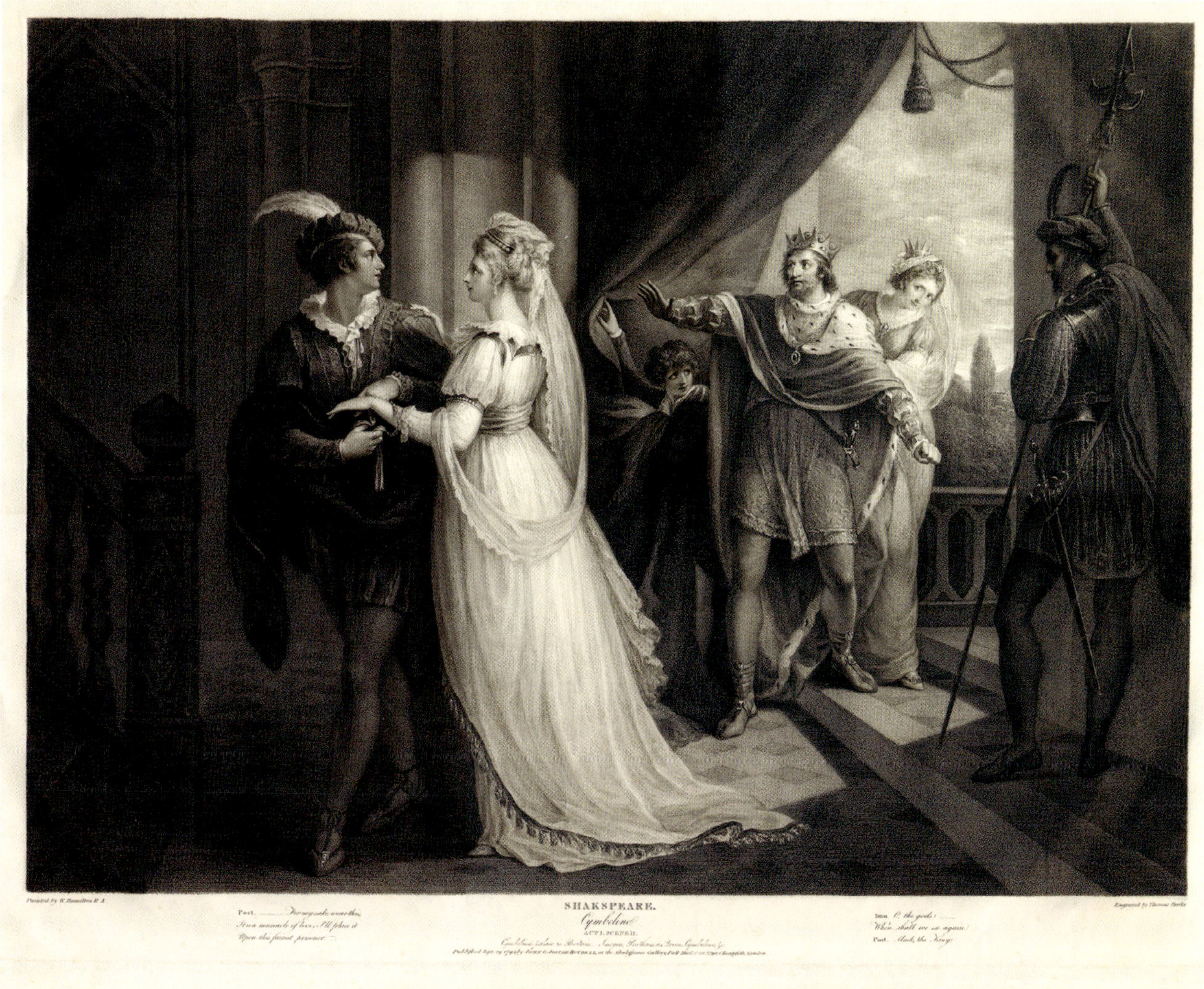


Plate 82
*Cymbeline* (detail shown below), engraved by Thomas Burke, 1795. Printed in black and white.

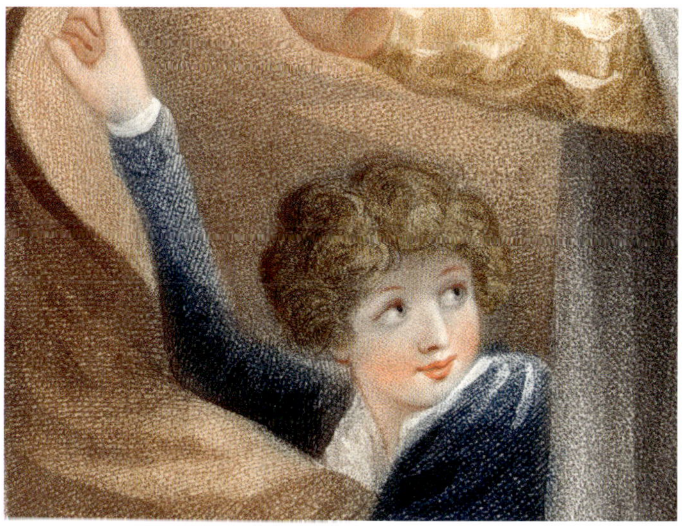

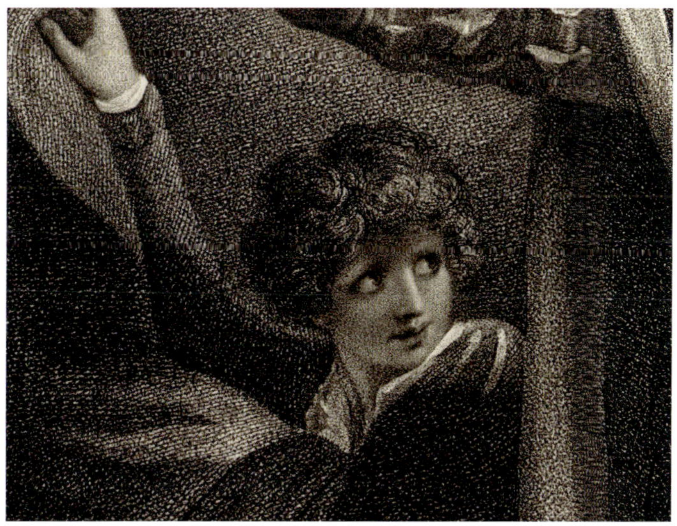

Boydell considered his *Scenes from Shakespeare* to be his tour de force. It was certainly his most lavish production, for which Boydell employed the best artists and engravers available, paying them well. The work was a financial disaster, and Boydell never recovered.

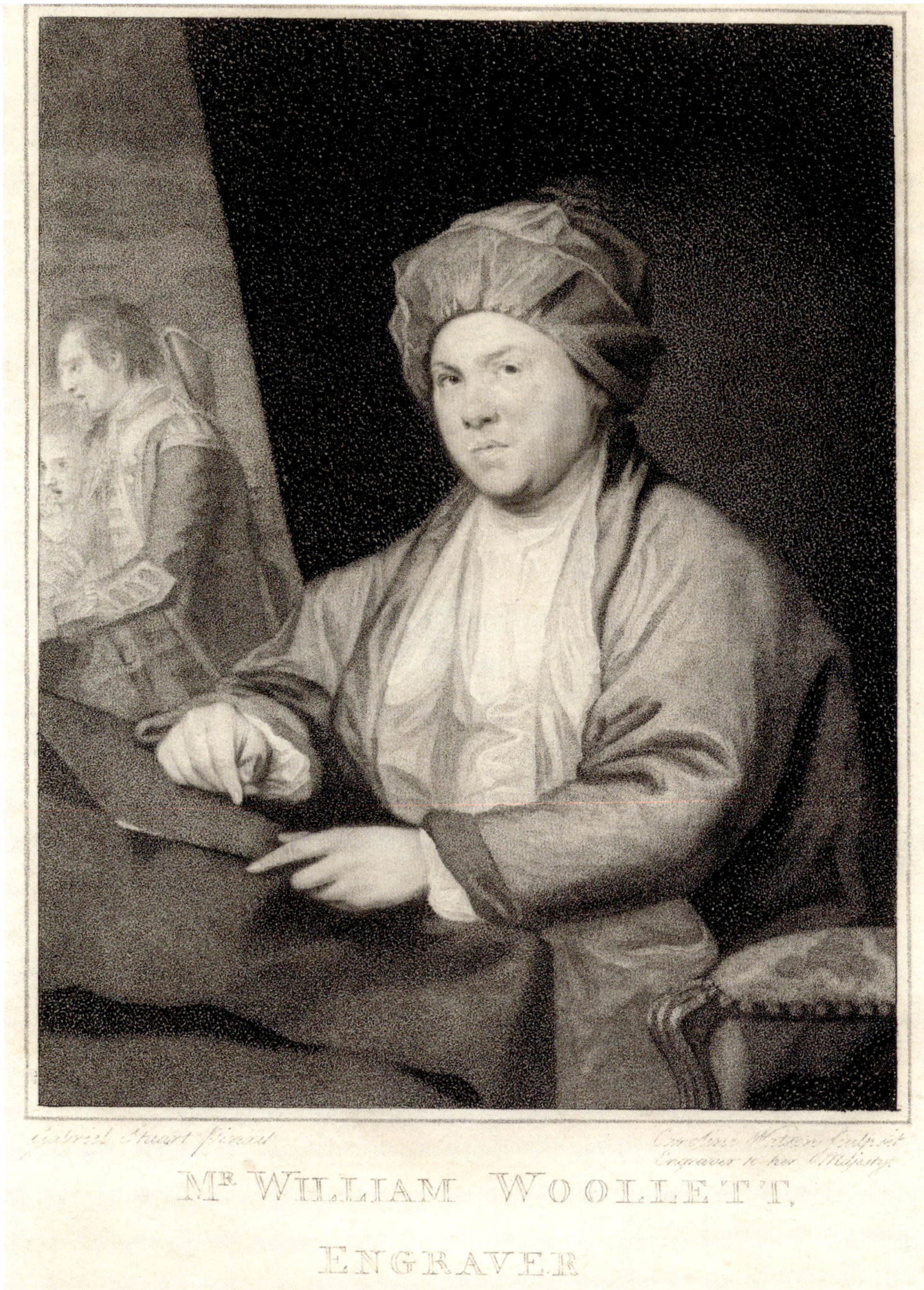


PLATE 83
*Mr William Woollett.* Born April 15th 1735. Died May 23rd 1785. Published Sept 1st 1785 by John Boydell, Engraver, of Cheapside, London.
Engraved by Caroline Watson, after Gabriel Stuart.
Stipple engraving, 15 x 12 cm (6 x 4.7 in.).

This is an interesting print for several reasons, not the least of them being that there were very few women engravers. Caroline Watson's father, James, was a mezzotint engraver (see plate 74, page 103) and her uncle, William, was a portrait painter, although Slater succinctly states that he was better at playing the flute.

The print is finely executed with good variation of tones. Caroline Watson also engraved in mezzotint and this print shows that influence, being densely stippled. The curtain behind Woollett is as dark as anything achieved in stipple. Woollett is shown working on a plate. Behind him, to the left, can be seen the side of the Benjamin West painting of the *Death of General Wolfe*, and this illustration shows how large the painting is. Notice, too, that the detail of West's painting is faithfully copied even though the painting is not a central feature of the engraving.

Woollett's engraving of the *Death of General Wolfe,* which was first published in 1776, nine years before this portrait was published, is discussed further on plate 51 (page 76).

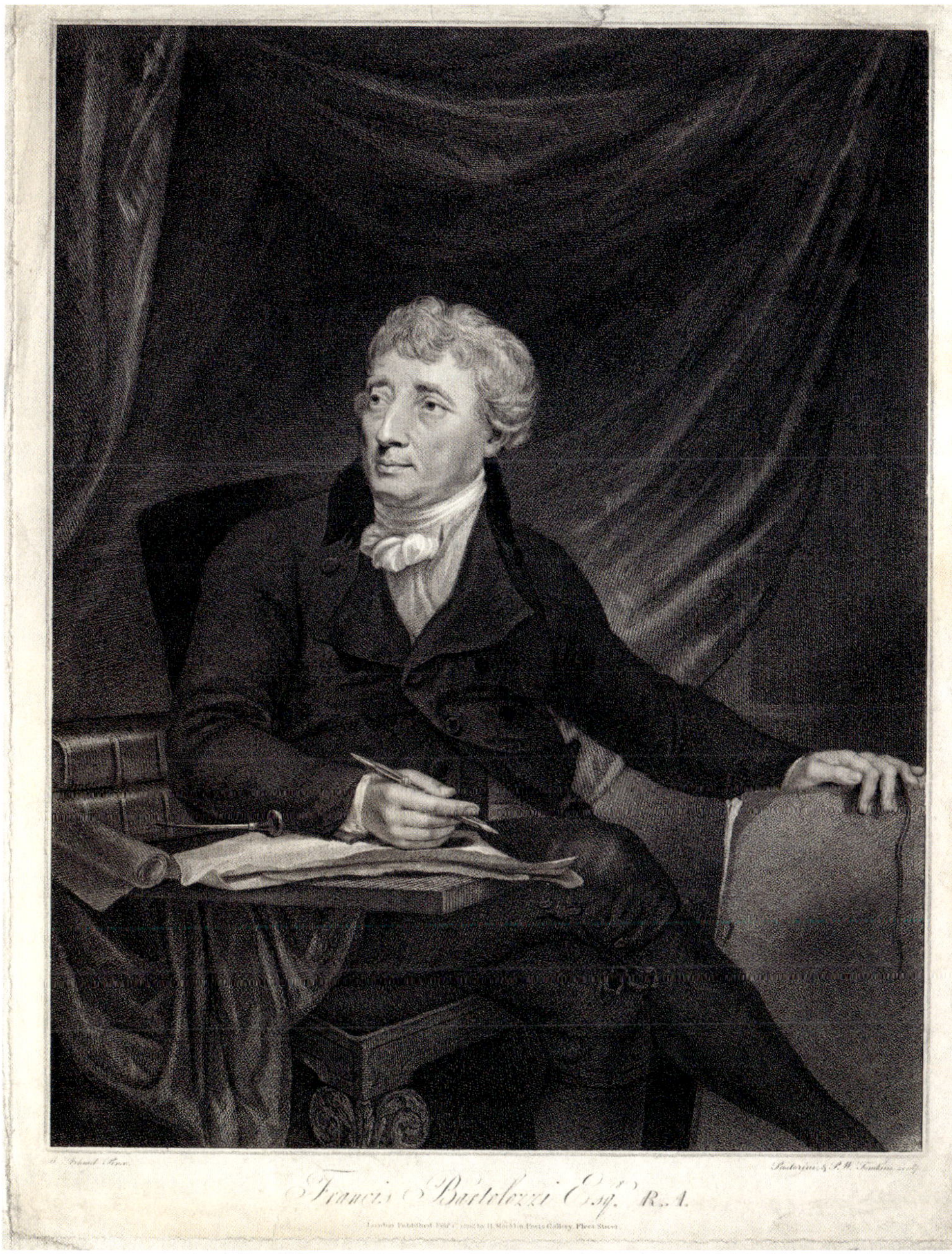


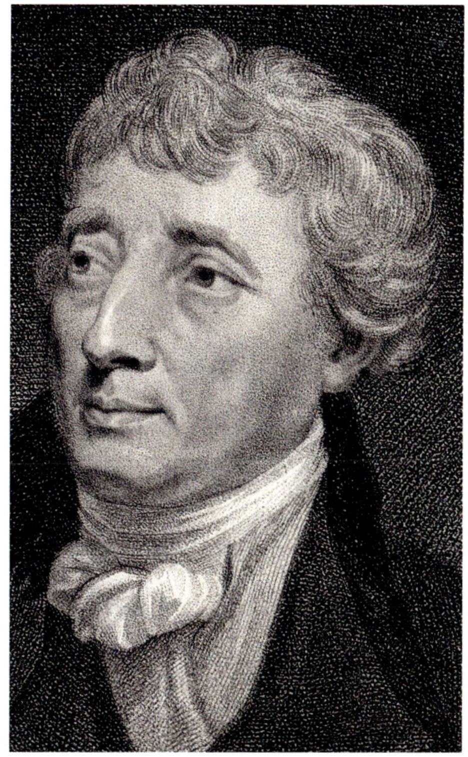

PLATE 84 AND DETAIL

*Francis Bartolozzi Esqr. R.A,* engraving by B. Pastorini and P.W. Tomkins after W. Arlaud. Published by H. Macklin in 1803.
Stipple engraving.
Plate: 51 x 38 cm (20 x 15 in.).

As already mentioned, Bartolozzi was one of the most prominent stipple engravers. He was Italian, born in 1727, and spent his early life working in etching, stipple and line engraving. He moved to England in 1764, and from then on he concentrated on stipple engraving. His most famous prints are after

Angelica Kauffman and Hans Holbein, many of them printed in red or sepia or in colours. He moved to Lisbon in 1802, the year before this print was published.

The portrait shows him with paper and pencil with a portfolio to his left. Just to his right is an engraving burin. There is particularly good definition in the face and hair. There is some use of line engraving in the darker parts of the print, and touches added to the hair. For that reason the print could be described as 'mixed method', but the bulk of the work is stipple.

It is unusual for a print to be engraved by two engravers. In this case, Pastorini was known for the line engraving, and Tomkins was a stipple engraver, and that is probably how they worked the division of labour.

Pastorini was also Italian-born and lived in London. He was one of the governors of the Society of Engravers, which was founded in 1803, the same year this print was published. Tomkins was a scholar of Bartolozzi.

PLATES 85 & DETAIL
*Helena Forman, Rubens's Second Wife* (detail), engraved by Louis Sailler after Van Dyck and George Farington, published by John Boydell in 1783.
Stipple engraving, 52.5 x 36.5 cm (the painting measures about 185 x 86 cm (72.8 x 34 in.)).

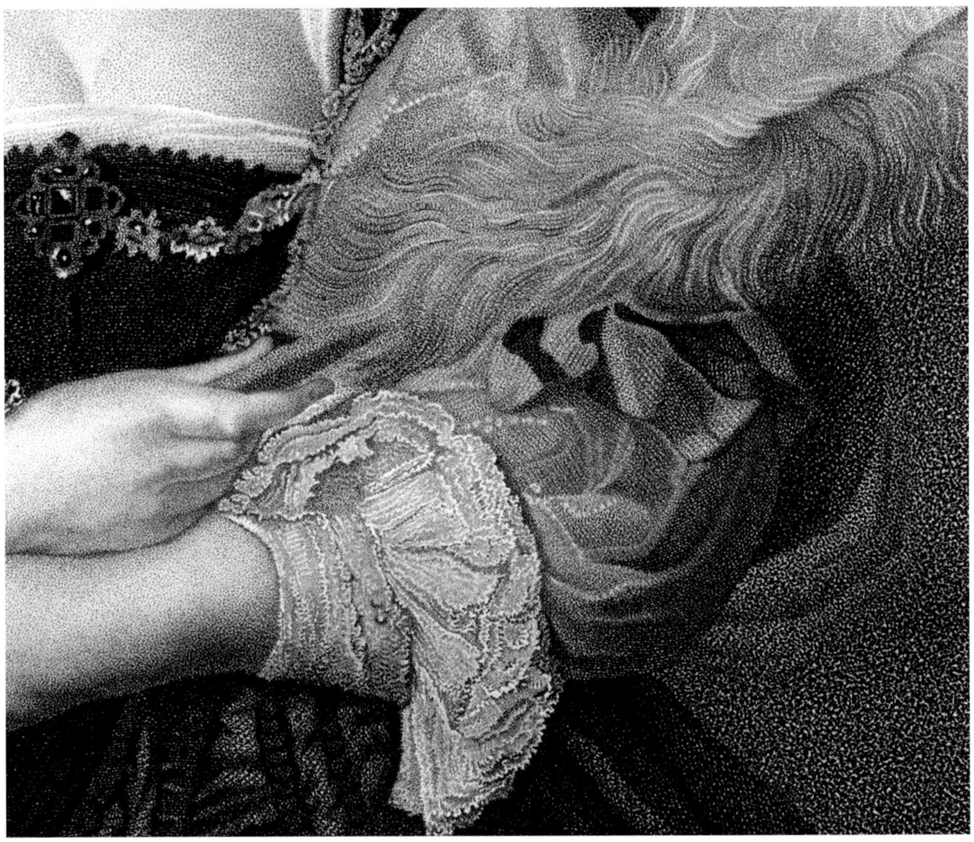

This makes an excellent contrast with the Rubens mezzotint, plate 75 (page 104). The effect of the lace, the feathers and jewels is quite the equal to the mezzotint. The textures of the dress and the hat are not quite so good, lacking the richness. This is unusually black for a stipple engraving. There is some shading added to the dress and hat with a burin.

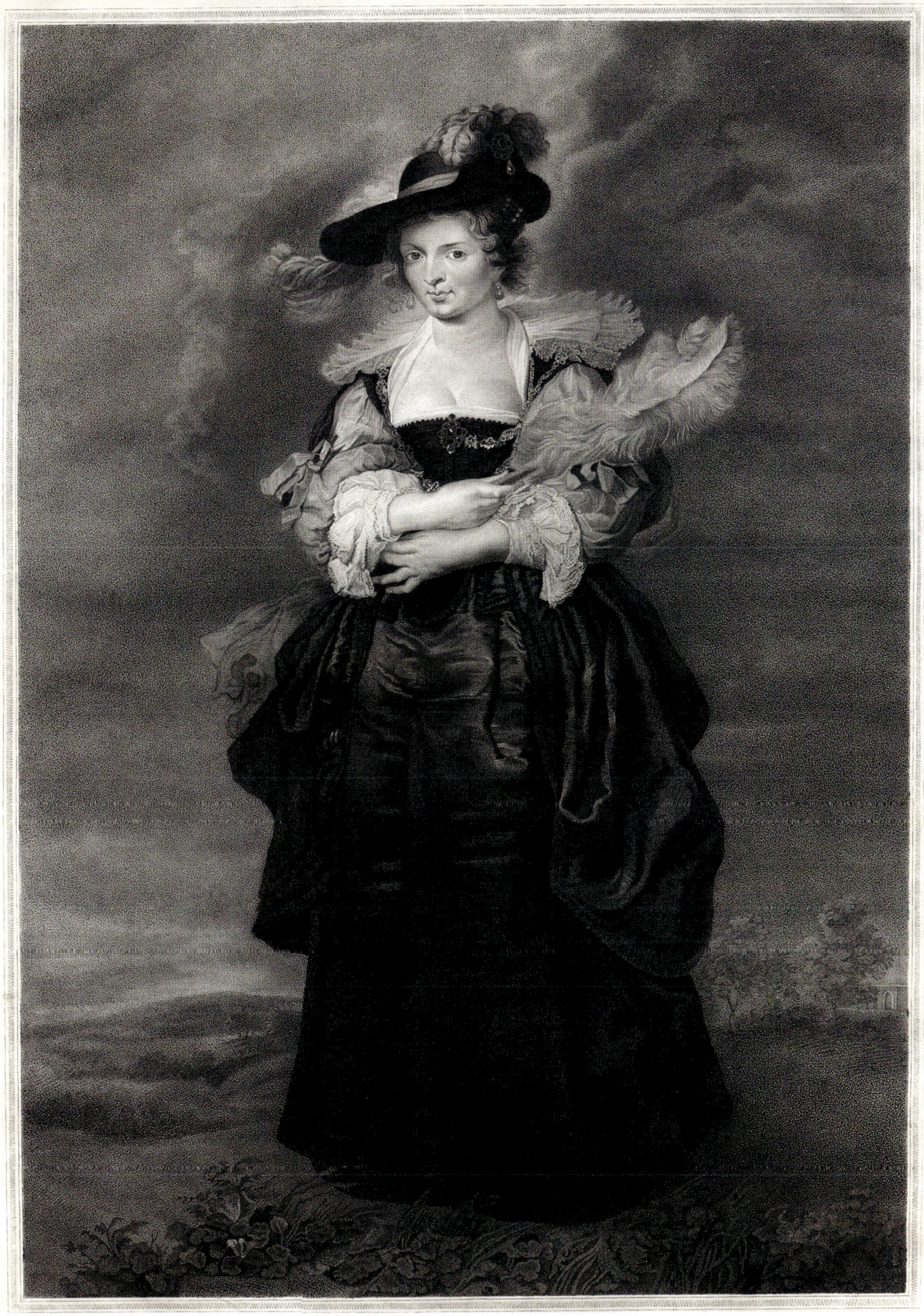

PLATE 86

*John Boydell Esq. Alderman of London.* From an original Picture by G. Stuart, in the Possession of Josiah Boydell, Esq. Drawn and Engraved by H. Meyer. Published June 21, 1814, by T. Cadell & W. Davies, Strand, London

Stipple engraving.

Image size: 21.4 x 19.5 cm (8.4 x 7.6 in.).

The plate is unusually large: 38 x 32.5 cm (15 x 12.7 in.).

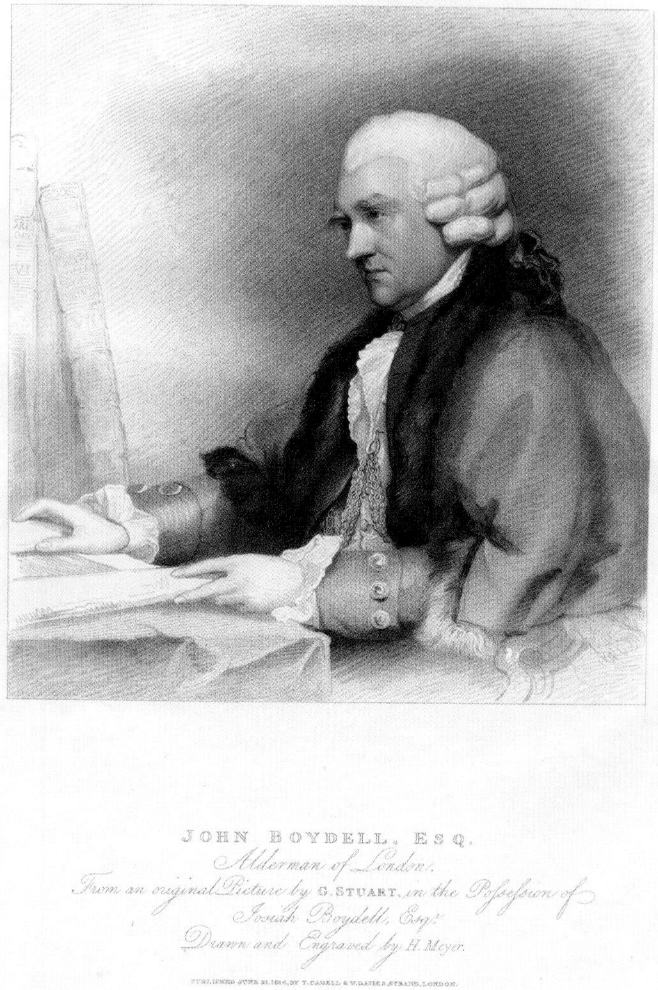


This is almost pure stipple engraving. The few fine lines in the eyebrows, the wig and the fur collar of the gown are very lightly etched.

John Boydell (1719–1804) was one of the most influential of all British printmakers and publishers, and there are several references to him and his prints throughout this book, mainly as a publisher. In this print, which was made ten years after he had died, can be seen two volumes of his prints beside his right hand. The titles on the spines of the books are in stipple, which is an unusual way of engraving such detail, and in fact are not clearly legible. Henry Meyer was another pupil of Bartolozzi who was known for his stipple engravings, but Meyer worked also in mezzotint.

Josiah, the owner of the original picture, was John's nephew and business partner. He became an Alderman of London when John died.

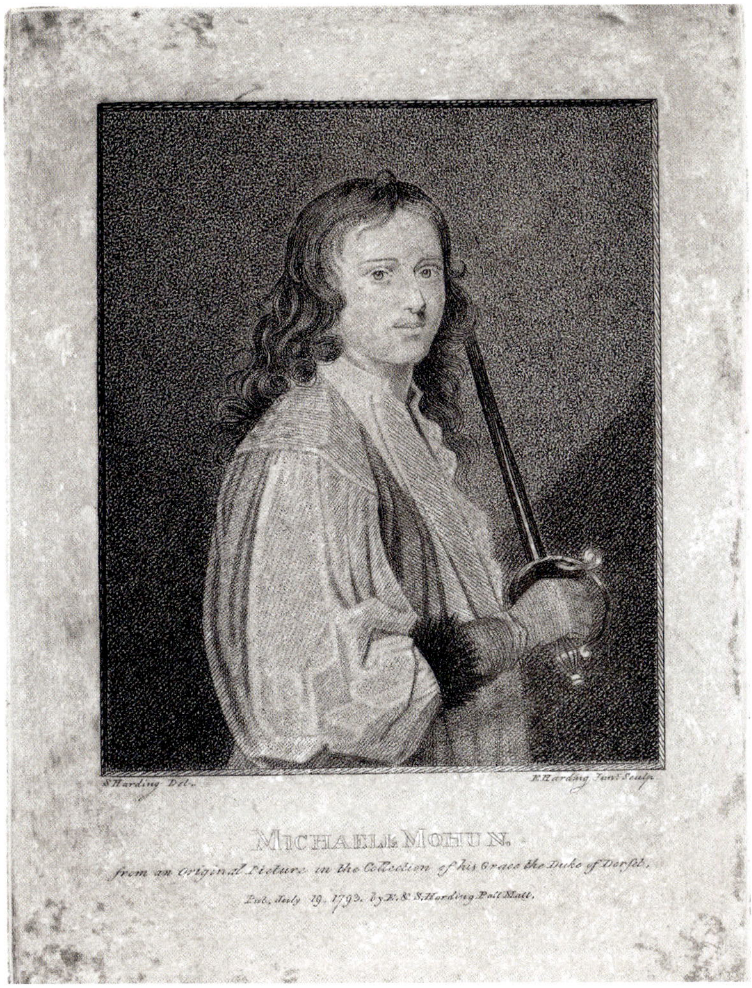


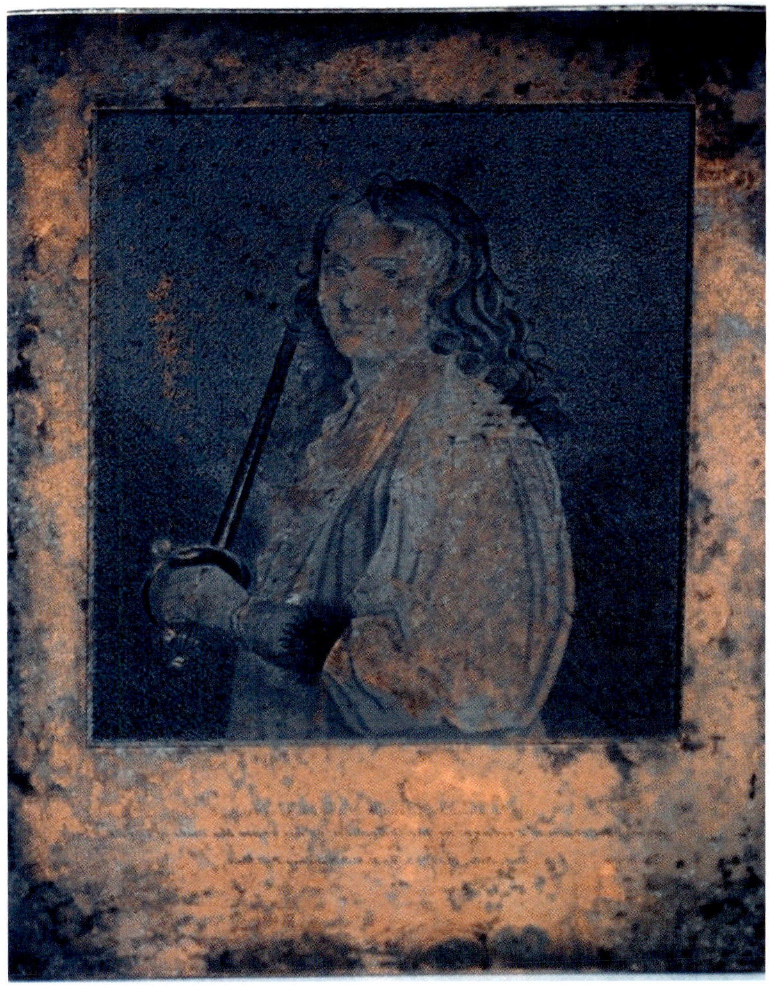

The problem here is that the copper plate was steel-faced which gives a harder surface, providing more prints. If it is not properly cared for, the steel will easily corrode, as has happened here: the plate is in a sad condition. The print is new and is better than might be expected. It was printed by Susanne Smith.

Michael Mohun (1620?–84) was an actor, who performed under Beeston at the Cockpit, joined the Royalist army, became a major and then returned to acting. The origin of the portrait is not known, but it is more likely to be taken from his acting career than the army.

Sylvester Harding was born in 1745, was apprenticed to a 'distasteful trade', according to Slater, and joined some strolling players. Aged 30, he went to London and took up miniature-portrait painting. He exhibited at the Royal Academy from 1775 to 1802. In 1786 he and his brother Edward, set up a book and print shop, publishing works themselves, including the *Biographical Mirror*. Edward junior (1776–96), the engraver, is the son of Sylvester, who was 16 years old when this portrait was engraved in the last quarter of his short life. Other sons were George Perfect, a watercolour artist, and Samuel, an engraver who also worked on the *Biographical Mirror*. They are not related to James Duffield Harding, who was the most famous artist of that name.

PLATES 87 & 88, THE PRINTING PLATE

*Michael Mohun,* engraved by Edward Harding Junior after Sylvester Harding from a picture in the collection of the Duke of Dorset.
Stipple engraving plate.
Pub. 19 July 1793 by E. & S. Harding, Pall Mall, for the *Biographical Mirror.*
Plate size: 19 x 14 cm (7.5 x 5.5 in.).

# SOFT GROUND ETCHING

Unlike normal etching, the ground is soft. Obviously. It had to be said.

The normal etching ground is made soft by adding tallow, which is a soft wax. It is important that the mixture is an even texture. The ground is laid onto the plate, as with etching, and again it is important that the ground is evenly, thinly coated over the plate. Next, a sheet of very thin paper is laid over the ground. The design is then drawn onto the paper with a pencil. Where the pencil strokes have been made, the paper will adhere to the ground. When the design is completed, the paper is carefully removed from the plate, peeled up from one end, lifting the ground with it. Various effects can be made by using pencils with different points; for example, a fine point will eventually make a fine line on the print. The softer the pencil, the less clear will be the effect on the print. Not all of the ground will adhere to the paper, so the effect on the print tends to be dotted rather than solid lines. Clear lines, like etching or engraving, do not happen.

Once the paper is lifted, the plate is subjected to acid in the same manner as etching, the completed parts stopped out as required.

The prints look like soft pencil drawings. They could be confused with stipple engraving, which are also dotted, but soft-ground etchings are usually much less formal, much more like freehand sketching. The main difficulty can be that they are even more similar to lithographs. The effect of each is intentionally the same. Soft-ground etchings, being printed from metal plates, should have plate marks, provided the paper is not trimmed.

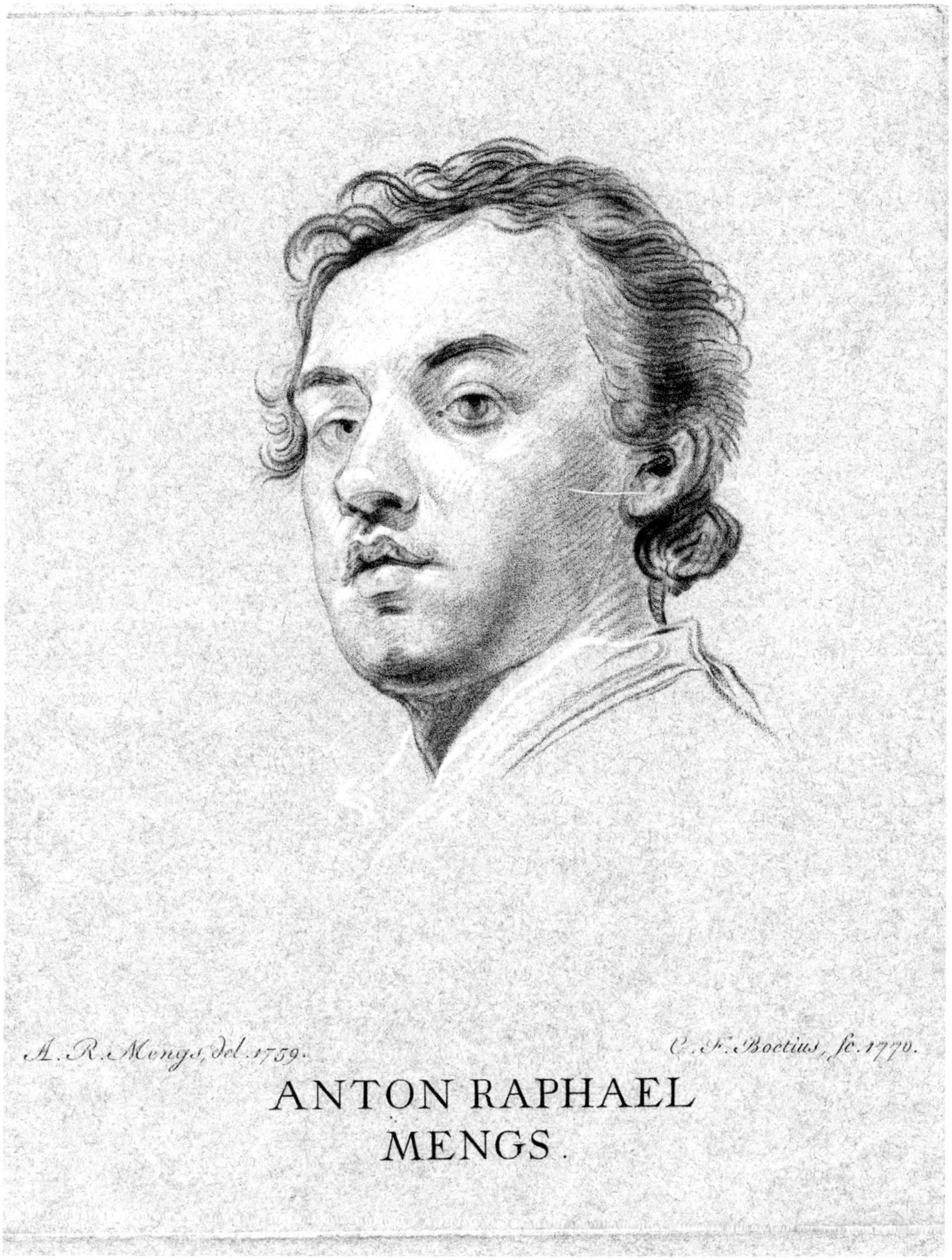


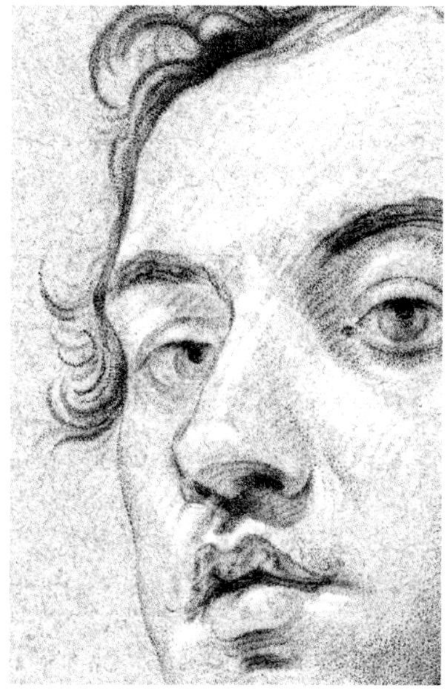

PLATE 89 & DETAIL

*Anton Raphael Mengs.* Self-portrait of the artist, engraved by Christian Friedrich Boetius, and printed in 1779
Soft-ground etching, 23.5 x 18 cm (9.3 x 7 in.).

This print is unusual for several reasons. It was made 20 years after the drawing, and both dates appear on the print. Very few prints of this period were made on anything other than white paper, whereas this is a flecked, textured blue paper. The white chalk highlights added at the time of printing were obviously intended to give the picture the appearance of being a drawing. Boetius is not well-known; most of his work was line engraving, and this print was probably an experiment to create something as close as possible to Mengs's drawing.

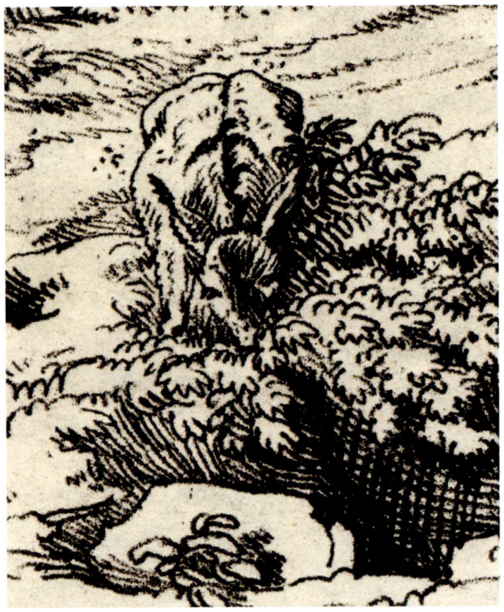

PLATE 90 & DETAIL

*Oak, near Bisham, Berks.* Drawn and etched by William Delamotte, signed within the picture, and dated 1805. One of a series of *Studies of Trees.*
Soft-ground etching,
45 x 34 cm (17.7 x 13.4 in.).

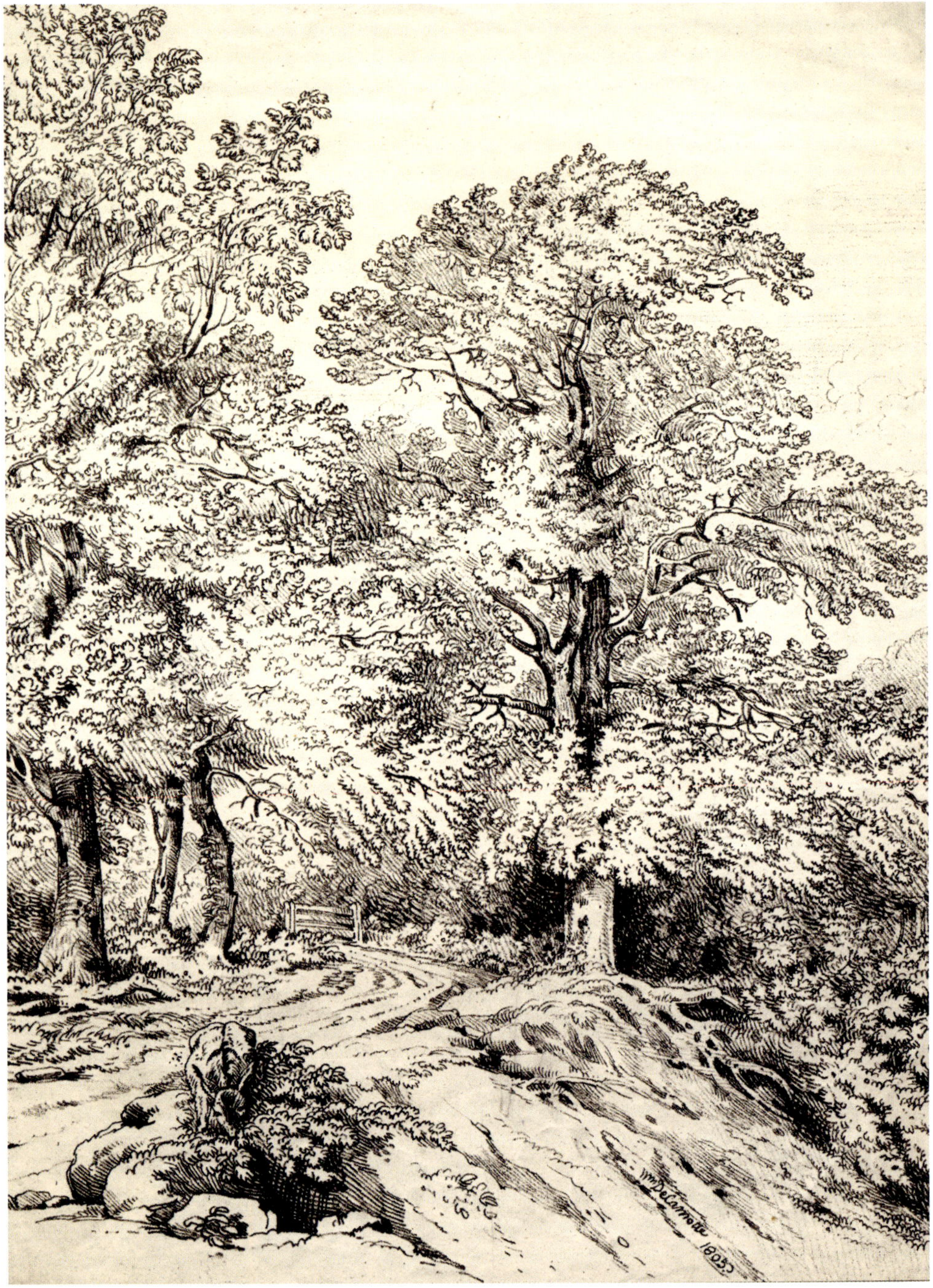

The effect of this print is intentionally a soft pencil, and could easily be mistaken for lithograph, especially in this case where all margins, and consequently the plate mark, are removed. Interestingly, Delamotte had produced lithographs before 1805.

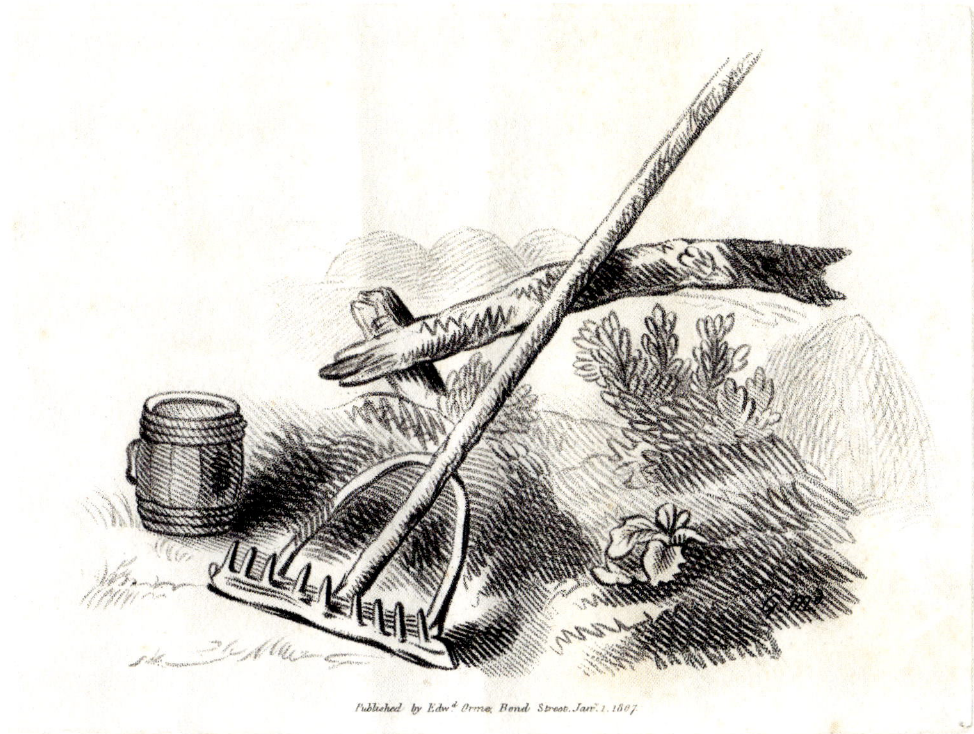


PLATE 91

Untitled rural scene, drawn by George Morland.
Published by Edward Orme in 1807.
Soft-ground etching,
16.5.x 21.5cm (6.5 x 8.5 in.).

A very simple picture, probably made for a book on drawing instruction with the deliberate intention of copying a drawing, this is a good example of the technique: it shows how the effect could look like a soft pencil drawing. The signature and publisher's imprint were done with ordinary etching; soft ground would not print such fine detail as this.

It could be a problem to decide how the print was made. It has a similar freehand pencil effect to that which can be produced with lithography. The print has a plate mark, which means it was produced from a metal plate; lithographs do not have plate marks. It is also made up of a lot of small dots, in a similar way to stipple engraving, but it is not stipple because the dots are irregular shapes.

An artist of the talent of Morland would have done the sketch in less time than it has taken to describe it. The engraver and the printer would have taken considerably longer.

# AQUATINT

There is more confusion over aquatints than there is over any other printing method, mostly because the title is not at all descriptive. 'Aqua' is a shortened version of 'aquafortis', literally translated as 'strong water', meaning acid. 'Tint' refers to tones of light and shade in the picture, and has nothing to do with colour. All of the earliest aquatints and many later ones were printed in one colour, usually either black or sepia. Much of the confusion arises because aquatints in colour can look very similar to watercolours.

The plate is engraved with acid, but there is little resemblance to an etching in the finished prints. Etching relies on lines, whereas aquatints are engraved in areas of tones. Close examination of an aquatint shows the engraved detail is the opposite way round to stipple, fine lines forming a pattern which is like wire netting of an irregular shape.

The engraver commences by laying a resin 'ground' on the copper plate, like etching. It isn't possible to create a fine line with aquatint, so the first part of most aquatint engraving is etching. When the business of aquatinting commences, the engraver removes an area of resin and, in its place, lays a powdered resin. The object is that the acid bites into the copper round the particles of resin, producing the tone in the tint. The difficulty is laying a suitable ground. This is done in several ways, depending on the choice of the engraver, or the style and subject of the print. The earliest engravers used a mixture of resin and spirit, with the consistency of varnish, which was spread evenly over the plate. As the spirit evaporated, the remaining resin dried and crazed in tiny particles. Paul Sandby used spirit grounds for his earliest prints, but it can be seen that he varied the size of the particles by using different mixtures of spirit and resin; the more spirit in the solution the more open the netting effect will be.

The first use of dust ground was laid by a shaker, like shaking salt or ground pepper. The difficulty was to make the ground even across the whole plate. An improved method was a dust box. The plate was laid inside, the box shaken and then time allowed for the dust to settle. The plate was heated sufficiently for the resin particles to adhere to the plate. The particles could be varied in size depending on the required effect, but most aquatint engravers relied on bite to create the right tone.

Like etching, the tones become darker with each immersion. The most simple aquatints are worked in four tones; fourteen is more usual, or indeed more for the most finely detailed prints.

The art of aquatinting was invented in France. Jean Baptiste Le Prince (1734–81), plate 92 (page 127), was probably the inventor of the dust process, but he has also been credited with the invention of aquatinting. His prints date from 1768, the year in which he took out a patent on the dust process. Slater suggests that Le Prince was not the inventor but merely improved on the method of laying the ground. However, he amassed a large sum of money from the patent, which he spent with more ease than he earned it, and, like so many artists and engravers, he died with many creditors. His work looks like pen-and-wash drawings, generally showing large areas of the same tone, with thick bold lines which are either etched or engraved. They were usually printed in sepia. At the time, the fashion in France lay in decorative subjects and domestic scenes, neither of which are best suited to aquatint. Stipple or mezzotint might have been an improvement.

Paul Sandby is usually regarded as the man who introduced aquatinting to Britain, but again this is not quite accurate; he was the first to produce a *series* of aquatint prints. Peter Perez Burdett produced three aquatints between 1771 and 1773, all of them being extremely rare, but Burdett is better known for his large-scale maps of Cheshire and Derbyshire, and a plan of Liverpool, his home town. In 1775 Sandby produced a set of 12 aquatints of South Wales, which he promoted by stating that aquatinting was 'a mode of imitating drawings on copper plates discovered by P. Sandby, R.A.'. The work is dedicated to the Hon.

Charles Greville, who is supposed to have brought the method of aquatint from France to Britain. Sandby continued to make important topographical prints until he died in 1809, and it was his tireless efforts and constant experimentation that did so much to promote the art of aquatinting in Britain. Sandby preferred to use a spirit ground, which we know was not Le Prince's method, so it could be argued that Sandby was using a new system.

Despite the fact that stipple engraving and mezzotints were being printed in colours at the time aquatinting started, it was some time before aquatints were colour-printed. James Malton first published a series of views titled *Picturesque Views of the City of Dublin,* in 1795, printed in monotone, but there is a colour-printed version published in 1798, which is probably the first colour aquatint book. In the normal way, aquatints were printed in two or three colours – the basic background colours, like blue, greens and browns – and any additional colour was applied by hand. This was usually the brighter colours, clothing in particular.

And so began a rich period of aquatinting. Over the ensuing 30 years there were some magnificent colour-printed aquatint books and separately published prints. Aquatint was ideally suited to topographical prints and any prints with a landscape or seascape environment, or sporting, military and marine subjects.

In the early 19th century, the style of aquatinting changed. Engravers began to use finer grounds so that the tones were even more detailed than 18th-century prints. Coupled with the use of colour printing, the prints began to look much more like watercolours.

David Cox produced *Treatise on Landscape,* which was illustrated with aquatints taken from his watercolours. The book did more to promote the use of colour aquatint than it did to instruct students of landscape, which was its original intention.

After Sandby, the most influential person in the promotion of aquatint was Rudolph Ackermann, the most prolific publisher of fine prints and colour-plate books from his premises in the Strand in London, starting in 1783, when he was aged just 19. He employed a team of colourists, who did the hand-finishing from a master copy, so that his prints were similar and not left to the discretion or the imagination of the colourist.

Ackermann was also an inventor, designing the suspension and steering gear of horse-drawn carriages. Regarded as an entrepreneur, his shop was the first in London to use gas lighting. The story goes that the public was dubious about the safety of gas lighting, and it was common for pedestrians to make a detour and pass his shop from the comparative safety of the opposite side of the street. During the Napoleonic Wars Ackermann was personally responsible for raising the vast sum of £100,000 for the aid of Napoleon's victims, and this sum was matched by the British Government, seemingly out of respect for Ackermann. Ackermann also invented a device that was attached to a balloon and used for dropping propaganda leaflets over France. He also designed Nelson's funeral carriage, which is shown in one of Ackermann's prints in the series *The Microcosm of London,* entitled *Greenwich Hospital – the Painted Gallery*, where the carriage may still be seen.

The method of aquatint was laborious and required great skill. Unlike etching, a near relation, there were very few artists who made their own aquatint plates; the task was normally given to professional engravers. There are records of relationships between artists and engravers being somewhat strained, and it is easy to imagine that an artist was never entirely satisfied with the engraver's results. The Daniells were a family of artists who were also fine aquatint engravers. William Daniell's epic work is the series *Voyage Round Great Britain,* which began at Land's End in 1814. Eleven years later, Daniell had completed a tour in a clockwise direction all round the coast, and returned to Land's End having made 308 aquatint views on the way. There is no other series which matches the *Voyage* for the variety of work. Some of the views represent scenes on hot summer's days, others are misty and damp days, and a few show stormy seascapes, all brilliantly executed. It is interesting that in the whole 11 years Daniell did not alter the style of his engraving at all; he was obviously content to continue with his customary style.

Samuel Daniell produced a series of African animals,

which are quite small, about 10 x 16 cm (4 x 6.3 in.), and the prints concentrate on the animal rather than the background, using not more than six tones of aquatint. It is recorded that Daniell could engrave one of these plates in a day, which is considered to be fast. From this, one can judge the time it must have taken to engrave a large, highly detailed aquatint plate.

Sadly, aquatinting was short-lived. Once lithography was established, the complexity of aquatint quickly saw its end as a commercially viable printing method.

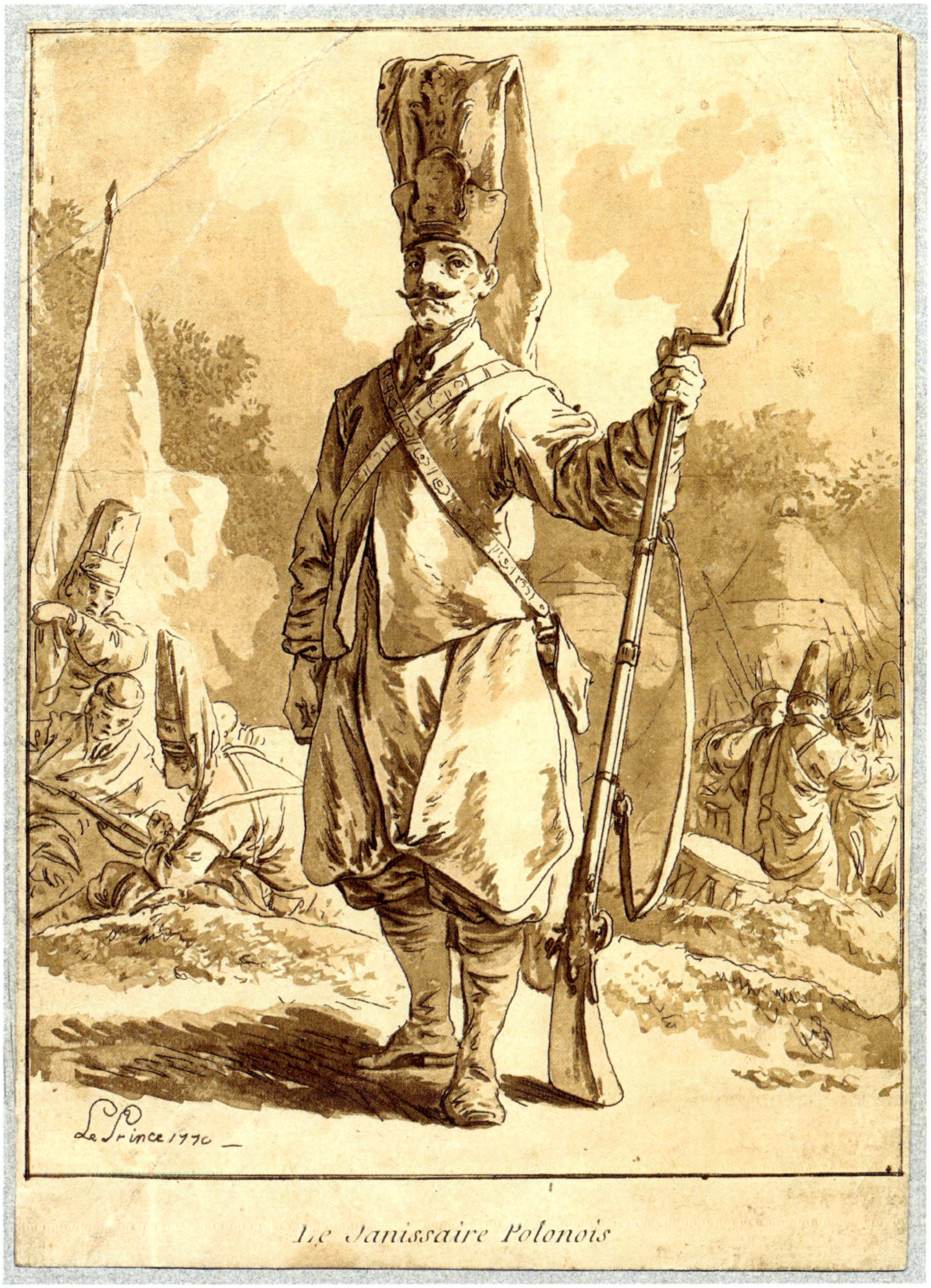


PLATE 92

*Le Janissaire Polonois,* aquatint by J.B. le Prince, 1770.
Image: 17.5 x 13 cm (6.8 x 5 in.).

This print is being shown here because it is the earliest aquatint in the collection, and among the earliest of all aquatints. It is not at all a typical example of aquatinting. At the time, the craft was in its infancy. Le Prince used a very fine resin dust, and even with a powerful magnifying glass the grain is not at all obvious, as it is with the later illustrations. In this case, the outlines are heavily etched, which, with the delicate and varied tones, gives the print the appearance of a wash drawing.

Le Prince was not the first to use aquatint, as some have suggested, but he was certainly influential in the developement of the dust process, and found ways to refine the method. His earliest aquatints were dated 1768, slightly earlier than this print. There is no doubt that Le Prince showed the method to Greville, who brought it to England.

Compare this with the next illustration, especially the detail.

PLATE 93 & DETAIL

*Overton Bridge. Over the river Dee, on the confines of Denbigh and Flintshire,* aquatint by Paul Sandby, artist and engraver. 'Publish'd according to Act of Parliament by Paul Sandby St Georges Row Sept 1st 1776.' Image size: 21 x 29.5 cm (8 x 11.5 in.). Collection of Sarah Baynton-Williams.

This is one of the earliest British aquatints, printed in sepia, as most early aquatints were. Sandby produced 12 aquatints of South Wales in 1775, the first series of aquatints in Britain. A year later he produced another 12 views of North Wales. The print of Overton Bridge is the first of the North Wales series, and, to my way of thinking, it is improved without the heavy aquatinted borders that were used for the South Wales views. The print is Sandby at his best, an inviting landscape with good animation, various people going about their everyday lives, a contrast to the formal promenading people in Woollett's view

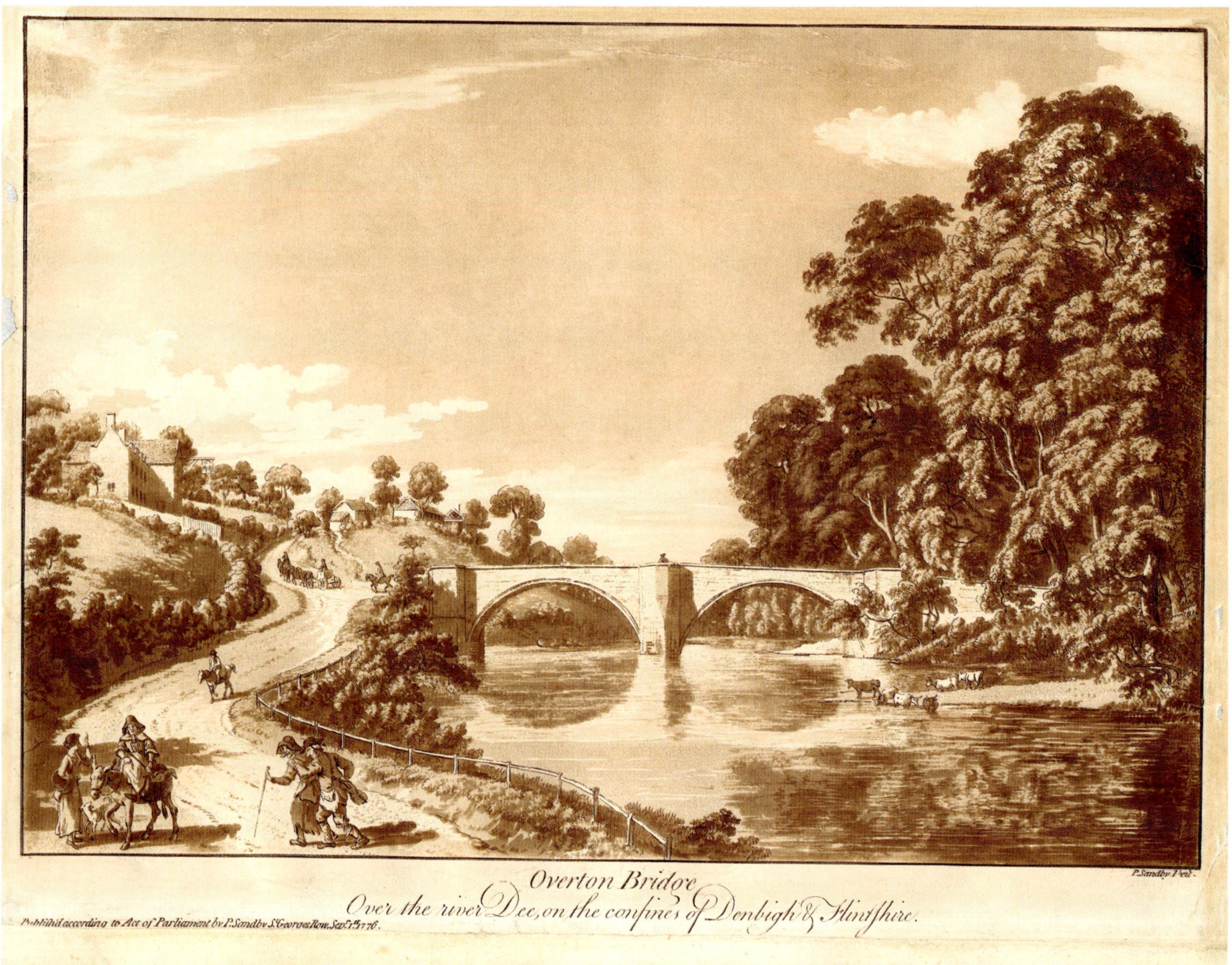

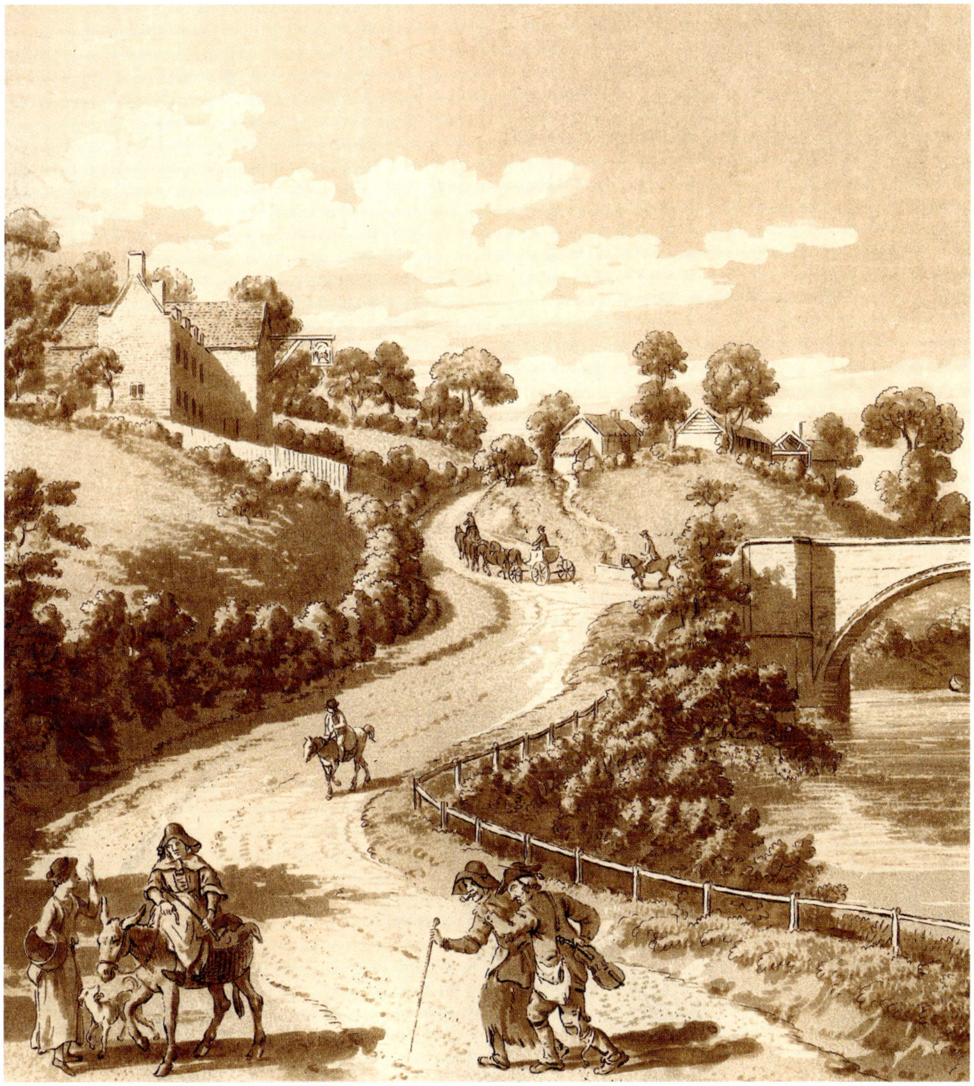

PLATE 93 DETAIL

of Whitton, plate 40 (page 62). The quality of the aquatinting is excellent, with wonderful tones and gentle variations. See how the sky gradually becomes lighter from right to left.

The bridge was built in about 1720. It was replaced with another one in 1816, of a very similar design, only higher above the water, probably to accommodate taller vessels. The building on the left is a public house, the Cross Foxes, a thought-provoking name, built in 1681 and not much altered. The road in the left foreground has been moved to a higher position, out of the way of flood water, to the left of the pub. While it is easy to pinpoint the position from which Sandby drew his view, it is not possible to see the view the way that he did because of the increase in trees and shrubs. This applies to a lot of topographical work; if you try to pinpoint an artist's position in the countryside, allow yourself at least twice the amount of time you think it will take.

The first edition of the *South Wales Views* was published by John Boydell.

The relationship between Sandby and Boydell may not have been a happy one. After the first edition, Sandby took over the publication himself, and took a lot more trouble to make the prints as he wanted them. The heavy aquatint borders, mentioned before, are about two centimetres wide and are a distraction from the picture. Sandby improved them greatly by lightening the tones. On the other hand, Sandby was possibly never content with his results, and he does some extraordinary things. There is one of his prints where he adds an extra bird to a group of six, a dot with wings in the distance, undoubtedly crows, above the tower of a castle. Comparison of the same prints rarely shows two that are identical; there is always some minor change, if only to the tone of the sepia ink. Sandby was always experimenting.

The plates for the two series are the same size. The borders being left out in the North Wales series, the image size of the prints is about three centimetres larger.

Also, as a contrast, the South Wales series consists of ten views of castles, one of a palace and one landscape. The North Wales series consists of five landscapes: three castles (two of them from a distance which blend into the landscape), a forge, a mill and a house belonging to Sandby's benefactor, Sir Watkin Williams Wynn.

Strangely, William Daniell, another master of aquatint topopgraphy, used aquatint borders for his epic *Voyage Round Britain*, published in 1825. These are much lighter in tone and do not distract from the print. Daniell was unlike Sandby in that he seemed to be so contented with his style. There are 308 prints in the *Voyage*, which took Daniell 11 years to produce, but he did not alter his style. Nor did Daniell make a single change to any of the plates once they were published.

Paul Sandby is an underrated artist and engraver. Gainsborough called him 'the father of the watercolour'. He was mainly responsible for the development of aquatinting in Britain. Born in Nottingham, Paul and his elder brother, Thomas, both worked for the Board of Ordnance early in their careers. Paul was appointed draughtsman to the Military Survey in Scotland and, while he was there, he began to make etchings. From small beginnings he rose to be a founder member of the Royal Academy. When he left the Board of Ordnance, Paul again joined Thomas, who was draughtsman to the Duke of Cumberland at Windsor Castle. Although he travelled a lot, Paul kept his ties with Windsor, and many of his prints and watercolours are of places in and around there.

The brothers had different talents. Thomas became deputy ranger of Windsor Park in 1746; he made alterations to the park and planned Virginia Water, but he was directed more towards architecture. He was the first professor of architecture at the Royal Academy. His main architectural works are Freemasons' Hall and Lincoln's Inn Fields, both in London. In 1777, he was joint architect with James Adam of His Majesty's Works.

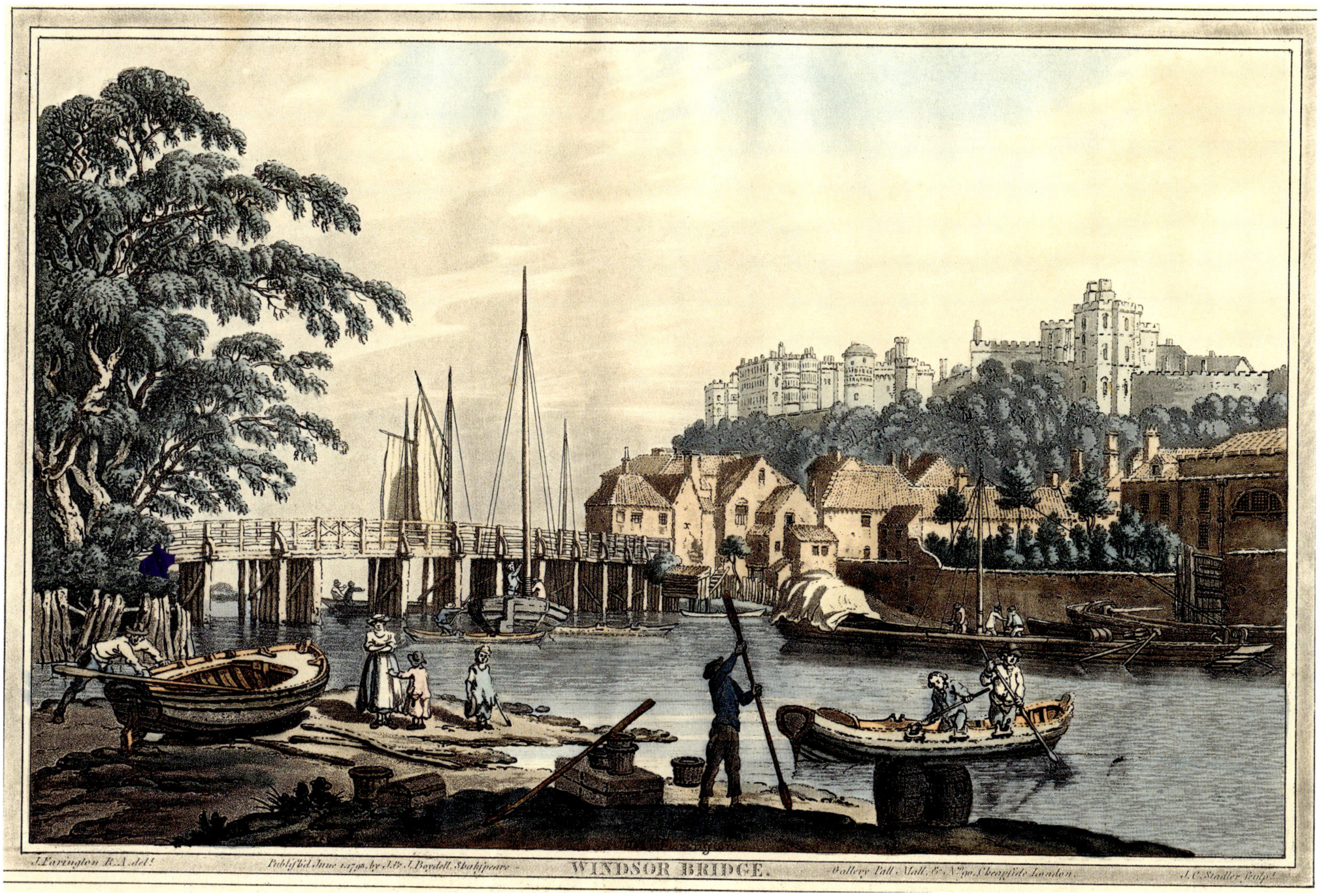


The print is a good example of a topographical aquatint of the second period, when colour printing began. This was printed in two colours, dark brown in the foreground and grey in the background, which creates a good effect of distance. The rest of the colour was added by hand. Farington excelled at river scenery; his views always provide a lot of detail and are clear representations of the subject.

PLATE 94

PLATES 94, 95 & DETAIL

*Windsor Bridge,* aquatint engraved by J.C. Stadler after Joseph Farington R.A., published by Boydell for *History of the River Thames*, 1793. Proof.

The complete set is 76 plates, most of them this size, some being double page.
The plate size of the proof measures 36 x 47 cm (14 x 18.5 in.). The size of the finished print to the outer border measures 21 x 31.5 cm (8.3 x 12.4 in.).

PLATE 94 DETAIL

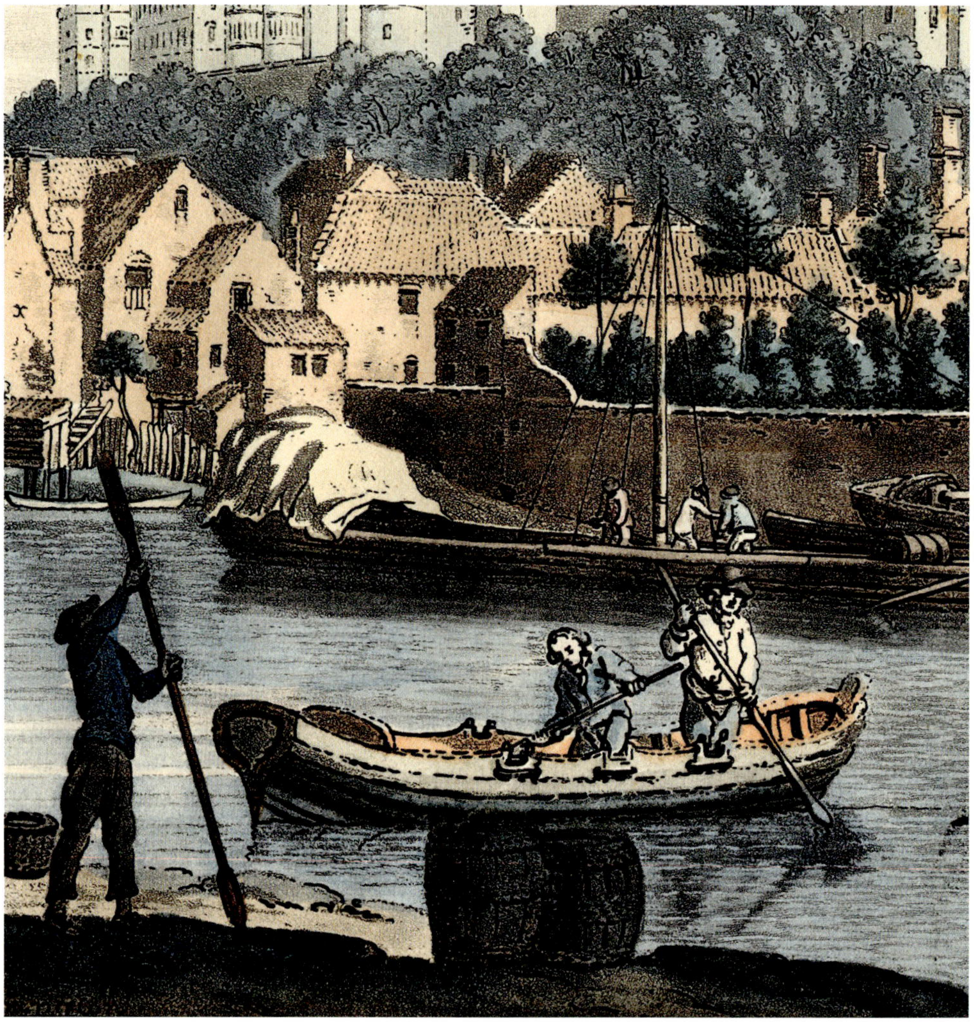

With it is a trial proof which was taken at a very early stage of the engraving, before the etched outline was completed, and before there was any detail to show the Castle. The engraver might appear to be working the wrong way round, leaving the main subject until last. The foreground is the strongest part of the picture, naturally, and therefore it would progressively become darker with each submersion in acid as the distant parts are introduced.

There are a few minor changes in detail from the proof to the published print. The figure in the foreground holds a pole which becomes an oar; the fence on the left is altered; Farington's signature below the boat on the left is later hidden with foliage. Detail of the rowing boat is slightly different: the lines of the planks at the side of the boat are not constant and the shading inside the bow is much altered.

The copper plate was unnecessarily large. The plate mark is about 8 cm (3.1 in.) outside the border of the print. It would need to be a very large paper copy for a plate mark to show.

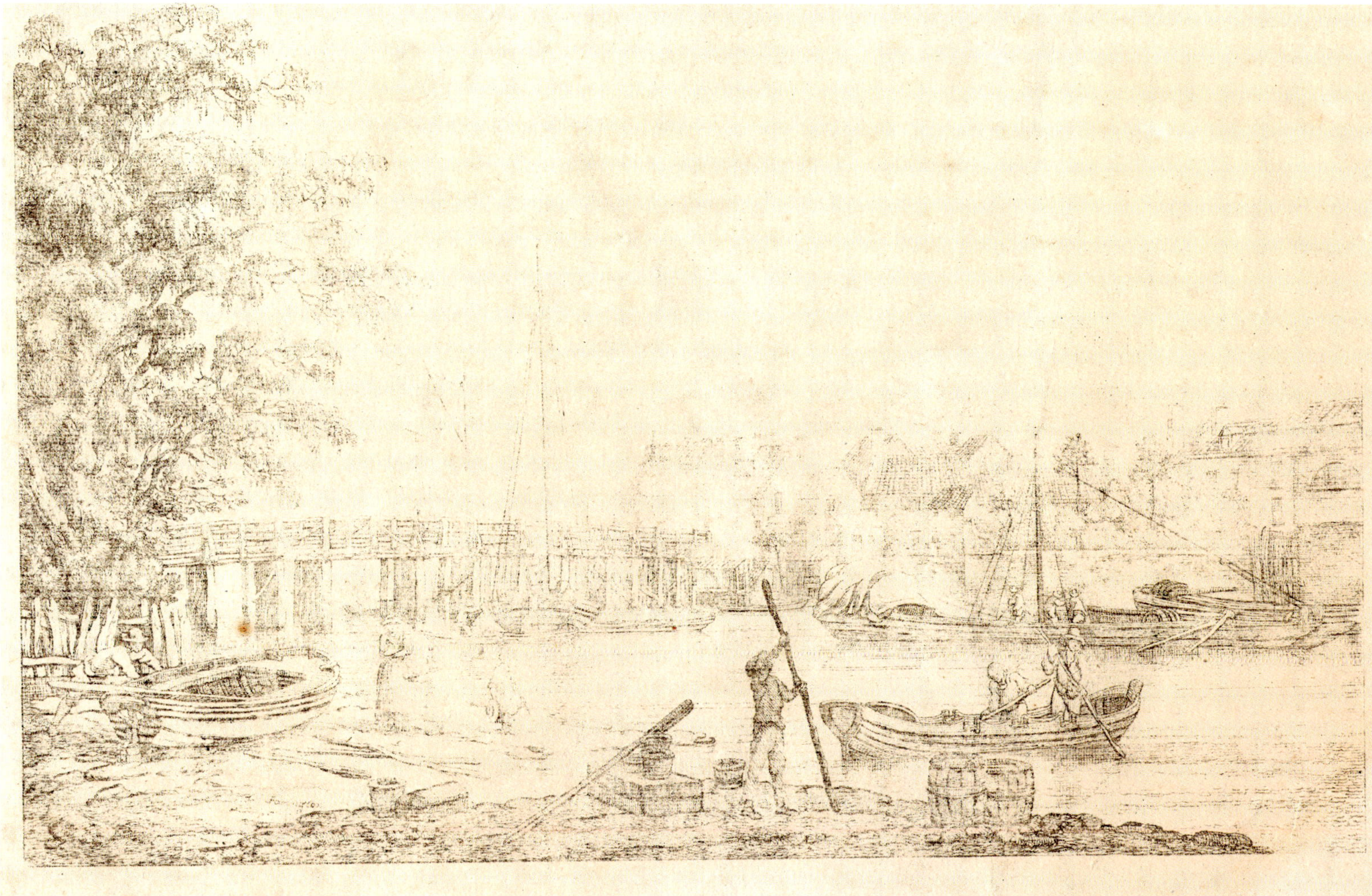

PLATE 95
The proof state.

PLATE 96
*Myrtle Cottage,* aquatint by D. Havell, 1817.
Plate size: 17.5 x 25 cm (6.8 x 9.8 in.).

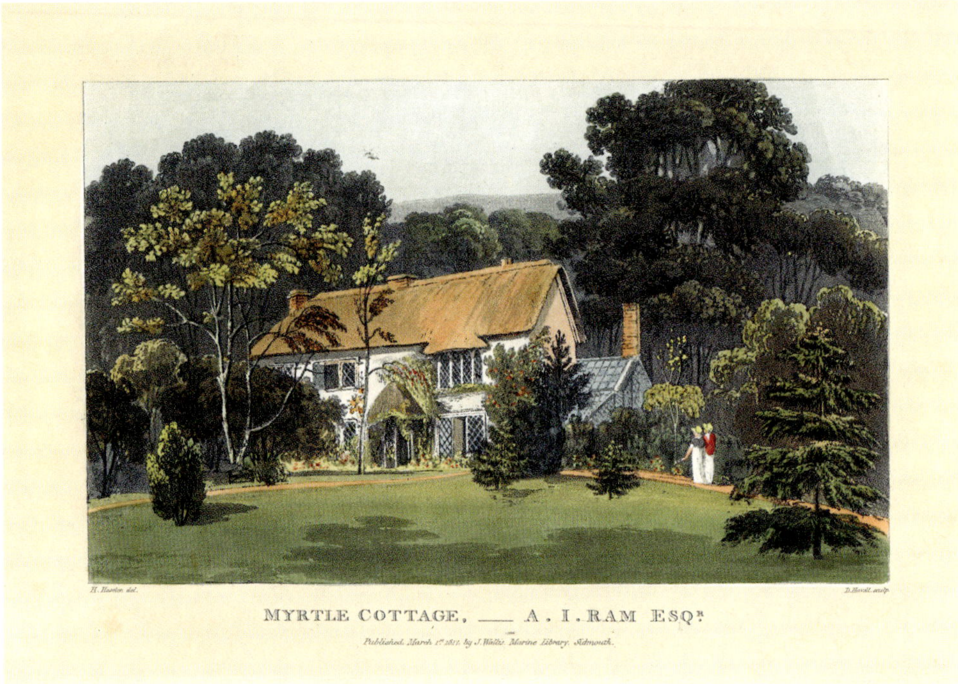


Two views, both engraved by D. Havell after H. Haseler, published by John Wallis at the Marine Library (now the Bedford Hotel) in Sidmouth, first issued in 1817 as part of the series *Sidmouth Scenery.*

The dates on prints only provide information about the date that the engraving was completed, and cannot be relied upon as accurate printing dates. In this case, the print of *Myrtle Cottage* (dated 1817) is a good early issue, partly printed in colour – black, blue and dark green – and finished with minimal hand-colouring – the yellow, the brown of the thatch and the chimney, and the clothing of the two women. The result is a good, clear impression, skilfully coloured with good variation.

The print of *Salcombe House* (dated 1816) has a watermark date in the paper of 1825, and would therefore have been published in 1825 at the earliest, or possibly several years later. In comparison with the print of *Myrtle Cottage* it looks very weak, normally a sign that the plate is worn, but even so the plate should produce a better impression than this. The focal point of the view is the house, which is far into the distance, and would never be as prominent as *Myrtle Cottage,* no matter how good the impression was. The main factor is that it was printed in sepia ink, which means that it was never quite as vibrant as it would be in black ink. All the colouring was done by hand, probably not very long ago. The colours are thin and washy, done with little variation. Besides that, sepia prints never seem to be enhanced by the addition of hand-colouring.

Below it is the plate that printed the *Salcombe House.* It is in good condition and is still suitable for printing good impressions. The finest detail hardly shows on the plate, which can be noticed in the sky in particular, but it is still enough to produce the light cloud effect on paper. John handmade the print.

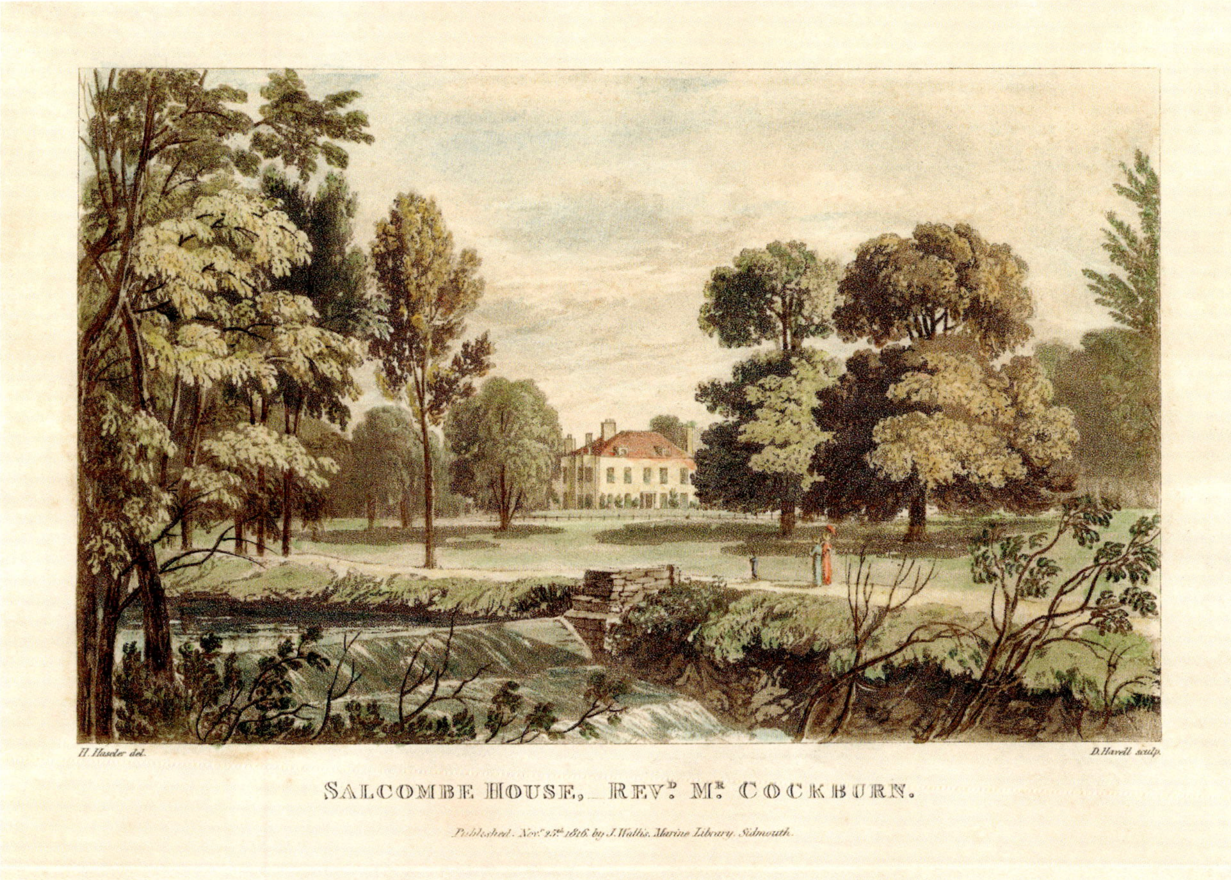


PLATE 97

*Salcombe House,* aquatint by D. Havell, with the printing plate (Pl. 98.) Plate size: 17.5 x 25 cm (6.8 x 9.8 in.).

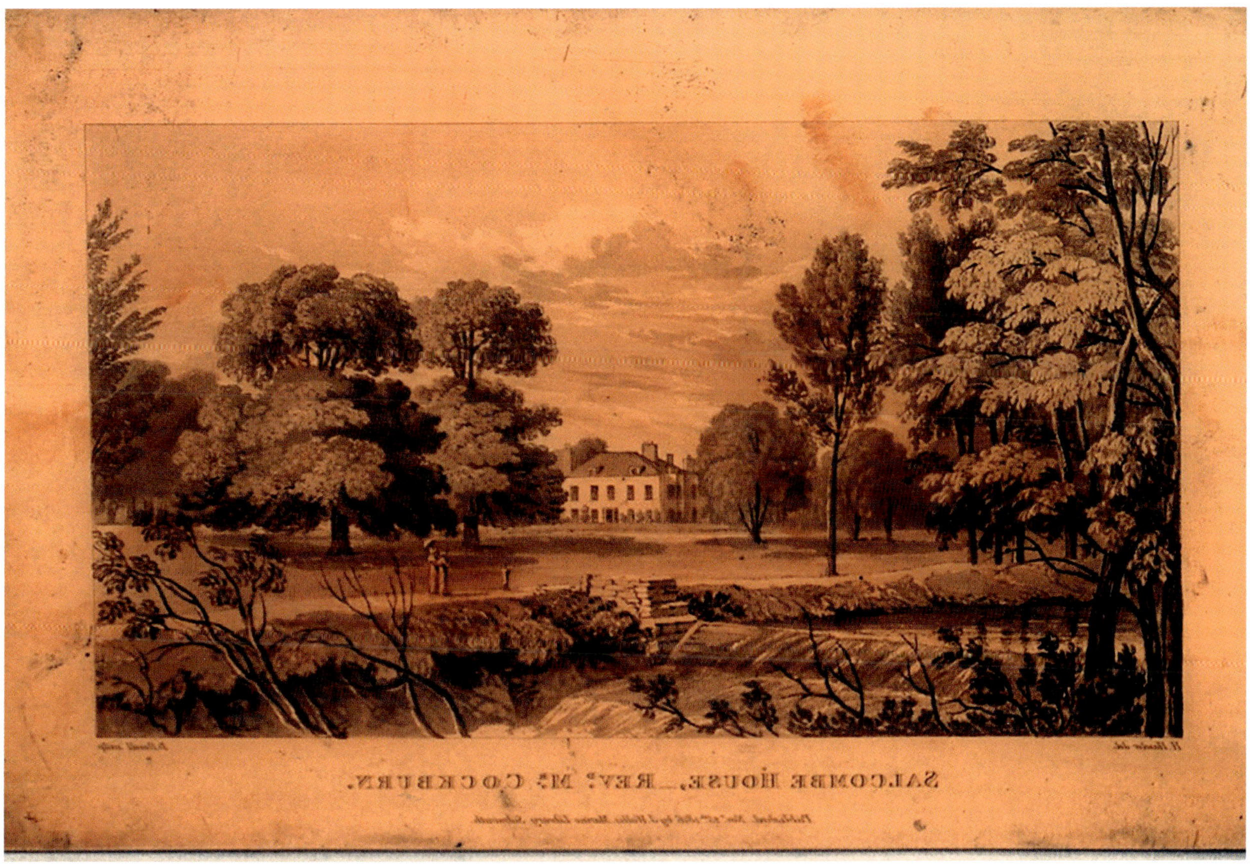

PLATE 98

The copper printing plate.

Identifying *Myrtle Cottage* has proved to be a problem. Myrtle is a shrub which grows profusely in the Sidmouth area, and was commonly used as a name for a house, appearing in various unpretentious combinations, usually with 'cottage'. Some large houses were called cottages. The Duke and Duchess of Kent lived for a short time with their baby daughter, who was to become Queen Victoria, at a massive house called Woolbrook Cottage, now the Royal Glen Hotel. We know that over the years the names of houses were changed to something more appropriate. The illustrated Myrtle Cottage is probably the house a little downstream from the ford on the east side of River Sid, towards Salcombe Regis.

Salcombe House, on the other hand, is not a problem. The building stands beside the River Sid, shown in the foreground of the illustration; the land between the river and the house is parkland. There is a hedge where the low fence is seen in front of the house. The house is little altered, other than that it is now called Hunter's Moon Hotel.

Reginald Lane, of Sidmouth Museum, has kindly provided some interesting information. The Revd Mr Cockburn was Sir William, Dean of York. The Dean was deprived of his benefice on a charge of simony, which is the crime of buying or selling holy orders or church preferment. He was reinstated because of the influence of Sir Robert Peel, who was probably related to the Dean's first wife. Later, the Dean's son, Robert, was dissuaded from marriage by his father, on the basis that the girl was too young. The Dean promptly married the girl himself. It was also rumoured that the Dean tried to sell Salcombe House to Robert when the house was not his to sell, but belonged to Charles Cornish, another influential Sidmouth man, and patron of John Wallis. He is probably related to Hubert Cornish, the artist of the *Long Picture of Sidmouth.* the seafront, published by Wallis in 1815. It is reported that Sir William Cockburn was the first man to be seen in Sidmouth with an umbrella.

The name of Salcombe House was changed by Mr and Mrs Fisher, who had been to see Ivor Novello's musical *Perchance to Dream* at the Drury Lane Theatre in London during the 1930s. The name of the house in the show is Hunter's Moon. During the performance they agreed that if ever they could afford a suitable house they would call it Hunter's Moon.

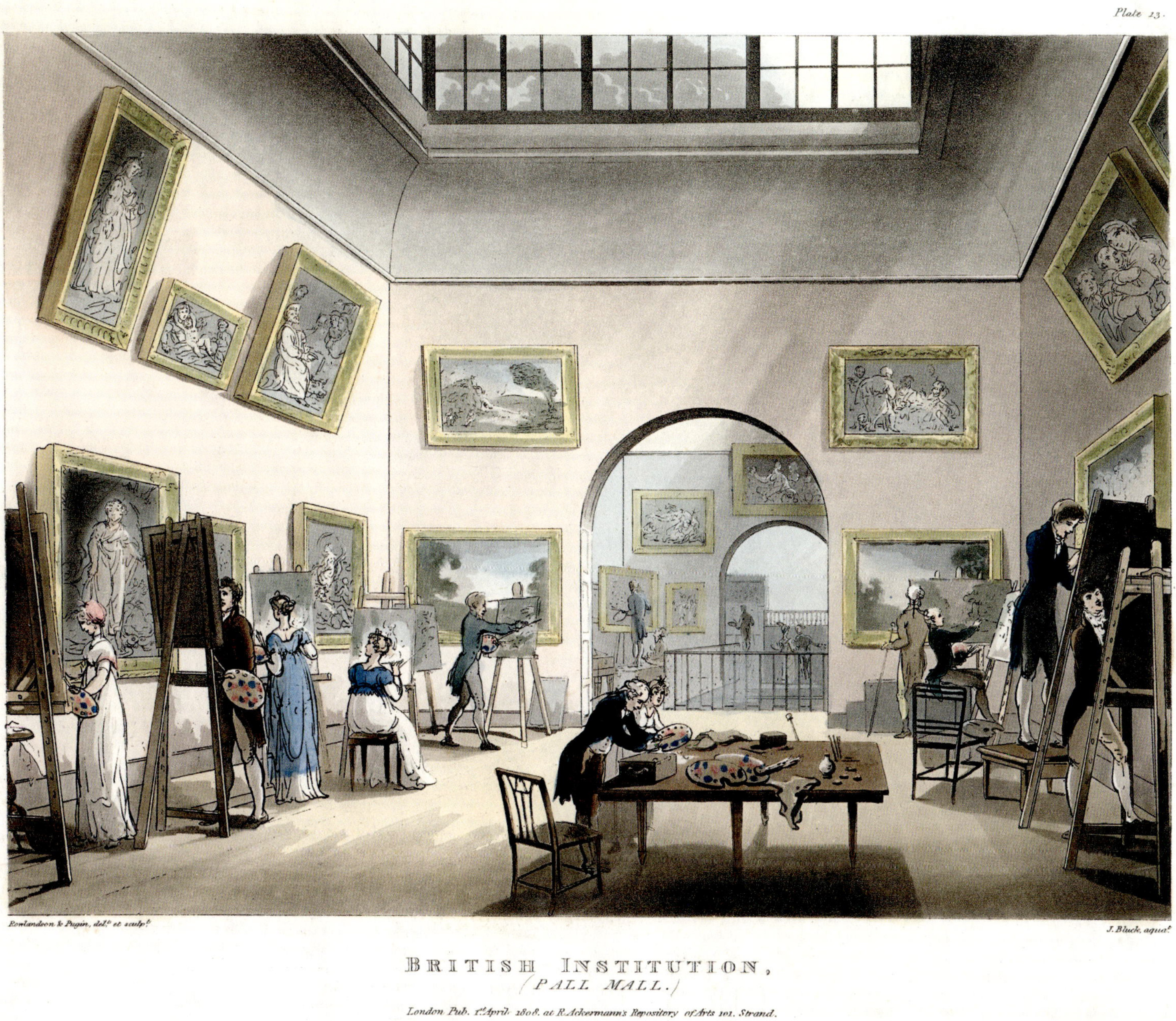


This is plate 13 from the epic series of 103 aquatint plates for *The Microcosm of London*, one of the finest colour-plate works and important as a major topographical documentary. Much of the success was due to the combination of Thomas Rowlandson, who drew the animation, and Augustus Charles Pugin (the father of the Houses of Parliament Pugin), who drew the architecture. They drew all the subjects for the series. In this case, they etched the outline for Bluck to complete the aquatinting. Bluck has used a very fine ground, noticeable in the shadows and in the paintings, the effect being like a wash.

The print has an additional interest. The building had earlier been occupied

PLATE 99
*British Institution, (Pall Mall.),*
aquatint by J. Bluck.
'Rowlandson and Pugin delt et sculpt. J. Bluck aquat.
London, Pub 1st April 1808, at R. Ackermann's Repository of Arts, 101, Strand.'
19.5 x 26 cm (7.6 x 10.2 in.).

by John Boydell as his Shakespeare Gallery. Its substantial dimensions are a guide to the misplaced faith that Boydell had in the *Scenes from Shakespeare*. The building must have been one of the first print shops to have a lantern light, seen also in the shops of Ackermann and Fuller. Boydell died before he was able to fund his financial recovery by lottery. His nephew, Josiah, sold the building in 1805 to the newly formed British Institution for Promoting Fine Arts in the United Kingdom, which was aimed particularly at helping young British artists and at rivalling the Royal Academy. It was closed in 1862.

PLATE 100
*S. & J. Fuller. Temple of Fancy.*
Aquatint, engraved by Smart & Sutherland, after W. Derby *c.*1815.
Plate: 16.5 x 23.5 cm (6.5 x 9.3 in.).

Again the print is credited with two engravers. In this case, Robert Smart worked only in etching, and any aquatinting required assistance. Thomas Sutherland produced many aquatint plates and worked for many of the famous publishers.

The print is another trade advertisement. The firm of S. & J. Fuller is remembered for their publication of fine prints and not for all the other interests that are shown in the print here. The firm was always at 43 Rathbone Place, Oxford Street, London, and flourished from 1812 to 1845. Like Ackermann and Fores, they specialised in fine aquatints of all kinds of subjects, especially sporting prints. They were fortunate in publishing the wonderful horse portraits, usually with the jockey up, of St Leger and Derby winners by John F. Herring, the most successful series of prints that they published. The first 12 St Leger winners that Herring painted, from 1815 to 1826, were all engraved by Sutherland. The first issues of these were published by Sheardown in Doncaster, before Fuller's took over the project in 1828. Before this date, Fuller's dropped the Temple of Fancy and became the Sporting Gallery.

The grand building is similar to other shops that were about at the time; the large lantern light in the roof was a big advantage in giving the best possible light in which to see the pictures properly. Not many prints are on show. To the left is a portfolio stand, and there are probably some prints to be seen in the glass cabinets. There are some books at the back, which would be Fuller's bound collections of prints.

By the way, it is quite usual for 'I' to be used instead of 'J'. The title of the firm is not a misprint.

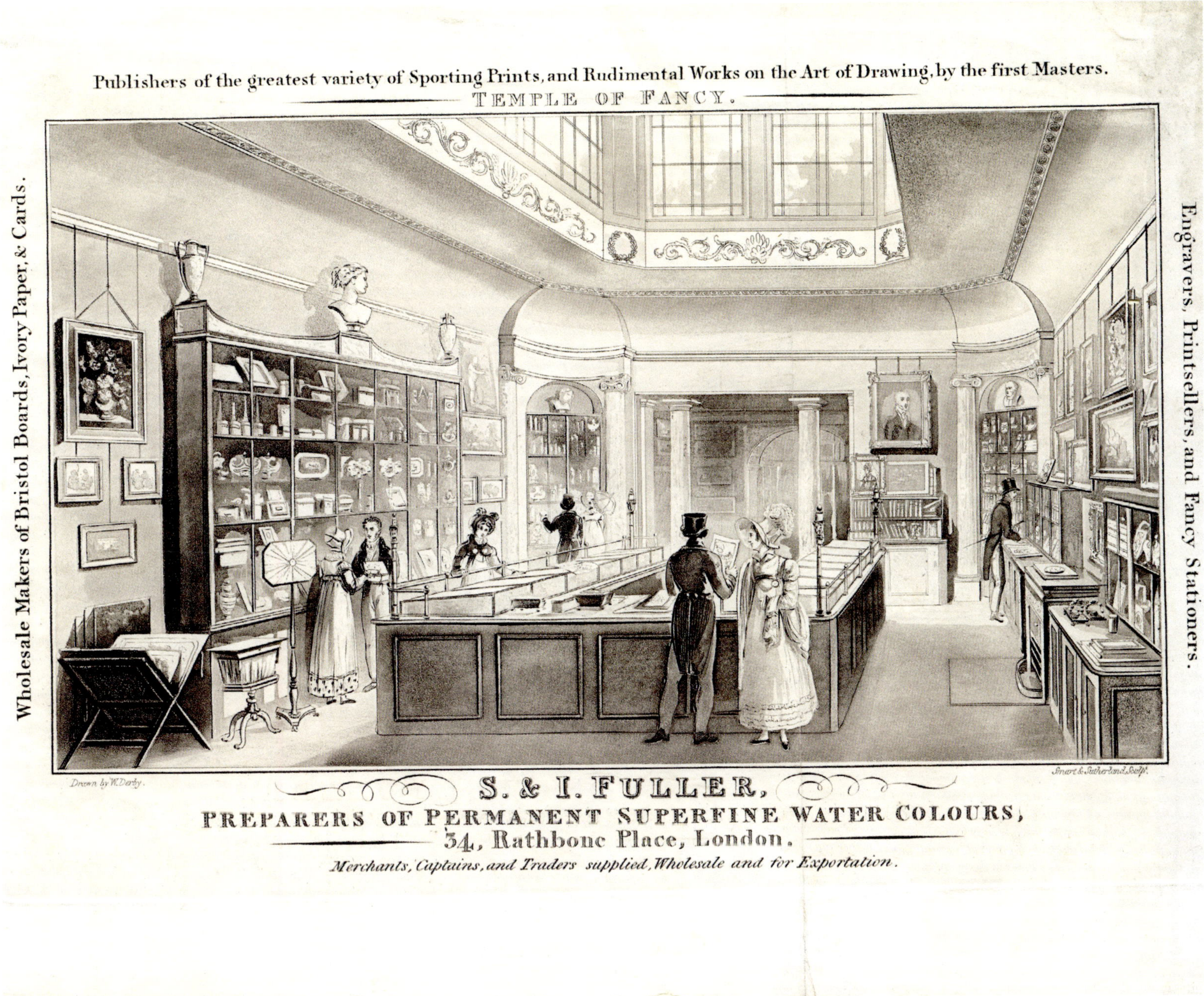
Publishers of the greatest variety of Sporting Prints, and Rudimental Works on the Art of Drawing, by the first Masters.
TEMPLE OF FANCY.
Wholesale Makers of Bristol Boards, Ivory Paper, & Cards.
Engravers, Printsellers, and Fancy Stationers.
S. & I. FULLER,
PREPARERS OF PERMANENT SUPERFINE WATER COLOURS,
34, Rathbone Place, London.
Merchants, Captains, and Traders supplied, Wholesale and for Exportation.

PLATES 101 & 102

*Dr Syntax reading his Tour.* Drawn and etched by Thomas Rowlandson. The engraver is anonymous. An illustration for William Combe's *Tour of Doctor Syntax in Search of the Picturesque.* Published by R. Ackermann. Plate 101 is dated 1817; plate 102 is dated 1819. There were several editions from 1812 until at least 1821.
Aquatint,
11 x 19.5 cm (4.3 x 7.7 in.)

The print is rather more typical of the work of Rowlandson than is seen in the *British Institution*, plate 99 (page 137). William Combe, described as 'with an indifferent reputation for honesty', was 30 years old before he took up a career in journalism. His success in this field was inconsistent, but he worked for journals regularly, and, in 1803, he was on the staff of *The Times.* Quite how he drew the attention of either Rowlandson or Ackermann is not clear. In about 1810 Rowlandson drew a series of illustrations concerning the events in the life of a touring schoolmaster. Combe was invited to provide the text. The schoolmaster became Dr Syntax, and it seems that Rowlandson's depiction of the character was actually based on Combe, even though the two men never actually met. The result was a very successful partnership.

On close examination it will be seen that these two illustrations were made from different plates, which indicates that Rowlandson or Ackermann thought that the original plates had become worn by the time of the edition of 1817. Al-

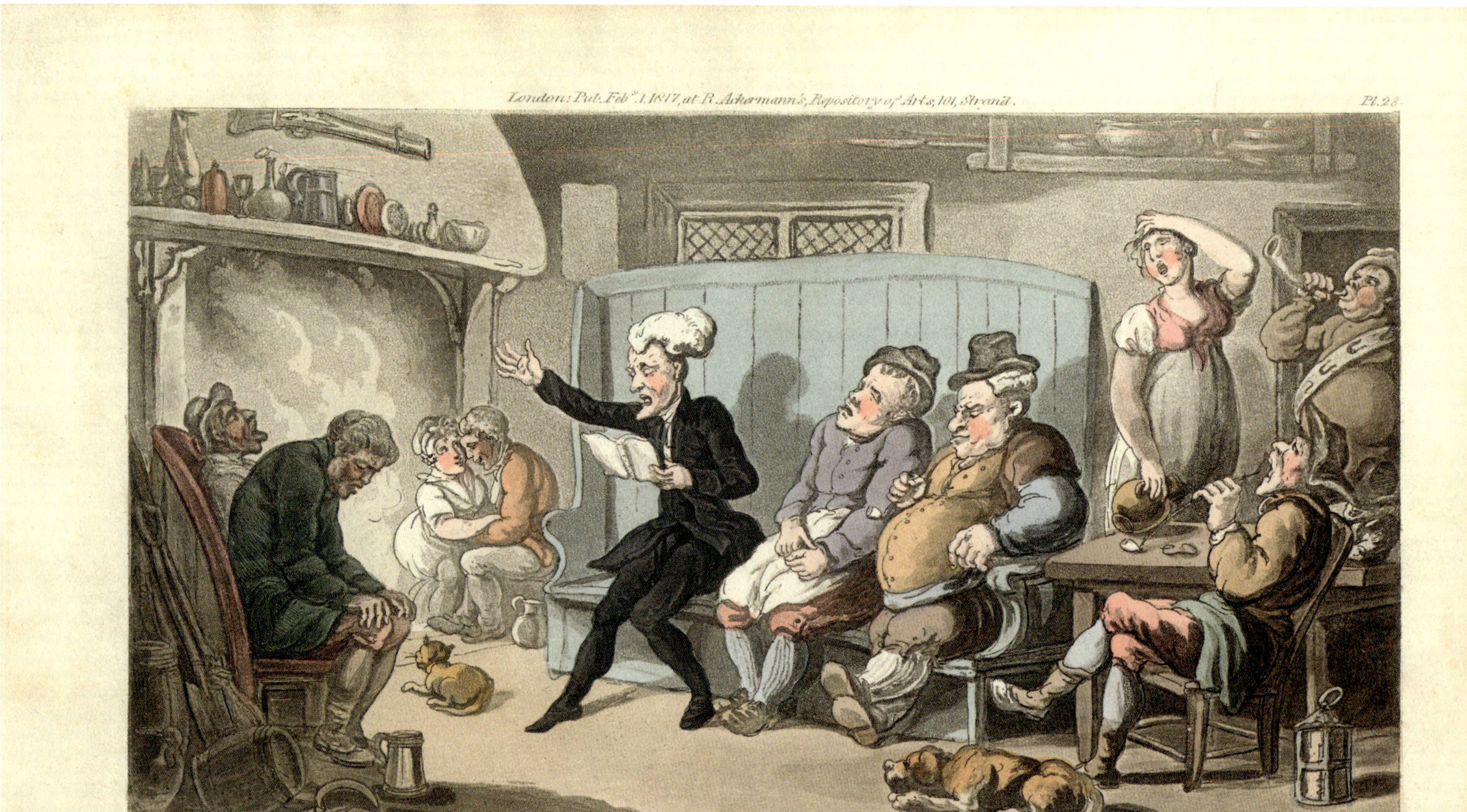


PLATE 101

though the composition is the same, there is hardly any detail which varies, except that, in the fireplace, the cauldron and the hanging hams are added in the 1819 print. The 1819 print is re-engraved with more darkly shaded tones. Lastly, even the colouring is the same; the same master copy would have been used by the colourist.

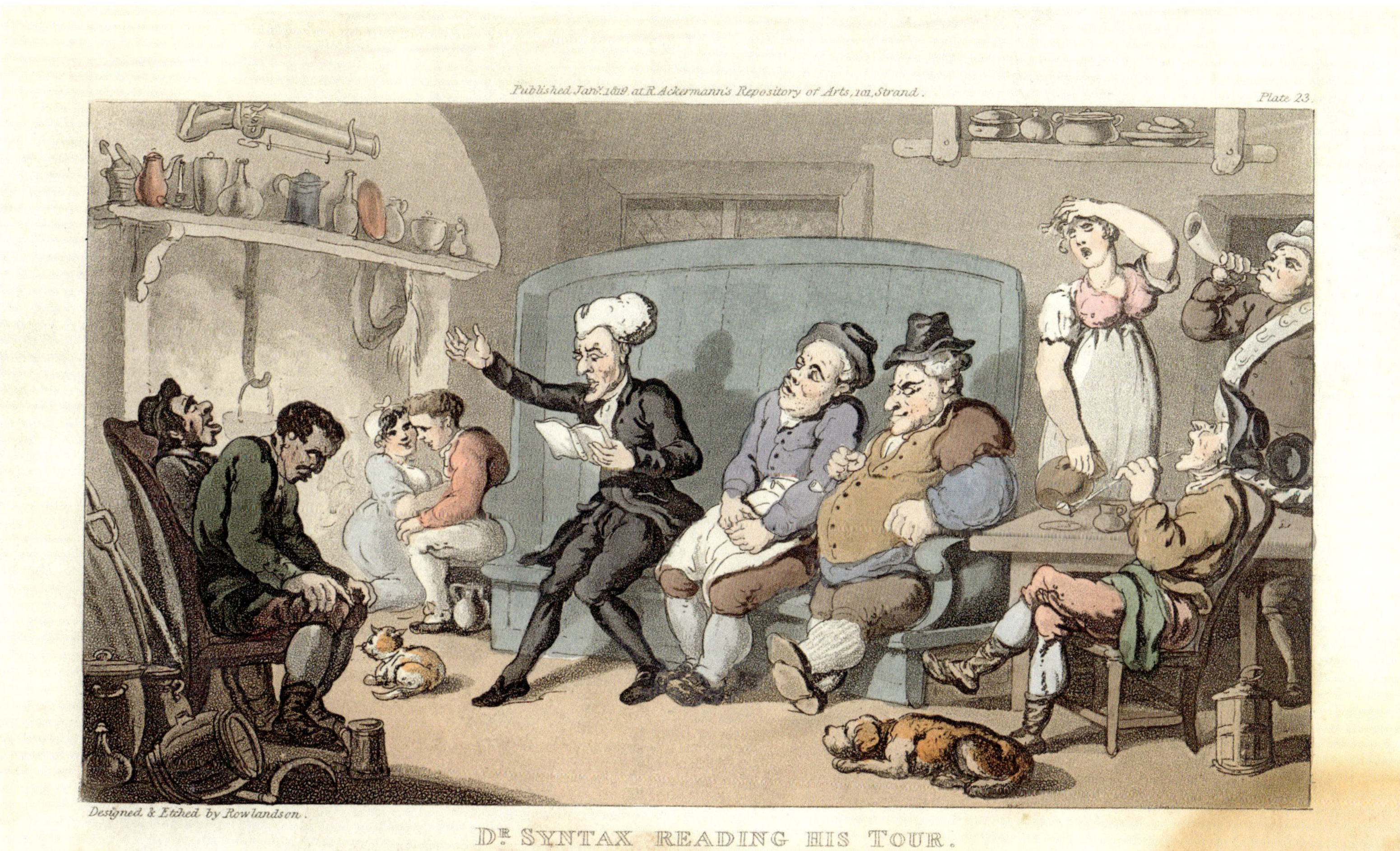


PLATE 102

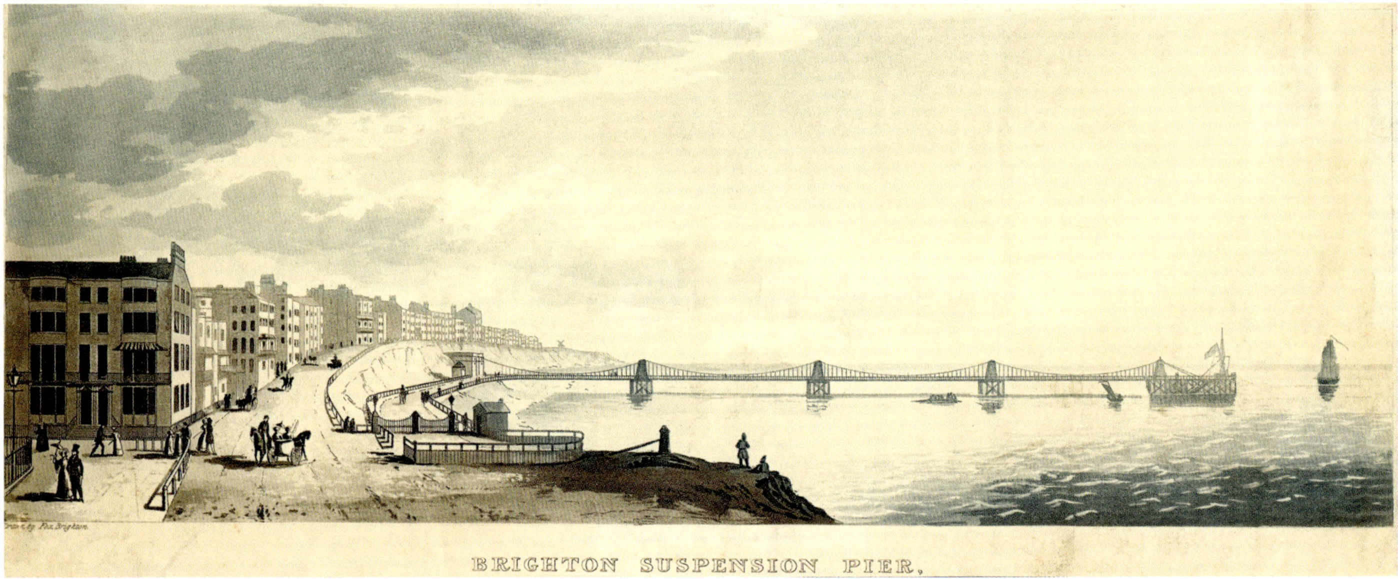


PLATE 103

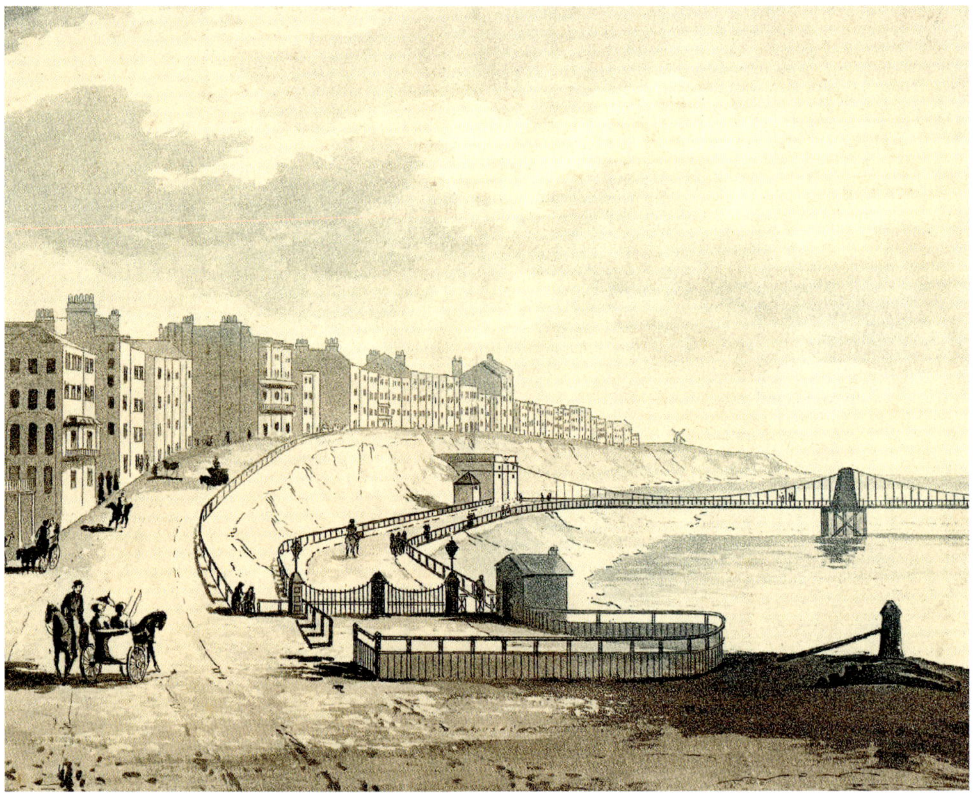

PLATES 103, 104 & DETAILS, AND 105

*Brighton Suspension Chain Pier.* Drawing by Edward Fox. The engraver is anonymous. Published by C. & R. Sicklemore, *c.*1825. Aquatint, 14 x 37.5 cm (5.5 x 14.7 in.)

These three prints were made from the same plate. The engraved detail is the same in all three. The difference is in the way they were printed and finished.

Plate 103 is shown in the state directly from the printing press without any hand-finishing. It was printed in blue and brown. In fact, it is not a particularly good specimen, which could explain why it was not finished. The sky is pale compared to the rich quality of plate 104, which was also printed in blue and

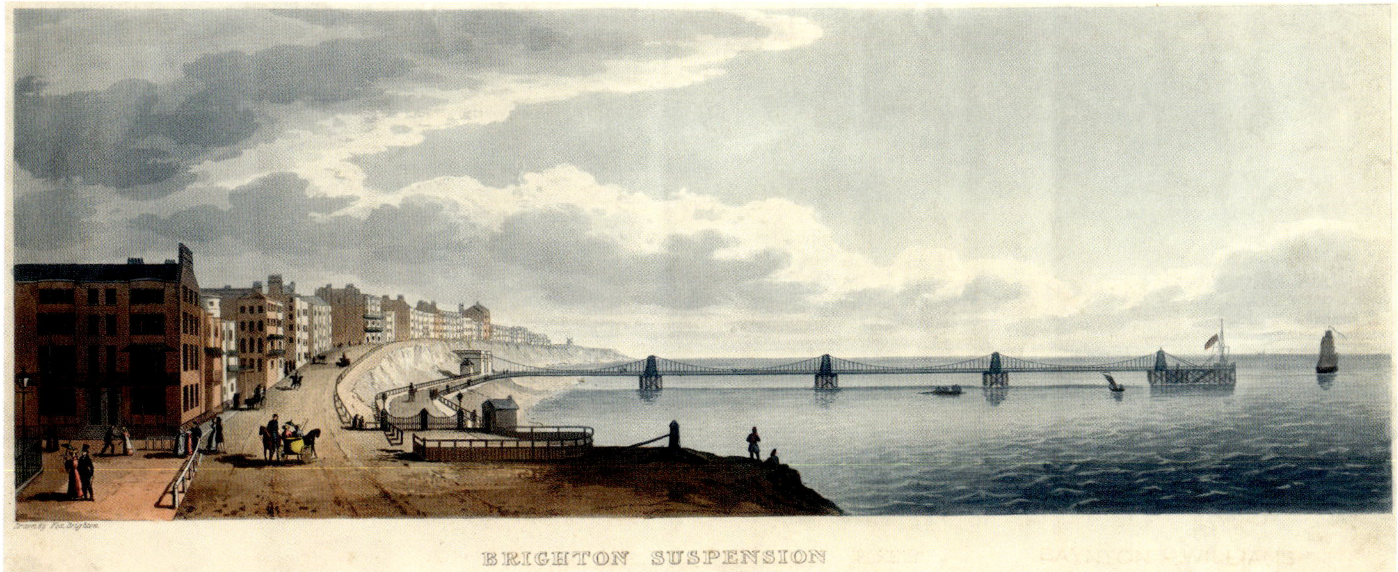


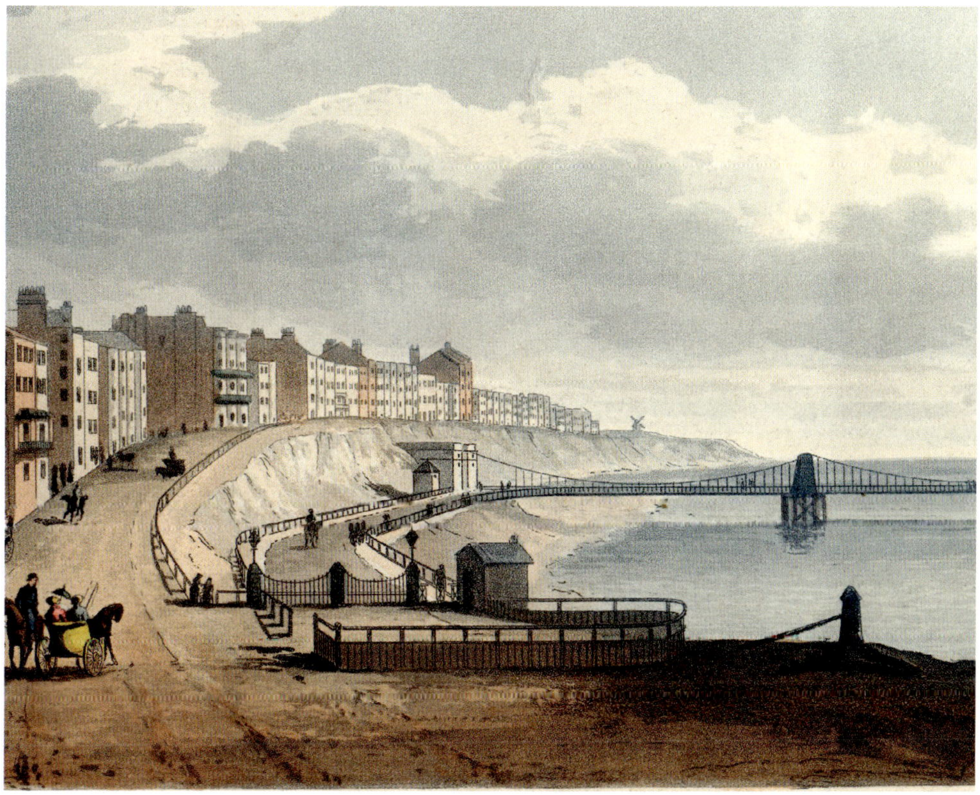

PLATE 104 AND DETAIL
Variant of *Brighton Suspension Chain Pier.*

brown, and then hand-finished. The added colour is mainly to the left side of the picture, to the buildings, the foreground and the people. To the right, the only additional colour is to the boats and the flag. The difference in the blue ink used is noticeable, with a far richer tone. Notice that the railings of the pier are blue, gradually turning to brown, giving emphasis to the perspective.

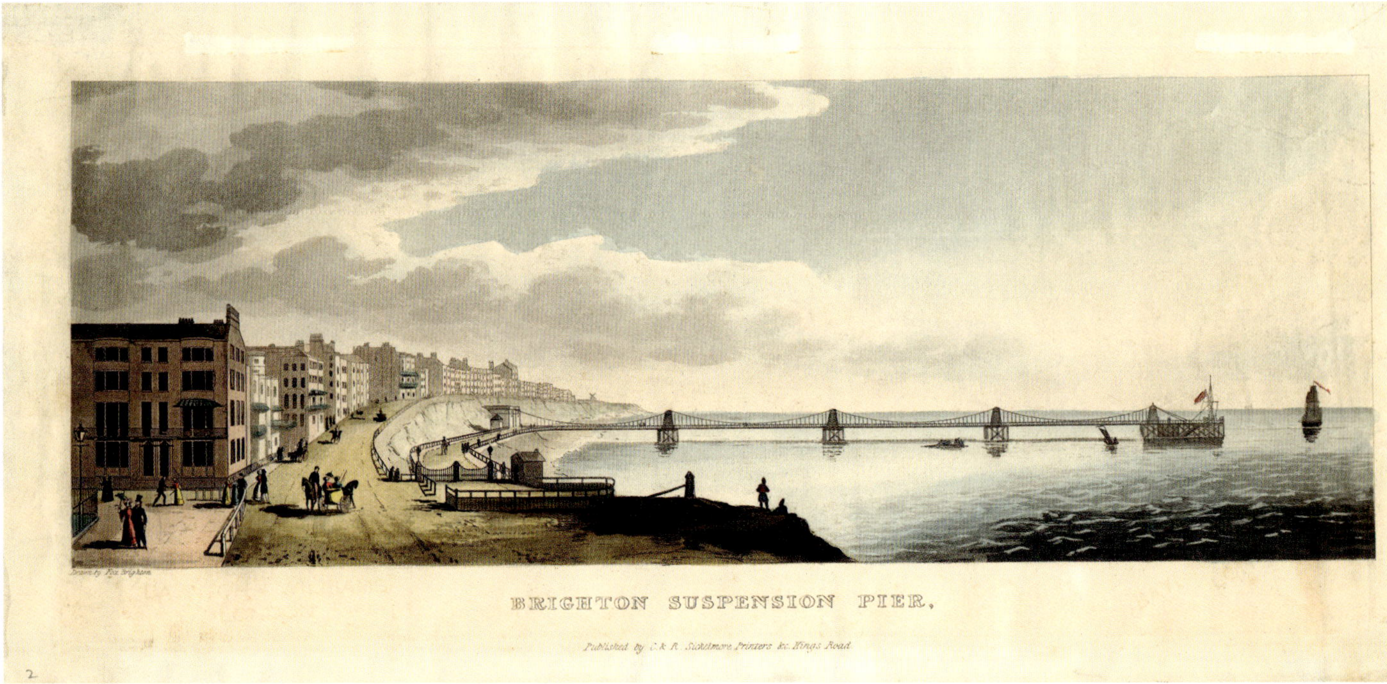

PLATE 105
Another variant of *Brighton Suspension Chain Pier.*

Plate 105 was printed entirely in black; all the colour was added by hand. The most noticeable difference can best be seen in the sky and the sea, the effect being light and delicate in the colour-printed examples, while in this print they are heavy masses, a dull effect, lacking perspective and giving the colourist no chance of giving the print the brilliance of plate 104. The picture becomes a dark stormy day.

In terms of value, plate 104 is worth three times as much as plate 105. Plate 103 is more of a novelty than a quality item, valued somewhere between the other two.

This view, from the Steine, appears to be one of the earliest views of the pier. The other prints of a similar date show more detail in the foreground.

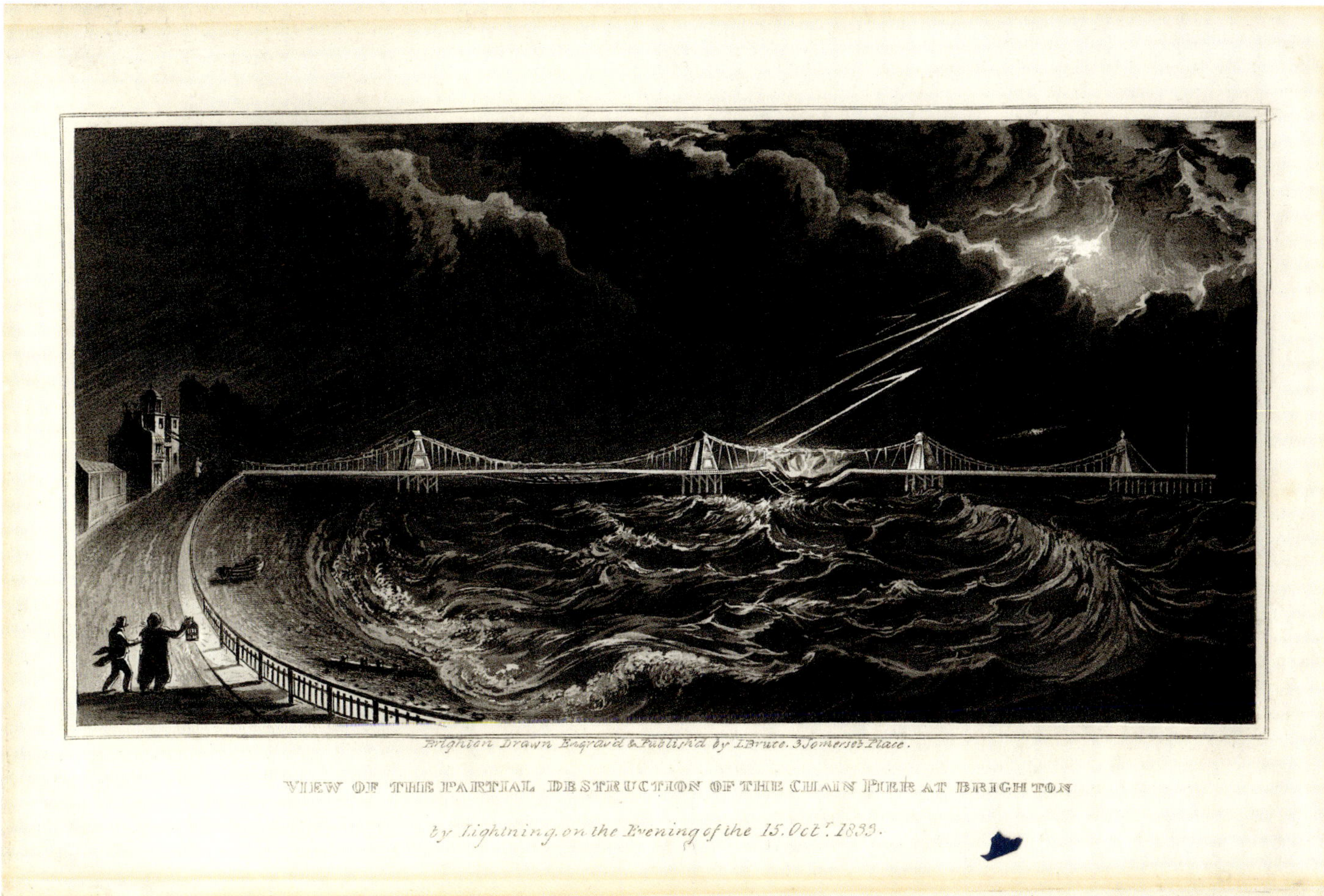


With the exception of the Pavilion, the Chain Pier drew the attention of artists more than any other Brighton subject. The storm was a major event in the chequered life of the Pier. Afterwards, it was restored, but was finally dismantled after another storm in 1896, when it was planned to build the Palace Pier.

The interest in this print is that it is so dark; the clouds are as black as any aquatint could be, like mezzotint. The clouds at the top right, the effect of the sea and the two men weathering the storm are well executed, making this a dramatic subject.

PLATE 106

*View of the Partial Destruction of the Chain Pier at Brighton by Lightning on the Evening of the 15. Octr. 1839.*
Aquatint drawn, engraved and published by J. Bruce, a prolific publisher of Brighton prints.
24 x 12.5 cm (9.4 x 5 in.).

# MIXED METHODS

It was quite common for intaglio prints to be engraved using more than one method. The obvious example is aquatint combined with etching, because it is not possible to make a fine line in pure aquatint. For this reason, I always think it pedantic to describe an aquatint as 'aquatint with etching'. In the same way, line engravers often used etching to do the initial outline detail of the work, before using the burin. In many of these cases it is only possible to detect the etching because there is an existing proof in etched outline only.

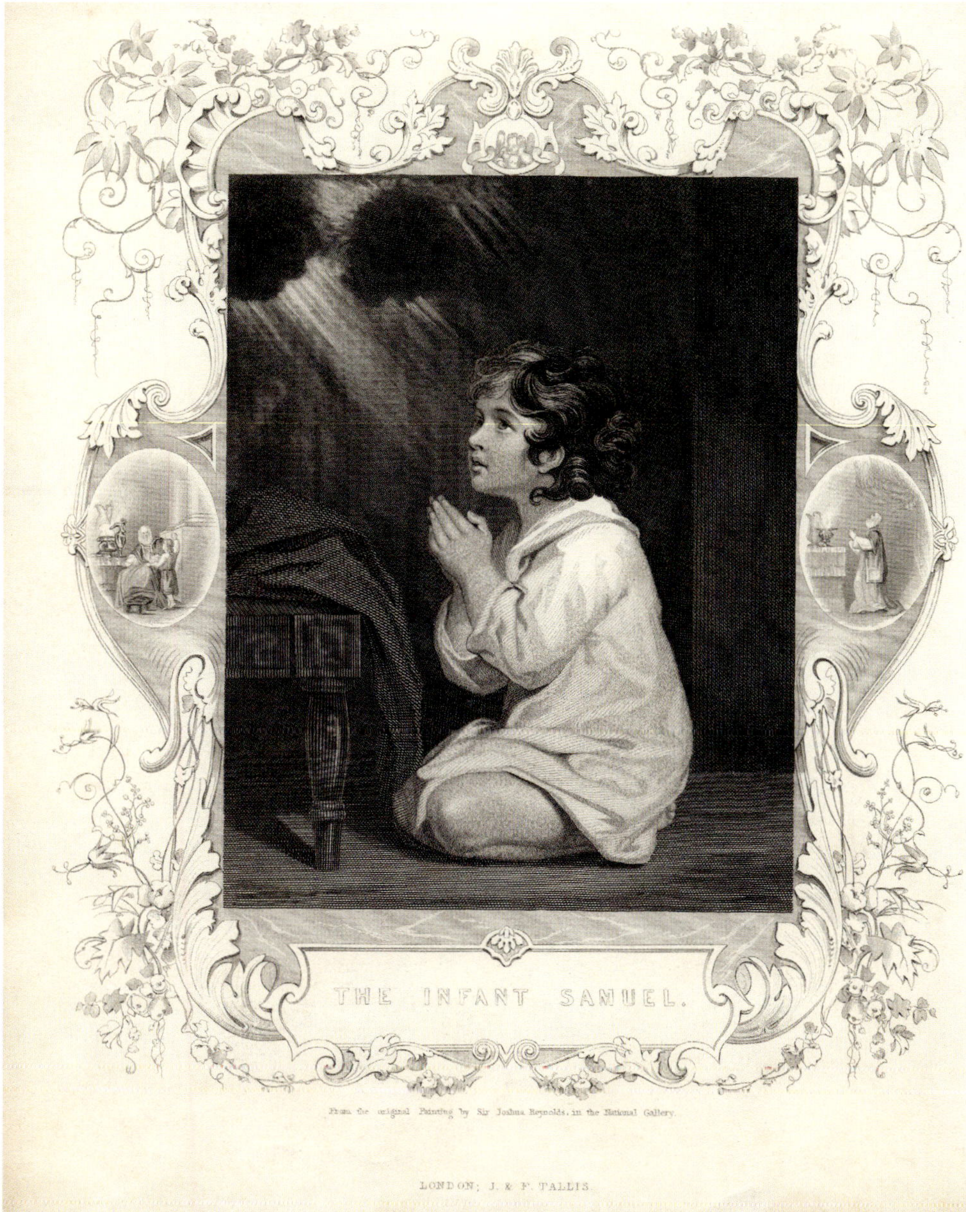


PLATE 107

*The Infant Samuel*, anon.
Anonymous engraving after Joshua Reynolds, one of a series of prints of paintings in the National Gallery.
Published by J. & F. Tallis, *c.*1850.
Mixed method, stipple and line engraving.
Engraved surface 22 x 16 cm (8.6 x 6.3 in.).

A contrast to the stipple engraving of Lady Morgan, plate 108, here most of the surface is engraved in line: the surrounding border, the background of the image, and the boy's hair. The face, the hands and the leg are all in stipple. The nightshirt might appear to be line as well, but in fact is stippled, with some line engraving added to the boy's right shoulder, where the shirt is shaded.

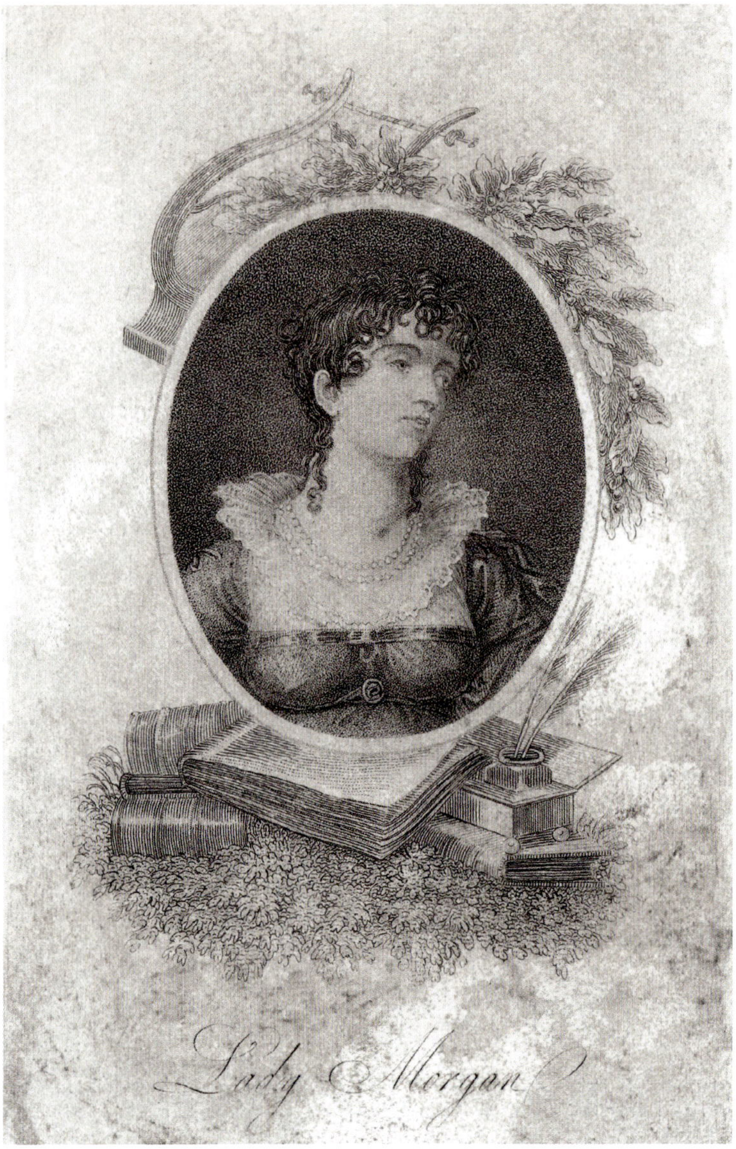


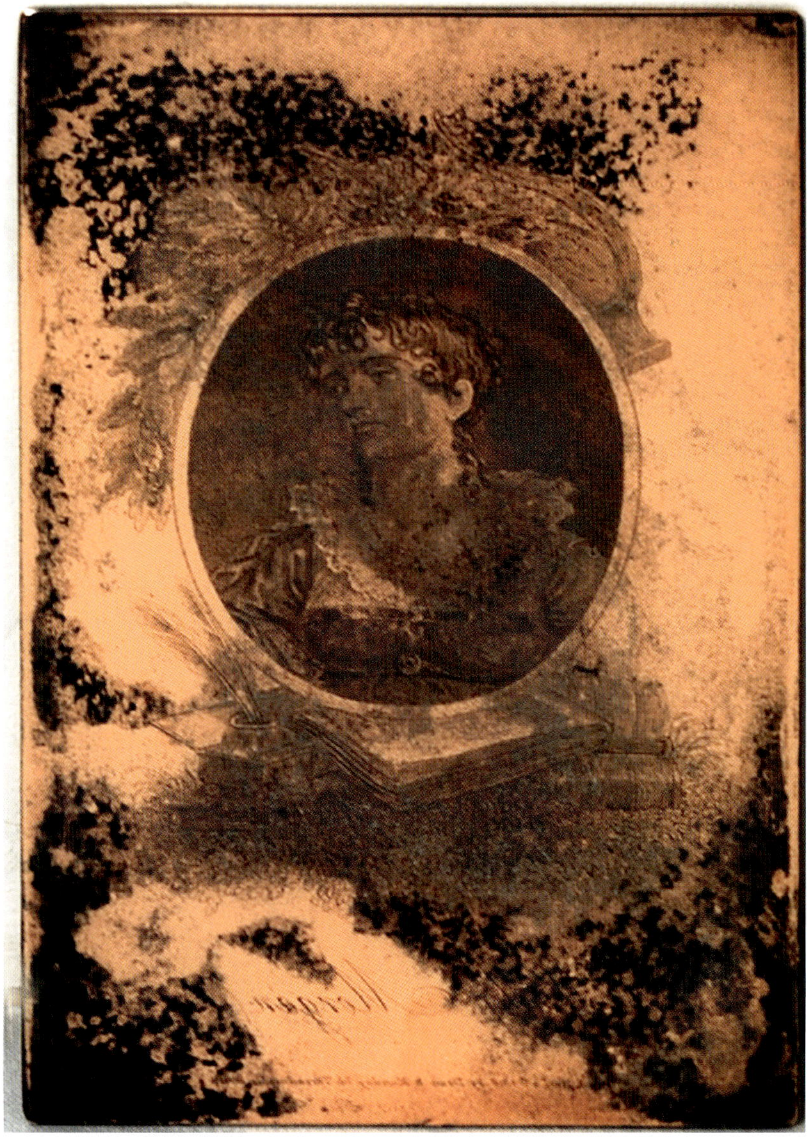

PLATE 108 AND THE PRINTING PLATE, PLATE 109
*Lady Morgan,* anon.
Published in 1816 as an illustration in *Ladies Monthly Museum* by Dean & Munday, Threadneedle St.
Mixed method: stipple and line engraving with etching plate, 19 x 11 cm (7.5 x 4.3 in.).

PLATE 109
The printing plate.

Another copper plate that has been steel-faced and has corroded. Again, the print was made recently by Susanne Smith.

The oval portrait is stipple engraving, the books and the harp are line-engraved, and the foliage at the top and bottom is etched. Where any two or more methods combine in one print the result is known as mixed method.

You do not need to know who Lady Morgan is to be able to guess she was an author. Surrounds like this were helpful in giving a few hints about the background of the subject, and add a lot of interest to prints. Her name is Sydney Morgan (c.1783–1859), daughter of Robert Owenson, and, in 1812, she married Sir Thomas Charles Morgan (1783–1843). Born in Dublin, she first worked as a governess before turning to literature; her reputation was made with *The Irish Girl* (1806). She was attacked in the *Quarterly Review* because of her patriotic opinions in her novels *O'Donnel* (1814) and *Florence M'Carthy* (1816). She wrote a book on France and another on Italy, travelling extensively in Europe.

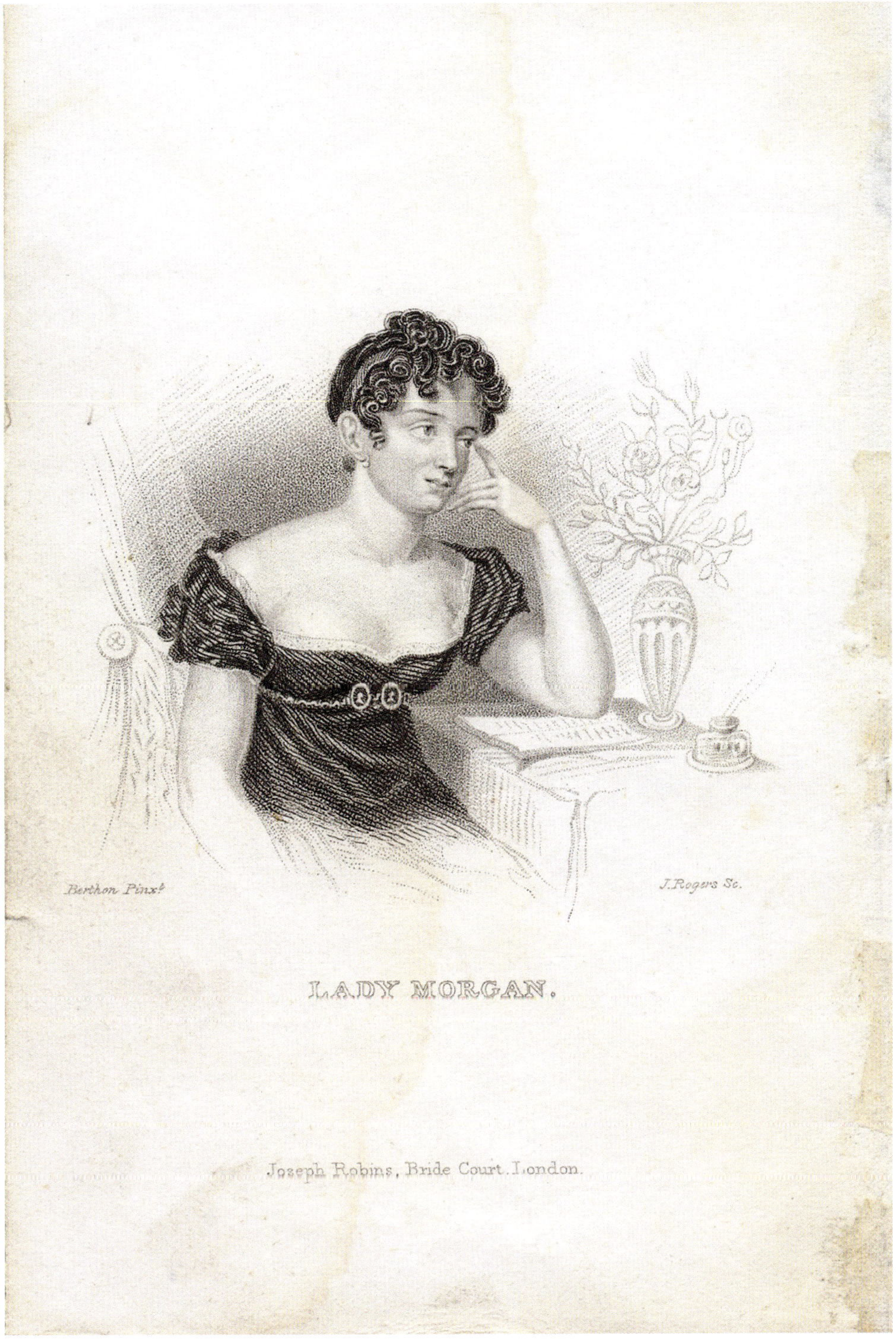


PLATE 110

*Lady Morgan.* Stipple engraving by John Rogers after Rene Theodore Berthon.
Published for the *Ladies' Pocket Magazine*, 1831.
Engraved surface 6 x 6.5 cm (2.4 x 2.5 in.).

A very similar portrait. In this case all the engraving is in stipple and the surround of the figure is very lightly engraved, which makes the subject stand out in the picture.

Berthon was French. The portrait could have been painted during Lady Morgan's visits to France in either 1821 or 1829.

Rogers was a well-known steel-plate engraver, and much of his work was done during the early 1830s, in his twenties.

# INTAGLIO COLOUR PRINTING

It is appropriate here to explain how mezzotints, stipple engravings and aquatints could be printed in colours.

There is an important difference between a print that was colour-printed and one that was hand-coloured. Unlike ceramics, for example, where hand-colouring is preferable, prints that are printed in colours are far more attractive, and have a greater brilliance and subtlety about them, not to mention a much greater value.

Colour printing mainly applies to stipple engravings, aquatints, mezzotints, and a few line engravings. Colour-printed etchings tend to be those which were printed at the end of the 19th century.

The method of printing in colour was laborious and expensive. It is important to understand that the same plate was used to make colour or monotone prints, and there was no need to make any sort of alteration to the plate. The difference was entirely in the inking of the plate. It was cheaper to produce monotone prints and then have them coloured by hand, and it was actually quicker, but the result was not nearly so effective.

Unlike modern printing, where each colour is printed from a separate plate, the method of colour printing in the late 18th century up to about 1850, was to apply all the coloured inks to the plate at once, so the plate goes into the printing press only once. The thick oily inks were slow to dry, so there was no particular rush to complete the inking. Extreme care had to be taken to ensure that the inks were correctly applied. Unlike painting, the printer did not have to tone the colours; the engraving did that for him, on the same principle as inking a monotone plate: the deeper the engraving the more ink lies in it. The colour of the ink does not alter the principle.

The ink had to be rubbed into the plate, leaving the surface clean, but in colour printing the difference was that the printer was applying inks to smaller areas, vastly more difficult than applying a single colour to the plate. To ink small areas, he used a small bundle of cloth attached to a stick, like a paintbrush, which was known as a 'doll', derived from the French 'à la poupée'. The printer had to take infinite care that one colour did not spread into another. On close examination there is sometimes some sign of spreading, but certainly not often. The temptation would be to use minimal quantities of ink, but this produced an inferior print, a poor impression. Once the inking was complete a print could be taken. And once the print had been taken the whole process of inking the plate had to be repeated before another print could be made. Anything that was as complicated as Boydell's *Scene from Shakespeare* (plates 80 & 81, pages 112-13) would require a day to produce one print. Most colour-printed prints are not so large or so complicated. Often the finest detail, like a person's lips, would be coloured by hand.

Many aquatints were printed in two or three colours with the rest of the colours added by hand. The printed colours were usually the large areas, sky and foregrounds in particular. Smaller detail, like clothes, were hand-coloured. Fox's *Brighton Suspension Pier,* plates 103–105 provides a good example.

The customary manner of description is to use 'colour' when a print is printed in colour, and 'coloured' when a print is hand-coloured. So 'colour stipple' means that it was printed in several colours; 'coloured stipple' means that it was printed in monotone and the colour was added by hand. There is, sometimes, some difficulty in detecting whether a print is colour-printed or hand-coloured. For the purpose of explanation, it is easiest to describe stipple engraving. Close examination of a particular detail, usually a face is the best, will show a multiplicity of dot. If the dots are black ink only, these dots are obviously going to remain black if the print is hand-coloured, whereas in a colour print the dots in the face will be flesh-coloured. As well as the two examples of *Scenes from Shakespeare* (plates 80 & 81, pages 112-13), plate 82 (page 111) stresses what happens when a monotone print is hand-coloured.

All this may seem complicated, a finer point for connoisseurs, but the colour-printed *Scene from Shakespeare* has a value five times that of the black & white example, so it is worth knowing the difference.

# LITHOGRAPHY

The discovery and exact history of most printing methods is somewhat vague. However, the development of the system of lithography is fully documented by the man who invented it, Alois Senefelder. His book on the subject was translated into English and published in 1819 by Rudolph Ackermann, who was always keen to explore the potential of modern inventions. Ackermann played a leading role in introducing lithography.

Senefelder initially followed his father's footsteps and became an actor, though without the same success. He turned his hand to writing plays. The first of these was a financial success, but he struggled to fund the cost of printing the second play, so he worked with the printer to reduce costs and to speed up the printing production, eventually only just recouping his money. The experience increased his interest in printing, and he set about trying to find a cheaper and more efficient method of printing typeset and music scores, and was not concerned with illustrations at this point.

In around 1790 he began to experiment with variations of the traditional printing methods, using wood and metals. He admits to failing in the attempt to engrave, and it appears he quickly found that porous stone had strong possibilities. He had numerous failures and disappointments before he perfected the basics of his method in 1798. Nor was the idea an instant success: lithographs made before 1820 are few and far between.

The process of lithography is simple and means that many artists can produce their own prints. The lithographer begins with a perfectly flat porous stone of a suitable size for the eventual print, and anything from 3 to 10 cm thick. It has to be thick enough not to be brittle, but light enough to handle reasonably easily, so it was certainly important not to use a stone any larger than it had to be. The picture, or lettering, or music score or whatever, is drawn onto the stone using an oily substance like an ink, in much the same way as an artist draws on paper with a crayon. So far it is straightforward. Now comes the technical part. The stone is then thoroughly dampened. The parts of the stone that have been drawn upon with the oily substance reject the water, the principle being that oil is incompatible with water. The oily ink on the stone remains unaffected. Next, the stone is inked with a roller. Printer's ink is another oily substance, and when the ink roller crosses the stone the chemical reaction is reversed. The ink adheres to the oily substance on the stone but the damp parts of the stone reject the ink. Once the whole of the stone has been evenly inked, it is ready to be printed.

The simply drawn illustration of the church from Ackermann's *Repository of Arts* was printed in exactly this manner. Compared to some of the later work, it is, perhaps, a little crude, but it has the appearance of a sketch drawn with a soft pencil. The method of printing was simple too. Inking a small stone like this would take a few seconds compared to the inking of an intaglio plate of similar size and of similar detail, which would take several minutes.

At the time of the discovery of lithography, there was concern among those who had mastered intaglio engraving that their craft was in jeopardy. A lobby resulted in a heavy tax being put on imported stone, and that is a plausible reason for the length of time that lithography took to come into general use in England. Intaglio engravers were right to worry about their futures. Once lithography had taken a stronghold, the intaglio printing methods began to fade away.

After 1820, lithography quickly developed, particularly in England and France.

The illustration (plate 123, page 164) of Harding's title page for *Sketches at Home and Abroad* is far from typical of the quality of the views in the series, perhaps intended as a stab at humour, or, as I see it, to point out the plight of a touring artist. Harding and Hullmandel had every reason to be pleased with the result of the views in the series. It is clear that at this time their friendship and common interest in lithography resulted in quick development. The friendship seems later to have foundered, however, probably because the two men were not able to share the credit for the development of lithography. They are both reported individually as the inventor of tinted lithography. In the preface to Harding's last work, *Picturesque Selections,* 1861, Harding states that he had spent his working life developing lithography to look like his drawings, and, with this series, he had achieved his ambition. There is, however, no recognition of his one-time collaborator, Hullmandel, suggesting that they may not have parted on the best of terms. *Sketches at Home and Abroad* is historically important. It was the first of the tinted lithograph works, and started a spate of fine lithograph-illustrated books. Shotter Boys, Samuel Prout and David Roberts are just three of the other names that spring to mind, all producing magnificent collections of lithographs.

## TRANSFER LITHOGRAPHS

In the middle of the 19th century, a discovery was made that simplified and reduced the time and cost of printing from plates. Transfer lithography is a combination of engraving and lithography. Because fine definition of engraving could not be achieved with pure lithography, the combination could work very well, especially for printing maps, in which lettering, like place names, had to be clearly legible.

The procedure is to print from the engraved plate in the normal way except that the print is made on a special transfer paper. While the ink is still wet, the transfer paper is laid over the lithograph stone, and the ink is transferred onto the stone. The stone can then be used to print as in normal lithography, and this was easier and faster than intaglio printing. Another benefit is that the metal plate does not wear. If an alteration needs to be made, as would often happen with maps, this could be done to the metal plate, and another transfer made onto the lithograph stone.

Detection can be difficult. The printing tends not to be quite as clear as intaglio printing, and is likely to be very slightly blurred compared to an engraved line. There will not be a plate mark.

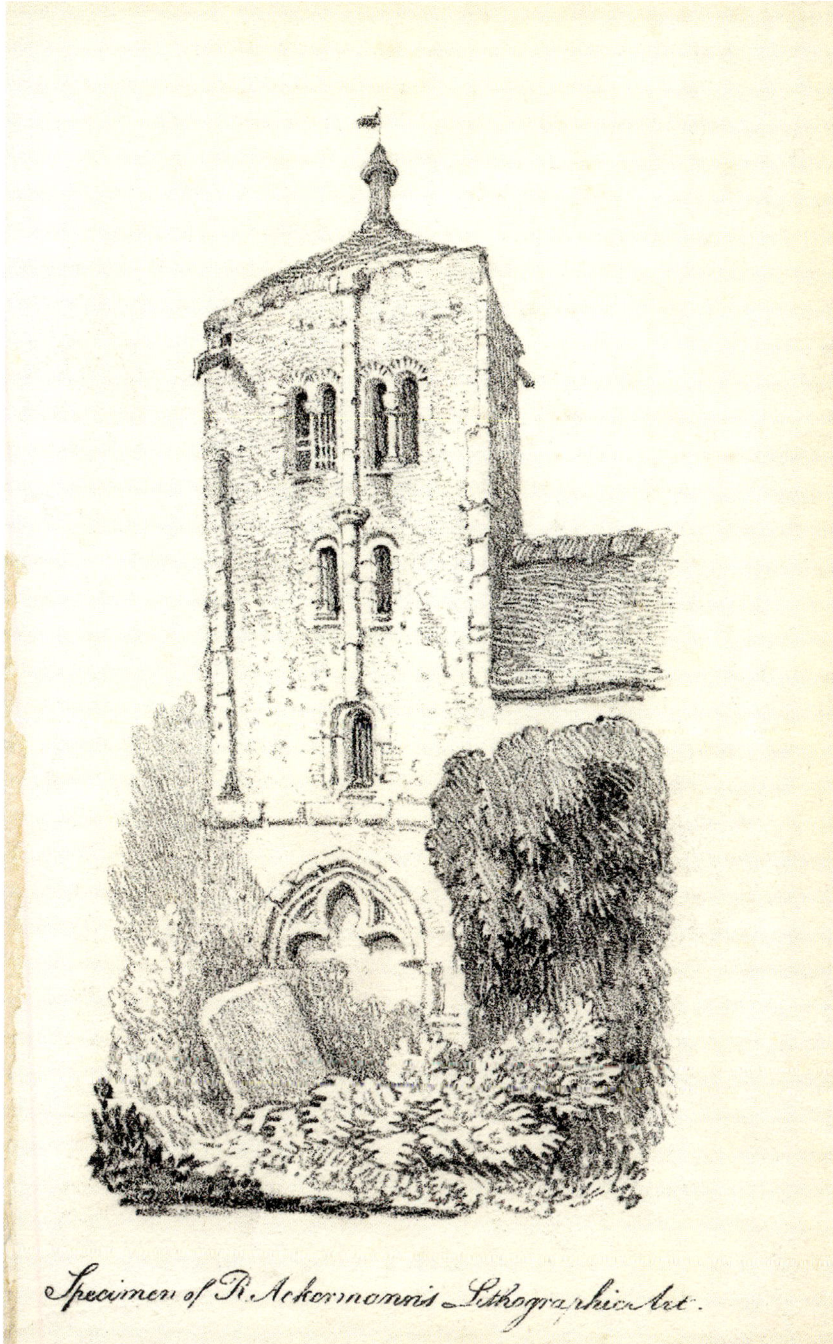


Extract from Ackermann's *Repository of Arts*, an extraordinary magazine which was published in monthly parts from 1809 to 1828 and covered a wide range of topical subjects. Ackermann installed his own lithographic press in 1817, and this is one of the first prints he produced – a very simple drawing. Ackermann presented five similar prints promoting the introduction of the art, and he was largely responsible for spreading the popularity of the art in Britain. Although Ackermann used a wide variety of printing methods for the illustrations, which were all of high quality, most of them are intaglio, either etched, line or aquatint.

PLATE 111
Specimen of R. Ackermann's *Lithographic Art,* 1817.
21 x 11 cm (8.3 x 4.3 in.).

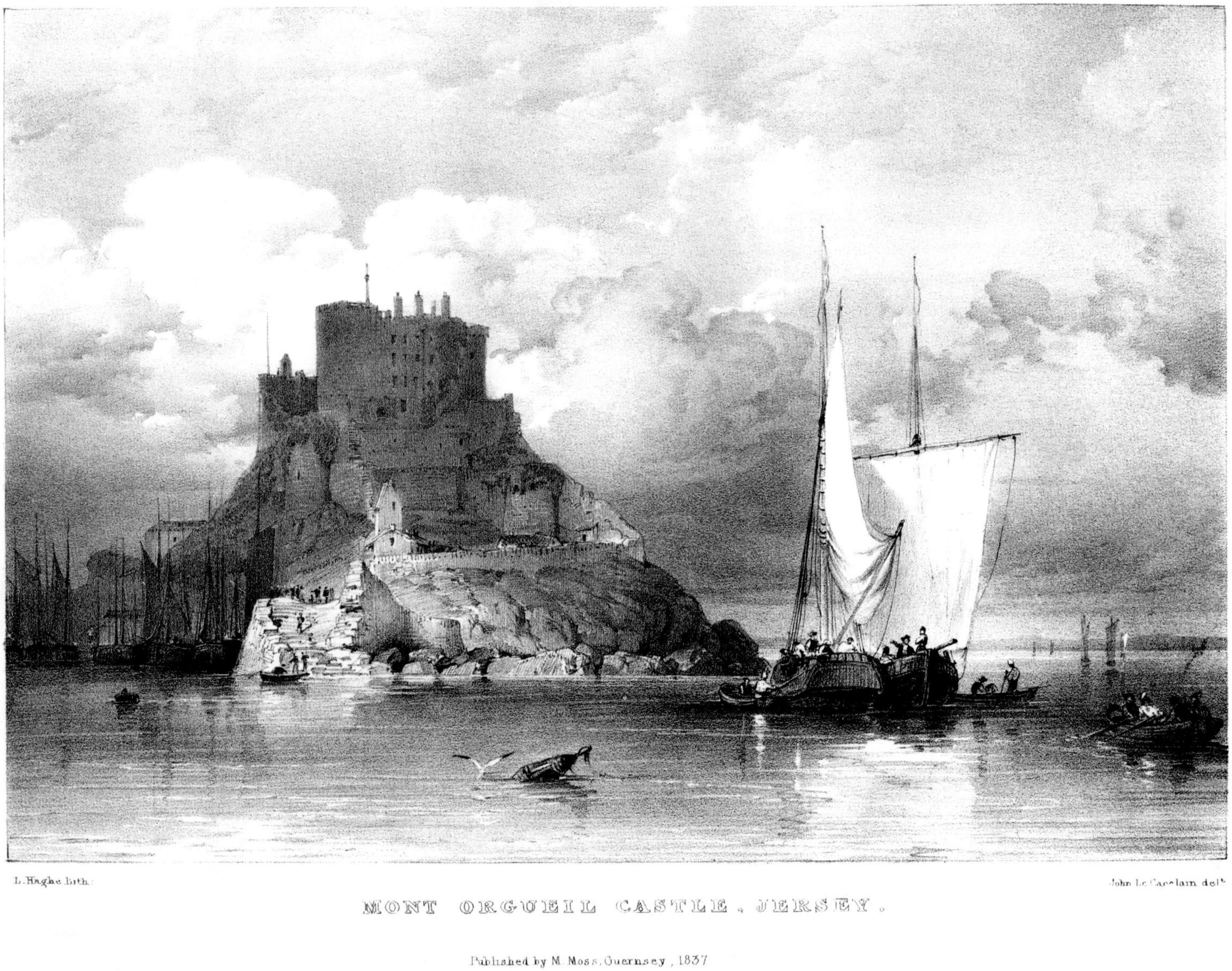


PLATE 112
*Mont Orgueil Castle, Jersey,* lithographed by Louis Haghe from a drawing by John Le Capelain, 1837.
From a series of the Channel Islands published by Mathew Moss.
Image: 17.5 x 24.5 cm (6.9 x 9.6 in.).

Lithography was well suited to topographical prints; this one has good contrasts of light and shade, as well as good perspective. The prints are the best topographical subjects of the islands, although the artist, John Le Capelain, is perhaps better known for the series of prints that were made to commemorate the visit of Queen Victoria in 1846, in whose scenes Le Capelain had to include numerous people. This print has more animation in it than most of the others in the series, which always makes the subject more interesting, particularly when the people are in action.

Moss appears to have sold the prints as separate publications and not bound sets, although there are bound collections put together at random – probably selections of the views made by the purchasers to suit their own interests or requirements.

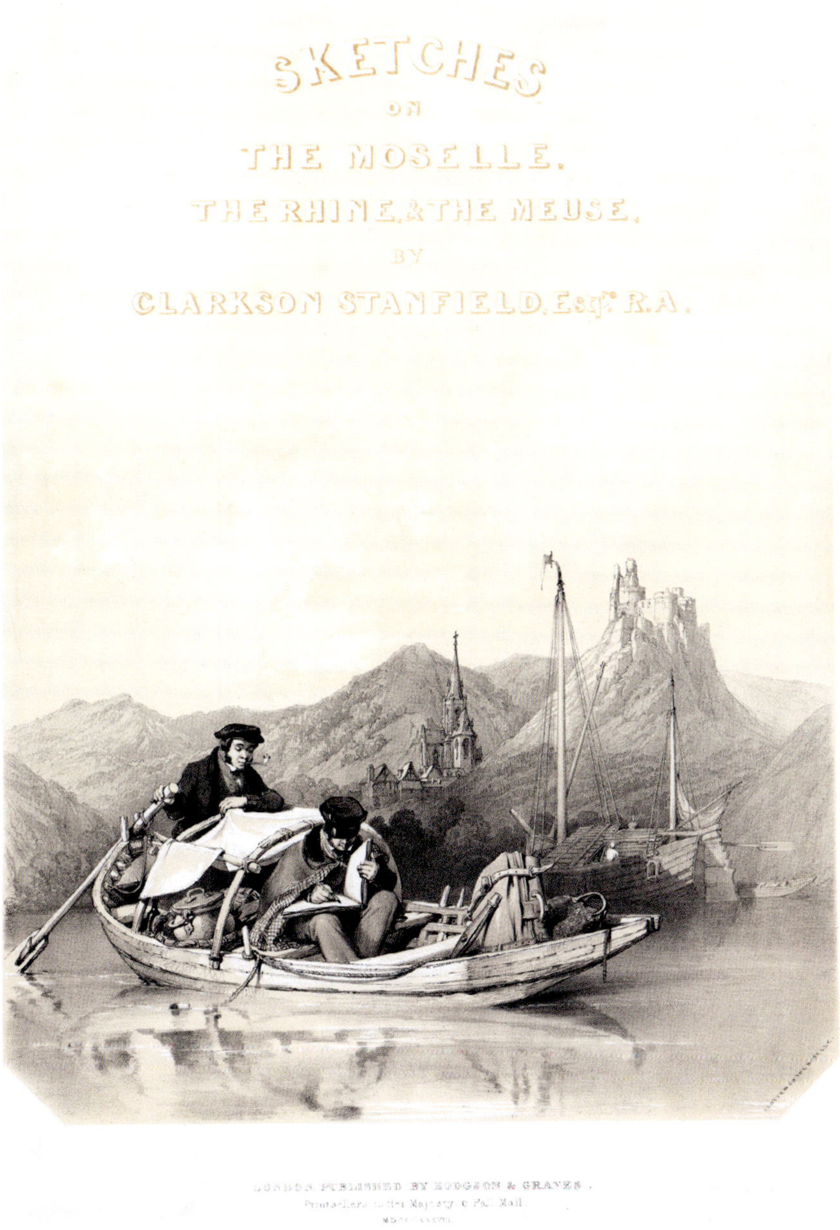


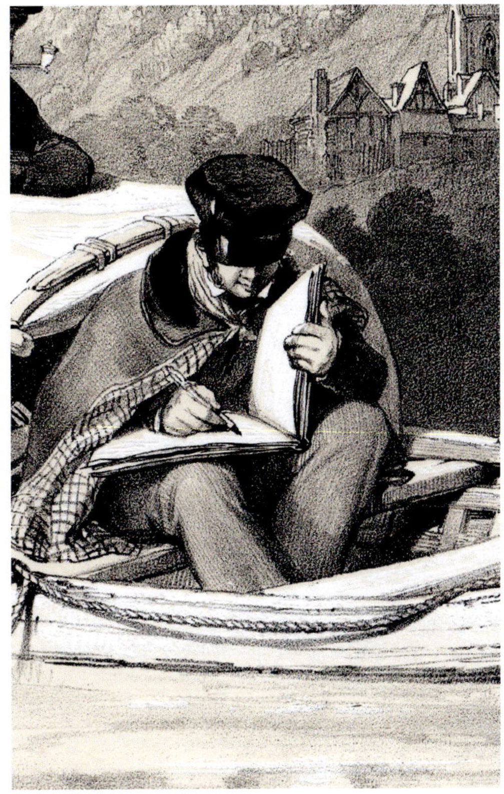

PLATE 113 & DETAIL.
*Clotton on the Moselle*, lithograph by Louis Haghe after Clarkson Stanfield R.A., the celebrated painter of landscapes and marine subjects.
The print is the title page of a series titled *Sketches on the Moselle, the Rhine and the Meuse*, published in London by Hodgson and Graves in 1838. Usually the name of the lithographer appears on the print; Haghe is credited only in the list of plates.
Tinted lithograph,
39 x 28 cm (15.3 x 11 in.).

In this print Stanfield is shown at work during his travels, his baggage beside him, and watched by a critical boatman.

Technically, this is described as a tinted lithograph, because there are added tints printed with separate printing stones. Cream is the main background colour, with a light brown for the outline to the title letters and, most particularly, a thick white to highlight the drawing book, the canopy, the structure of the boat and the reflections on the water.

The bound set of 26 plates, including this title, was published for £4. 4shillings, or £10. 10shillings coloured and mounted. In this case mounted means that the print is laid on thick card, trimmed to the image, the printed title and credits removed, giving the impression of a watercolour.

PLATE 114

*Hampton Church,* lithograph by N.O. Green, published by G. Rowney, *c.*1850.
Tinted lithograph, 33 x 25 cm (13 x 9.8 in.).

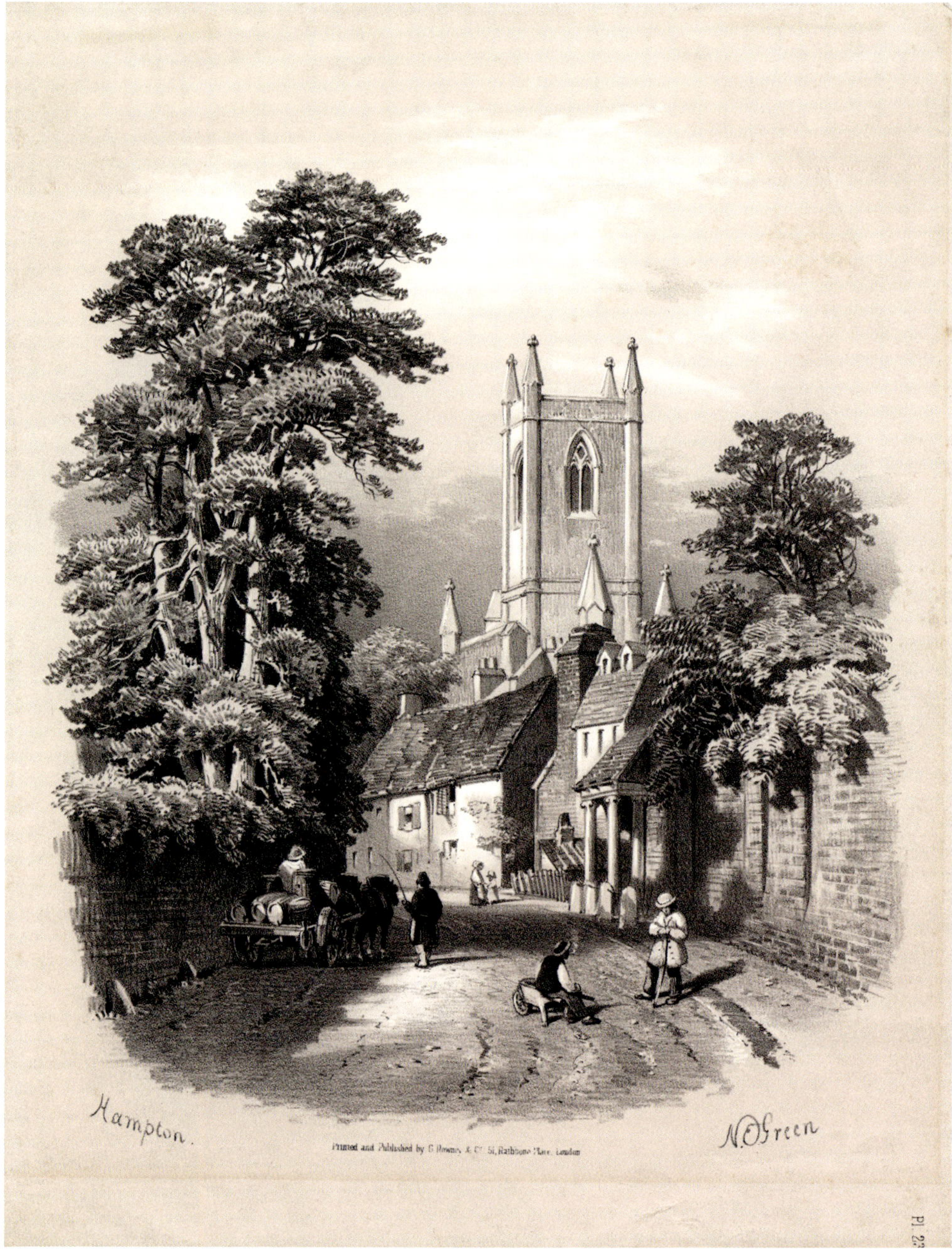


The system here is similar to the Stanfield print of the Moselle, but the result is quite different. The grey tinted colour might be taken to be a coloured paper, but the tint was printed with a separate stone, onto white paper. By leaving areas so that the white of the paper shows, the lithographer has created the effect of whitened highlights. The master of this technique was Harding, as we see in the next illustration.

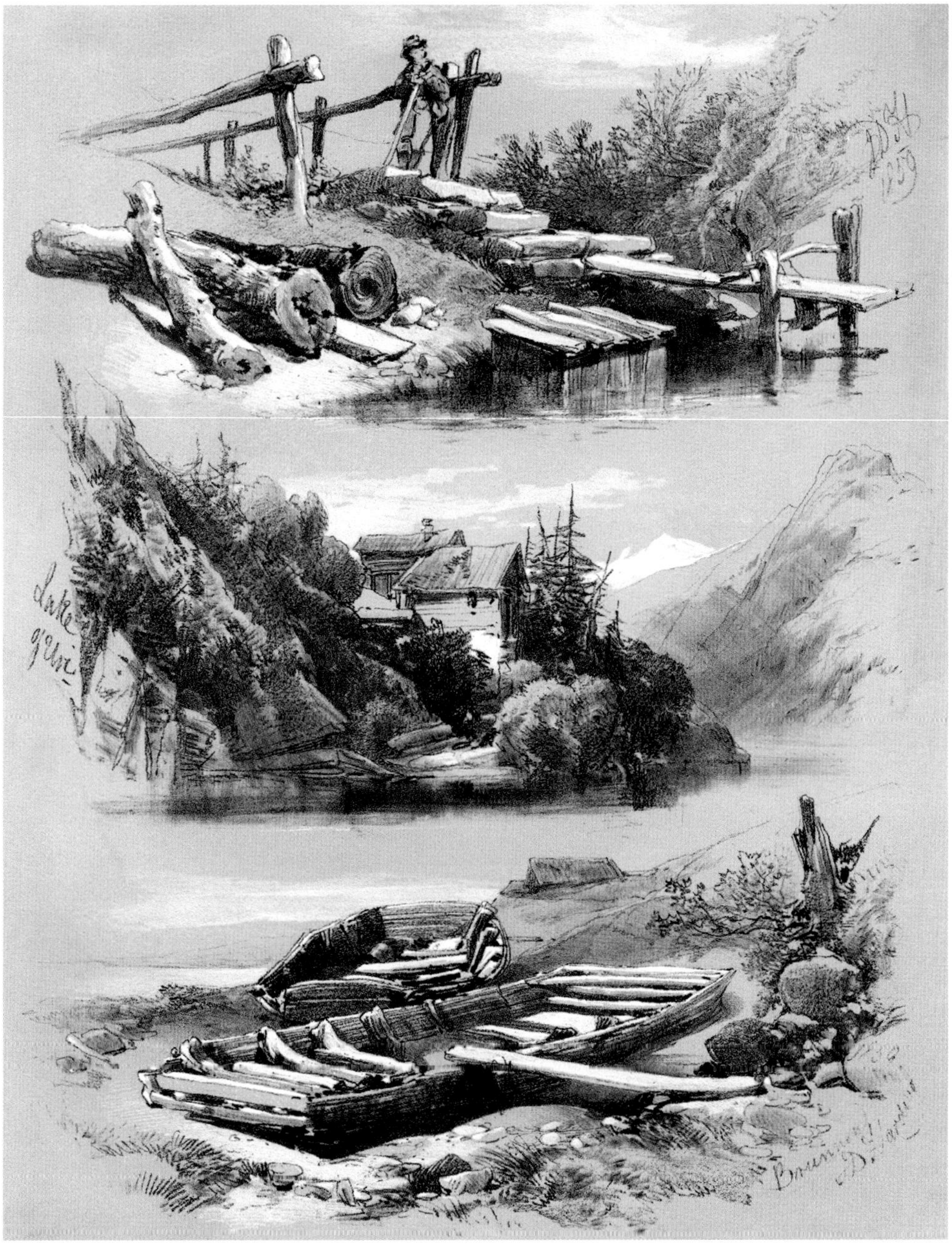

PLATE 115

*Swiss Scenery for Picturesque Selections,* tinted lithograph by James Duffield Harding, for the series *Picturesque Selections,* published in 1861, 25 years after *Sketches at Home and Abroad.*
38 x 27 cm (15 x 10.6 in.).

These three scenes are all of Switzerland. The top is untitled, the centre is of Lake Uri, and the bottom is Brunnen. As usual, Harding signed with his initials and a date, in this case 1859.

In the preface to the portfolio, Harding states that he had striven all his working life to perfect his lithography, and with this series he had achieved his ambition of producing lithographs that were faithful copies of his drawings. Unfortunately, it was to be his last work; he died in 1863. It seems that his relationship with his collaborator Hullmandel had reached a low ebb; there is no mention of the fact that the two men had spent so long in perfecting the art of tinted lithographs. These two and Louis Haghe were the main people responsible for the development of lithography in Britain.

The prints in the *Picturesque Selections* series are mainly sketches like these unrecognisable places. They are a complete contrast to the highly detailed townscapes that were shown in *Sketches at Home and Abroad.* Harding's technique is interesting. Like the previous illustration, the paper used is white and has a grain to it. The grey tint is printed. Even close up, the white highlights look exactly like Chinese white, and are actually slightly embossed into the paper, making the white stand out in relief. Even the grey tint shows through the white in places. The distant snow-capped mountain in the view of Lake Uri looks just as though it has been added with a brush. The top and the bottom views show moon reflections brilliantly.

And finally, the paper is laid onto thicker card, just as drawings often were at this date.

PLATE 115 DETAIL

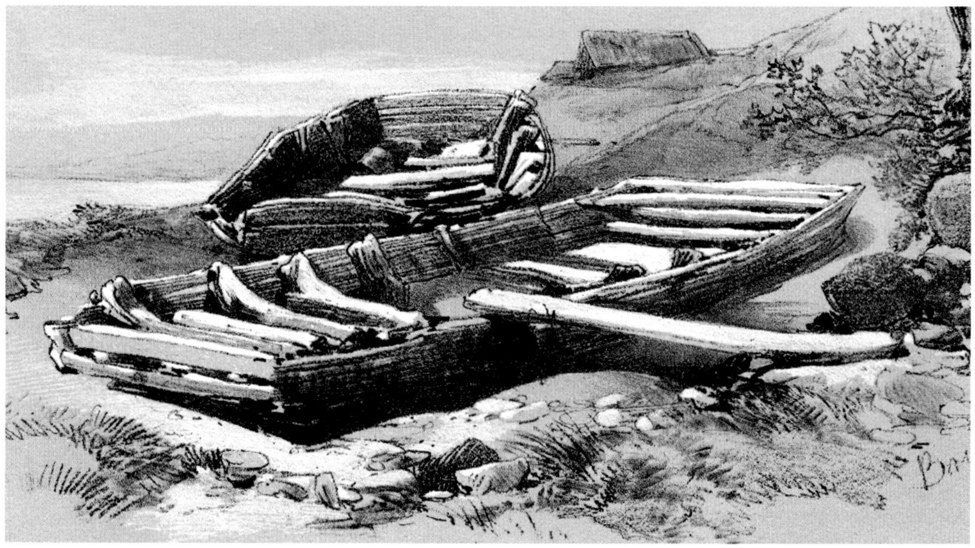

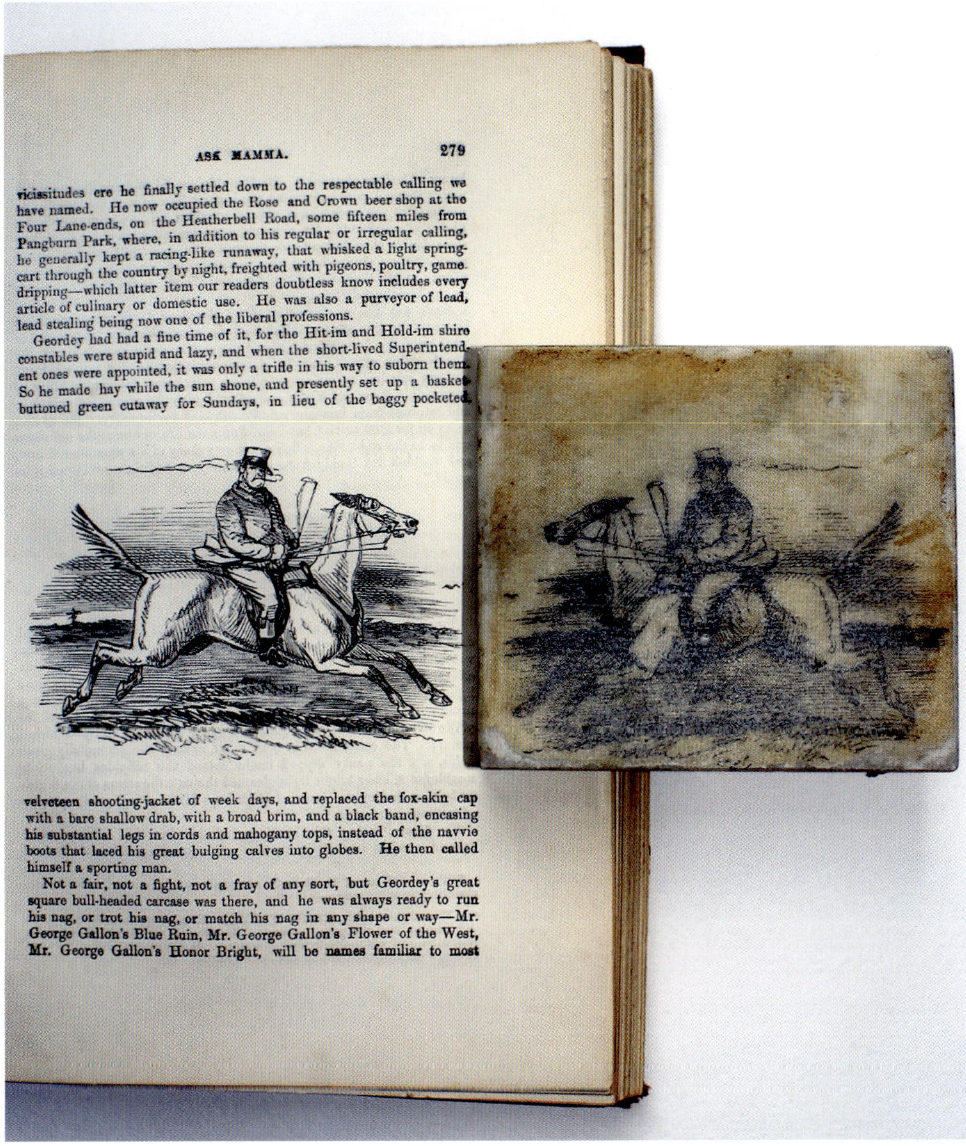


PLATE 116 & 117

Lithograph stone (with the book); an illustration from *Ask Mama,* by John Leech, 1858.
8.5 x 9.5 cm (3.3 x 3.7 in.).

An illustration by John Leech combined with the text for Robert Smith Surtees's *Ask Mama,* 1858. The print is not titled, which is customary for illustrated novels. In the list of plates the title is given as 'Mr Geordy Gallon'. But the strange thing is that the illustrations are described as woodcuts, which this is clearly not. There were probably some editions of *Ask Mama* where the illustrations were printed with transfer lithographs for simplicity. There is no difference between the book illustration and the lithograph stone: the two are identical in every line.

John Leech provided ideal illustrations for Surtees's later books, and the combination made the books extremely popular. Surtees was a very keen horseman, as good at describing sporting events as Leech was at drawing them. Strangely, Surtees did not like to see his name in print; the only one of his books to bear his name is *Horseman's Manual,* a general treatise on the laws relating to horses.

PLATE 118
Commercial lithographic printing stone. *c.*1880.

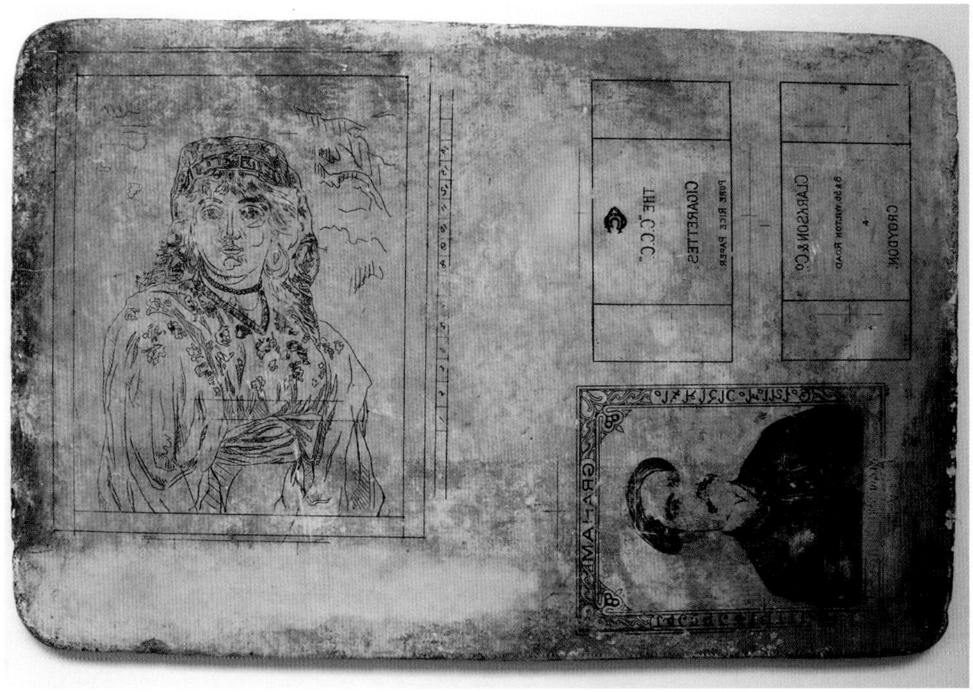

It appears that there are three separate items being printed from the stone, the cigarette packaging, the portrait of the woman, and the portrait of the man, both of whom could be of Turkish origin. The portrait of the man has 'Graham' written in the top border, and 'Manchester' in the bottom border, almost illegibly. Unfortunately, the stone has not been properly cared for, and has been scraped and chipped. The texture has the smoothness of polished marble. It is only 15 mm thick, less than half the usual thickness of a lithograph stone. This means that the stone is easier to use, being lighter, but it is also much more fragile and easily broken. The overall size is 46 x 30.5 cm. It was generously given to the Baynton-Williams Collection by Eric Morten, bookseller, of Didsbury, Greater Manchester, so it probably comes from a Manchester printers. It was in use in about 1880.

PLATES 119, 120 & 121
*Arundel Church,* drawn by Samuel Prout, lithographed by J.D. Harding, printed by Day & Son, 1844. This is one of a large series titled *The Baronial Halls and Picturesque Edifices of England.* 17 x 26 cm (6.7 x 10.2 in.).

Another example of how the same print appeared in various different guises. First, it was published as a plain lithograph and, shortly afterwards, as a tinted lithograph.

*119)* This was printed in black only. It is the earliest, printed in 1844. It is described as 'In Lithotint by J.D. Harding; Published by Chapman and Hall; from a Sketch by S. Prout'. Lithotint is a slight variant on normal lithography only in that the ground is laid with a brush instead of crayon or chalk. It was invented by Harding's compatriot, Charles Hullmandel. The word is confusing. Perhaps it was chosen as a parallel to aquatint. It should not be confused with tinted lithograph. Harding was a master of lithography, normally working on his own pictures.
*120)* A yellow tint is added. The names of Chapman & Hall and of Harding are removed. Day & Son become the printers.

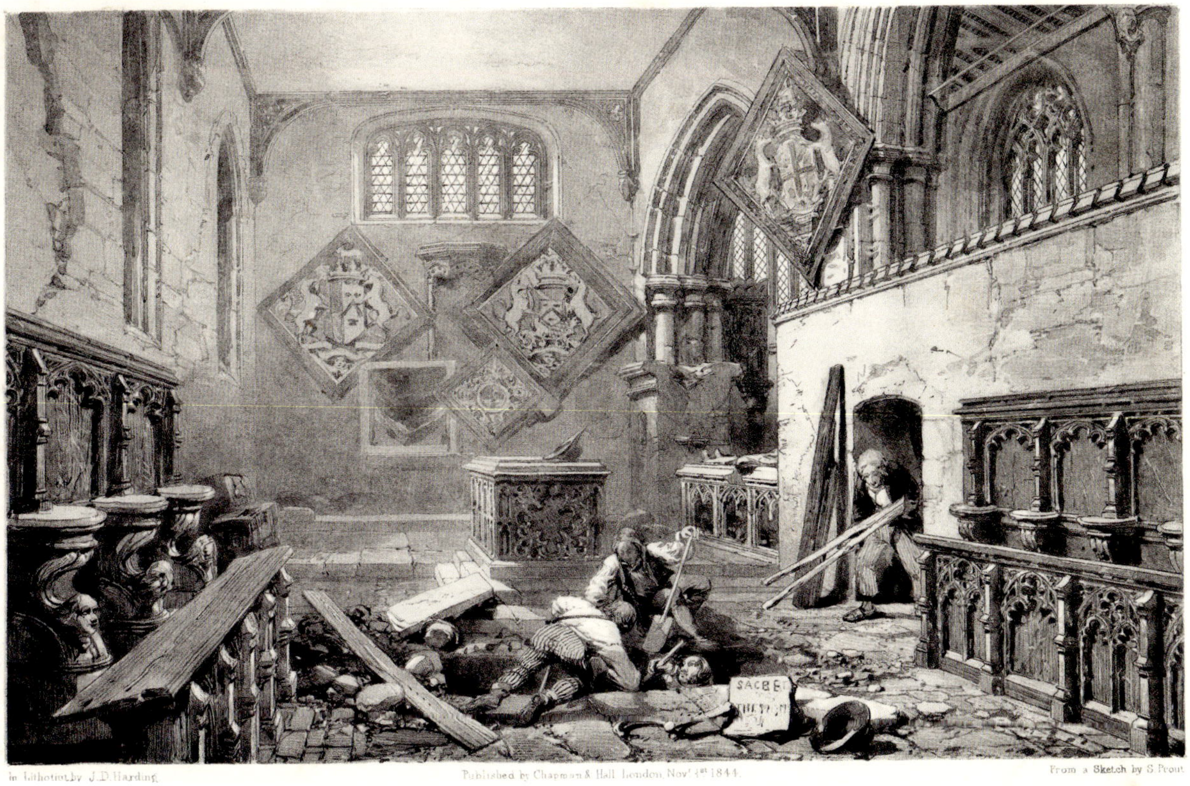


PLATE 119

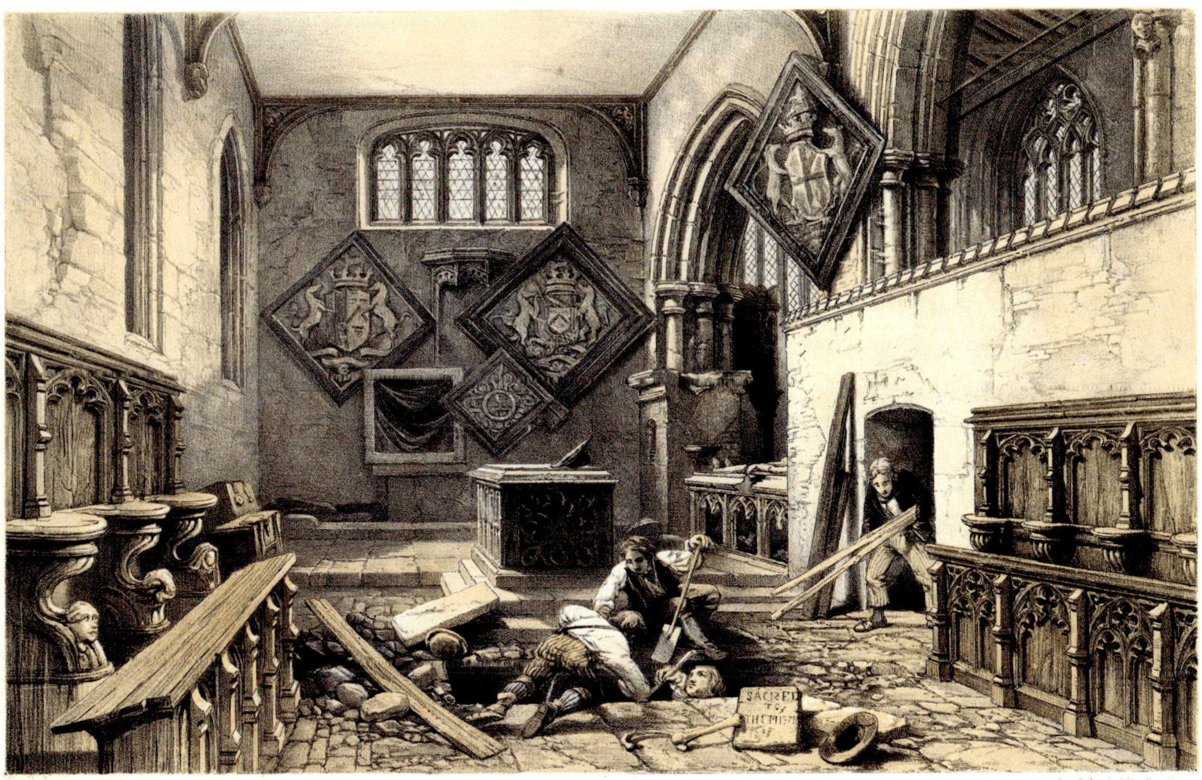


PLATE 120
Variant of *Arundel Church.*

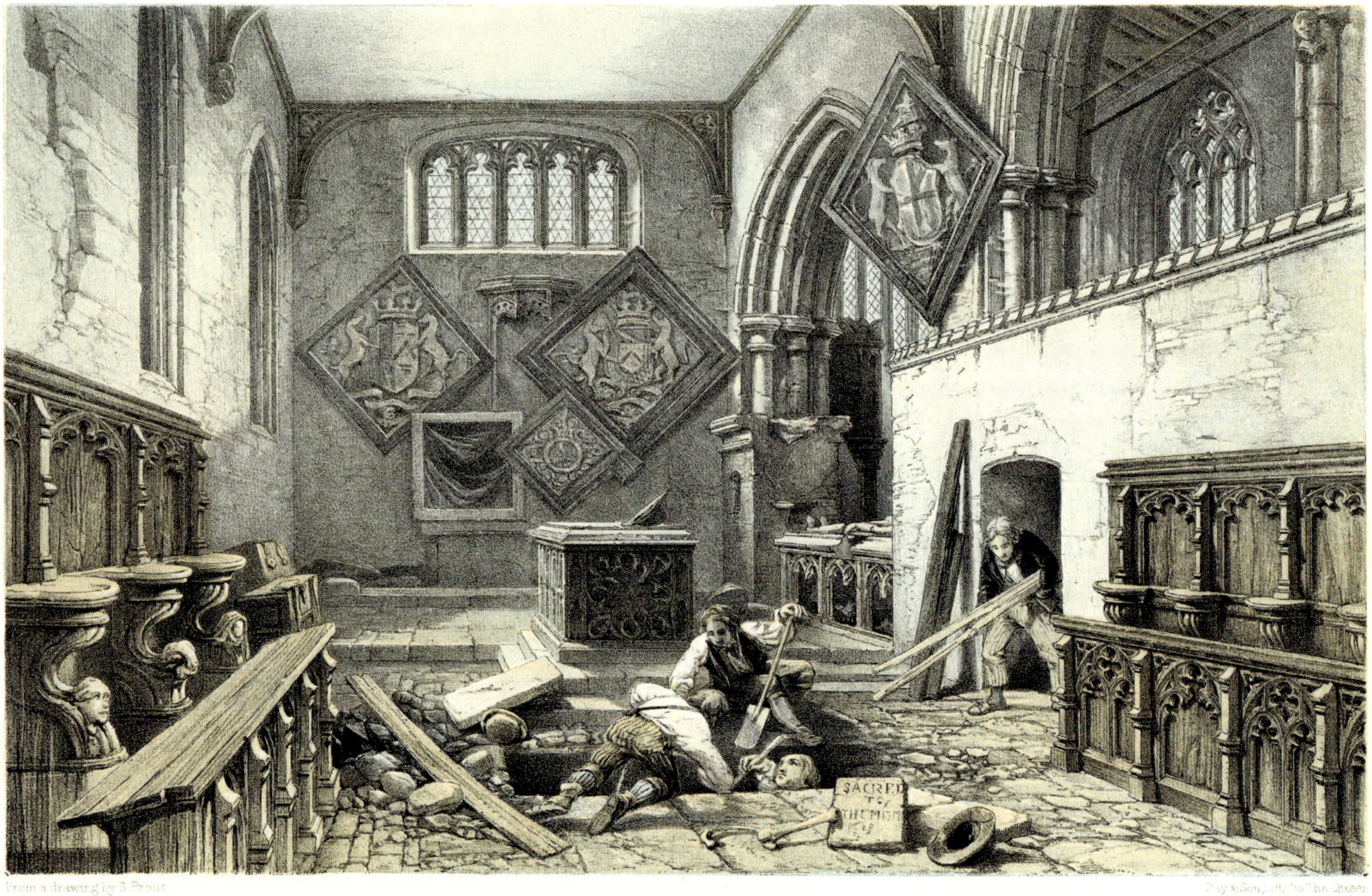

PLATE 121
Another variant of *Arundel Church.*

*121)* A further blue tint is added.
Plates 120 & 121 are described as tinted lithographs, which does not mean they are fully coloured, but simply that a coloured tint (or tints) is added. In this case, the clarity of detail is greatly improved in the later editions, particularly noticeable in the coats of arms on the back wall, and the lettering on the stone slab in the foreground. More importantly, the introduction of the yellow tint shows up the detail more, perhaps making it look too hard. The blue tint makes it look softer and adds to the sense of space.

The title of the print is not quite correct. The 14th-century Arundel Church is overpowered by Arundel Castle on one side and by the 19th-century cathedral on the other, standing between the two. What is peculiar is that the chancel shown in the print is the Fitzalan Chapel. The Fitzalans became the Dukes of Norfolk, the premier Catholic earls. The chapel was divided from the Protestant church by a wall, but the wall was eventually removed and replaced with a wrought-iron and glass screen, so you can see from one to the other. There is a gate in the screen but that is rarely unlocked. The chapel has the tombs of many members of the family. The print shows the digging of the grave of Lord Henry Thomas Howard.

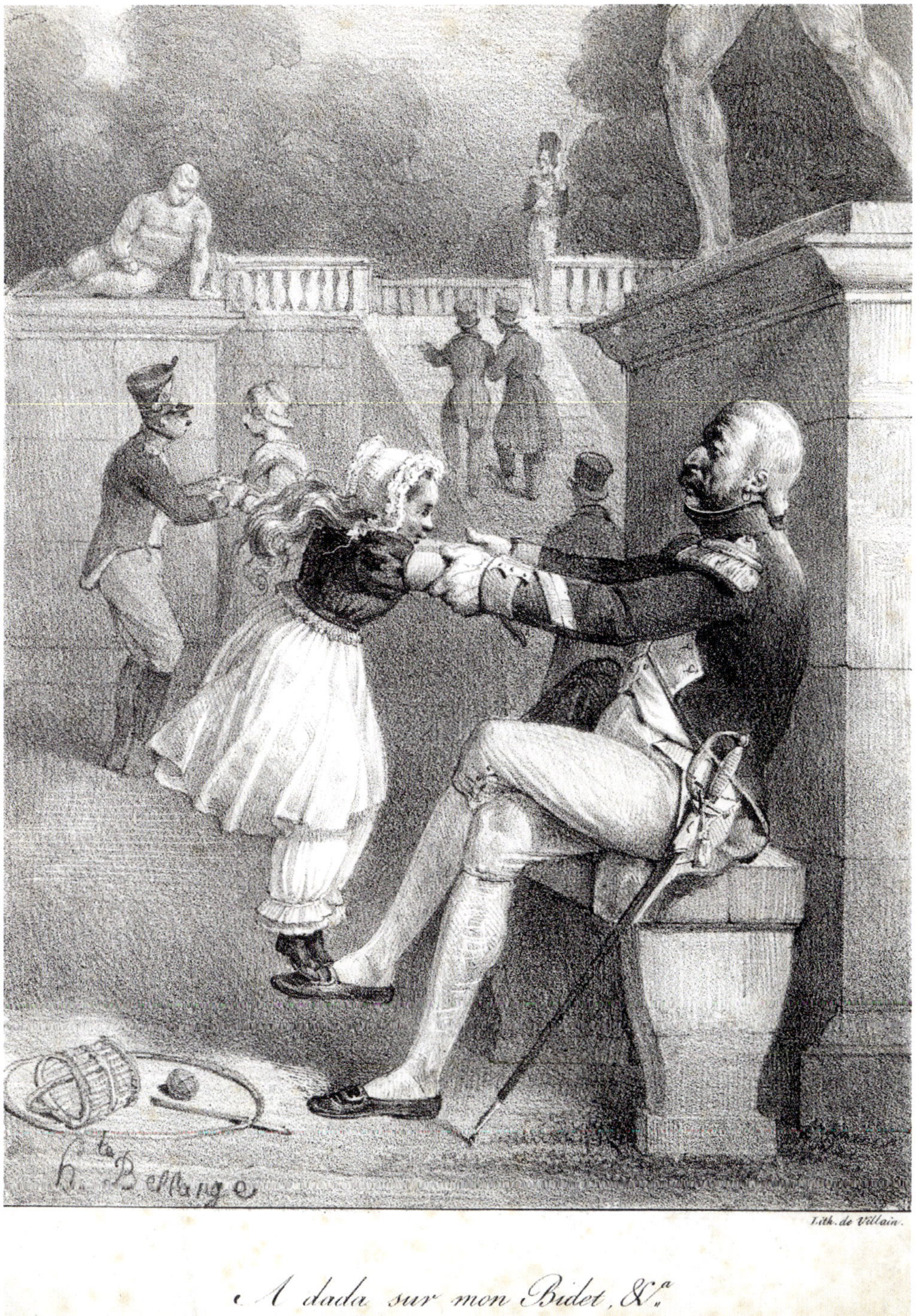


PLATE 122

*A dada sur mon Bidet, &c,* lithograph by Villain after Hippolyte Bellange, published *c.*1825. 22 x 16.5 cm (8.6 x 6.5 in.).

This is an illustration for a French nursery rhyme. Bellange is better known for his paintings of military subjects, influenced by the wars of the first Napoleon. In his youth he produced some of his own lithographs.

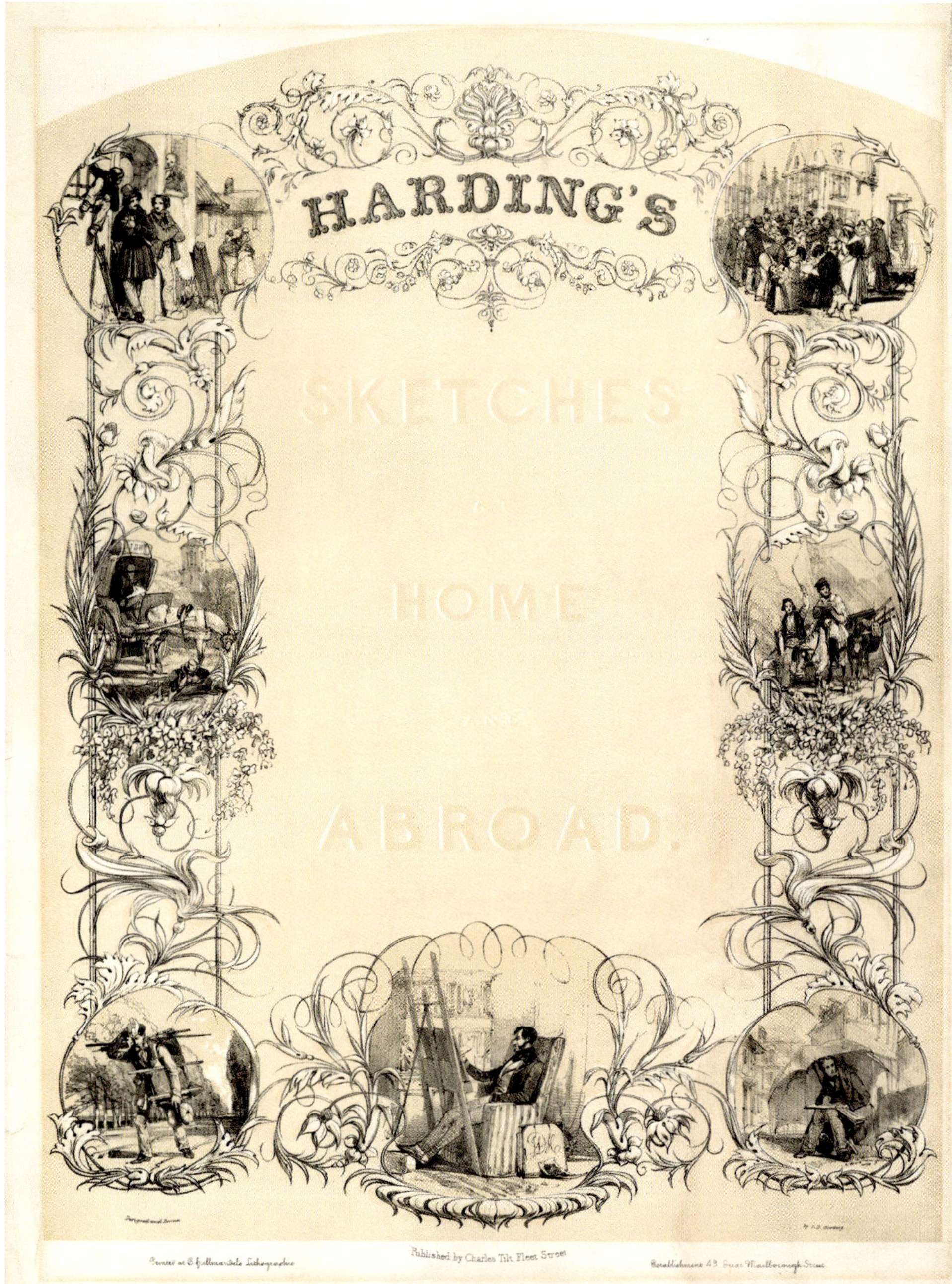


PLATE 123
Title page of J.D. Harding's *Sketches at Home and Abroad,* lithograph by C. Hullmandel. No date, but 1836.
Designed and Drawn by J.D. Harding.
Printed at C. Hullmandel's Lithographic Establishment
Tinted lithograph,
45 x 34 cm (17.7 x 13.3 in.).

This is the least effective print in the series. It is, however, a very good example of a tinted lithograph, developed by Harding and Hullmandel. The book was the first to use an added tint stone, seen here to great effect. The variation of the depth of tint is clear to see, and in this case there is very little of the white paper showing beneath the tint. The use of the tinting for the title does not work at all well, as the lettering does not show clearly. The views that are contained within the book are among the best topographical lithographs to be produced. The vignettes are amusing sketches, like soft pencil drawings, a contrast to the finely detailed work in the next illustration.

See plates 11–17 (page 25), where the vignettes are shown in detail.

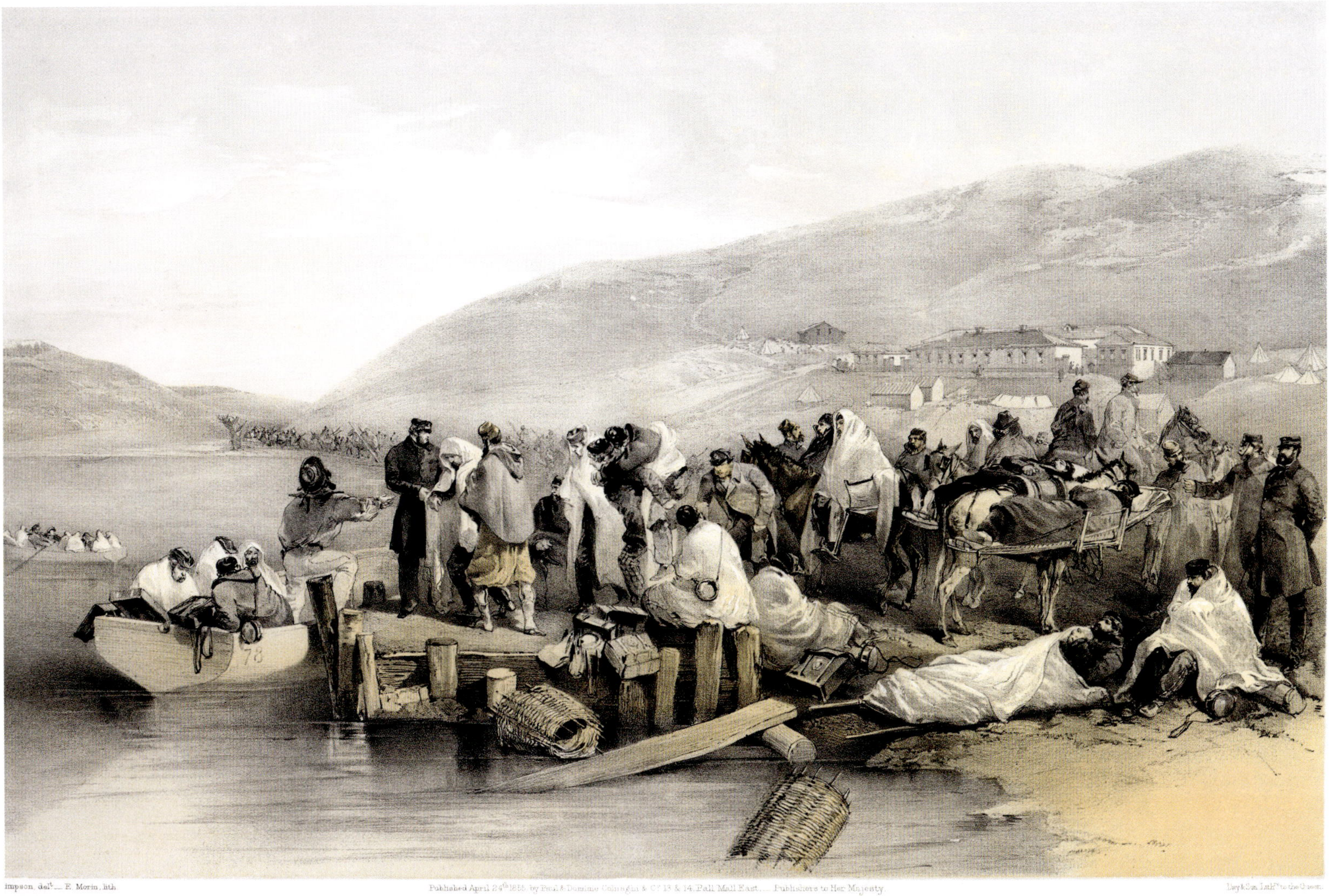


There were 80 prints like this in this series, not all of them as detailed as this, but equally masterly examples of print production, a huge achievement on Simpson's part, resulting in a very comprehensive and unglamorous record of the event, never attempted before. Yet it was also the last series of fine prints to be made of a momentous event. From the point of view of pictorial history, the war was significant because Roger Fenton made a photographic record, the first time this had happened. It was, in my biased view, a retrograde step in the history of printing art. On the other hand, making prints from photographs was a huge technical advance.

PLATE 124
*Embarkation of the Sick at Balaklava,* tinted lithograph by E. Morin.
Drawn by William Simpson for his series of the Crimean War, titled *War in the East.* The lithograph is by E. Morin, the printing was by Day and Son, and it was published by Paul and Dominic Colnaghi in 1855.
29 x 44 cm (11.4 x 17.3 in.).

# MULTI-BLOCK COLOUR PRINTING

George Baxter (1804–1865) was the son of a printer ,and he worked in his father's business in his youth before becoming an apprentice to a wood engraver in London. He set up his own engraving business in 1827. He became interested in the idea of colour printing, and spent many hours experimenting before he perfected his method – though perfected might not be the right word: his method was so complicated that he must have had a lot of failures, but he managed to print many perfect examples.

Baxter is regarded as being the first to develop the system of printing in colours using 'separations', using a separate block for printing each colour – the basis of modern colour printing. In fact, there had been colour printing on a small scale as early as the middle of the 15th century, using colours to print large ornamental capital letters. Baxter's technique was slightly refined by the use of intaglio plates for producing the fine detail. He used woodblocks to print each of his colours and normally at least one metal plate, usually aquatinted, to provide the fine detail. Unlike modern printing, Baxter used as many as 27 blocks for one print, because he was not able to alter the tone of a colour, which meant, for example, that he had one block for dark red and another for light red.

One of Baxter's main problems was obtaining correct 'register', which means that each block had to be perfectly positioned to print the colour in the right place. Even being slightly out of register would show on the prints, with colours either overlapping or not quite meeting as they should. The British Ordnance Survey maps were not printed in colours until early in the 20th century because of the difficulty of correct register; until then it was considered preferable to colour their maps by hand.

Baxter was a stickler for perfection. It would be interesting to know what percentage of the prints he made, or started to make, were relegated to the wastepaper basket in relation to the number that were sold. There is no question that he was a successful printer, but his business acumen might not have been all that was desired: he became bankrupt in 1865, two years before he died. This was despite selling licences allowing other printers to use his method. One of these was Abraham Le Blond, whose work was very close in style to that of Baxter, and it is one of Le Blond's prints and the complete set of woodblocks which are illustrated.

Baxter's method was primitive by modern standards, but it was the start of printing separations, one colour at a time, a principle that remains with us 150 years or so later.

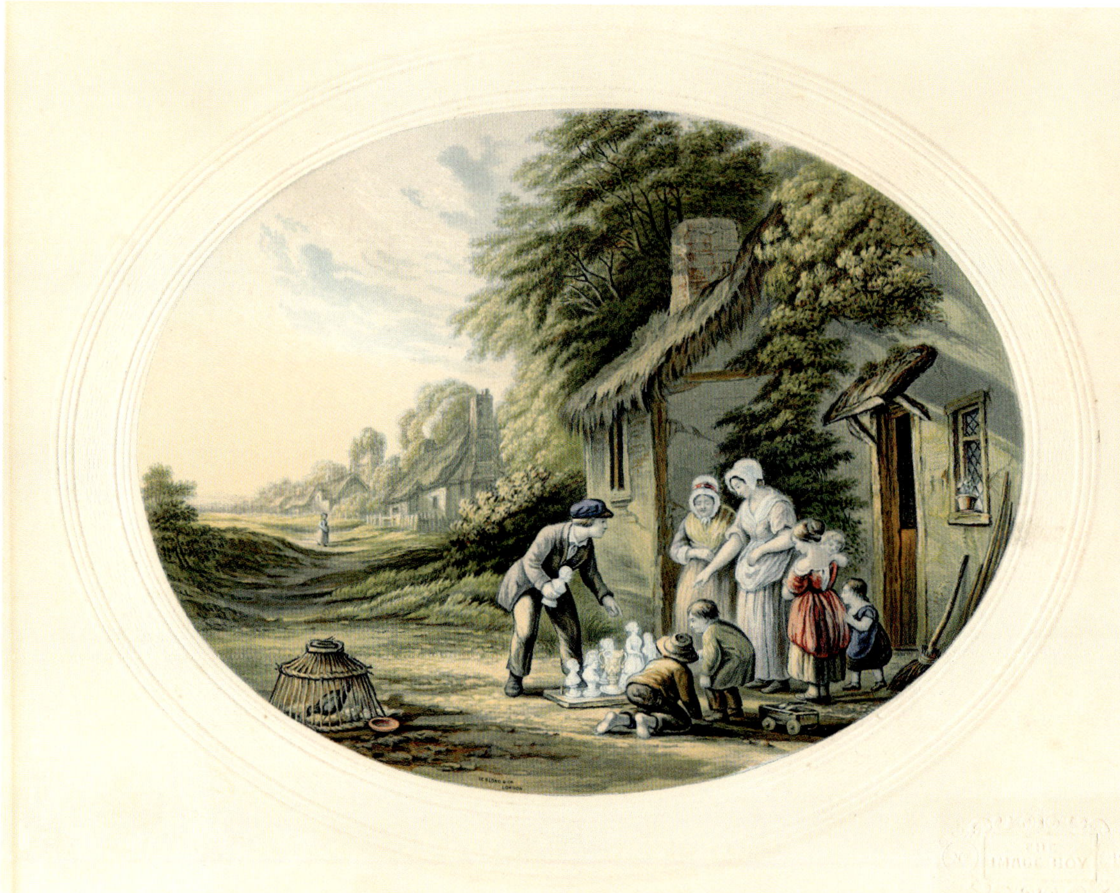

PLATE 125
*The Image Boy*, print by Le Blond, *c.*1860.
Multi-block colour printing, 13 x 17 cm (5 x 6.7 in.).

Brothers Abraham and Robert Le Blond, published prints using George Baxter's method, under licence. They are known particularly for the series of ovals, *The Image Boy* being one.

The 14 woodblocks each printed a separate colour included the print. There would also have been a metal plate for printing the fine background detail. Notice that the blocks are not uniform in shape. Each woodblock is marked with the colour that it printed, and a number to indicate the order in which it was used in the printing. As an example, the dark crimson block printed the dark parts of the girl's dress, the hat band of the older woman and the bowl by the chicken coop. It is numbered five, and would be the fifth colour to be printed. It was not possible to tone a colour, so a light crimson was used to print the light parts of the girl's dress, the brickwork in the chimney, the flowerpot on the window sill, and a minor amount of shading in the tree and the shrubs beneath.

The inks were slow to dry, and were usually left for a day before the next colour was added. So, 14 woodblocks plus the metal plate makes 15 working days to make one of these prints.

The oval border and the title are embossed, a tecnique known as 'blind-stamp'. The title is in the bottom right corner, and because there is no ink involved in the blind-stamp, it does not show up well.

PLATE 126

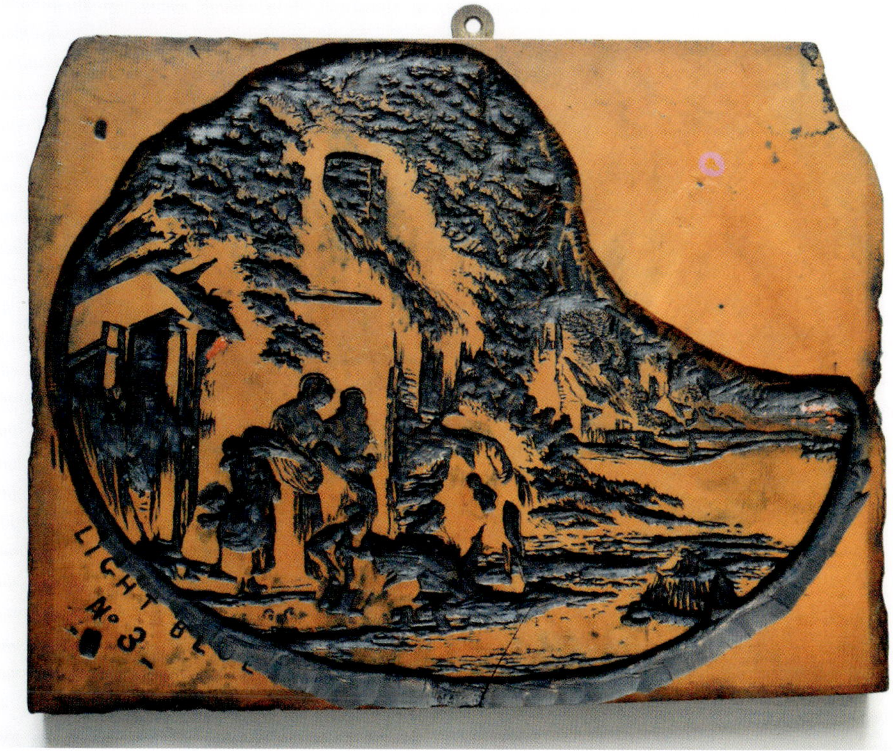

PLATE 127

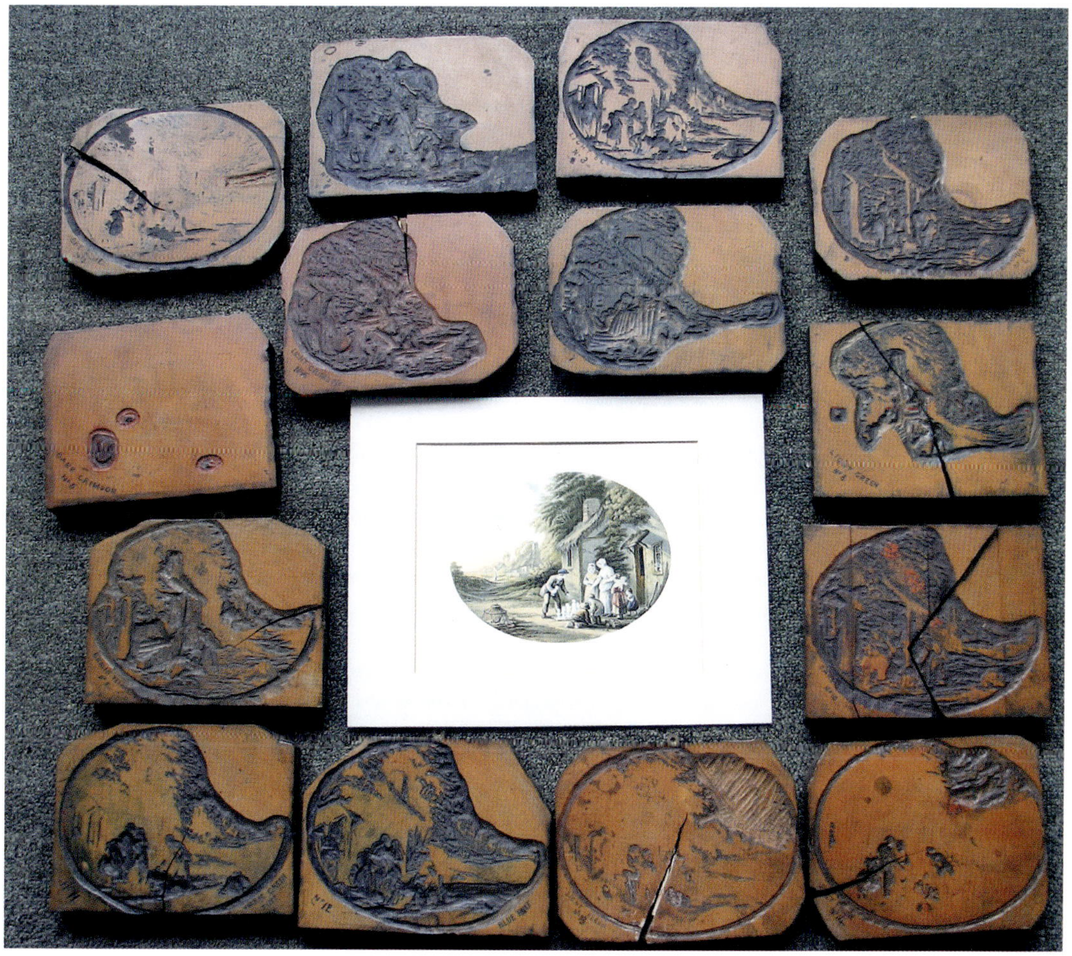

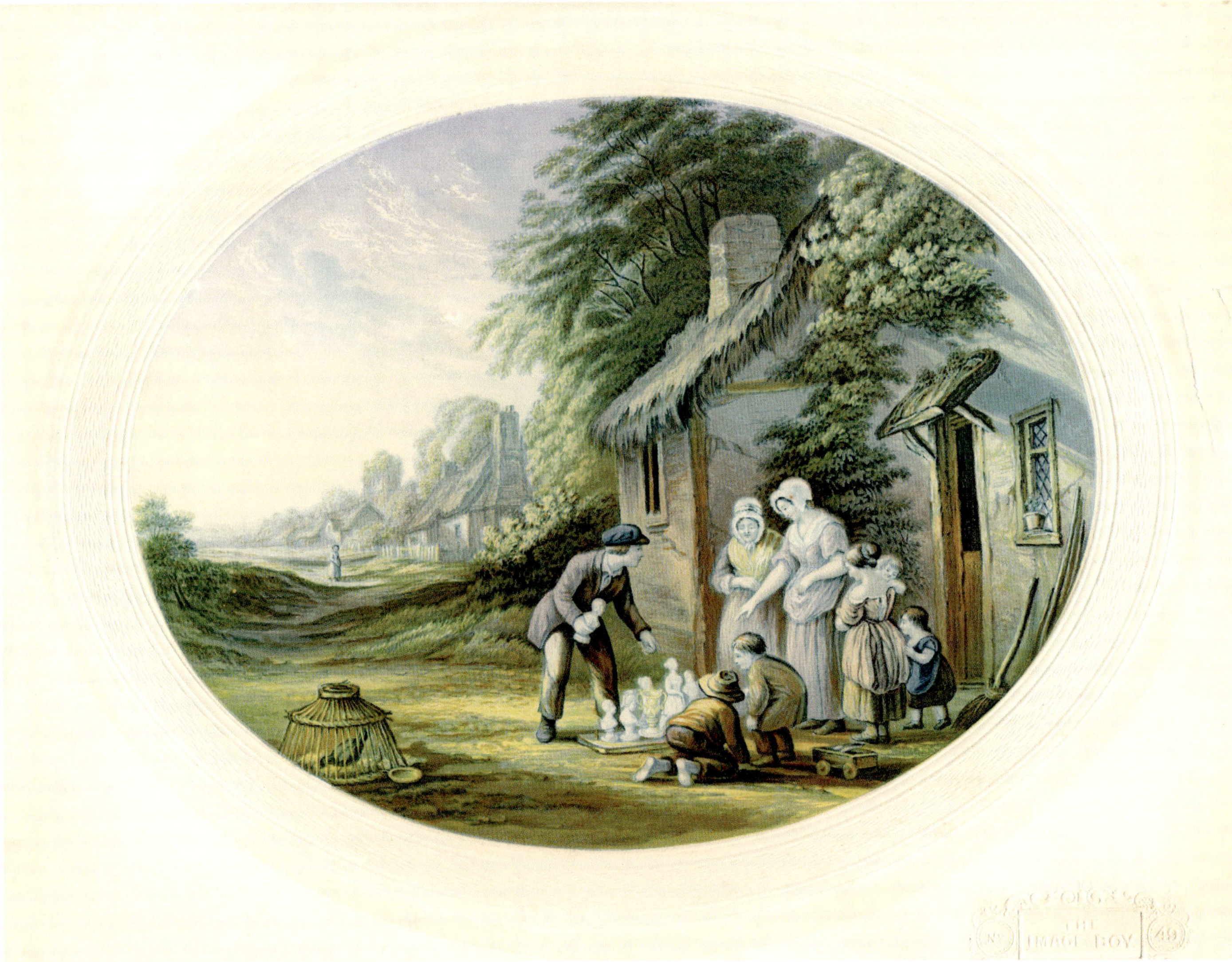


PLATE 128
Faded print.

The second illustration of the print of *The Image Boy* is a badly faded example. It shows how important it is to look after prints properly, and keep them well away from sunlight.

# GLASS PICTURES

More often than not these are described as 'paintings on glass'. A few of them are. Most are made with prints stuck onto glass. When this is done properly, the effect is very good.

The method was to stick the print onto glass, usually with a thin varnish. When the varnish dried, the paper was dampened and carefully rubbed away, leaving just a thin layer of paper, about the same thickness as tissue paper, though the varnish makes the paper even more transparent. The print was then coloured with an oil paint, which has much more body to it than normal water or gouache colour, much richer than normal print colouring. Because the paper is transparent, the colour shows through it clearly, and because the print is as near as it can be to the viewer, the finest detail of the print shows clearly.

Another method, perhaps not quite so effective, was to soak the paper in turpentine before laying it onto the glass. The turpentine made the paper translucent, which meant the tedious business of rubbing the paper was avoided. However, the colour did not show through the thicker paper so well.

The most effective prints were mezzotints and stipple engravings. The greater the density of ink, the richer was the result. Many of the subjects were classical. Even more were less desirable biblical subjects. There were glass pictures made of most subjects; the choice for the collector is wide. Their appeal is very personal.

There was, of course, a large disparity in the quality of the colouring. Some of it was applied in an amateurish manner, laid onto the paper with haste and little variation. Strangely, this is sometimes acceptable, because, if the print is sufficiently dense, the detail of the ink provides the necessary variation.

# TRANSPARENT PRINTS

The idea here was to make light show through the paper when the print is held against light. The system was not, therefore, suited to all subjects. Some simple prints can be used. I have seen an ordinary print of the elevation of a house, which might be ignored: when held up to a light, however, the building appears to be at night time with glowing lights in the windows. Usually the subjects are much more dramatic than this.

The method was to use a varnish, applied to both sides of the paper where required, to make the paper transparent. Depending on the thickness of paper, several coats of varnish could be applied.

One of the most effective transparent prints that I have seen is, again, of an elevation of a building. To the back of the print was laid a sheet of tissue paper that had been richly hand-coloured in red and yellow. When the print is held up to light, the whole building is engulfed in fire, the windows glowing and the roof burning ferociously. Subjects like this produce the best result, where there is an intensity of light or fire.

These prints are rare, mainly because they were published separately, unprotected, which inevitably means that they become damaged. They need to be very carefully handled. I do not suppose I have had ten good ones in stock in the last ten years.

Similar to transparent prints, but with little by

comparison in quality or effect, are prints where holes are made in the paper so that light shows through. Sometimes, appropriately coloured tissue papers are stuck to the back. The most effective that I have seen was a collection of charts of the stars, showing the zodiacs in detail, made early in the 19th century and in mint condition. More often, good prints have been spoiled, particularly as they were very attractive to careless children!

# PROOFS, LETTERS AND STATES

This selection of engravings was made for the purpose of showing how apparently similar prints can vary, just slightly. These prints are not sufficiently valuable for their to be any appreciable difference in value between an early state and a late state. With more important prints there can be a substantial difference in values. However, these prints have been chosen to explain how changes were made and also the differences in the lettering – detail that can make such a difference.

The prints are four pairs, each pair being slightly different from each other, mainly because of the lettering. In one pair the view has been considerably altered.

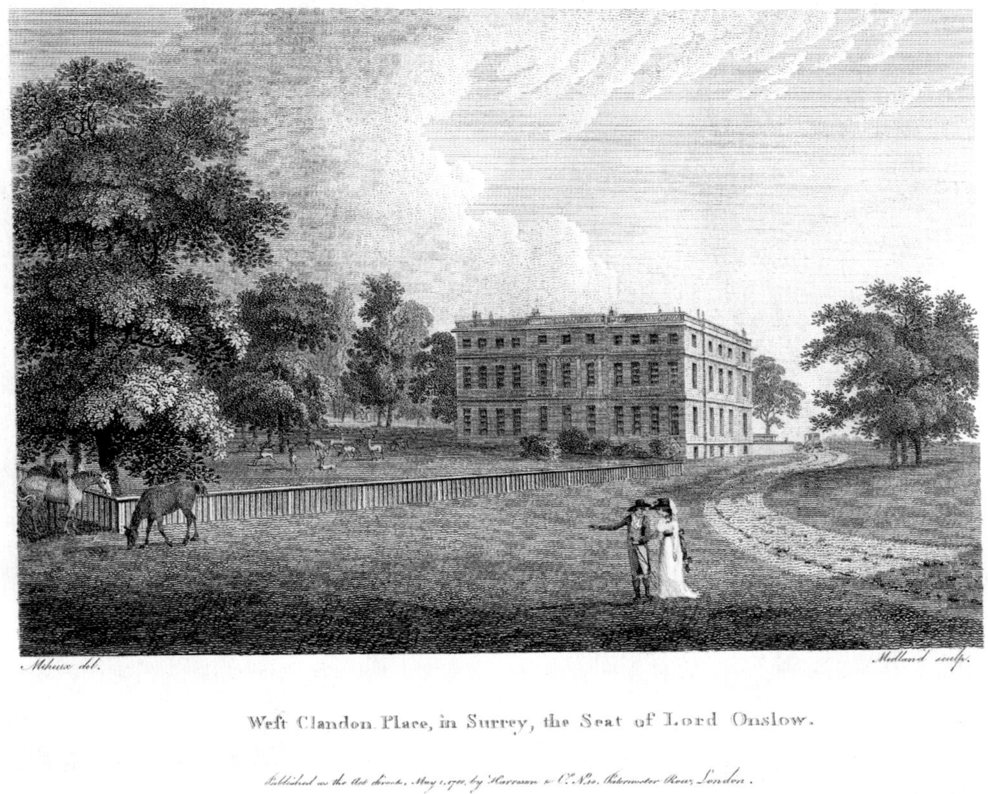


PLATE 129

*West Clandon Place, in Surrey, the Seat of Lord Onslow.*

'Meheux del. Medland sculp. Published as the Act directs, May 1, 1788 by Harrison & Co, no 18 Paternoster, Row London.'

Plate size: 15 x 20 cm (6 x 7.9 in.).

The lettering of the title is described as 'open letters' because each letter is white at the centre, engraved in outline without any engraving inside the outline.

PLATE 130

Variant lettering, *West Clandon Place, in Surrey, the Seat of Lord Onslow.*

For some reason, the whole layout of the lettering has been altered for another edition, published five years later. Even though Onslow still owned the house his name is omitted and the title shortened to West Clandon Place (shaded letters) Surrey (open letters). 'Shaded letters' means that the inside areas of the letters are engraved, in this case with fine horizontal lines.

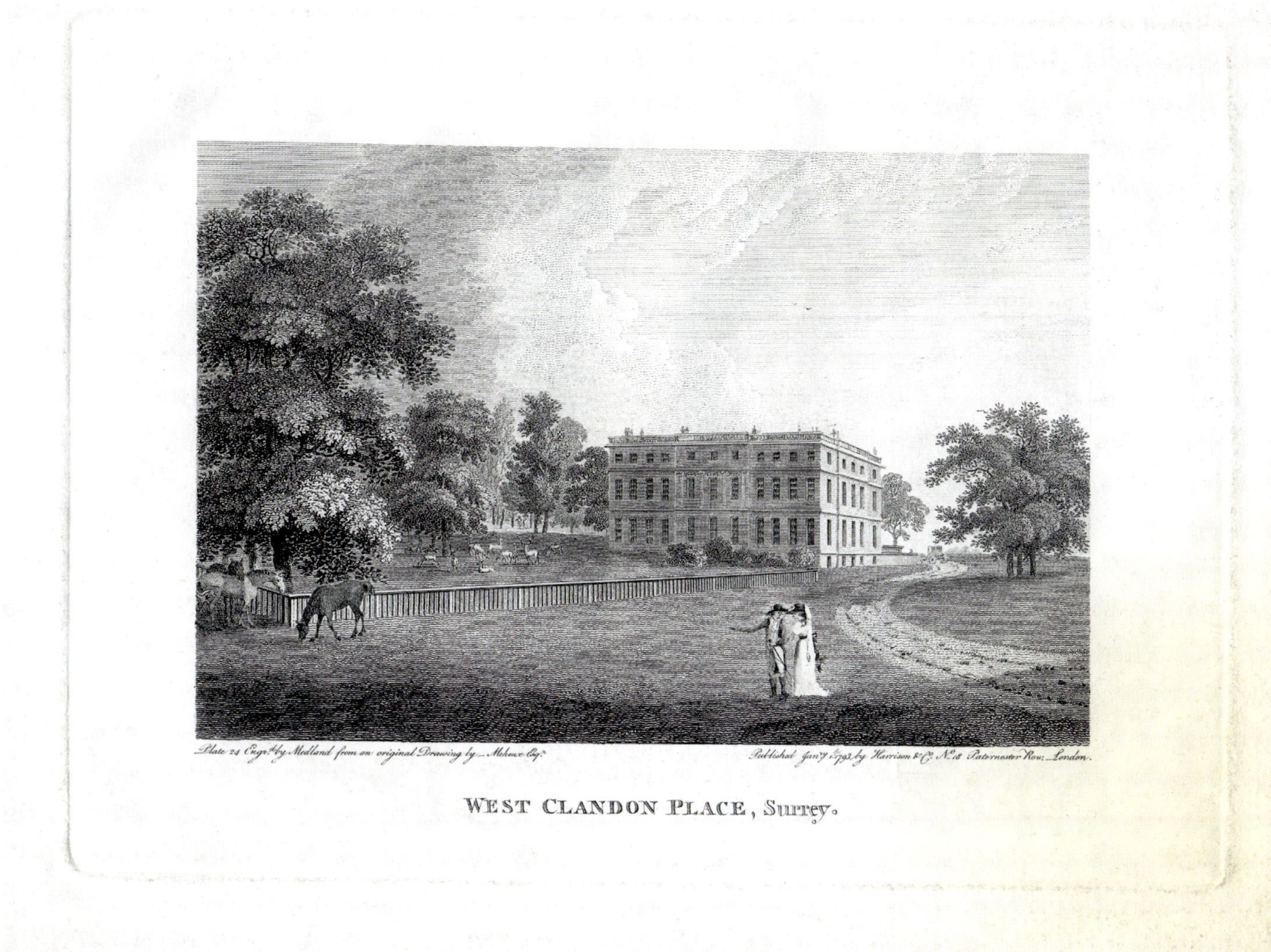


Beneath the image on the left: 'Plate 24 Engrd by Medland from an original drawing by—Meheux Esqr.' Where a word has been abbreviated, as Engrd, it was the custom to raise at least one letter beyond the letters that have been omitted. It has become the modern custom to underline those letters when the print is catalogued.

Beneath the image on the right: 'Published Janry 1st 1793 by Harrison & Co, No 18 Paternoster Row, London.'

The view was published in *The Copper Plate Magazine*, or *Monthly Cabinet of Picturesque Prints*, consisting of 'Sublime and Interesting Views in Great Britain & Ireland Beautifully engraved by the Most Eminent Artists from the Painting and Drawing of the First Masters'.

There are no changes to the image. The inking of the plate is the same, so that the actual images are remarkably similar.

By coincidence, the next pair of views is also by Medland after Meheux, but not the same publisher.

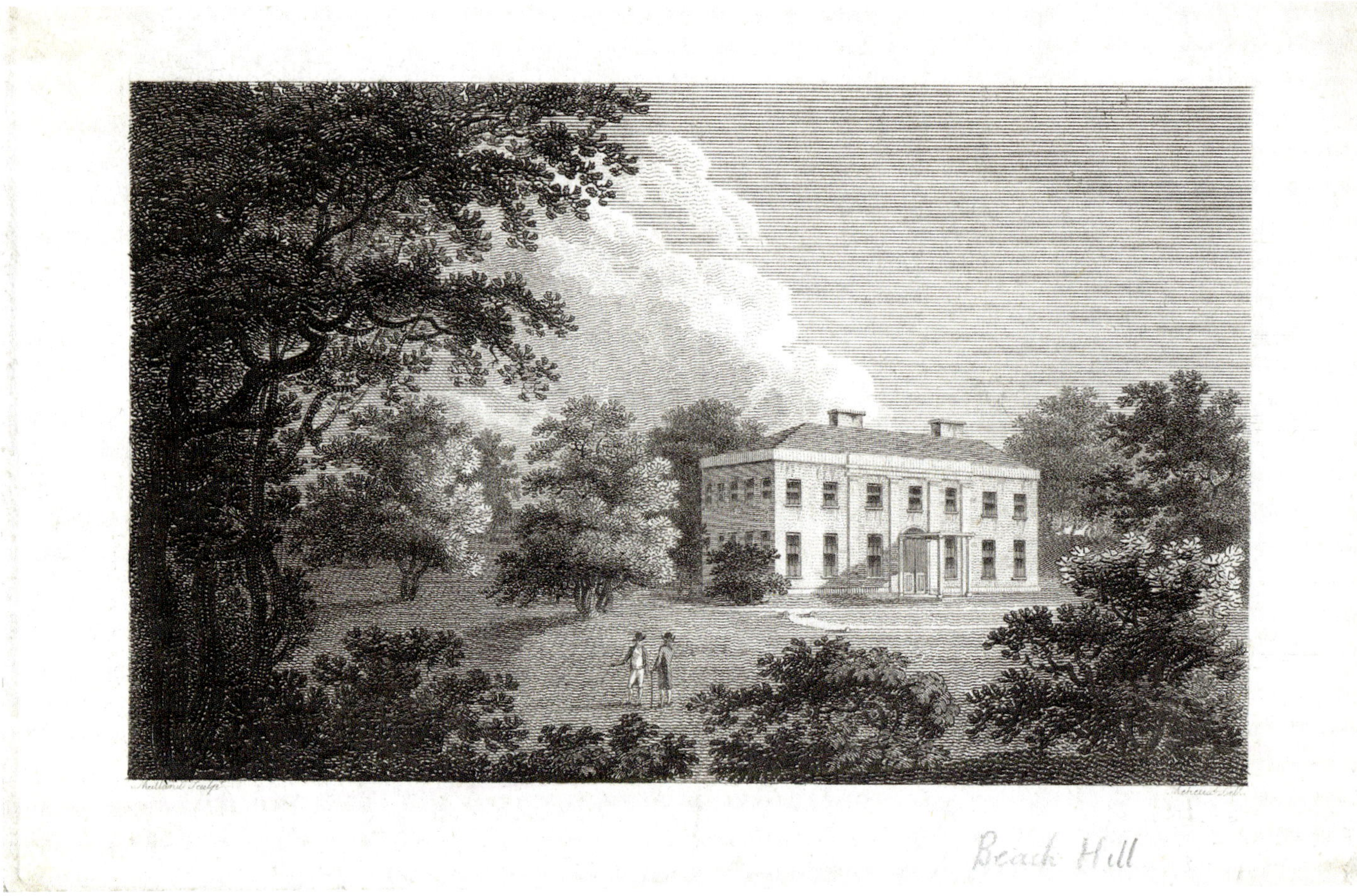

PLATE 131
Beach Hill.
Image size: 10 x 16 cm (4 x 6.3 in.).

This print is a proof before title. It is not a proof before letters because the names of the artist and engraver are present beneath the corners of the image in minute scratch letters, so small that it needs very good eyesight to be able to read them. The artist's name is on the right, the engraver on the left, which is the opposite way round to normal.

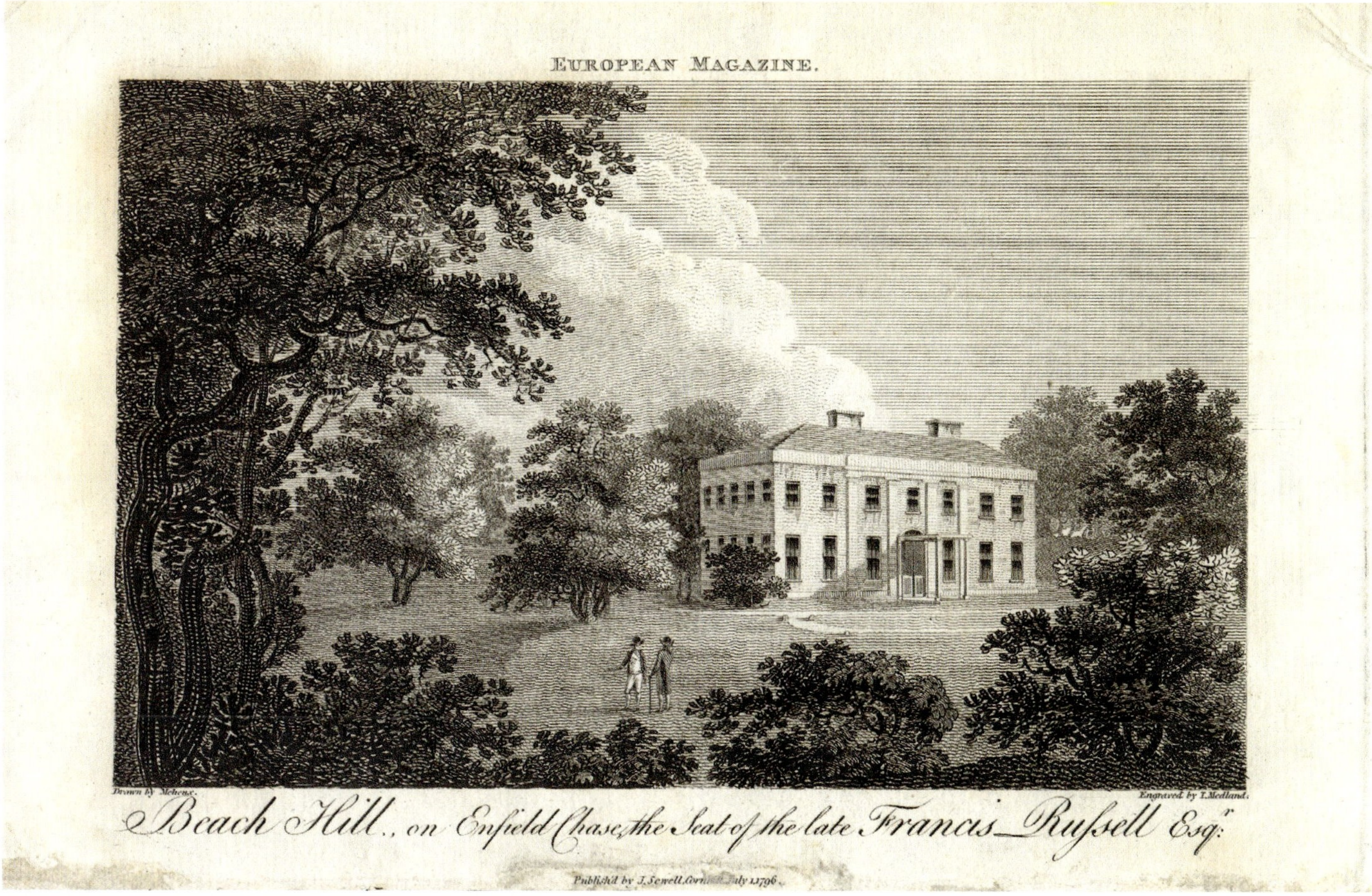


PLATE 132
*Beach Hill on Enfield Chase, the Seat of the late Francis Russell Esqr.*
Published edition.
Image size: 10 x 16 cm (4 x 6.3 in.).

A print complete with title, and credits to the artist, the engraver and the publisher. Beneath the image on the left is 'Drawn by Meheux' and on the right is 'Engraved by T. Medland'. Centrally, beneath the title, is 'Publish'd by J. Sewell, Cornhill, July 1, 1796'. Credits are often as brief as this and raise questions for the inquisitive. Who was Francis Russell? Who was Meheux? He is probably John Meheux, who was an active painter and engraver at the time, but he could be a gifted amateur. John Sewell is well-known as a publisher of the *European Magazine,* and he published many prints of the same kind as this one.

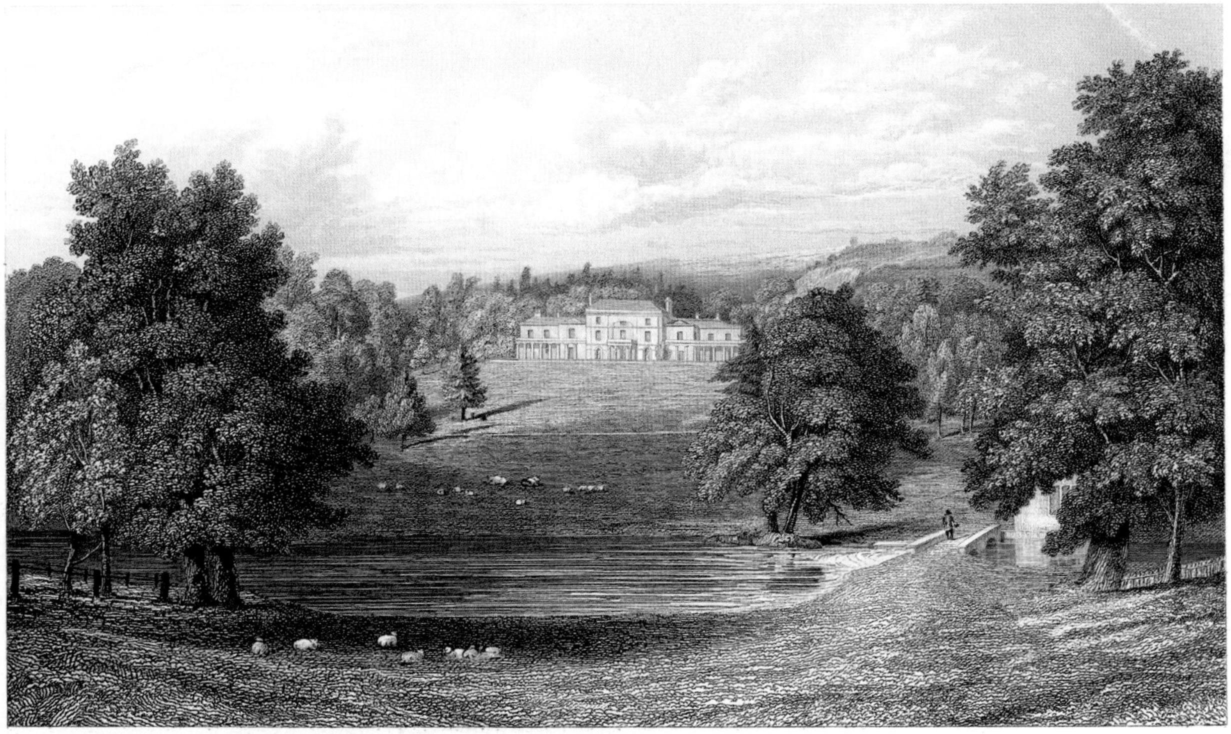

The next two pairs of prints were made for Brayley's *History of Surrey*.

PLATE 133
*Abinger Hall.* Proof before letters.
Image size: 11 x 18.5 cm
(4.3 x 7.3 in.)

Proof before all letters simply means that there is not lettering on the print, only the view. It was important for the engraver to make prints during the course of his engraving, as this was the best means of judging his progress.

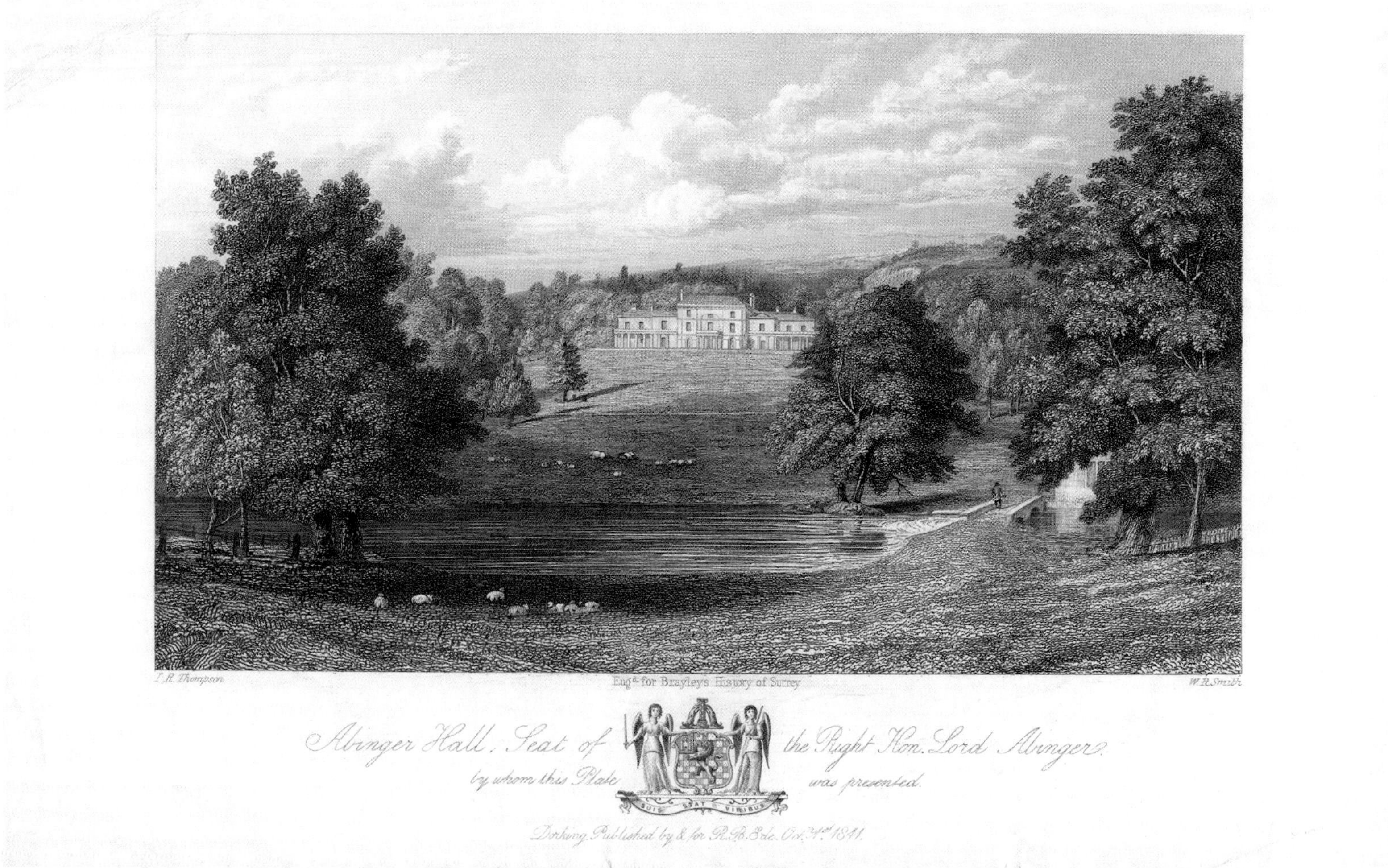


It is unusual for the names of the artist and the engraver to appear alone, without any indication of how they contributed to the print. All of the lettering so far is in script. Beneath the image at the centre is: 'Engd for Brayley's History of Surrey'. In the centre of the title are the arms of Lord Abinger. There do not appear to be any differences in the engraving of the image, so the proof before all letters has the image in the published state, or final proof state.

PLATE 134.
*Abinger Hall.* First published edition.
Image size: 11 x 18.5 cm (4.3 x 7.3 in.)
First published state.
'Abinger Hall, Seat of the Right Hon. Lord Abinger by whom this Plate was presented.
Dorking, published by & for R.B. Ede Octr 1st 1841
I. R. Thompson [artist] W.R. Smith [engraver].'

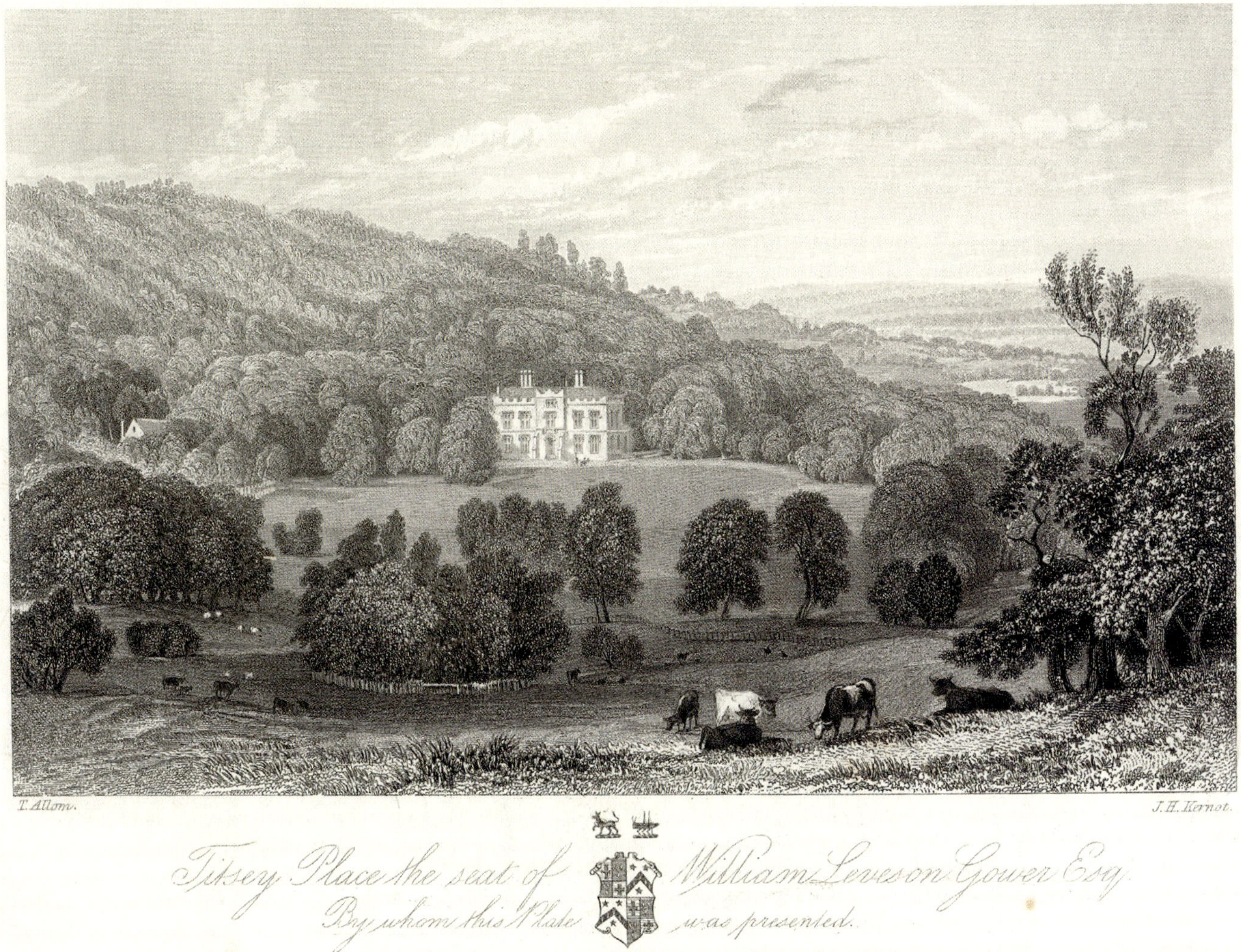


PLATE 135
*Titsey Place.* First published edition.
Image size: 11 x 17 cm
(4.3 x 6.7 in.).

'Titsey Place the seat of William Leveson Gower Esq. By whom this Plate is presented.' His coat of arms is shown in the centre of the title.

'Thomas Allom' [artist]; 'James Harfield Kernot' [engraver]. Again they are shown in name only. All the lettering is script. The arms of Mr Gower are shown at the centre of the title.

This is the first published state of 1841, but is without the publisher's imprint.

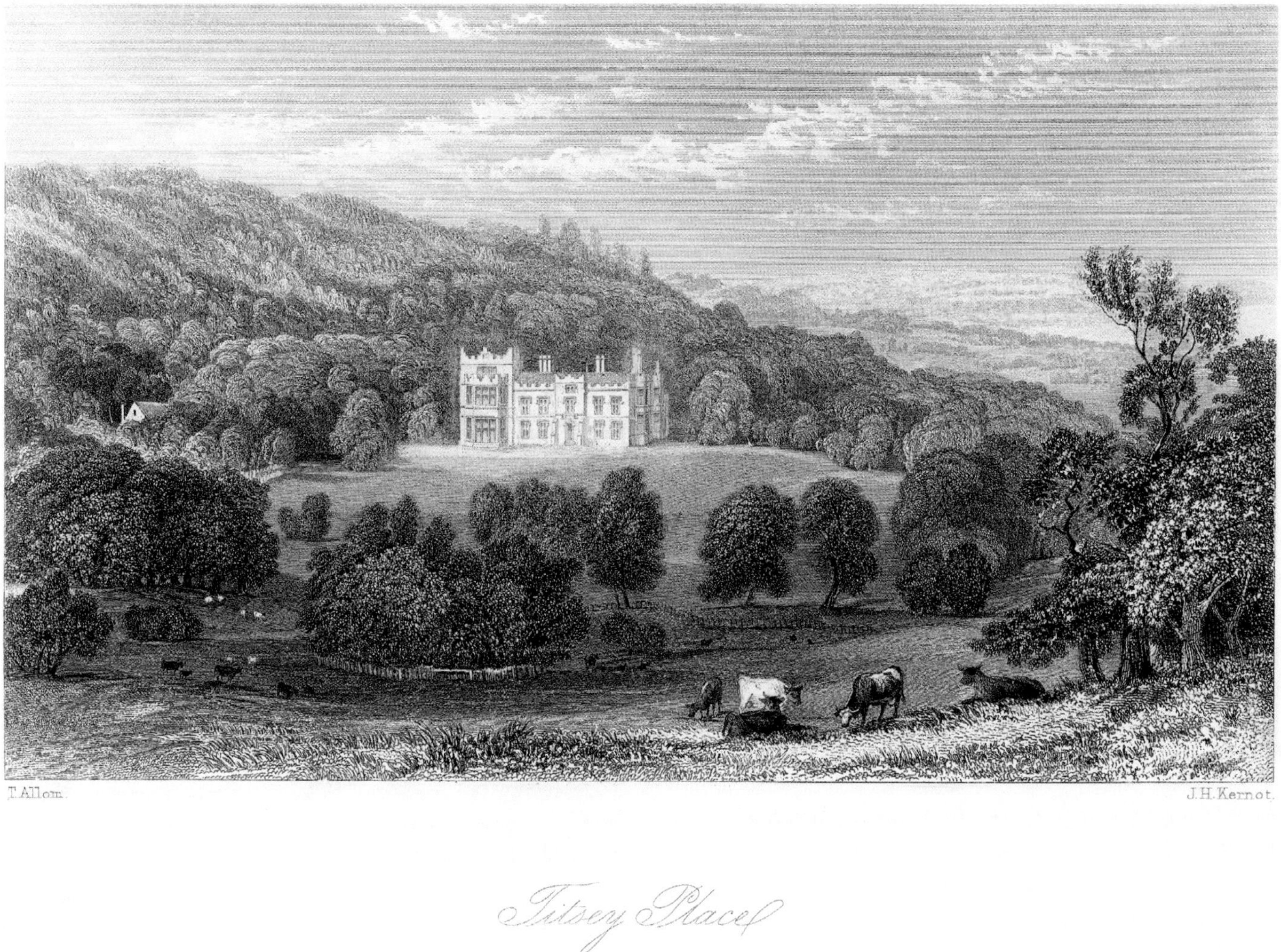


The second view has the title with the name of the house only, and the names of the artist and the engraver and the publisher, who then were Vertue and Co. This is a later edition of about 1860, probably the second state. Apart from the titles there were very few alterations to the plates in the *History*. This is an exception. The house has a new wing on the left side, and a very large chimney on the right side. Shading has been altered to the area of ground to the left of the tall tree on the right, and shading is reduced on the right side of the tree. The sky is much improved with white floating clouds. It is understandable that the house should have been altered, but the other re-engraving would have taken a lot of work and a long time for the engraver without producing much reward. If Mr Gower paid for the alterations it might be expected that his name be still on the plate.

PLATE 136
*Titsey Place.* Later state.

PLATE 137
Etching. Printed from cancelled plate, with remarque.
E. Messonier. Signed within image and dated 1876.
Published 1911 by C. Klackner, Old Bond Street, London.
Plate: 21 x 23.5 cm (8.3 x 9.3 in.).

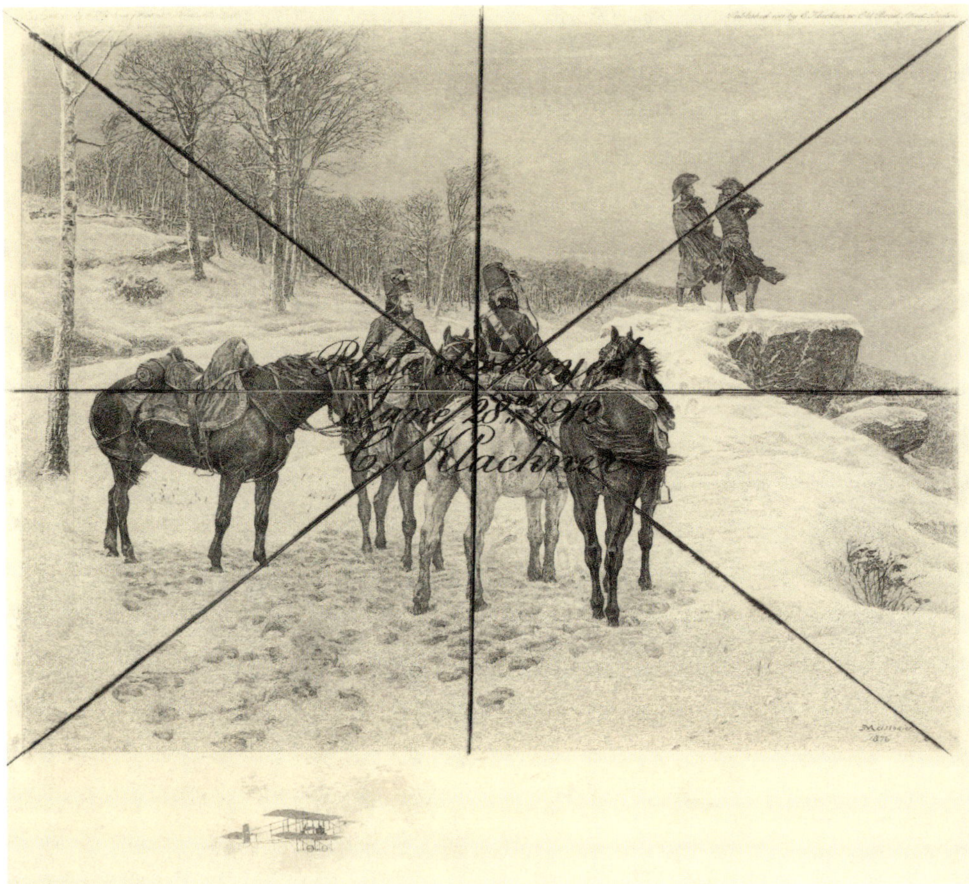

The plate has been scored with four lines, and at the centre is 'Plate destroyed June 28th 1912 C. Klackner'. This is an oddity. Why should a print be made from a cancelled plate? Perhaps it was for no other reason than to prove to the publisher's customers that the plate had been cancelled. Little care was taken with the printing and the result is a poor impression. The remarque of the biplane in the margin is obviously an addition to earlier issues of the print. There is a second publisher's imprint at the top left corner which is illegible. There is surplus ink in the left margin.

The additional picture of the biplane in the bottom margin is known as a 're-marque', an idea which began in the latter half of the 19th century, when remarques were pencil drawings, often in watercolour, executed by the artist to make the print unique. Later remarques began to be printed, which defeats the original object, but adds another point of interest to the picture. In this case the aeroplane is out of keeping with the Napoleonic soldiers in the picture.

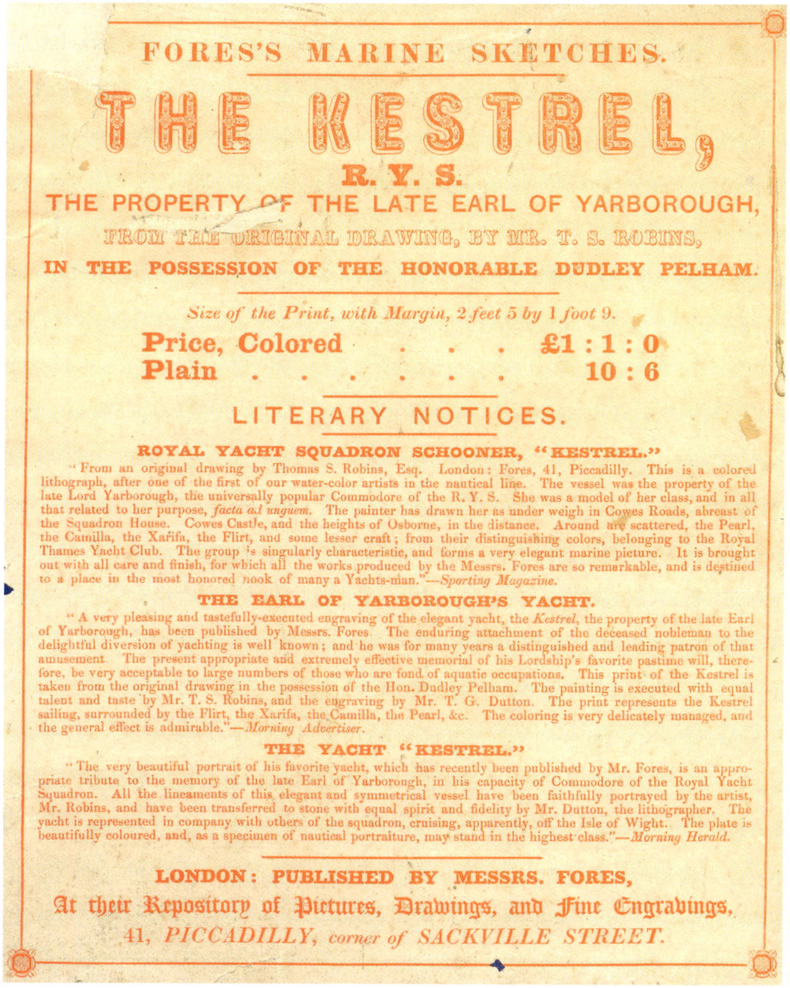
FORES'S MARINE SKETCHES.

THE KESTREL,

R. Y. S.

THE PROPERTY OF THE LATE EARL OF YARBOROUGH,

FROM THE ORIGINAL DRAWING, BY MR. T. S. ROBINS,

IN THE POSSESSION OF THE HONORABLE DUDLEY PELHAM.

*Size of the Print, with Margin, 2 feet 5 by 1 foot 9.*

Price, Colored . . . £1 : 1 : 0
Plain . . . . . . . 10 : 6

LITERARY NOTICES.

ROYAL YACHT SQUADRON SCHOONER, "KESTREL."

"From an original drawing by Thomas S. Robins, Esq. London: Fores, 41, Piccadilly. This is a colored lithograph, after one of the first of our water-color artists in the nautical line. The vessel was the property of the late Lord Yarborough, the universally popular Commodore of the R. Y. S. She was a model of her class, and in all that related to her purpose, *facta ad unguem.* The painter has drawn her as under weigh in Cowes Roads, abreast of the Squadron House. Cowes Castle, and the heights of Osborne, in the distance. Around are scattered, the Pearl, the Camilla, the Xarifa, the Flirt, and some lesser craft; from their distinguishing colors, belonging to the Royal Thames Yacht Club. The group is singularly characteristic, and forms a very elegant marine picture. It is brought out with all care and finish, for which all the works produced by the Messrs. Fores are so remarkable, and is destined to a place in the most honored nook of many a Yachts-man."—*Sporting Magazine.*

THE EARL OF YARBOROUGH'S YACHT.

"A very pleasing and tastefully-executed engraving of the elegant yacht, the *Kestrel*, the property of the late Earl of Yarborough, has been published by Messrs. Fores. The enduring attachment of the deceased nobleman to the delightful diversion of yachting is well known; and he was for many years a distinguished and leading patron of that amusement. The present appropriate and extremely effective memorial of his Lordship's favorite pastime will, therefore, be very acceptable to large numbers of those who are fond of aquatic occupations. This print of the Kestrel is taken from the original drawing in the possession of the Hon. Dudley Pelham. The painting is executed with equal talent and taste by Mr. T. S. Robins, and the engraving by Mr. T. G. Dutton. The print represents the Kestrel sailing, surrounded by the Flirt, the Xarifa, the Camilla, the Pearl, &c. The coloring is very delicately managed, and the general effect is admirable."—*Morning Advertiser.*

THE YACHT "KESTREL."

"The very beautiful portrait of his favorite yacht, which has recently been published by Mr. Fores, is an appropriate tribute to the memory of the late Earl of Yarborough, in his capacity of Commodore of the Royal Yacht Squadron. All the lineaments of this elegant and symmetrical vessel have been faithfully portrayed by the artist, Mr. Robins, and have been transferred to stone with equal spirit and fidelity by Mr. Dutton, the lithographer. The yacht is represented in company with others of the squadron, cruising, apparently, off the Isle of Wight. The plate is beautifully coloured, and, as a specimen of nautical portraiture, may stand in the highest class."—*Morning Herald.*

LONDON: PUBLISHED BY MESSRS. FORES,

At their Repository of Pictures, Drawings, and Fine Engravings,

41, *PICCADILLY, corner of SACKVILLE STREET.*

PLATE 138

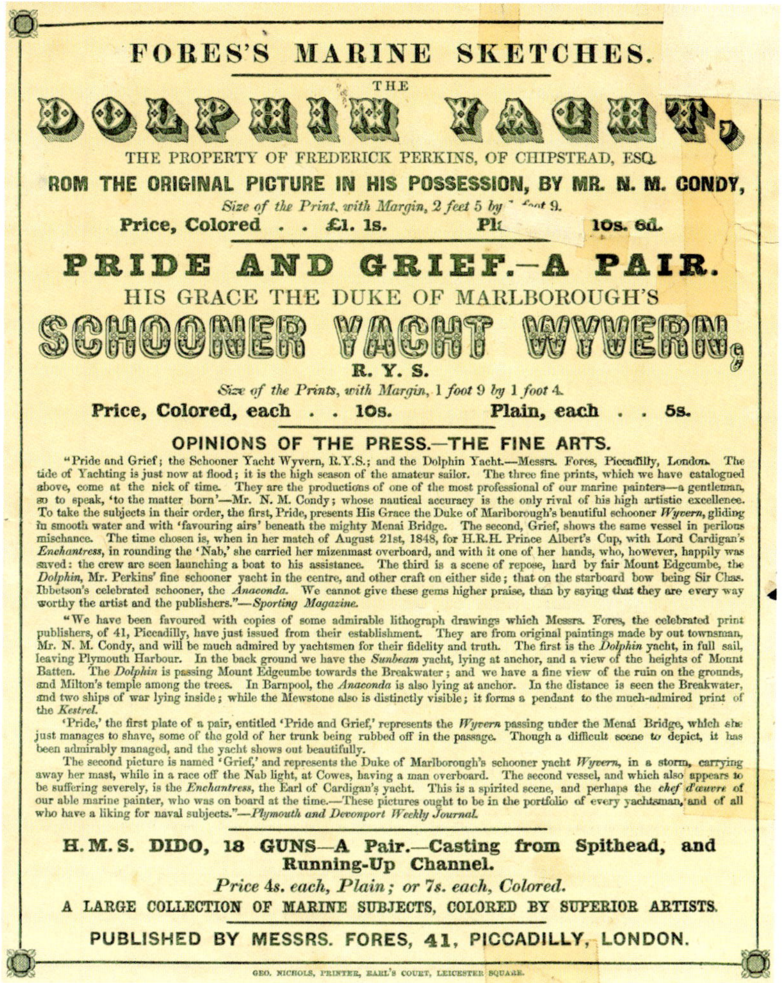
FORES'S MARINE SKETCHES.

THE

DOLPHIN YACHT,

THE PROPERTY OF FREDERICK PERKINS, OF CHIPSTEAD, ESQ.

ROM THE ORIGINAL PICTURE IN HIS POSSESSION, BY MR. N. M. CONDY,

*Size of the Print, with Margin, 2 feet 5 by ' foot 9.*

Price, Colored . . £1. 1s. Pl 10s. 6d.

PRIDE AND GRIEF.—A PAIR.

HIS GRACE THE DUKE OF MARLBOROUGH'S

SCHOONER YACHT WYVERN,

R. Y. S.

*Size of the Prints, with Margin, 1 foot 9 by 1 foot 4.*

Price, Colored, each . . 10s. Plain, each . . 5s.

OPINIONS OF THE PRESS.—THE FINE ARTS.

"Pride and Grief; the Schooner Yacht Wyvern, R.Y.S.; and the Dolphin Yacht.—Messrs. Fores, Piccadilly, London. The tide of Yachting is just now at flood; it is the high season of the amateur sailor. The three fine prints, which we have catalogued above, come at the nick of time. They are the productions of one of the most professional of our marine painters—a gentleman, so to speak, 'to the matter born'—Mr. N. M. Condy; whose nautical accuracy is the only rival of his high artistic excellence. To take the subjects in their order, the first, Pride, presents His Grace the Duke of Marlborough's beautiful schooner *Wyvern*, gliding in smooth water and with 'favouring airs' beneath the mighty Menai Bridge. The second, Grief, shows the same vessel in perilous mischance. The time chosen is, when in her match of August 21st, 1848, for H.R.H. Prince Albert's Cup, with Lord Cardigan's *Enchantress*, in rounding the 'Nab,' she carried her mizenmast overboard, and with it one of her hands, who, however, happily was saved: the crew are seen launching a boat to his assistance. The third is a scene of repose, hard by fair Mount Edgcumbe, the *Dolphin*, Mr. Perkins' fine schooner yacht in the centre, and other craft on either side; that on the starboard bow being Sir Chas. Ibbetson's celebrated schooner, the *Anaconda.* We cannot give these gems higher praise, than by saying that they are every way worthy the artist and the publishers."—*Sporting Magazine.*

"We have been favoured with copies of some admirable lithograph drawings which Messrs. Fores, the celebrated print publishers, of 41, Piccadilly, have just issued from their establishment. They are from original paintings made by out townsman, Mr. N. M. Condy, and will be much admired by yachtsmen for their fidelity and truth. The first is the *Dolphin* yacht, in full sail, leaving Plymouth Harbour. In the back ground we have the *Sunbeam* yacht, lying at anchor, and a view of the heights of Mount Batten. The *Dolphin* is passing Mount Edgcumbe towards the Breakwater; and we have a fine view of the ruin on the grounds, and Milton's temple among the trees. In Barnpool, the *Anaconda* is also lying at anchor. In the distance is seen the Breakwater, and two ships of war lying inside; while the Mewstone also is distinctly visible; it forms a pendant to the much-admired print of the *Kestrel.*

'Pride,' the first plate of a pair, entitled 'Pride and Grief,' represents the *Wyvern* passing under the Menai Bridge, which she just manages to shave, some of the gold of her trunk being rubbed off in the passage. Though a difficult scene to depict, it has been admirably managed, and the yacht shows out beautifully.

The second picture is named 'Grief,' and represents the Duke of Marlborough's schooner yacht *Wyvern*, in a storm, carrying away her mast, while in a race off the Nab light, at Cowes, having a man overboard. The second vessel, and which also appears to be suffering severely, is the *Enchantress*, the Earl of Cardigan's yacht. This is a spirited scene, and perhaps the *chef d'œuvre* of our able marine painter, who was on board at the time.—These pictures ought to be in the portfolio of every yachtsman, and of all who have a liking for naval subjects."—*Plymouth and Devonport Weekly Journal.*

H. M. S. DIDO, 18 GUNS—A Pair.—Casting from Spithead, and Running-Up Channel.

*Price 4s. each, Plain; or 7s. each, Colored.*

A LARGE COLLECTION OF MARINE SUBJECTS, COLORED BY SUPERIOR ARTISTS.

PUBLISHED BY MESSRS. FORES, 41, PICCADILLY, LONDON.

GEO. NICHOLS, PRINTER, EARL'S COURT, LEICESTER SQUARE.

PLATE 139

The verso.

Unlike the advertising bill from Slater, which draws attention to all aspects of that business (plate 54, page 80), this bill is confined to promoting just six lithographs of yachts, although Fores published a wide range of subjects. The prints were offered plain or hand-coloured. Notice that the difference in price is doubled for the colouring.

The prints were lithographed by T. G. Dutton, now regarded as one of the leading marine printmakers. On the bill, Dutton has one mention, but it is Thomas Robins and N.M. Condy, the artists, who attract the attention. The journalist from the *Morning Advertiser* does not know his engravings from his lithographs.

Originally, S.W. Fores, founded in 1785 and always in the vicinity of Piccadilly in London, began by publishing cartoons and caricatures. In the early 19th century, they turned to specialising in some of the finest sporting and marine prints.

PLATES 138 & 139.

Advertising handbill. Fores's Marine sketches. Lithograph, *c.*1850.

Printed on both sides, one side in green, the other in red.

25 x 20 cm (9.8 x 7.9 in.).

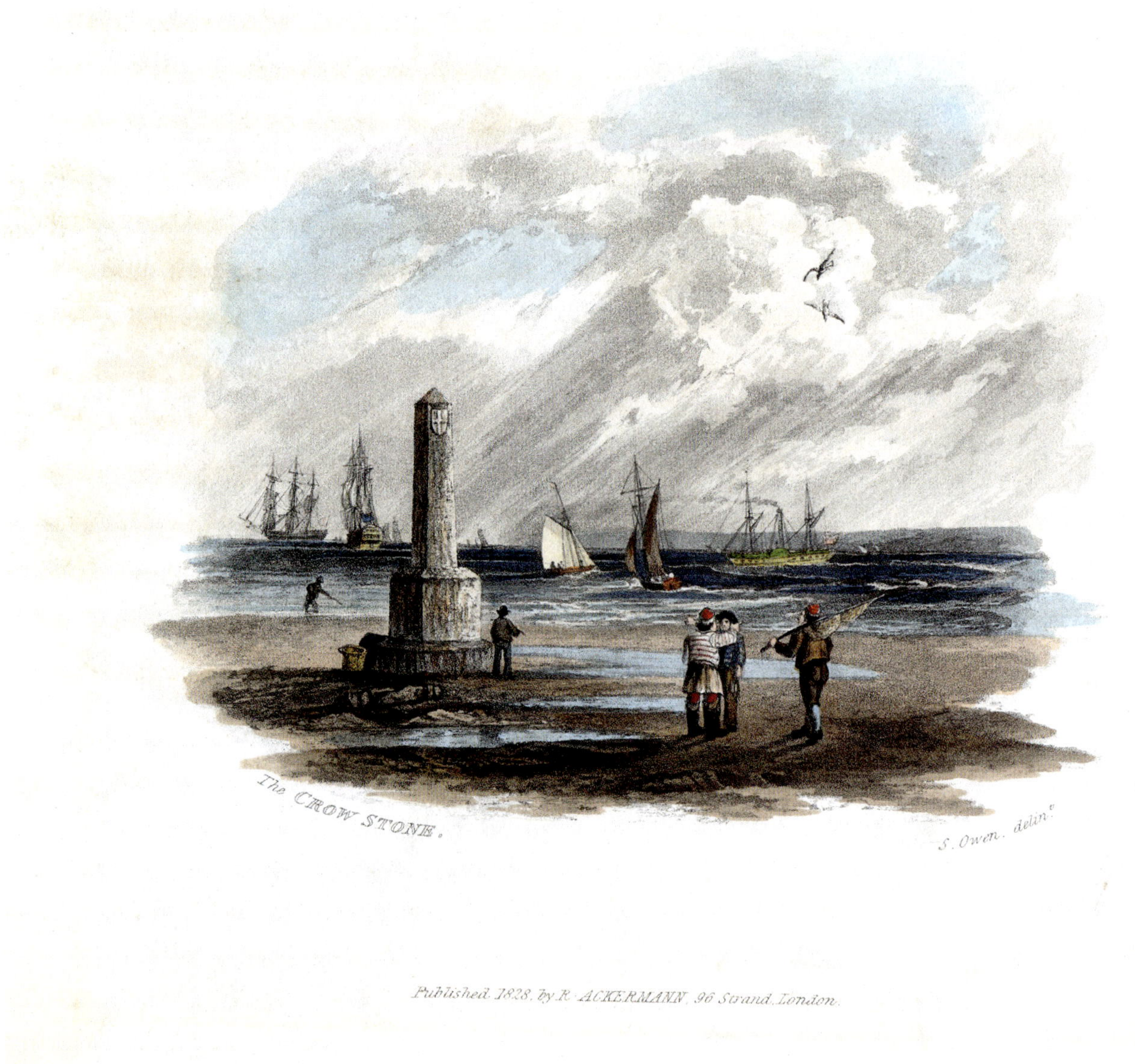


PLATE 140.

*Crow Stone,* drawn by Samuel Owen, aquatint probably engraved by him. Published by Ackermann in 1828, one of his last publications, and one of the finest of all colour-plate books.
Aquatint.
Vignette: 12 x 15 cm (4.7 x 6 in.).

The print is the tailpiece of Westall and Owen's *Picturesque Tour of the River Thames.* The print is Martin Hardie's favourite aquatint. It is almost pure aquatint. Only the rigging of the ships is etched, because it is not possible to produce a fine line in aquatint.

The print is quite different in style to the others in the series, being less formal. The colouring is by hand, whereas the others are colour-printed and finished by hand. It is very simply coloured, mostly in blue and brown, with a little brighter colour for the small details such as the clothing and the hulls of the two central sailing boats. The grey clouds are left uncoloured and would not be enhanced with additional colour. A slight fault is that there are traces of 'offset', the lines across the sheet, which is transference of ink from the text on the opposite page of the book.

If I had to choose my favourite print from this collection, this would certainly be a contender. It makes a fitting tailpiece here, too.

# INDEX

With the exception of the two prints by Paul Sandby, the illustrations are all taken from the author's collection, selected as good examples of the printing methods and to show the different characteristics of each method. Very few names of printmakers are represented here, and the subject matter of the prints is narrow compared to the huge range that can be found in specialist print shops.

The following is an index of names of engravers, artists and publishers. The names of subjects of portraits are also shown; those who are not concerned with printmaking are in [ ].

# GLOSSARY OF TERMS

After: followed by name, indicates the artist of the original picture from which the print was made. See also 'By and after'.

Aq.; aqua.; aquat.; aquaforte; aquatint: seen after name, indicates aquatint engraver. Sometimes seen after the name of an etcher.

Aqua fortis: literally *strong water*, nitric acid, used for etching and aquatint.

AQUATINT (intaglio): Form of etching, using acid to incise the plate, producing areas of tone, whereas etching works in lines.
Span: 1775 to 1830. Particularly suited topographical, shipping, military and sporting prints.

Bite: the incision made by acid in metal plates (intaglio). The longer the plate is subjected to acid, the more 'bite' will occur, and the darker will be the effect on the eventual print.

Blind stamp: an embossed mark without ink in the margin, intended as the publisher's approval. Modern prints sometimes have a coded number of the edition. Some private collectors have their own blind stamps as proof of ownership.

Block: a piece of wood or stone used for printing.

Body colour: thick colour, a gouache, sometimes used to heighten colours in prints. More often refers to watercolours.

Burin: an engraving tool for cutting into wood or metal plates.

Burnisher: a cloth pad for polishing metal plates.

By and after: the same person was the artist and the engraver of a print.

Camera obscura: an aid to artists. A box that works in a similar manner to a box camera, dark inside, an image being projected through a lens onto a sheet of paper at the back of the box, enabling an artist to trace an accurate image. The method is known to have been in use in the $16^{th}$ century. It was ideal for quick sketches of topographical subjects.

Capriccio: a fantasy picture, usually a landscape. Originated in Italy. The principal exponent in Britain was George Smith, known as Smith of Chichester, who had many prints made after his paintings of what one would think was a typical English landscape.

Cartouche: an ornamental feature, a framework, usually containing a title or description of the print.

Colour or coloured: an important difference. 'Colour print' describes a print that is printed in inks of different colours. 'Coloured print' means hand-coloured.

Contemporary: a word that is so misunderstood it is rarely used. It means 'of the period,' so 'contemporary colouring', for example, means that the colouring is the same age as the print. It does not mean 'modern'.

COPPER ENGRAVING, COPPERPLATE ENGRAVING (intaglio): a print made by cutting lines in a copper plate.
Span: 1550 to 1830

Copper plate: a flat metal plate used for most intaglio prints until about 1820, when steel plates came into use.

Copperplate lettering: perfectly formed writing, usually refers to manuscript.

Copy: when a print or a book is described as a 'good copy', it means a good example of an original – not a reproduction. A 'copy of an original' means that another print has been made, based on the original, not necessarily identical.

Copyright: as we understand it, this is quite modern. There were early attempts at protecting the rights of printmakers, none totally successful. William Hogarth tried to stop his work being copied, and helped in producing an act of parliament, with the result that some 18th-century prints have 'published according to Act of Parliament' in the publisher's imprint.

Cropped: margins trimmed close to the printed surface.

Cross-hatching: cutting lines across each other to create a dark texture. Applies to line engraving.

Cut: trimmed within the plate mark or within the image.

Delineavit, del., delin., delint.,: seen after a name, indicates the name of the artist who produced a drawing, not a painting, from which the print was made; the delineator. Literally, 'He drew it'. (Latin).

Eng.; engr.; eng'd: followed by name it means engraved by.

ENGRAVING: usually refers to line engraving. Describes any form of intaglio method, e.g. etchings, aquatints, stipples, and mezzotints, which are also described as 'engraved'.

Et.; Etch: seen after name, it means etcher.

ETCHING: the first intaglio method to use acid to 'bite' into the plate. Similar to line engraving, but more freehand in appearance. Suited most subjects. The earliest known etching is dated 1513. Flourished from around 1550 to 1750, revived in the middle of the $19^{th}$ century.

Facsimile: literally an exact copy, produced in the same way as the original. Now the word is misused, and, in the context of prints, means a photographic reproduction. Sometimes a facsimile is used to restore a badly damaged print, or to make up an incomplete book.

F.; fec.; fecit: literally, he made it.

Folio: a container for storing prints, as portfolio. Also book size: fol.

Foxing: small brown spots found in paper, caused by impurities in the paper becoming damp. Can be removed.

Frontispiece: the illustrated page at the front of a book. Many of them are fine printed works of art.

Graver: an engraver's tool for cutting into woodblocks or metal plates, also known as a burin.

Ground: an acid resistant substance laid over metal, for etching and aquatint, preventing the acid biting in unwanted parts of the plate.

Hachuring: parallel lines which represent one tone or shadow. Used in maps to represent hills. Unlike 'hatching,' the lines do not cross.

Hatching: shading by series of parallel lines crossing

each other, not always at right angles.

Image: the printed surface of a picture.

Impression: printed ink on paper. A printer takes an impression. Also used to describe the quality of a print, as in 'good impression' or 'early impression.'

Imprint: the lettering beneath the image of a print.

Ink: early printers made their own inks, so there was no precise consistency in colour or texture. It was thick and oily, and slow to dry.

Intaglio: an Italian word meaning 'cut into.' In printing it refers to any method where the surface of a metal plate is 'cut into'. That includes all types of etching, line engraving, mezzotint, stipple and aquatint. The opposite of 'relief'.

Inv.; invent.; inventit: followed by name, literally 'he invented it'. Originally designed by that person.

Laid paper: made in a sieve, a flat tray with fine wires close together in one direction and, at right angles, wires at about 3 cm intervals. The lines show in the paper when held up to the light. Paper was made in this way until about 1780, when 'wove' paper was made, which does not have wire marks.

Laid down: describes a print stuck onto another paper or card, usually detrimental to the value.

Landscape shape or format: any print which is wider than it is high. Portrait shape is higher than it is wide.

Late issue, or impression: a print made a length of time after the first edition or that shows signs of wear.

Letters: printed words beneath an image.

LINE ENGRAVING (intaglio): the image produced by incising lines in a metal plate with a tool. The method suited all sorts of subjects and remained in use for a long period. The span of copper was from 1550 to 1830. Steel plates were used after that.

LITHOGRAPH: a print made from a flat surface, usually stone, not requiring engraving. The earliest use was 1790; it flourished from 1820.

MEZZOTINT (intaglio): instead of working on a polished plate, the mezzotint engraver roughened up the surface with a roulette. At that stage, the plate would effectively print entirely black. The engraver then put in tones of light by smoothing out the surface, using a scraper to cut away the rough surface. The pure white areas had to be completely smooth. Mezzotint was ideal for portraits and produced excellent textures of distinctive clothing. Span: 1650 to 1830.

Original colour: generally used to describe hand-colouring of black & white prints, and simply means that colour was added within a short time of printing. Some printers and publishers employed their own colourists, but early colourists were mostly independent, especially map colourists. The perfect word to describe original is 'contemporary', meaning 'of the period'.

Outline colour: refers to maps. Boundaries are coloured. Other features are left uncoloured.

Pinx.; pinxit: indicating the name of the artist of the original painting from which the print has been made.

Plate: flat metal sheet from which a print is made.

Plate mark: indentation in paper where the edge of an intaglio plate presses into the paper during printing.

Pub.; pub'd: abbreviations of published.

Published as the Act directs, or Published according to Act of Parliament: seen in conjunction with the imprint in the middle and late 18th century. The Act was passed in 1735 to protect artists against having their work copied without consent, a protection from inferior engravers – an early form of copyright. William Hogarth was largely responsible for the completion of the Act, and presented a strong lobby.

Resin: the basic ingredient of a ground.

Sc.; sculp.; sculpsit: seen after a name, it indicates the engraver.

Separate publication: refers to a print that was not bound into a book.

Sepia: reddish brown. In prints it refers to the colour of the printing ink.

Shaved: margins reduced in size, cut close to the image.

sic.: the preceding word or words are correct or correctly spelt, copied from the original, no matter how unlikely it may seem. It usually appears in square brackets [sic].

Signed: when an artist's or an engraver's name appears anywhere on a print, it is described as 'signed' even when it is printed and formally lettered. From the end of the 19th century manuscript signatures were sometimes added to the bottom margin.

SOFT GROUND ETCHING (intaglio): a variation of etching. Paper is laid over a soft ground and the image is drawn onto the paper with a soft pencil, which makes the paper adhere to the ground. When the paper is lifted the ground is lifted as well, exposing the copper, which is then subjected to acid. The resulting print is like a soft pencil drawing. Used for domestic and rural scenes. Span: 1780 to 1830.

State: used when there is an alteration to the plate, e.g. 'second state', and usually means that something has been added to the original image. Sometimes alterations are minuscule, especially in proof states, so a print can be described as 10th state when in fact it is a very early impression, even the first published state.

STEEL ENGRAVING (intaglio): line engraving, using steel plate. Used for most subjects. Span: 1820 to 1860.

STIPPLE ENGRAVING (intaglio): engraving method in which the image is entirely comprised of multitudes of tiny dots, punched into the plate. Suited portraits and domestic scenes, especially when printed in colours. Flourished from 1780 to 1830.

Stopping out: refers to etching and aquatint where more ground is applied to the plate to protect it from further 'bite.'

Topography: views of places.

Variant: in prints, this can mean two or more engravings taken from one artist's painting, viz. West's *Death of General Wolfe*, plates 51 & 52 (pages 76 & 79). Or it can mean more than one engraving of the same subject.

Watermark: a mark sometimes seen in paper when held to the light. The mark might be a motif or a papermaker's name, sometimes with a date. To make the mark, a wire design is put into the tray during paper manufacture so that the paper is slightly thinner.

Wove: A type of paper made with very fine mesh, without the lines which show in 'laid' paper. Invented in 1755 but not in general use until about 1790.